SHOCKINGLY CLOSE to the TRUTH!

SHOCKINGLY CLOSE to the TRUTH!

Confessions of a Grave-Robbing Ufologist

JAMES W. MOSELEY & KARL T. PFLOCK

59 John Glenn Drive
Amherst, New York 14228-2197

Published 2002 by Prometheus Books

Inquiries should be addressed to
Prometheus Books
59 John Glenn Drive
Amherst, New York 14228–2197
VOICE: 716–691–0133, ext. 207
FAX: 716–564–2711
WWW.PROMETHEUSBOOKS.COM

06 05 04 03 02 5 4 3 2 1

Library of Congress Cataloging-in-Publication Data

Moseley, James W.
Shockingly close to the truth : confessions of a grave-robbing ufologist / James W. Moseley and Karl T. Pflock.
p. cm.
Includes bibliographical references and index.
ISBN 1–57392–991–3 (cloth : alk. paper)
1. Human-alien encounters. 2. Unidentified flying objects. 3. Alien abduction. I. Pflock, Karl T. II. Title.

BF050 .M665 2002
001.942—dc21

2002018951

Printed in Canada on acid-free paper

To Gray Barker, who should have lived to see this. —J. W. M.

This one's for Pop, who'd have loved it. —K. T. P.

The forceps of the mind are clumsy forceps
and crush the truth a little in taking hold of it.

—H. G. Wells

Acknowledgments 9

A Note on Sources 11

Prologue. The Truth Is Out There, Maybe
Jim Moseley 13

Prologue. The Time Machine
Karl Pflock 19

PART 1. The 1950s: S.A.U.C.E.R.S. and SPACE BROTHERS

1. In the Beginning . . . 25
2. Tracking the Elusive Flying Saucer 35
3. Inside the Spaceships 59
4. Attack of the Saucer Men 87
5. The Straight Straith and Other Mysteries Revealed 104
6. Grave Robbing for Fun and Profit 128

PART 2. The 1960s: SWAMP GAS and HIGH HOPES

7. Adrift in a Saucering Sargasso 155
8. What a Gas: I Become an Expert 178
9. The Great Con and the Morning After 194

PART 3. The 1970s: CRASHED SAUCERS and KIDNAPPERS from SPACE

10. We're Baaaaaaack! 221
11. Greetings (Again!), Fellow Saucer Fiends 234
12. Ufology Snatched, Crashed, and Mutilated 248

PART 4. The 1980s: COSMIC BABBLEGATE

13. Roswell, MJ-12, and All That 259
14. Conned Again and Other Follies 269
15. The Marvelous Mr. Ed 285

PART 5. The 1990s and BEYOND: VIRTUAL REALITY?

16. Trust No One! (Especially Your Abductologist) 299
17. "I Don't Care What the People Say . . ." 312
18. Millennial Musings and Parting Shots 323

Epilogue. The Fact 328

Appendix. The Straith Letter (December 1957) and Special *Saucer News* Adamski Exposé Issue (October 1957) 331

Sources of Further Enlightenment 353

Index 361

We wish we could thank by name everyone who has contributed, knowingly and otherwise, to this book. Unfortunately, it would require a volume larger than this to do so, for literally they are all the saucer fiends, anti-saucer fiends, and hopeful innocents and Space People of all sorts who wandered in off the street and dropped in from Where- and/or Whenever to make ufology what it was, is, and (maybe) will be. Without each and every one of you, this book never would—never could—have been perpetrated. Please accept our heartfelt thanks and, as appropriate, apologies.

There are a few special earthlings and others whose important contributions demand particular mention and thanks: Tom Benson, for taking so much of his limited time to mine his files on a rush basis for many of the one-of-a-kind photographs included herein, and for loaning us the original special Adamski exposé issue of *Saucer News* from which the appendix to this book was reproduced; Ufotoonist Matt Graeber, for his enlightening, inspirational, and very funny visual insights into the Essential Ufology and his selfless efforts to help us sell this project; Antonio Huneeus, for his helpful suggestions and continuing support; Carlos Mentira and Harry Lime, for their sage insights and other contributions over the years; our agent, Cherry Weiner, for putting up with us; Meghann French, our editor at Prometheus, ditto; Mothman, just for being himself; Gray Barker, ditto; Al Bender and his Three Men, the same; and last but by no means least, James Villard, who knows what he did.

This isn't a scholarly work. It's a very personal recollection of more than fifty years of UFOs, ufologists, ufology, and "ufoology." So we haven't larded it up with footnotes and other stigmata of the scholar at work, although where we thought it appropriate, we have provided in text the information necessary for the reader to locate sources of quoted material and the like.

This is not to say our book doesn't have a solid factual and documentary foundation. At the age of ten or thereabouts, Jim Moseley decided the best way to accurately track his activities was to keep a diary, and this he has done almost daily up to the present time. This is a rather unusual habit in this day and age, and it has come in very handy indeed for pinning down exact dates and, equally if not more important, Jim's spontaneous, contemporaneous reactions to and observations on events, people, publications, ideas, and more, as well as precise language used and exact claims made by others, taken down immediately after the fact.

We've also had the benefit of about 150 pages of single-spaced, typed notes that Jim made during his 1953–54 cross-country flying saucer research odyssey and the months immediately following it. As the reader will learn, Jim made the journey and kept his meticulous notes in anticipation of writing a book about saucers. That book never was written, but its spirit definitely haunts these pages. The notes are the foundation for our section on the 1950s and provided very interesting new ufological information and insights which are published there for the first time.

In addition, we've drawn heavily upon bound volumes of Jim's (in)famous ufological periodical, now known as *Saucer Smear* and previously as *Nexus* and, in its heyday, *Saucer News,* which is unmatched as a running, "as it happens" social history of ufology. The bound set, which continues to grow, includes every issue published and much additional material. It's a gold mine rich in saucer lore, fact and fantasy, feud and folly, and will one day be added to the Gray Barker Collection in the Clarksburg-Harrison County Library in Clarksburg, West Virginia, which is open to all interested researchers.

Of course, we also took advantage of the research and writings of others. All these sources and more are listed in our bibliography ("Sources of Further Enlightenment"). Of particular value to us were Jerome Clark's monumental *UFO Encyclopedia*; David Jacobs's *UFO Controversy in America*; Loren Gross's amazing multivolume labor of love *UFOs: A History,* covering the years 1896 and 1946–1959; and Curtis Peebles's *Watch the Skies!*

Should the reader come upon something he or she remembers differently and feel moved to discount our version, we respectfully suggest it be kept in mind that little in "saucerdom" is exactly what it seems. Also, it should never be forgotten that we make no claim that this book is anything but *Shockingly Close to the Truth!*

I do have a serious interest in UFOs, and I did have a serious interest even back when I was doing hoaxes, but my approach *is not serious. I like to enjoy myself.*

—J. W. M.

It used to be that just about every "objective" book about UFOs started out by informing us that the modern flying saucer era began on June 24, 1947, when a private pilot named Kenneth Arnold spotted "nine gleaming objects" flying at very high speed in a loose formation near Mount Rainier in the state of Washington. Arnold likened the motion of the objects to that of a saucer skipping on water, and some ingenious headline writer coined for him the term *flying saucer,* which has stuck with us ever since.

This being an unusual sort of UFO book, I won't start out that way. Nor—even though it was the incident that caused me to pay serious attention to UFOs—will I give an account of the next Big Event in the saucer saga, the case of Capt. Thomas Mantell, a Kentucky National

Guard fighter pilot who may or may not have been "zapped" by interplanetary invaders when, in January 1948, he flew too close to one of their craft. Nor will I say much about the month of July 1952, when the air force received over fifteen hundred UFO reports—notably the famous incident in which unidentified radar blips indicated saucers were flying crazily at fantastic speed over Washington, D.C., no less!

While I was mildly interested, I pretty much slept through most of that, and it wasn't until late 1953 that I became actively involved with UFOs. Having met a professional writer who offered to coauthor a book with me—look, it's happening to me again!—I went off on a two-month, cross-country automobile trip, interviewing perhaps a hundred people who had some spectacular UFO experience, as written up in the early saucer books, or who, as celebrities in their particular fields, had made exciting public statements on the subject.

There never was a book, but I still have about 150 pages of typed, single-spaced notes concerning the interviews I made on that trip, which Karl Pflock and I have drawn upon in writing this tome. What we now call the UFO field or "ufology"—The Field—was just getting started. There were very few UFO conventions and very few experts and alleged experts. The only supposedly large-scale UFO investigation outfit in the country, perhaps the world, as of 1952 was the International Flying Saucer Bureau (IFSB), headed by Albert K. Bender, an eccentric factory worker in Bridgeport, Connecticut. Bender published a very small quarterly magazine called *Space Review,* which had several hundred subscribers, including a few overseas—thus, I suppose, the "International" in the IFSB's name. Bender was just getting out of The Field as I was getting into it—in that, in the fall of 1953, he supposedly was "hushed up" in a spectacular way, revealed in detail further along in this book.

Just about the only good thing to come out of the IFSB was that Bender found a pen pal among the handful of British *Space Review* subscribers, and this lady eventually became his wife. The happy couple later moved to California and into the deep obscurity they so richly deserved.

In those days, educated people with advanced degrees shunned The Field like the plague, quite rightly believing such an association would ruin their reputations. But as the years went by, this situation changed somewhat. The Field's hard core still consists of only a few thousand fans, but by now there have been many dozens of people from various realms of literary and scientific endeavor who have made significant contributions (and "contributions") to ufology, both in lecturing and in writing. Stanton T. Friedman, M.Sci., UFO lecturer and former nuclear physicist, comes immediately to mind. Sadly, I have had to learn the hard way what I should have known long ago through common sense: A good formal education, even a Ph.D., does not by any stretch of the imagination guarantee objectivity, competence, integrity, or even sanity. As The Field has grown in size and complexity, and despite and even because of the efforts of some of the aforementioned worthies, the overall situation has become more and more muddled, with no objective solution to the UFO mystery yet in sight.

I was never quite dumb enough to believe the ravings of Al Bender, but UFO fandom, like anything else, is no fun unless one accepts at least *some* of its enthusiasms as being true. At first I was a believer in the Interplanetary Theory, or Extraterrestrial Hypothesis (ETH), which is still the most popular, at least in the United States. I accepted the stories of live little men from "out there" that were popularized by an organization called the Aerial Phenomena Research Organization (APRO) from the 1950s through the 1970s—these tales not to be confused with the stories of *dead* little men in crashed saucers, which go all the way back to the late 1940s, of which the notorious and fabled Roswell, New Mexico, incident of 1947 has become the best known.

I concluded that little men who look almost like us logically should come from a nearby planet almost like ours, so by the early 1960s I was convinced Mars was the answer. I was all the more astounded when I learned the "canals" or straight-line markings on the Red Planet had been photographed through telescopes, showing, it seemed, they were not an optical illusion. A little more thought on my part would have caused me to realize the camera can be fooled as easily as the eye. Alas, there are no canals on Mars, and now the breathlessly touted "faces" there have disappeared the same way, dissolved by higher-resolution pictures of the Martian surface.

So, the flying saucers aren't from Mars—or any other planet in our solar system. Then where *are* they from—assuming, of course, we are dealing with a genuine mystery and not just a bunch of hoaxes and misinterpretations? The answer, according to my current thinking, is what I somewhat facetiously call the 4-D Theory. The wonderful thing about this "theory" is, unlike others, it simply can't be disproved, since in essence it assumes *anything* is possible. Needless to say, it can't be *proved,* either, thus the quotation marks around *theory.*

If we are dealing with "magic," then there's no problem in believing entities can walk through walls to abduct hapless earthlings. *Of course* they can read our minds; keep our mail from being delivered; engage in shameless interdimensional, interspecies sex; and generally carry on in all sorts of illogical and disturbing ways. They thus represent a scenario so totally unknown and frightening that no government on Earth dares to admit They—whoever *They* are—even exist.

Well, I don't totally believe those last two paragraphs myself. What I do find curious is that the "aliens" used to fly around in craft that were about twenty to fifty years ahead of the cutting edge of earthly technology. Recently, the gap has narrowed considerably. Either we earthlings are getting smarter in a hurry, or the "aliens" have slowed down their progress, or—as many would have it—we, especially in the United States, have benefited marvelously from the use of technology taken from captured spaceships. So now, when something utterly amazing flies by, one doesn't know if it is ours or Theirs without getting a good look at the pilot!

But that doesn't sound right to me, either. Our government—*any* government—is far too inept to keep important secrets for very long. I therefore go back to the core of *my* version of the 4-D Theory, which is that, in some strange, distorted way, the saucer occupants are a reflection of *ourselves*. As one researcher so aptly put it, They are *too much like us* to be interplanetary visitors. They display aspects of the objective and of the subjective at the same time. Whatever may be the case, I do not believe The Answer will be found in our lifetime, or at least not in mine.

Nonetheless, the trip has been fun. As much as I would like to know The Answer, I have seldom given in to frustration, as many so-called saucer researchers have done. A great many sane, objective, thoughtful people have entered The Field over the years, stayed awhile, found out there are *no* easy answers, and gone on to other interests. Those who stay on are mostly the crackpots, however well educated; the money-grubbers; and the ego-trippers—and, of course, there are large overlaps among these categories. I consider myself sane and have a reasonably secure ego, but at the same time I have made very little money from UFOs over the years—though I would have no objection to doing so. (Thanks for buying this book!)

To me, the *people* in The Field are as interesting as the underlying phenomenon, if any. It is mainly the foibles and fantasies of the ufologists themselves that have held my attention over the years and in the various incarnations of my UFO magazine. I have stepped on many toes, been threatened with lawsuits several times—though none has ever been filed against me—and, in general, I deliberately have made myself unpopular with The Field's leading lights, simply because, though I *do* take the subject seriously, I don't take the people in The Field—least of all myself—seriously.

Just remember this: In a thousand years, *none* of this will make any difference (probably).

What are UFOs? The short, honest answer is, We don't know. But who in The Field can leave it at that? Not I.

—K. T. P.

Jim Moseley is my time machine, transporting me back to the days of my youth, when the flying saucers were real and most of the people chasing them were not.

Although Jim is *much* older than I, my serious interest in saucers predates his a bit, going back to the summer of 1948 or 1949, when I was a lad of five or six. At a backyard birthday party for the son of one of my dad's bookstore employees, I sat in awe, listening to several of the partygoers' fathers talk about "those flying saucers"—more particularly, the discovery by the military of a crashed flying saucer *with dead little men from another planet in it!* This was at least months before the first such story saw print, and the Roswell tale didn't acquire its dead ufonauts until the late 1970s.

I was hooked.

Of course, it didn't hurt that my father was interested in such things, too, in an open-minded but hardheaded way, and that he'd begun my "corruption" at an early age by reading the classics of science fiction to me, a chapter or two a night. Pop ordered saucer books for me through his bookstore as they came out, and we talked and speculated about what UFOs were and, if they were real, where they were from and why they were here. Throughout the 1950s, we never missed the latest science-fiction films, not a few of which featured flying saucers and their usually malevolent operators—among them *Earth versus the Flying Saucers, The Thing (From Another World!), Invasion of the Saucer Men, It Came from Outer Space, Invaders from Mars,* and *The Day the Earth Stood Still,* in which a saucer bearing the stern but benevolent Klaatu and his indestructible robot sidekick, Gort, actually landed on the White House lawn. Well, it was on the Ellipse, a park across the street, but that sure was close enough.

In the summer of 1951 or 1952, when I was eight or nine, I saw a UFO, or what I'm sure would have stacked up as one if the sighting had been investigated. I won't go into the details here, but my dad and I and two of my friends and their father saw a silent, very strangely behaving flying object as we were returning home from a day of fishing at a reservoir south of San Jose, California, my hometown. After carefully considering all the possibilities—bright planet, airplane, rocket, helicopter, fireworks, flares, even a balloon—it was a UFO as far as we were concerned. I seem to remember my dad, an old crime and general-assignment newspaperman, talking about our sighting with a reporter friend of his on one of the local papers, but I don't think anything ever came of it.

I devoured all the serious UFO books I could talk my dad into buying for me, from Keyhoe's *Flying Saucers Are Real* to Ruppelt's *Report on Unidentified Flying Objects.* I diligently studied the articles about saucers, pro and con, in such decidedly nonkooky magazines as *True, Flying, Look, Saturday Evening Post,* and *Life.* "Have We Visitors from Space?" an article in the April 7, 1952, issue of the latter, which I carefully clipped and still have today, had me saying, "Yes!"—as did a 1954 "Special Issue!" of the thinking kid's comic book *Weird Science-Fantasy,* an "Illustrated [boy, was it!], Factual Flying Saucer Report" in which the intrepid editors issued "A CHALLENGE TO THE UNITED STATES AIR FORCE!" demanding it "TELL US THE **TRUTH** ABOUT THE FLYING SAUCERS."

I also read several of the not-so-serious saucer books, in which the authors told of their contacts with golden-haired Space Brothers and shapely Space Sisters; their travels to other worlds aboard the saucers and their huge, cigar-shaped mother ships; and the Brothers' warnings of our impending self-inflicted doom, in those days, usually global nuclear war.

As a guest of a neighbor—the father of one of my playmates and a true believer if there ever was one—I even attended a lecture by one such "contactee," a woman whose name I no longer recall (Dana Howard?). Yawn.

While I found the contactees' photos of alleged Venusian scout ships and such interesting—and fantasized a bit about the Space Sisters—I simply couldn't take the contactees' yarns seriously, however much I would have liked to. I was cursed. My brain wouldn't let me get away with self-delusion, at least not for long.

Speaking of self-delusion, along about 1957, a couple of friends and I determined to get the U.S. Air Force to "TELL US THE **TRUTH** ABOUT FLYING SAUCERS." Naively, we figured we would do better at prying same from the air force if we didn't present ourselves as a bunch of teenagers asking for "everything you know about flying saucers." So we founded the National Committee for Investigation of UFOs (NCIUFO), with Yours Truly as director. Much to our disappointment, but not really to our surprise, all we got were a few releases from the air force press desk in the Pentagon, with saucer-report and case-"solved" statistics and the usual "the Air Force takes UFOs seriously, but . . ." rhetoric. We also cranked out a couple of newsletters, but soon lost interest when we were unable to generate enough paying subscribers to cover the cost.

A few years ago, ace UFO-document sleuth Robert Todd showed me that the air force seems to have taken us seriously, at least as a nuisance. Good old NCIUFO, "Director—K. T. Pflock," was included on lists of pesky UFO organizations in two classified air force intelligence staff studies written in 1958 and 1959. It would have been exciting to know this at the time, but to be honest, it probably wouldn't have mattered much. Real Earth girls had by then preempted the Space Sisters in our youthful affections.

Jim Moseley notes in his prologue that he figuratively slept through the exciting early days of flying saucers. Well, over the years and until relatively recently I have done something similar. With one exception—more about this as our story unfolds—apart from rather casually regarding the antics and claims of the contactees and a general, amused awareness of such goings on as the monster gatherings of saucer devotees at places like Giant Rock in California's Mojave Desert, not to mention Jim Moseley's huge 1967 convention in New York City, I paid little attention to anything I didn't regard as Serious Stuff and cared virtually not at all about the sociology of The Field. I only vaguely recall hearing or reading about Jim and his *Saucer News*, now *Saucer Smear*, back then.

Apparently, my ever-vigilant, if all too fallible Not-Serious Filter bleeped them out. (Sorry, Jim!)

So this collaboration has permitted me to go back in time and fill in the blanks as well as to explore much Serious Stuff, gaining significant insights not only into The Field and its denizens from the 1950s right up to today, but also into quite a number of historically and substantively important UFO cases and claims. It has been an enriching, enjoyable, enlightening adventure. I hope it will be at least half as much so for our readers.

Oh, almost forgot. In my epigraph I implicitly promised to offer my views on the nature of UFOs. Well, today, everything from livestock mutilations through crop circles, Bigfoot, and channeled alien masters to *chupacabras* and abductions with nary a strange craft in sight has been dragged under the big top labeled "UFO." All these phenomena are interesting. Some *may* even have a basis in not-so-mundane fact outside the imaginations of the alleged "experiencers" and those who investigate their reports, not to mention those of a hoax perpetrator or three.

As for me, give me the ol'-time UFOs: nuts-and-bolts vehicles, flying saucers from another world embraced by the warmth of a star not unlike our own, piloted by sentient beings who explored our planet and solar system, studied and perhaps experimented with us—just as we would were we to come upon such interesting places and curious beings as we sailed among the stars.

Note well my use of the past tense. If, as I'm subjectively certain it does, some fraction of UFO-report data arises from observations of such craft and their occupants, it is my guess they were here and left some time ago—arriving in the early to mid-1940s, departing in the mid- to late 1960s or early 1970s. They came here because Sol and his planets seemed cozily familiar: Perhaps beings like us dwell there! They studied our entire system and us quite closely. Once in a while a couple of grad students got drunk and buzzed the natives. On occasion an ambitious scientist overstepped a bit and interfered with the locals—the famous and in my opinion very real 1961 abduction of Barney and Betty Hill comes to mind.

Then they left.

So I speculate, based upon a careful though yet far from complete consideration of the data and informed by a strong gut feeling and, admittedly, a bit of nostalgia.

Klaatu, please come back!

The 1950s: S.A.U.C.E.R.S. and Space Brothers

Part 1

I do not mind lying, but I hate inaccuracy.
—Samuel Butler

It is far easier to make up things than to stick strictly to the Truth. So it is that close *is about as near to Truth any of us ever gets. By some odd alchemy this usually brings out what really matters.*

—J. W. M.

I was born James Willett Moseley in New York City on August 4, 1931, just about the time the Great Depression really was getting into gear. There was no Depression in our household, however, as my father was a general in the United States Army and my mother had inherited a moderately large fortune from a steamship line founded by her father.

My parents soon separated, but nevertheless I ended up attending almost a dozen schools all around the country, just like an army brat. For a couple of years I was the only day student at an all-boarding prep school in Arizona, and later I was one of a dozen boarders among some three hundred students at St. Albans in Washington, D.C. I was an only child, at all times and in all respects brought up by my mother to be different and somewhat more lonely than other kids—but always within the rules of our rather privileged class.

In 1949, at seventeen, I graduated from a New Jersey prep school and went directly to Princeton University, simply because I was expected to do so. I had no enthusiasm for any of it. I vaguely wanted to be a writer, but really had no specific direction in mind. I *was* different, but not quite in the ways my mother would have liked. I was perhaps the original Rebel without a Cause.

Mother died in December 1950. Thus at nineteen I became the beneficiary of a large trust fund, the corpus of which is now mostly gone. Although I was doing very well academically, as of that moment I did not see any further reason to hang around Princeton. I was happily aware that I didn't *have* to do anything, so for a while I simply did nothing, except for some recreational drinking and girl chasing.

This quickly palled, and I became desperately bored. So began a rather frantic and neurotic search for something—anything—interesting to do, which in no small degree, if in a more laid-back form, has characterized much of my life since. I even briefly took a couple of salaried jobs when the boredom was at its most suffocating. Mainly, I looked for real business investment opportunities and tried very hard to get in touch with various people who were or might be organizing interesting expeditions to exotic places. I was only too well aware that, since I had no degree in anything and no particular skills, I would probably end up having to pay to tag along on any real or semireal expedition. In this I wasn't disappointed.

The first of my pay-to-go treks was to South Africa in late 1951, with the then-well-known and photogenic Italian explorer Attilio Gatti (remember the "Man of Distinction" magazine ads?). In late December 1952, I embarked on a wider-ranging adventure, more than five months of road and air travel in some twenty African countries and then up through Italy and France and on to England, arriving in London in time for the coronation of Elizabeth II. I then flew to New York and, via the George Washington Bridge, headed back to my furnished room in exciting Fort Lee, New Jersey.

Soon after my return to the States, an old friend sent me a clipping from a Miami newspaper. The article told of writer-adventurer-explorer Ken Krippine, regular contributor of true-adventure tales to *Argosy* magazine, popular lecturer on his exciting travels to wild and dangerous lands, and all-around interesting guy. I immediately set about trying to connect with Krippine and his colorful partner, Dick Weldy, who, a few years later in Peru, lost his beautiful wife, Pilar, to John Wayne (but that's a story for my next book).

Making contact with these two characters took a lot of time and effort to accomplish. However, I was then well into what I now wryly think of as my Intellectual Period, so I was semiconstructively occupied. I was very seriously interested in various fields of philosophy, science, history, and mathematics, and wrote a number of what I rather grandly labeled "Philosophical Outlines." The seventh of these, drafted on October 2, 1953, revised and expanded a couple of weeks later, and typed in final form on November 1, 1953 (the significance of these dates will soon become apparent), was entitled "Flying Saucers."

My interest in the subject had become more than casual one day in early 1948, when I was attending St. Albans. A boy my age who lived across the street excitedly told me a deliciously chilling story he had just heard on the radio. A military pilot, while chasing a flying saucer upward to high altitude, had been "zapped" and killed when his plane crashed to the ground. This was the famous Thomas Mantell case. I was quite impressed. I had already heard and read other saucer reports and was mildly interested in the subject. The Mantell tragedy convinced me there really could be physical aliens capable of intruding into our airspace and even killing one of our pilots, though of course I realized it might just have been an accident.

Subsequently, I bought and carefully read the first spate of UFO books. All were aimed at making the case that, as the title of the first saucer book by leading early UFO-age figure Donald Keyhoe (in fact, the first saucer book, period) proclaimed, *The Flying Saucers Are Real* (June 1950)—and piloted by beings from another planet. Others that I studied back then were Gerald Heard's *The Riddle of the Flying Saucers: Is Another World Watching?* (December 1950 in the United Kingdom and April 1951 in the United States); Frank Scully's super-best-seller *Behind the Flying Saucers* (September 1950), which laid out all the key elements of the crashed-saucer mythology; Keyhoe's second and best-selling tome *Flying Saucers from Outer Space* (1953); and the book that launched the colorful career of "Professor" George Adamski and the saucer-contactee subculture, *Flying Saucers Have Landed* (1953), by Adamski and recently deceased Irish Lord Desmond Leslie.

So it was that, as I pursued Krippine, I quite naturally spent some time pondering the UFO mystery. These excerpts from "Philosophical Outline #7" reveal the essence of my thinking at the time:

There has been a great deal of speculation, particularly during the last few years, concerning certain strange objects that have been seen in the skies by competent persons. . . . The number of sightings has been extremely large, especially in the United States, and some date back as far as the last century. Although the hundreds of eyewitness reports on the subject vary in many details, the types of objects seen seem to boil down to two main kinds: long, cigar-shaped objects appearing like space-ships, and round, saucer-shaped objects which often move erratically and at high speed. . . . Undoubtedly, hoaxes, mirages, and legitimate objects (such as balloons) of one sort or another, do account for a high percent of the sightings. However, there definitely has been no theory advanced that will account for all the sightings. A small [*sic!*] but persistent minority (about 20% to 25%) have defied explanation up to the present time. From what I have read on the subject, there seems to be only one theory that will explain this "unexplainable" 20% or 25%, and that is: that there are intelligently-controlled objects watching us from the skies, and that these objects are sent and controlled by a form of life that exists on one or more of the many planets that surround our own . . . .

To many, the outer-space conclusion may indeed seem . . . fantastic. . . . However, it is my opinion that there is neither anything absurd nor frightening about the idea that we are being watched by creatures from another world. There are millions of planets in this vast universe. It seems to me that the probability of ours not being the only one capable of supporting intelligent life is far greater than the probability that our planet is the only one on which such life can be sustained. Granted this, it follows that the life on some of these inhabited planets will be of an intelligence inferior to ours, while the life on others will be of a superior intelligence. . . . It follows that the inhabitants of those planets more advanced than us would have almost certainly learned the secret of inter-planetary travel, since we ourselves are on the verge of such travel (and barring catastrophe, we will likely make our first flight to the moon within 20 years [How's that for calling it!]). . . .

. . . On another planet evolution might have taken a course similar to our own, or it might have progressed in a way that to us would be fantastic or even inconceivable. Although the most likely story is that they [the saucer beings] are "humanoid" forms of some sort, I tend to disbelieve all the stories that have been reported concerning the finding of the dead bodies of little men three feet tall; I feel quite sure that if these stories were true, they could never have been hushed up and ridiculed as thoroughly as they have been. We must conclude therefore that we as yet know nothing concerning what these creatures look like. However, in regard to their minds, we have much better (though nevertheless indirect) evidence to go on. From the way the saucers have con-

> ducted themselves, it seems obvious that the intelligence guiding them is not warlike, but is merely bent on studying us from a distance, at least for the time being. . . . The most thrilling thought of all is that perhaps they are biding their time, and when they are ready, or when they feel we are ready, i.e., sufficiently advanced, they will communicate with us. If and when such a thing happens, the human race may advance a thousand years within a very few years, provided we are willing to listen to the superior wisdom and kindly advice of an alien planet. The possibilities of such a meeting and intercommunication are endless. Instead of fearing these creatures, we should all hope for the day when the mystery will be ended, and our visitors from outer space will give us the benefits of their higher civilization.
>
> If, however, at the present time or in the near future the general public were ever to seriously believe that our planet is being watched by creatures from another world, I feel that a panic might develop, the like of which has never been seen. It is therefore possible, though not likely, that certain scientists and top government officials already have proof that these flying saucers are from another planet, and for fear of starting a panic they refrain from announcing this information to the public. However, my guess is that, while the qualified investigators of the saucer reports may suspect the origin of some of these saucers is not of this earth, they have not as yet any conclusive evidence to that effect; . . . it may be a very long time before we will ever to be able to prove that they exist—if they do exist. In the meantime, the only sensible course for one to follow is to keep an open mind in regard to the various conflicting theories in this fascinating field. But one should definitely hold the view that as the evidence now stands, the outer-space theory is by far the most believable of all explanations that have been presented so far. . . . The space-ship idea is fantastic. Yet, so is Einstein's concept of the universe, as well as the Hydrogen bomb and many other realities of our modern world. Let us then not reject the theory merely because it is unpleasant or strange, for truth can indeed be stranger than fiction.

Enter Ken Krippine. He and Weldy finally came up to New York in October 1953, just as I was setting down the above profundities. I first met with them on October 5. We talked about possible future projects Krippine had in mind and how I might participate. I ended up signing a contract with him, under which he would take me on a Peruvian jungle expedition beginning in February 1954. This would cost me about four hundred dollars.

Krippine, now long dead, was the sort of character who was quite proficient at "living off the land." He immediately realized I was a rather naive guy, with a car (a spanking new, dark blue Hudson) and money, who would make a great "follower." I ended up driving him to two lecture engagements in New England, and soon after, we flew to Detroit for another. I even drove him to Philadelphia so he could hook up with a girlfriend who was threatening to dump him (he married her years later). Krippine ran out of his own money early on, and I ended up footing all the bills.

It didn't take long for me to see I was being taken advantage of. After much cajoling, I got Krippine to sign a statement that my four hundred bucks for the Peruvian trip was paid in full, this being the approximate amount I was out of pocket on his expenses by then.

I don't recall which of us first brought up the notion of a book collaboration or who suggested it be about flying saucers. Likely Krippine posed the book idea, and I suggested saucers. The first mention of this scheme I've been able to find is my diary entry for October 22, 1953:

> If I want to do the necessary research, Krippine will write a book on flying saucers under my name, using my research and some fraudulent material which he can dig up. [This turned out to be the briefly notorious Head Man from Outer Space tale, about which more later.] If he does this, I will be launched as a writer! If I decide definitely to do the research . . . I will make, from my books on the subject, a list of places saucers have been seen, and by whom. Then I'll drive to California & back, interviewing people who have seen them. This will solve my problem of what to do till February.

Thus from youthful boredom and ambition was born a lifetime of involvement with flying saucers and the curious and endlessly interesting and amusing subculture which has grown up around them.

I quickly set about carefully combing through the five books on the subject I had in my library, putting all the most interesting cases and their pertinent details on four-by-six file cards. These I arranged geographically, so that I could interview as many people as possible as I drove across the country to the coast and back.

As I planned and began packing for my journey, it dawned on me that, while I was pretty well steeped in facts, I really didn't know much about the key "saucerian" personalities and the saucer-enthusiast clubs that were beginning to spring up around the country. I sat down in the middle of my room, surrounded by half-packed bags and clutter. I needed a crash course in saucerian lore and celebrities. What was I to do?

Strangely enough, I get some of my best thinking done when I am in disorganized situations—which is a good thing, since that's often the case. It wasn't long before I remembered a local newspaper story about an area man who claimed to have witnessed and photographed a spectacular saucer. I thought I might have clipped and saved the item.

While I engaged in the usual boyhood mischief, I also developed a not-so-usual habit of clipping out interesting news stories. These I pasted in scrapbooks.

The only organization one could claim for these volumes was that they were chronological. So, remembering the story had appeared about a year back, I pulled out the 1952 volumes and started paging through them, working backward.

As I got into August, a bell began to ring in the back of my mind. By the time I'd thumbed back to June, the subconscious memory link was explained. I found the clipping. The man who photographed the saucer was August C. Roberts, of Jersey City. I'd seen his name in a photo caption in Adamski and Leslie's book, a caption that wrongly identified the photograph with the event reported in the newspaper. (As we shall see, Adamski very frequently was less than careful about such trifling details.)

It seems Roberts was on a sky-watch tower when he and fellow civil defense aircraft spotters James Leyden and George Conger spied an incredible thing hovering over the New York City skyline. Roberts told a reporter it looked like a huge shiny coin, tilted with its edge toward them. It hovered briefly, then vanished in a burst of tremendous speed.

Before it zipped away, Roberts grabbed Leyden's Brownie camera and snapped two photos. Unfortunately, the shutter was set on "time," so he got only blurred images on the film. Nevertheless, the paper had run the two photos with a lengthy story.

Roberts's sighting had been accompanied by "a strange feeling, like nothing I ever felt before," he was quoted as saying. He also said that, for no logical reason, he felt certain what he had seen was an interplanetary spacecraft.

That decided me. I was confident Roberts would be the man who could give me some leads on saucers and others who had seen and believed in them. A check in the telephone book showed no listing for an August C. Roberts in Jersey City, so the next day, November 1, I contacted J. B. Foley, the head of civil defense for that city. Foley told me Roberts was unmarried and boarded at his sister's house. Foley gave me the address and telephone number, telling me he thought Roberts an honest man but a "crank" when it came to flying saucers.

When I finally got Roberts on the phone, he didn't sound at all wacky. I wasn't sure if I was disappointed or not. He told me the paper had misquoted him, that he had no definite opinion as to what the object had been, and that he would gladly show me his extensive UFO files. He suggested we meet that evening, November 5, at the home of a gyroscope technician also interested in flying saucers. He said this man, Dominic (or Dominick; he spelled it both ways) C. Lucchesi, likely could give me several leads to sources of information and interviews in California, as he had corresponded with saucer buffs out there. But then Roberts added a strange note. He and Lucchesi were uneasy, he said, because of an incident involving a friend of theirs who had been "hushed up."

That evening, in Lucchesi's book-lined apartment, I was treated to a bizarre promenade of various UFO theories and bits of information. My diary entry reads:

> My interview with Roberts was weird. The whole thing was taken down on a tape recorder. Roberts . . . [and Lucchesi] said they are members of a saucer club which was recently broken up in an odd way, supposedly by the government, because the president of the club, in Connecticut, had gotten too close to the truth about saucers—which supposedly will be revealed in Dec. or Jan. I will see Roberts again on Sunday. He is a "bug" on saucers but apparently sincere, and he has set me to really thinking! There really *is* something to this saucer business! . . .

Roberts and Lucchesi told me they had belonged to the International Flying Saucer Bureau (IFSB), which collected and studied information about saucers. Supposedly, Albert K. Bender, the head of the organization, had by some accident come across accurate information about the origin and purpose of the strange craft and had been told to stop his investigations—possibly by the government, my hosts thought.

Bender told his friends this warning had been delivered to him by three men in black suits and black homburgs. Whoever they were, they had confirmed the secret information Bender had stumbled across, then had severely threatened him, or so he claimed. He was so frightened by the visit, the two told me, that he became physically ill. He refused to tell Lucchesi and Roberts who the three men were, what agency they were from, or, of course, the secret they had sworn him to keep.

Roberts and Lucchesi were concerned they, too, might be visited, put under some sort of security regulations, and silenced. If this happened, they thought, they would have to give up their saucer studies. It seemed to me they were more than a little overanxious, but I was quite intrigued by the Bender tale and what have come to be known as the MIB—Men in Black.

Once Lucchesi and Roberts were comfortable that I was what I claimed to be, merely an aspiring author, they relaxed and opened up further, even suggesting I call them "Dom" and "Augie." Soon my head was spinning with saucer lore and names, phone numbers, and addresses of saucer luminaries. Besides giving me leads to many interesting personalities on the Coast, they also provided local and perhaps even interplanetary information. My notes from that mind-boggling session read in part:

> (1) "Earth to tilt due to ice cap at South Pole and destroy civilization as it did 5,000 years ago. Saucers here to prevent this."
>
> (2) "Lucchesi's friend in Pennsylvania had contact with female saucer occupant, was given strange black box which may be extremely dangerous. Box isolated in unpopulated area."
>
> (3) "Saucers may come from inside the earth, where cave dwellers are alleged to pilot these craft."
>
> (4) "Apposition [*sic*] of Mars and frequency of saucers."
>
> (5) "Saucers historical. Get Charles Fort's book."

When Fort came up, Dom climbed onto a chair and pulled a thick volume from a high shelf of a huge bookcase. It was the classic *Books of Charles Fort,* a single-volume compilation of four separate books written by a man who had enjoyed tweaking establishment science with accounts of phenomena it could not explain. Aside from his tongue-in-cheek "proofs" that Earth was flat and the Moon only thirty-seven miles away, Fort, who died in 1932, immediately impressed me with his years of gathering mountains of unexplained events. Among these are hundreds of accounts of unidentified flying objects antedating by years, even centuries, the recent reports that had begun in earnest in 1947 and reached a peak in 1952.

Clearly, Fort impressed other UFO writers, for his material has provided boundless filler and "validation" for their books and articles. I mention him not only because of this, but also to note that Fort's writings seemed to me then to confirm my strong but tentative conclusions about flying saucers and their origins, and even much of what I was hearing as Dom, Augie, and I talked far into the night. Although the stories they told me were fantastic, many of them more than just bordering on the unbelievable, here was Fort, who had spent most of his life carefully gathering such inexplicable data. He quoted from learned journals and other scholarly sources. The solidity of his findings seemed unimpeachable.

I certainly had discovered a cure for my boredom! As I noted in the year-end summary of my 1953 diary: "From the first, I loved this work, for not only was I keeping busy, but I was aiming toward a definite goal—the publication of my book—and at the same time investigating a subject that deeply interested me."

Driving home from my meeting with the two "saucerers," I decided I should postpone beginning my research trip until I'd had a chance to look into the Bender and other local stories first. I felt this would at least be good practice for future interviews, as well as giving me a better grounding in The Field. Little did I know that the following Sunday, with Augie Roberts, I would conduct my first case investigation, involving what seemed a nearly averted crash of a UFO, complete with amazing and genuine physical evidence.

Man, if you gotta ask, you'll never know.

—Louis Armstrong

I put the next couple of days to good use. First, I contacted a number of people who had reported saucer sightings in the greater New York City area.

The most significant of these was Associated Press reporter Saul Pett. His July 22, 1952, night sighting of a large, swiftly moving red-orange disk from his home in River Edge, New Jersey, had been favorably mentioned by both Donald Keyhoe and Desmond Leslie. I remember being very impressed by Pett. He was sure he'd seen something extraordinary, but steadfastly refused to say it was a flying saucer. He simply said he did not know what he saw and really had no way of knowing. He also commented, "I wasn't frightened at all, because the thing looked so peaceful and so serene. There wasn't any appearance of menace."

Pett was a levelheaded, thoughtful fellow. I hoped other witnesses would be half as sensible. Adding to my positive impression of Pett and my growing conviction that the flying saucers indeed were real was that two friends of mine, Ted and Ruth Hunt, had seen something similar on the same night, near their home about five miles from Pett's. At my request, they signed a sworn statement before a notary public. I was sure this would lend substance to my book.

ORTHODOX SCIENCE SPEAKS

I also decided it would be worthwhile to find out what scientists thought about UFOs. After all, who else but scientists to get to the bottom of the mystery? So, to start with, I interviewed Dr. Hugh Rice, a research consultant at New York's Hayden Planetarium. Rice said his guide on the matter was a recent book by Prof. Donald Menzel of Harvard. (This was *Flying Saucers*, the first of Menzel's debunking books, which I had not yet read.) It was Rice's opinion that Menzel had sufficiently explained saucer sightings with his temperature inversion theory. He suggested that others in science agreed and told me he couldn't think of any "real" scientists he could recommend to me who would admit the outer-space theory was credible.

I was disappointed, not because Rice didn't think flying saucers were real and came from another world, but because he seemed so ill-informed on the subject and yet didn't hesitate to dismiss it out of hand. His attitude struck me as grossly unscientific, which at the time I found odd in a professional scientist. I asked him if it wasn't the business of science to explain all unexplained phenomena. He agreed, but said that there was not enough evidence on saucers to study them.

In my notes on this meeting I wrote, "In all sincerity I believe that the reason orthodox science as a whole takes such a dim view of saucers is that they are, as a group, as unscientific as Dr. Rice is." To this I appended something from a newspaper article from a couple of years before. It seems a Rev. Louis Gardner of Los Angeles had written to Albert Einstein, asking his opinion on flying saucers. The great scientist replied, "Those people have seen something. What it is I do not know and I am not curious to know." Not much has changed in the fifty-plus years since, and, while I no longer believe UFOs are ships from outer space, I still deplore the unscientific attitude of most scientists on the subject, although over the years I have met a few—very few—whom I found to be truly scientific in their outlook.

A PICTURE IS WORTH...?

Another line of inquiry I began at that time was into the authenticity of the rather amazing photos in the Leslie-Adamski book *Flying Saucers Have Landed.* These included the one snapped by Augie Roberts, which I could easily investigate locally, and the seemingly too-good-to-be-true shots of saucer-shaped "scout ships" and huge cigar-shaped "mother ships" taken by Adamski.

The photography experts I consulted on the Adamski pictures were unanimous in the opinion that all could easily have been faked with a lampshade with a brass dome (the scout saucers), cardboard cutouts (the mother ships), light reflections, and double exposures. The experts explained and demonstrated this to my satisfaction. I considered the views of these two men particularly important, since both were inclined to believe flying saucers were ships from outer space. Of course, that it was possible the photos could have been faked didn't prove they had been.

As for the photograph by Augie Roberts reproduced in *Flying Saucers Have Landed,* I had first learned from the newspaper article and had it confirmed by civil defense boss Foley that it wasn't taken during the incident described in the caption. Needless to say, this made me suspicious. Roberts explained that the photo in the book was one he had taken in 1949 and sent to Adamski for publication after Adamski had contacted him on reading about the 1952 incident. He said he'd written Adamski about the mix-up, adding that he had not sold his saucer photos, even the one he had provided Adamski. Then, to my surprise, he declared he thought Adamski probably was a fraud and *his* pictures fakes.

Roberts gave me prints and the negatives for his 1949 and 1952 snaps, which I then had examined by a third expert. This fellow found that the negatives hadn't been tampered with, but nonetheless he was sure the photographs were "clever fakes," though he couldn't prove it. I, on the other hand, had been impressed by Augie's naive genuineness and was more inclined to believe he wasn't a hoaxer. If what he had captured on film were phony saucers, I thought, Roberts was most likely a hoax victim, not a perpetrator.

Augie, who dropped out of active involvement in ufology in 1960 or thereabouts and died in 1994, was a peculiar fellow. He was painfully shy and remarkably credulous, making him equally susceptible to saucer scams and practical jokes perpetrated by friends, Lucchesi and me included. He was fond of saying, "I believe in everything and nothing"—by which he meant he believed in the possibility that any UFO story, no matter how wild, might be true. A semi-successful professional photographer, he amassed a vast library of saucer, saucerian event, and ufological personality photos, coming to be known as "the flying saucer photographer" and contributing numerous illustrations to many UFO books and magazines.

Augie was intensely interested in saucers from the moment he heard of Kenneth Arnold's sighting in June 1947. In 1949 he snapped his first UFO picture, the one discussed above. In April 1952 Al Bender announced formation of the International Flying Saucer Bureau. As soon as he heard about the IFSB, Augie signed up.

The same year, Roberts became a member of a Jersey City Civil Defense skywatch team, which he joined specifically in the hope of seeing a flying saucer. Sure enough, in July 1952 one put in an appearance, and Augie got the photograph—showing a nondescript zigzag of light across the night sky—that appeared in the local paper, was picked up by the wire services, and brought him to the attention of George Adamski—and me.

The NEW HAVEN FIREBALL and the GREAT HUSH-UP

The morning of Sunday, November 8, Augie piled into my Hudson and we headed for New Haven, Connecticut, where on the evening of August 20 a fiery flying object of some sort had rammed through a twenty-gauge steel billboard and hurtled on. Roberts, who investigated the event immediately after it happened, told me the thing had torn a large hole in the sign, leaving fragments of itself behind on the jagged edges of the hole.

As we drove, I elicited more information from Augie about the weird Al Bender IFSB hush-up story. It seemed that besides Bender himself, the key members of the IFSB were Roberts, Lucchesi, and a Clarksburg, West Virginia, man named Gray Barker, who was the group's chief investigator and published his own UFO magazine, the *Saucerian.* Bender's outfit included a good number of space and saucer enthusiasts, some of whom, including Augie, wrote UFO articles for (as I thought of them then) semi-science-fiction magazines such as *Fate.* Another IFSBer later to become well known in ufological circles was IFSB International Council member George W. Fawcett, whose first appearance in the group's publication *Space Review* curiously enough announced he was ending his saucer investigations after five years of intensive work. (Quitting and then, after a time, returning to The Field is one of ufology's odd little rituals.)

Augie repeated the tale of Bender's three menacing visitors in black, adding that Bender had been told to stop publishing *Space Review*, disband the club, and cease his UFO investigations. This, Roberts said, had been done. While, obviously, Bender could not reveal what the awful truth was that he'd been ordered to stop probing into and talking about, he did tell Augie that one of his visitors said "they"—meaning, Roberts thought, the U.S. government—had no power to stop what was going on, which I took to mean an invasion from another planet or something equally horrific. When the truth was made public sometime in the following two months, Augie said, it "will be fantastic."

Roberts had given me a couple of copies of *Space Review*, which I found to contain a harmless mishmash of truth and fiction about saucers. I couldn't understand why the government or whoever had sent the Men in Black would bother with Bender and his IFSB, especially since, at the time, the air force seemed to be becoming progressively more open about the UFO information it possessed. But there it was in black and white on page one of the October 1953 *Space Review*, complete with a strange use of quotation marks:

> STATEMENT OF IMPORTANCE
>
> "The mystery of the flying saucers is no longer a mystery. The source is already known, but any information about this is being withheld by orders from a higher source. We would like to print the full story in Space Review, but because of the nature of the information we are sorry that we have been advised in the negative."
>
> We advise those engaged in saucer work to please be very cautious.

I determined to meet and interview Al Bender as soon as it could be arranged.

As Augie and I neared New Haven, I steered the conversation back to the wayward fireball. Two witnesses, Lorrayne and Margurete DiMeola, lived in a house just a few yards from the signboard. About 8 P.M. on the night in question, they heard a whizzing noise, saw a bright flash that "lit up the sky like daylight," and heard a very loud explosion. The windows of their home rattled, and its lights dimmed for an instant. When the DiMeolas rushed outside, they saw heavy black smoke rising from a hole in the nearby billboard. According to these two ladies, before long, the fire department and police ballistics experts showed up and examined the damage, finding no trace of gunpowder or other evidence of a bomb.

A newspaper account Augie showed me related that a fiery object was seen to swoop out of the darkening sky, crash through the steel billboard from behind, and keep on flying, across the road and, depending upon who was being quoted, back into space, or toward a mile-distant hill called East Rock, or dropping into a much closer field. Another account told of a startled and unfortunately unidentified motorist who reported seeing a red ball of fire a few inches in diameter blast through the sign and flash across his path, about thirty feet in front of his car. It tore through the top of a tree on the far side of the road, just missed telephone wires, and disappeared in the direction of East Rock. A search of the area where some thought the object had fallen turned up nothing.

A few days after the incident, local saucer enthusiast Joseph Barbieri removed the section of the billboard holed by the object. Roberts took me to see Barbieri, who told me he'd found traces of metal from the UFO around the edges of the hole the object had made. He collected these and sent them to Coral Lorenzen, head of the then relatively new Aerial Phenomena Research Organization (APRO), a private UFO research group that was to become very well known and influential in The Field. Lorenzen had the material analyzed by a Milwaukee lab. Barbieri showed me a copy of the lab report, in which the stuff was identified as copper.

When Augie and I went to have a look at the billboard, we discovered it had been repaired. However, we also found that the object seemed to have grazed a wooden support in which it had embedded bits of itself. We cut away several small pieces of this "impregnated" wood, one of which I kept (but have long since lost). Roberts later arranged to have the "alien" material analyzed by the laboratory at the Bendix plant where his friend and IFSB associate Dominick Lucchesi worked. The Bendix lab also identified the material as copper, noting that it was of very high quality.

After poking around the sign, Augie and I visited the DiMeolas, who confirmed what Roberts had told me. We also talked with the operator of a gas station that, together with the DiMeolas' house, closely bracketed the abused signboard. He was sure he saw the destructive UFO fall into a field on the other side of the road, yet nothing had been found there.

Following up after our investigative trip, I spoke with local police, the newspaper reporter who covered the story, and several others, all of whom told me no explanation had been found for the incident. I also learned that a Colonel Emerson of Baton Rouge, Louisiana, had somehow received some of the UFO fragments. The colonel was a reserve army officer, a research chemist with Kaiser Aluminum, and a saucer enthusiast. Emerson told me he, too, found the fragments of the mysterious object to be copper. He also pointed out that, if the object had indeed kept on going after hitting the sign, then it must have had power applied to it after the collision. Otherwise, he said, it wouldn't have had sufficient energy to keep going after impact. In other words, it must have been under some sort of intelligent control.

There also were rumors that some samples of the UFO metal had been analyzed at the Oak Ridge nuclear weapons laboratory, although I was never able to confirm this. Of course, IFSB potentate Al Bender also obtained samples, probably from Augie Roberts, and supposedly had his own analysis done. Not long after, the mysterious three men in black arrived at Bender's door and took their first steps into UFO lore.

A couple of days after my fireball baptism into ufological field research, I drove back to Connecticut, this time alone and to Bridgeport to interview Bender, my way prepared by Dom and Augie. An owlish and nervous little man with black hair and black horn-rimmed glasses to match, Bender was not at all forthcoming. However, through close questioning and the intentional and unintentional hints and allusions he threw out, I learned quite a bit.

Bender claimed to have been visited by a trio "in government service" who told him that, in an article he recently had tried to publish, he accidentally hit upon the answer to the saucer mystery, and that therefore he must drop his UFO investigations. The "solution" to the mystery seems to have been that we were about to be attacked by the saucers, which were based in the polar regions. They were not interplanetary after all, but either the work of the Soviet Union or, and more likely, some other earthly group, perhaps even a mysterious, until recently hidden and highly advanced race. The saucers definitely were not American-made, and the government was helpless against them. A public announcement was coming "within six months." (This is another ufological tradition. An announcement from the government revealing the Truth about UFOs has been imminent more times than I can remember. Unless I missed it, we're still waiting for one.)

Bender professed to be very frightened by the government men and their confirmation that his information was true. Well, who wouldn't be? Coming from a character like Bender, though, I found the whole thing more amusing than terrifying.

There are those in ufology who still believe Bender really was hushed up, probably by government agents (over time transmuted in both Bender's tellings and those of others, notably Gray Barker and John Keel, into much more than that). The New Haven billboard incident was the proximate cause of this intimidation. The hurtling gadget was an American missile of some sort—either gone astray during a classified experiment or accidentally launched by one of our warplanes. Bender and his associates had physical evidence that could cause problems for the government. So a clever hush-up was carried out to take advantage of the flying saucer mystery and Bender's paranoia, perhaps the first—but not the last—time a fake UFO cover-up was used to protect government secrets and careers.

Maybe. There's no doubt in my mind Bender was truly obsessed not only with saucers but also science-fiction and horror films, the occult, and who knows what else. While he may actually have believed his story, may even have been visited and threatened, I thought it more likely then, and still do, that he cooked the whole thing up to provide a dramatic way to cloak personal reasons for disbanding his club. I think Gray Barker, who was to exploit the "Bender Mystery" and the Men in Black for all they were worth, probably had it right. In a November 20, 1954, letter to New Zealand ufologist Harold Fulton he wrote, "There is little mystery connected with it [Bender's tale] other than the mystery of Al's own mind and imagination. I think that it was a persecution complex, developed, perhaps, out of being unable to cope with the administrative details of his large organization, his inability to solve the saucer mystery, and possibly some deep-seated psychoses. . . ."

Anyway, the IFSB folded and, as far as I know, the New Haven fireball case is still on ufology's unsolved list. Together, these two possibly connected episodes seem to sum up ufology: genuinely mysterious events that always remain somehow just beyond solution while becoming impossibly tangled in a web of wacky human failings and yearnings. I didn't realize it at the time, but looking back, I think the Bender and fireball affairs and the people involved planted the seed that before long grew into the amusedly jaundiced take on the subject that has stayed with me to this day. Back in 1953, though, the youthful earnestness reflected in "Philosophical Outline #7" was strong and fresh and more than a match for my cynical side.

MY SAUCERING ODYSSEY BEGINS

I returned to my furnished room in Fort Lee a bit apprehensive about what I'd gotten into, but also exhilarated. Wacky and weird or not, "saucering" was great fun, and in a few days I would be off on an interesting, rambling road trip, something I still immensely enjoy.

Before I hit the highways, though, I had two more local interviews to do. The first of these was with airline pilot Robert Adickes, who in April 1950, while flying a TWA DC-3 near South Bend, Indiana, made one of the most famous saucer sightings of the early UFO age. As the airliner droned through the night sky, First Officer Robert Manning spotted a glowing orange disk coming up from behind and to the right. He immediately called it to Captain Adickes's attention. At first the saucer was at an altitude lower than the DC-3 and appeared to be about a half mile away, a distance it held as it rose to the liner's altitude. Adickes told me he estimated it to be about fifty feet in diameter and that it definitely was a solid object.

For some time, the saucer paced the plane at a speed of about 175 MPH. Adickes turned off the cabin lights and asked his nineteen passengers to take a look. Most saw the UFO and gave descriptions closely matching those of the flight crew. Adickes tried to ease his plane closer to the saucer, but it always slid away at the same rate, maintaining its distance. Then the pilot decided to bank abruptly toward the disk. As he did so, the saucer made a sudden ninety-degree turn and rapidly flew away, disappearing in the distance in ten to fifteen seconds. The sighting had lasted about four minutes.

Adickes was very impressive, calm, reasonable, and solid, just the sort of man you'd want piloting a plane you were aboard. This made his conviction that the saucers were from another planet seem absolutely reasonable and made me feel I was on the right track.

On the heels of my talk with Adickes was an interview with a Mr. Brewster, a guided-missile expert and an assistant to the president of Republic Aviation, then a major aircraft manufacturer on Long Island. I told him what I'd learned from Adickes and about the Bender story. He seemed favorably impressed by the former and very doubtful about the latter. Most interesting and exciting to me, though, was that Brewster had done a great deal of saucer investigating—officially, for his company. He said that as a result of this he was convinced no one, not even the air force, had any definitive answers as to what the saucers were or how they were propelled.

Brewster also made quite a point of telling me he thought I would have a hard time getting anything useful out of the air force and in getting any consistent ideas of the performance and appearance of saucers, since in his opinion UFO reports, even the credible ones, were so conflicting. As I was soon to learn, he certainly was correct—about the latter.

Bright and early on the morning of November 14, I drove southward to Washington, D.C., where I hoped to gain access to air force UFO files and interview several important saucer witnesses and famed saucer author Maj. Donald E. Keyhoe.

Keyhoe, a retired Marine Corps officer and U.S. Naval Academy graduate, had left active duty a few years after being injured in a plane crash. In 1926 he went to work for the U.S. Commerce Department as a public affairs flack. The following year, he landed a plum assignment as an aide to Charles Lindbergh during the triumphal tour of the country following his solo flight to Paris. Keyhoe recounted his experiences on this trip in his first book, *Flying with Lindbergh* (1928), beginning a quite successful career as a book and magazine writer.

It was Keyhoe's piece in the January 1950 issue of *True* magazine that catapulted him into ufology and forever after made his name all but synonymous with flying saucers. Called "The Flying Saucers Are Real," this article proclaimed we were under surveillance by beings from another world, who'd been hanging around for at least a couple of centuries. Keyhoe laid out all the essential elements of what became known as the extraterrestrial hypothesis, or ETH, generating tremendous controversy and equally tremendous magazine sales. A few months later, he expanded his article to book length, and under the same title, it became a huge success, selling a half million copies. Keyhoe's second saucer tome, *Flying Saucers from Outer Space,* had been released just as I was getting into The Field and was already on best-seller lists when I drove into Washington.

Keyhoe was the first person I contacted after getting settled in my hotel. Though I had a fairly informative telephone conversation with him, I had the sense that since I was planning to write a saucer book, he considered me a rival he had no intention of helping. He was, he said, too busy to see me for several weeks, but promised to arrange to meet "in December or January," if I would write and remind him.

During our chat, I asked Keyhoe what he thought of George Adamski's claim of meeting and conversing with a man from Venus. He replied that he didn't think much of it, and "to put it politely, Adamski had a vivid dream."

It was obvious my "rival" wanted me to think he had the inside track on all the hot saucer dope. Without prompting, he hinted darkly that there were certain questions I might ask him which he could not answer, and that these questions could concern a new investigation he was pursuing. I assumed this might involve important new evidence for the ETH or perhaps a new theory altogether, an impression Keyhoe did nothing to discourage.

In June 1954, when I was on the second of many research trips to Washington, I finally managed to entice Keyhoe into seeing me. He came to my room at the Ambassador Hotel. It was a very short meeting, during which Keyhoe did most of the talking, asking questions clearly aimed at assessing what I knew about saucers and determining if I had any edge on him. Finally, satisfied I posed no commercial threat, he left, commenting that *he* had sources that no one else had, sources who were giving him the inside scoop on what the government knew and was hiding about saucers.

Although young and rather naive, I wasn't impressed. I felt—correctly, I still believe—that Keyhoe routinely made too much of too little, at least in part just to sell books. After all, he was a professional writer who got his start in the pulp magazines of the 1920s and 1930s. I suppose that is where he picked up a literary device he used in his saucer books and which I hated, and still do: fictitious characters and fictitious "reconstructions" of fictitious conversations dramatizing UFO cases and Keyhoe's own musings on the Significance of It All.

So I wasn't at all impressed with his alleged insider sources. Unlike most in the saucer game, even then I understood the essence of the "need to know" philosophy of the military, especially the intelligence and other sensitive branches. Keyhoe's big-deal insiders were for the most part Pentagon public information officers (PIOs). Why would a PIO be given access to top secret information about UFOs—if there were any such information—when he might spill the beans to an unauthorized person, inadvertently or otherwise? These PIOs, some of whom I got to know rather well over lunch in the Pentagon cafeteria and about whom Keyhoe made such a fuss, were perhaps the military people *least* likely to fulfill any writer's dream of sensational inside scoop, about flying saucers or anything else. That's why I never tried to press them for information beyond what they were authorized to provide.

I will admit that, when I began my research, I was under the impression from Keyhoe's writings that I'd need a special air force clearance to get anywhere on saucers in official Washington, a clearance that Keyhoe seemed to have. Before leaving New Jersey on my cross-country trip, I had written President Eisenhower, whom my father had known very well in the army. When I made my first visit to the Air Force Office of Public Information in the Pentagon in November 1953, a day or two after talking with Keyhoe on the phone, I hadn't received a reply from the president (and never got one; perhaps Bender's intimidators picked it off). To my surprise and secret amusement, during our meeting the following June, Keyhoe said he'd been told I had met with Ike and been given "exclusive info." Since, as I've already noted, Keyhoe left apparently assured of my commercial insignificance, it's likely I'd disabused him of this titillating notion. Still, I wonder if he ever really entirely shed himself of it.

Anyway, one day in mid-November 1953, I strode confidently up to the air force Pentagon press desk and asked the duty PIO, a young lieutenant, to see anything he had available on flying saucers, expecting to be told to take a hike. To my utter surprise, I learned that no clearance of any kind was needed to see the reports on UFO cases investigated by the air force—including those Keyhoe had used for his books. All that was withheld were the names of the witnesses and others interviewed in connection with the sightings, as well as any sensitive information about military equipment, unit locations, procedures, and the like.

Not only was I permitted to read the files, I was even allowed to make detailed notes from them. (I later discovered some of the confidential military stuff had inadvertently been released to me, but I never disclosed any of it.) I also was told that there should be no trouble arranging for me to visit Project Blue Book, the air force's saucer investigation group at Wright-Patterson Air Force Base in Ohio, and while there to see not only additional saucer reports but also photographs of UFOs. It was obvious that ace saucer-truth-seeker Keyhoe had been overplaying the secrecy and inside-info angles to add excitement to his storytelling and pull in paying readers.

While on a second visit to the Pentagon in late January 1954, I found public access to case reports had been severely restricted and was advised I would not be allowed to visit Project Blue Book (though I finally was able to do so in 1962, one of the few private saucer researchers ever to be so privileged). I was told on the QT that the newly restrictive policy was largely due to Keyhoe's ravings in *Flying Saucers from Outer Space* and his complaints that I'd somehow been given special treatment. So it was that I, a rank newcomer to saucering, had quite innocently and indirectly made a contribution to The Field's conviction that the government knows and is covering up the Shocking Truth About the Saucers—an angle central to Keyhoe's pronouncements, which he promoted and exploited for the entirety of his long ufological career.

SAUCERS over the NATION'S CAPITAL

Among the cases I looked into while in Washington in late 1953, was one Keyhoe had made much of in his latest book, the famous Washington National Airport radar-visual incidents of the summer of 1952. I was able to interview Harry Barnes, the senior air traffic controller at National during these events, and James Ritchey and James Copeland, two other controllers who were involved. At the Civil Aeronautics Administration (CAA), I picked up a pamphlet called "A Preliminary Study of Unidentified Targets Observed on Air Traffic Control Radars," which was an attempt to debunk the events of 1952 as having been caused by weather phenomena, namely, the temperature inversions of which Professor Menzel was so fond. I found the pamphlet—though not necessarily the explanation it advanced—ludicrous. At the time, I noted the report "impresses me as having been written by imbeciles to be read by imbeciles."

The three CAA air traffic controllers, U.S. government employees, were generally reluctant to say much, and all said they were "obliged" to stand by the official position that the blips they saw on their scopes were caused by temperature inversions. Copeland and Ritchey seemed quite sincere in this and neither bought the saucers-come-from-space notion. Barnes, on the other hand, had different ideas. He made it clear that, as a CAA employee, he felt he was not free to express his personal opinion on what UFOs were. He then added he was obliged to stand on both the CAA report and Keyhoe's account of the incidents. Puzzled, I pointed out the dramatic differences between the two. Barnes replied that I "may draw my own conclusions," by which I understood that he meant the CAA was playing down the interplanetary angle, while Keyhoe was playing it up. After we finished the formal interview, Barnes couldn't resist telling me his own opinion, off the record. After all these years, at last it can be told: Barnes was certain the UFOs he tracked were solid objects, probably intelligently operated vehicles from outer space.

Through the air force press desk, I managed to arrange an interview with Maj. Lewis Norman, an air force radar expert whose views Keyhoe cited in support of his interpretation of the Washington National case.

With some amusement, Norman told me Keyhoe "had badly misquoted" him. Then he went on to tell me things that largely bore out the author's claims. For example, Norman told me a temperature inversion of nine to eighteen degrees would be required to produce what was seen on radar in July and August 1952, yet the inversions on those nights were only one to two degrees. He did explain, however, that a greater inversion at some distance could still have been responsible. Nonetheless, he thought there was "a very good chance" the Washington National UFOs were solid objects. In fact, he said, he thought it was "a very good possibility that the saucers come from outer space." Coming from an air force radar expert and former pilot who had chased UFOs that turned out to be "IFOs"—ordinary things like balloons and airplanes—this made a great impression on my receptive mind.

Before leaving Washington I interviewed several more UFO sighters. Among them was the one person who may clearly have seen the saucers the CAA and air force radars had picked up, and another man, a private pilot, who made a quite impressive sighting more than two years before.

About two o'clock on the morning of July 18,1952, Elmer Chambers, the chief engineer for Washington's Radio WRC, was leaving the station's transmitter when he spotted five huge disks flying in trailing line formation, swiftly descending toward the ground. He told me all glowed orange, and all carried a single pulsating light. These identical lights pulsated in unison about once a second. Suddenly, the saucers executed a right-angle turn (a standard saucer maneuver), and began flying horizontally. They then made another ninety-degree turn and shot almost straight up into the night sky.

Bertram Totten, at the time a private pilot for sixteen years, told me he flew above a saucer in broad daylight. On the afternoon of March 26, 1950, Totten was flying a light plane by himself near Washington National Airport. His altitude was five thousand feet. Out of nowhere and about one thousand feet below, a classic saucer appeared—circular, about forty feet in diameter and ten feet thick, aluminum in color and glittering on top, with no windows and no sign of hatches or other openings. Totten told me the UFO was on a course that crossed his, and as the thing was about to pass under him, he dived his plane toward it, hoping for a closer look. As he did so, the saucer accelerated at a terrific rate, tilted slightly upward, and disappeared in a few seconds, moving at a speed Totten estimated at four to five hundred miles an hour.

Both Chambers and Totten impressed me. As I put it in my notes, they were "solid," and "not the type" to make things up. What's more,

Totten was black, a factor that seemed to me to militate against his story being a hoax, given the state of race relations in the early 1950s.

SAUCERS over the OLD SOUTH,...

After interviewing Totten I was on the road again, headed for South Carolina. I left Washington feeling my time had been well spent. I had acquired much detailed information from the air force on cases I was planning to look into and had learned about several others. The bonus from this was discovering the truth about the air force's approach to public disclosure was quite different than claimed by Keyhoe and others in The Field. I had obtained firsthand information from key witnesses in both well-known and lesser-known cases, some of which I was sure no one else had. I had spoken with Keyhoe and gotten something of a measure of him. All in all, I felt sure I was on my way to both literary success and a solution to the mystery of the flying saucers, which, with the misplaced optimism of youth, I thought would come in fairly short order. In this I was not alone. The Field in those days was sure all the answers were just around the corner, if, perhaps, locked up in some Pentagon safe.

In South Carolina, I hoped to gain access to the sort of evidence that could provide a major step toward solving the saucer mystery, a motion picture of a formation of flying saucers. It seems that one evening almost exactly a year before, a Long Island man visiting friends in the Landrum, South Carolina, area had shot about forty feet of 8 mm color film. It showed eleven UFOs traveling rapidly east to west across the sky, the fading rays of the setting sun behind them. The photographer, David Bunch, was accompanied by his wife, aunt, and friends Mr. and Mrs. C. F. McLean of nearby Tryon. All saw the saucers, which Mr. McLean spotted first and called to the attention of the rest.

I interviewed the McLeans in Tryon. Mr. McLean, a Southern gentleman of the old school, was one of the most reputable of witnesses I had yet encountered. He told me the saucers were metallic and glowing, but that at times one or more of them seemed to disappear "in place" and then reappear. The number visible at any one time varied between four and eleven. McLean told me that before his own experience he vehemently disagreed with his son Clyde, the editor of a shipyard newspaper in Mississippi and an enthusiastic "saucer fiend." The elder McLean had been made a believer by his sighting and was convinced the saucers were from outer space.

Bunch gave his film to McLean, who passed it along to his son, who in turn told Donald Keyhoe about it. Keyhoe arranged for the air force to be given the film for analysis in exchange for two copies, one each for the senior McLean and Bunch. McLean told me the copies were much darker than the original, making it difficult see the saucer images clearly. (Thus I encountered still another persistent ufological theme, the saucer film or photos given to the air force, with poor copies being returned to the witness or the originals lost or returned with the best segments removed.)

Unfortunately, while McLean had his copy during my visit, he had no projector, and it was impossible to make out anything on the tiny 8 mm frames with the naked eye. I hoped to have Bunch screen his copy for me when I returned to New Jersey, but as I have no recollection or record of this occurring, I doubt that it ever did.

On the same evening Bunch shot his film, November 16, 1952, and a short while after that incident, hundreds of people in the Florence, South Carolina, area—including an air traffic controller, whom I interviewed by phone, and the crew and forty-two passengers of an airliner waiting to take off from the Florence airport—reported seeing a huge, white, elliptical saucer pass overhead at a speed "faster than a jet." After interviewing the controller by phone, I decided this provided some indirect support for the McLean-Bunch sighting, even though Florence was almost two hundred miles from the Landrum-Tryon area. Obviously, I thought, the saucers were operating all over South Carolina at that time.

...SIGHTED by a WOULD-BE WRITER from NEW JERSEY, and...

On November 23, while checking things out in the Florence area, I interviewed Mr. and Mrs. W. J. Hutchinson. I set up the interview with a telephone call to Mrs. Hutchinson, who told me she had seen saucers "many times." This made me wonder, as I'd never heard of a genuine case of someone who had seen UFOs more than once or twice.

During the interview that evening, Mrs. Hutchinson said she, her husband, "and the whole neighborhood" had seen saucers at least a dozen times during the past two years—and that she had seen one go over just before I arrived! Now I was *really* wondering.

She then suggested we step outside to see if there were any more around. As we walked out the front door, she claimed to spot one, which I missed. Just as I was about to write her off as a charter member of the lunatic fringe, another appeared. And I saw it! It was a white light, with the same magnitude as the average star, moving rapidly south to north at a very high altitude in the night sky. A few seconds after this UFO disappeared in the north, still another appeared. This one was like the first in all respects except that it had a blinking red light encircling the central white one. Both passed in total silence.

Needless to say, I was pleased, dumbfounded, and very excited. However, being a good investigator, I immediately contacted both the Florence airport and Shaw Air Force Base, about thirty miles distant. I learned that two F-80 jet fighters were in the vicinity at the time, flying at twenty-five thousand feet and traveling the same direction as "my" saucers. I also learned that no UFOs had been reported or tracked on radar.

Gloom. Still, I wasn't 100 percent convinced. The UFOs seemed to me far bigger than aircraft lights would have appeared at that altitude, and those I spoke with at the airport agreed that if the jets were low enough for their lights to seem so large, we probably would have heard the roar of their engines.

Even so, I reluctantly had to conclude that what I saw most likely were the F-80s, and on further questioning, the Hutchinsons admitted that *all* the "saucers" they'd sighted finally disappeared in the direction of Shaw AFB. Moreover, *all* their sightings were of lights in the night sky. On top of this, they were "saucer minded" in the sense that they were eager to see UFOs. Of course, observers of this sort are strongly disposed to jump to conclusions.

If what I'd seen that night were airplanes, I could see how untrained observers could easily be fooled, myself a case in point. It seemed to me that a good number of what ufologist J. Allen Hynek later labeled "Nocturnal Lights" sightings could be chalked up to misidentification of high-flying planes and other all too earthly devices.

Gloom.

...SHOT AT by a FARMER

My spirits were lifted when I followed up on a tip provided by Mr. McLean. In Tabor City, North Carolina, I spoke with an acquaintance of McLean's, Horace Carter, the Pulitzer Prize–winning editor of the *Tabor City Tribune*, the local weekly newspaper. The February 4, 1953, edition of Carter's paper had carried a story about farmer Lloyd C. Booth, who shot at and seemed to have hit a saucer that got too close for comfort. Carter said Booth was a fine, upstanding guy, to which he said he'd attested in a sworn statement for the air force. The newspaperman told me where I could find Booth, and I was on my way.

Booth had a farm and owned a gas station near Loris, South Carolina, just across the state line from Tabor City. He was a World War II veteran—antiaircraft artillery, appropriately enough. We met at his station, where he told me a fascinating story.

Around midnight on January 29, 1953, Booth heard a commotion among his farm animals. When he went to investigate, he saw a flying saucer behind his barn, south of his position. It was only about seventy-five feet above the ground, barely clearing some trees, and moving eastward at "about a walking pace." Booth followed it, even running out front to get a better look. He saw two lights in back and a lighted "window" in front, but could see nothing inside the UFO. There were no identifying markings and no visible means of propulsion, though Booth heard a faint hum, like that of an electric motor.

This peculiar chase lasted for at least twenty minutes and covered about a half-mile. During this time, Booth yelled for his family to come outside, but apparently wasn't heard. Then he decided to shoot at the saucer with his .22 pistol, "to see if it would respond. And it did." He heard his first bullet bounce off the object, and "the thing took off," zipping away at what he estimated to be "a good six hundred miles an hour." By the time he fired a second shot, the saucer was well out of range, and he missed it.

I asked Booth where he thought the saucer had come from. He said he believed it was from some other country and not from space. He added that there had been several saucer sightings in the area before the shooting incident, but none afterward, so he figured he'd frightened them off.

Booth's story reminded me of several of the saucer hoaxes that had received a lot of publicity. However, as I wrote in my notes, "due to the local reputation of Booth, for honesty, church-going, etc., and due to the stature of Mr. Carter, I cannot make any conclusion other than that this particular incident is true. Mr. Carter had just recently won the Pulitzer Prize when this incident occurred, and I do not feel he would have risked his reputation on a saucer hoax. Of course, Booth may be lying, but I feel that is extremely unlikely." This may say more about the youthful me than it does about the veracity of the trigger-happy farmer.

MONKEY from MARS, "ROCKET SHIP" from...? and an EARLY ROSWELL

My next stop was Atlanta, which at the time was fertile saucer ground. There had been numerous recent sightings in the area, and adding spice to the mix was the "monkey from Mars" hoax. This involved local barber Edward Watters, who on a bet had shaved a monkey, killed it, and chopped off its tail. Then he and a friend drove out into the country, laid the "Martian" in the middle of the road, and waited for a car to come along, so they could flag it down and claim they'd accidentally hit one of several little men from a saucer that had been hovering nearby. Unfortunately for the hoaxers, they stopped a police car.

Before long, the prank was confessed, and Watters paid a forty-dollar fine for violating a sanitation ordinance by leaving a dead animal on a public highway. An amazing number of people seem to have bought the story, some still believing it even after Watters had admitted the truth. (Here we have still another ufological "convention," one with which I've had direct, confessed-hoaxer experience: an admitted hoax isn't that at all. It's part of The Cover-Up.)

Moving from the ridiculous to the genuinely mysterious, I interviewed Eastern Airlines pilot John Whitted, who lived in Atlanta. As all saucer fiends know, in July 1948 he and Capt. Clarence Chiles had one of the most famous UFO sightings of all time. On an unusually clear night near Montgomery, Alabama, Chiles and Whitted saw and, they thought, were almost hit by a huge, wingless, windowed, fire-spitting, rocket-shaped UFO that roared out of the sky directly ahead of their DC-3, swooping by very fast and very close, then pulling sharply up and disappearing into a cloud bank.

According to saucer lore, this was the case that convinced air force investigators the saucers were from outer space. This led to the famous Project Sign (predecessor to Project Blue Book) "Estimate of the Situation," a top secret report that stated this conclusion and got all the way to air force chief of staff Gen. Hoyt Vandenberg before being consigned to the classified trash. Which, I guess, is just as well, since according to what I've read in years since, the two pilots probably saw a giant meteor, or bolide, that actually was many miles away and much higher than their plane. On the other hand, they did say the thing pulled up, a very un-meteor-like thing to do.

Perusing the flying saucer file at the *Atlanta Constitution,* I learned that a saucer of some sort had landed on the Fulton County farm of Ralph Horton—and that Horton had "captured" the thing. Of course, I lost no time getting out to see Horton, who obligingly hauled the saucer out of the woods behind his house, where he'd tossed it after the excitement had died down.

It seems that in July 1952, some of Horton's neighbors saw the gadget fly over their property before it landed in his yard. Soon after he retrieved it, Horton called both the air force and the Atlanta airport, asking if they had any interest. When he described what he had, he was told there was no interest, that he could do what he liked with it.

"It" was a box-kite-like contraption made of wooden sticks and tin or aluminum foil with a weather balloon attached. In a phone call to the Atlanta airport, I confirmed that it was a device used by the air force to determine wind velocity and direction at various altitudes. It was sent up attached to a balloon and tracked by radar, the beams of which the gadget reflected very well.

I photographed Horton with the "saucer," which he then offered to me. I took it with thanks. Unfortunately, it got lost in the shuffle over the years. If I'd held onto it, it might have been I rather than my Esteemed Coauthor who cracked the infamous Roswell saucer-crash case, which involved a bunch of such gadgets, adorned with weirdly marked tape. Sigh . . .

A BELIEVING BRIGADIER and a CURIOUS COLONEL

From Atlanta, I went on to Pascagoula, Mississippi, where among others I interviewed Clyde McLean, who indeed proved to be a true believer, but a very nice fellow. He and his wife had seen a UFO about a year before and reported it to nearby Keesler Air Force Base. They were convinced they'd seen something from another planet.

On a visit to Keesler AFB to check on the McLeans' sighting, I spoke with Brig. Gen. J. P. Kerkendall, the deputy base commander. About two years before, the general had a spectacular sighting of his own, and he told me he believed UFOs were real, solid objects but had no idea where they were from. The fact that I was able to speak with an air force general about the subject on the record, especially given his views on saucers, raised even more doubts in my mind about what Keyhoe and others had been writing about air force secrecy and debunking.

Crossing the Mississippi into Louisiana, I stopped in Baton Rouge to interview Col. Robert Emerson, with whom I had spoken about his analysis of fragments from the New Haven fireball. While Emerson clearly was a man solidly grounded in science—he was a research chemist—and a high-ranking army reserve officer, I found his views to be a bit far out, even for a willing believer such as I was at the time. He told me he had no trouble at all with the great variety of saucer shapes and sizes reported. He said they might be "as diverse as the different kinds of fishes in the sea. Creatures from different planets no doubt use different types of spaceships, and perhaps creatures from the same planet use different types for different purposes." He added that he thought "the saucer visitors are 'tourists' passing through our atmosphere, and therefore have a desire to watch us but not to communicate with us."

LIGHTS over LUBBOCK

Rather bemused, I left Emerson and pressed on to Texas. After stops in Dallas and Fort Worth, I arrived in Lubbock, intent on digging into the famous Lubbock lights case of August 1951. This involved numerous sightings of mysterious, softly glowing lights flying in formation or, at least, large groups over the town and five photos of such lights, in an orderly *V* formation, taken on two nights by Texas Tech freshman Carl Hart Jr.

The most significant sightings other than Hart's were those of four Texas Tech professors, one of whom I interviewed. Dr. W. L. Ducker, then head of the Department of Petroleum Engineering, said he really didn't know what he and his colleagues saw, and he refused "to go out on a limb and hazard a guess." However, he was quite sure that Donald Menzel's reflection-refraction theory was wrong, and he proceeded to explain why at great length.

Ducker also had serious doubts about Hart's photographs. For one thing, the formation they showed wasn't anything like the loosely grouped objects he and his associates had seen. Also, the lights in the photos were much brighter, and there was only a little blurring in one photo and none in the other four, even though Hart said the formation he saw was moving quickly. The professor also had heard some unflattering things about Hart that suggested to him the kid might have been hoaxing, especially since he took his photos after other sightings had been reported in the local media and saucer excitement was running high.

Next stop, Carl Hart, by then a junior at Tech. He showed me his negatives, on which the images were so small I could see nothing useful. He also gave me eight-by-ten prints. While Hart was quite cooperative, he struck me as a not particularly serious fellow.

I followed up with William Hams, the reporter-photographer on the *Lubbock Avalanche Journal* who covered flying saucer stories for the paper and arranged for Hart to sell his pictures to *Life* magazine. Hams was convinced Hart wasn't hoaxing, and he showed me the August 30, 1951, edition of his paper, published the day after Hart snapped his famous photos. At least four people reported seeing the lights that night.

I wasn't sure what to think. From what Ducker told me about what he'd seen—large numbers of faint lights in no regular formation—it was obvious this wasn't what Hart photographed. The photos showed lights in a very precise shallow *V* formation, suggesting they were on a solid, flying-winglike object. Adding to the confusion, Ducker said the air force intelligence officers who had interviewed him seemed convinced Hart's photos were not of the "real Lubbock lights." Yet the public air force report said there seemed to be no reason to believe Hart faked them. So the air force appeared to be declaring possible fakes to be genuine, just the opposite of what they would have been doing if they actually were trying to hush up the saucer scare.

Years later, I heard that what the professors and many other Lubbock residents saw were migrating birds, plovers, reflecting the glow of city street lights. The evidence for this was quite convincing, but that still leaves Hart's photographs. Were there real UFOs operating over Lubbock at the same time the plovers were passing through?

A COUPLE of NOT-QUITE ORTHODOX SCIENTISTS

At the Lowell Observatory in Flagstaff, Arizona, my faith in science—or, at least, some scientists—was bolstered. There I was very fortunate to be able to interview two great astronomers, Clyde W. Tombaugh, discoverer of the planet Pluto, and E. C. Slipher, a renowned authority on Mars.

Tombaugh, a friendly and unpretentious man, was very open and quite willing to discuss saucers, what they might be, and where they might be from. Perhaps this was because in 1949 he had a remarkable sighting of his own, as well as later sightings, including several of the strange green fireballs seen over New Mexico in 1948 and 1949.

The 1949 sighting occurred on August 20, at about 10:45 P.M.

Tombaugh, his wife, and his mother-in-law were sitting outdoors at his home in Las Cruces, New Mexico, gazing at the stars. Suddenly, at the zenith, Tombaugh saw about ten faint, rectangular, symmetrically arranged, yellowish-green lights, which he thought were on a single object. This strange phenomenon moved very fast to the south-southeast, disappearing from view in about three seconds at thirty-five or forty degrees above the horizon. The lights dimmed out gradually before disappearing. His wife also saw the object and said she detected a very faint glow coming from the thing as a whole. Tombaugh didn't see this, but was sure it was a single object because the lights maintained exactly fixed positions in relation to each other.

He said he was quite unnerved by what he saw, and therefore failed to study it in the scientific manner he should have. However, he was quite emphatic in rejecting the temperature-inversion explanation advanced yet again by Harvard astronomer Donald Menzel. While Tombaugh definitely believed what he and his wife saw in August 1949 was a solid object, he was unwilling to suggest it was a spaceship from another world.

The affable astronomer also described his other sightings to me. There were green fireballs, for which he offered no explanation, and a light in the daylight sky, five or six times brighter than Venus and moving just as the 1949 object had. Tombaugh had no doubt there was intelligent life on other planets, though not in our solar system, and he said he felt extraterrestrial visitation certainly was possible. He made it very clear that he believed flying saucers should be subjected to serious scientific investigation.

Dr. Slipher told me that modern science was pretty well agreed that there were canals on Mars. Where scientists differed was over whether they were natural river valleys or artificial constructions. His view was that they were the latter, as the pattern they exhibited was such that they seemed very unlikely to be natural formations. Therefore, Slipher thought "that at some time in the past the surface of Mars was networked by intelligent minds," who built the system to irrigate vegetation. "We cannot," he said, "explain their appearance or behavior as natural features, i.e., they were artificially built." Thus there once was intelligent life on Mars, life that through ingenuity could still exist, by perhaps having gone underground.

Given his breathtaking declarations about the Martian canals, I expected Slipher to be open to the idea that the flying saucers might be coming here from the Red Planet or, if not, then maybe from a world outside our solar system. However, he surprised me by saying he generally agreed with Menzel, that is, that all saucers could be explained as natural phenomena or misinterpretation of conventional things such as balloons and airplanes.

Well, Slipher *did* turn out to be wrong about the canals . . .

The matters I relate
Are true lies.

—Jean Cocteau

As I drove southwestward out of Flagstaff toward Prescott, Arizona, and Los Angeles beyond, I was more certain than ever that the flying saucers were from another planet, quite possibly Mars. Still, my investigations so far also had raised a host of questions in my mind. It wouldn't be long before these were joined by additional and serious concerns arising from what I learned about who and what were behind some of the most spectacular saucer tales of all.

FLASHBACK: WINSLOW, ARIZONA

A major objective of my trip was to get as much inside information as possible on the claims of George Adamski, whose new book (with Desmond

Leslie), *Flying Saucers Have Landed,* was causing quite a stir. The "Professor," as he liked to be styled, was an uneducated but intelligent, clever, and charming Polish immigrant. In the 1930s and 1940s, he had been a semisuccessful Southern California guru, the founder of a mystical-religion cult called the Royal Order of Tibet. In the early 1950s, at the age of sixty-one, he was the first to claim contact and communication with benevolent Space Brothers, and during the next couple of years he came into his own as *the* flying saucer "contactee." His first contact, after many saucer sightings beginning in 1946, was a meeting with Orthon, a man from Venus. This supposedly took place in the Mojave Desert on November 20, 1952, precisely 10.2 road miles northeast of the crossroads town of Desert Center, California.

Adamski's claims of receiving wisdom from other worlds; trips into space, to the Moon, and even to Saturn aboard flying saucers and their mother ships; and so on, as ghostwritten for him in *Flying Saucers Have Landed* and two other books, defined contactee-ism for all who followed in his and Orthon's footsteps. He was remarkably adept at turning attacks upon himself and his tales to his advantage, not to mention getting a lot of mileage out of stories that proved easy to rip apart from any sort of reasonable, scientific point of view. Yet despite everything I came to learn about the man, I never had any dislike for him, which suggests at least one reason why he was so successful.

When I set out for California, I still had an open mind about Adamski and his claims. True, his photos of scout-ship saucers and the like seemed too good to be authentic, and on examination by experts, it was clear they could have been faked without much trouble. True, the likelihood that spacemen would be essentially physically identical to earthlings wasn't great, even if they were from our solar system. True, Venus seemed an unlikely home for any sort of life as we know it, let alone long-haired, blue-eyed Space Brothers. Still, there was something about the Professor's story that I found compelling. Maybe it was because, if it were true, the riddle of the saucers was solved, and in a very positive way. Then again, maybe at the time I was just a sucker for a tall tale well told.

Driving through spectacular Oak Creek Canyon on a beautiful December day, I thought back on my last interview stop before Flagstaff. This was the Route 66, Santa Fe Railroad town of Winslow, Arizona, where I met with Alfred C. Bailey, one of the six witnesses to Adamski's alleged conversation with Orthon. Also present at the interview was Lyman Streeter, a friend of Bailey's, who at first was so paranoid about being quoted that he refused to give me his name. Both men said they had made saucer sightings on their own, as well as, in Bailey's case, with Adamski. Streeter made what in my estimation were even wilder claims about his personal communications with the saucer people.

Bailey, a Santa Fe Railroad man, told me that, because of his saucer "work," many people in Winslow considered him a crackpot. It had gotten so bad even his sister wouldn't speak to him. With this preamble, he said that, as claimed in Adamski's book, he, his wife, and four others—a Dr. George Hunt Williamson and his wife, of Prescott; Alice K. Wells, owner of Palomar Gardens, the place in California where Adamski lived and held court; and Lucy McGinnis, the Professor's secretary (and girlfriend?)—waited about a mile or mile and a half away while Adamski had his chat with the spaceman. Shortly before Adamski went down the road to the rendezvous he "sensed" was coming, Bailey and the others had seen a huge, cigar-shaped mother ship, floating high above and moving slowly toward the southwest, as if leading the way to the encounter site.

However, contrary to Adamski, Bailey said he never saw Orthon or the small saucer-shaped scout craft in which he landed, even through binoculars. All he saw were "flashes of light" in the direction of the spot where Adamski was supposed to be, which made him think it was possible the small saucer actually did land. Yet Adamski's *Flying Saucers Have Landed* reproduced affidavits in which all present swore they had witnessed the historic meeting. The book also included a rather detailed sketch of Orthon, made by Alice Wells "while watching the interview through binoculars." Hmmm . . .

Streeter chimed in, telling me the photo in *Flying Saucers Have Landed* labeled "Flying Saucer Passing Low Over Trees" was taken by Adamski rather than the man to whom it was credited, a Sgt. Jerrold E. Baker. Streeter claimed (and I later confirmed with Baker) that Adamski had credited the photo to Baker in order to give the impression others were taking pictures of the same kind of saucers he had captured on film. Streeter also asserted that the photo was not of a real saucer, but had been faked by Adamski. This inspired Bailey to add that, to his knowledge, another photo in the book titled "Desert Center, California, 20 November 1952," supposedly showing Orthon's saucer as a tiny, indistinct blob partially hidden by a hill in the far distance, was not taken on the day of the encounter. Hmmm . . .

Yet Bailey insisted on clinging to the possibility that an actual contact with a Venusian had occurred, refusing to have any part in discrediting

Adamski. Despite this, he admitted Adamski's account was "not true in all details" and added that he and Streeter were "drifting away" from the Professor because he supposedly had recently claimed he was "the second coming of Christ."

Streeter then dropped his own bombshell. He said a principal reason for his doubts about Adamski was that the message conveyed by the spaceman through the Professor was cryptic, whereas it should have been crystal clear and "of the sort we can all understand, in English or a recognized Earth code." I asked why he thought this. Well, you see, he had made numerous contacts with spacemen by radio, all in English or International Morse Code! In fact, he, Bailey, and Bailey's fellow witness Williamson had written a book about these contacts. It was called *The Saucers Speak* and was to be published later in December. In these communications, Streeter told me, the Space People said they looked similar to us; that many are "among us" on Earth, unnoticed; that they are mentioned in the Bible; that they worship God, but differently than earthlings do; and so on. Hmmm . . . !

"DOCTOR" WILLIAMSON, I PRESUME?

In Prescott, I met with George Hunt Williamson and his wife, Betty. It turned out Williamson held no doctoral degree, as attributed to him by Adamski. However, he was deeply interested in anthropology and, he claimed, possessed extensive knowledge of the ways of various tribes of Plains Indians, acquired by years of living among them. At twenty-seven, Williamson was barely older than I, and was employed at a local radio station. As I was to learn over the next few years, there was both much less and much more to "Dr." Williamson than met the eye.

Concerning the Adamski affair, at first all Williamson would say was that his part in it was correctly represented in Adamski's book, and if he were asked to sign his sworn statement again, he would do so. I finally got him to open up a bit, and he admitted that all he saw of the meeting—through low-power binoculars—was Adamski talking with "someone, who could have been anyone," and "nearby, something that might have been a saucer." He also said he'd seen the mother ship, and his description was consistent with that given by Bailey and Adamski. He added that, though he believed Adamski had talked with a man from Venus, he could not be certain of it. "But of course," he said, "the Professor would have no reason to lie." Hmmm . . .

I then asked about *The Saucers Speak.* It turned out Williamson and Bailey were the book's coauthors, with Streeter appearing in its pages as "Mr. R," the ham radio hobbyist who had initiated radio contact with the Space People. Williamson was quite willing to discuss what he had learned from his radio—and Ouija board!—contacts with the Space People (all of which he later "admitted" actually were psychic communications). It seemed that the spacemen rejected Darwinian evolution in favor of divine creation, that they came from "many different planets within and outside our solar system," yet all looked "more or less like we do," that they felt Earth was going through a "difficult period" and they wanted to help us, so there were "millions" of them on our planet, passing unnoticed and even intermarrying with Earth people, and so on. *Hmmm . . . !!*

NEXT STOP, CARLSBAD

After interviewing another Prescott resident about eight disks he and two friends had watched do "impossible" maneuvers for over twenty minutes the previous May, I pressed on to California. Somehow, the maneuvering disks story, which only a couple of weeks before I would have found exciting, seemed very tame after what I'd heard from Williamson, Bailey, and Streeter. As I drove, I decided it would be a good idea to do one more interview before confronting the great man himself.

In Carlsbad, a small town on the California coast north of San Diego, I met with D. J. Detwiler, the man who processed Adamski's saucer photos. I found him to be most accommodating. A professional photographer and photo processor, he had met Adamski about ten years before, when Detwiler was at Palomar Gardens photographing the café there. He assured me Adamski's saucer photos were not faked through double exposure or other such technical tricks, which he said he had affirmed in a sworn statement not included in the Professor's book. He quickly added that, of course, this didn't mean the things photographed were genuine flying saucers. He then qualified this qualification by declaring Adamski was a very poor photographer and likely not clever enough to fake such pictures. "His photos are often terribly over- or underexposed, and he's made other equally bad technical errors."

During his adventure near Desert Center, Adamski had used a camera that employed cut film in holders. Orthon asked to take one holder away with him, and Adamski obliged. About three weeks later, on

December 13, a Venusian scout ship appeared over Palomar Gardens and Adamski's film holder was tossed out of an open porthole, landing at his feet. (It was this saucer that Jerrold Baker supposedly had photographed as it was departing.) Detwiler told me he developed the returned film in Adamski's presence. When the image of strange hieroglyph-like markings, apparently a message of some sort, appeared, it seemed to Detwiler that Adamski was genuinely "surprised and excited." (Given that the contactee was such a poor photographer and assuming his surprise and excitement were genuine, they could just as easily have been inspired by his delight that a hoax image he'd made came out at all, as because he was amazed that Orthon had brought him a message from Venus.)

Detwiler told me he firmly believed saucers were real and "probably came from outer space." He also thought Adamski had taken genuine saucer photos and regretted he had not "stuck to photographing them in the air instead of claiming the personal contact with a man from space." This, Detwiler said, branded Adamski a crackpot, which Detwiler thought he was, though "he is perfectly sincere in telling the story of his contact with the spaceman. Adamski believes what he is saying, but the account isn't therefore necessarily true."

To his curious semi-endorsement Detwiler added that he felt Adamski was a kind and humble man, that he had not made much money from saucers, "not even from his book," and that he was "a very fine man in general." All this was seconded by a minister, whose name I no longer remember, who was present during the entire interview and claimed to know Adamski fairly well.

MEETING of MINDS at PALOMAR GARDENS

Prepared by my interviews of several of Adamski's key followers and my other research into his claims, I arrived at Palomar Gardens early on the afternoon of December 15, having called ahead and received a gracious invitation from the Professor himself to "stop by whenever it's convenient." Despite its rather exotic name, the place was just a small hamburger joint about three thousand feet up the slopes of Mount Palomar, on the road to the famed observatory. It was situated on a fairly large piece of land owned by Alice Wells, and there were several cabins adjacent to it; Adamski lived in one of them. Also on the property was a homemade observatory dome housing the larger of the contactee's two telescopes. Although he claimed never to have said he worked at the real observatory on the mountain peak above, the Professor discouraged such impressions only when pressed to do so.

The parking lot was nearly full, and when I entered the café, which had only a four-stool counter and three or four small tables, I found the place similarly crowded. I immediately discovered that, while it was lunchtime, the real draw was the gray-haired, rather distinguished-looking gentleman seated at one of the tables. Except for those of the counterman and the fry cook banging around in the kitchen, all eyes were upon this soft-eyed, well-tanned man, and all ears were lent to his words.

Professor Adamski was holding court. I found a free corner of the lunch counter to lean on and listened, while taking in the crowd and the large black-and-white prints of Adamski's saucer photos that adorned the opposite wall. The Professor radiated an aura of humility and goodwill, even in the face of some rather rough heckling from a skeptic who left shaking his head and grumbling under his breath not long after I arrived.

I spent about four hours listening and observing, as I nursed a couple of Cokes and nibbled a grilled cheese sandwich. During that time, the crowd of mostly avid admirers remained about the same size, twenty to twenty-five, but people came and went. So Adamski repeated his account of his meeting with the Venusian and the events leading up to and following it at least five times, while answering many questions put to him, most in tones of near reverence. While the Professor was hardly a polished speaker, he did have a great sense of the dramatic that more than made up for this. He also had a way of gazing upon his listeners that gave each of them the flattering sense that he was speaking directly and almost only to each of them. I confess I felt it, too.

As the Professor's audience finally dwindled to a handful, I moved forward and introduced myself. Adamski said something like, "Ah, yes, Mr. Moseley. So good to meet you." After warmly shaking my hand and inviting me to join him at his table, he rummaged in a pocket of his windbreaker jacket and pulled out a letter, which he handed to me. It was from George Hunt Williamson, forewarning Adamski of my visit and describing me as "a snoop." My expression must have telegraphed my consternation. Adamski laughed, patted my hand in an indulgent, fatherly fashion, and said, "Never mind Ric. He's a suspicious fellow, but not me."

We talked for about an hour, as three or four others listened. I asked him questions from a long list I'd prepared in advance, based on his book; my interviews with Bailey, Streeter, Williamson, and Detwiler; and what I'd been told by the photo experts. Not once did Adamski seem to take offense. His attitude in the face of my obvious doubts was that of one who had been chosen to have a Great Truth revealed to him, a truth he had faith his doubting interviewer would someday come to accept.

After I'd exhausted my list, we discussed a variety of topics, including the "Head-Man from Outer Space" tale, which Ken Krippine had related to me when we met briefly as I was passing through Beaumont, Texas. I later found out this was the bogus information Krippine had said he would use to spice up our book, but at the time I thought it legitimate. In brief, the story was that the crew of a Pan American Grace (Panagra) airliner on a Lima-to-Miami flight had not only seen a flying saucer close up, but had clearly seen its alien pilot. This creature had no body, but was just a large, strangely misshapen head with weird tentacles and other strange things sprouting from it. It was too horrible for the human mind to fully comprehend and thus defied clear description.

I told Adamski the story, and he didn't bat an eye. He said the being's appearance was distorted due to the angle of view and gases between it and the viewers. This was something Adamski had experienced himself, only to realize the spaceman he was seeing "looked quite normal" when the angle of view and other conditions changed. He added that, in "three to six months," the government would tell the truth about saucers, and if I wrote a book about head-men from outer space, I would look very silly. "Actually, all spacemen look very much as we do," he said, "with only minor variations."

There was much, much more, spun out by the contactee almost at random, including: a Venusian visitor who came to the café posing as an earthman, identifying himself to Adamski with the secret Space Brother handshake; the Venusian who worked for the Los Angeles district attorney for a short while, after deeply gouging a piece of heavy-gauge steel with his thumbnail to prove his origin; a six-hour motion picture that showed not only saucers but beings on another planet, which had to have either been brought to Earth by spacemen or taken by Earthmen on Venus (since it was on 35 mm film, Adamski said he believed the latter); Adamski's having gone Einstein one better by studying the fifth dimension, which the Professor called "cause" (Adamski's explanations were beyond me); that the 1951 science-fiction film *The Day the Earth Stood Still* was "95 percent true" and showed the actual interior and exterior of a flying saucer; that the account of captured crashed saucers and dead little men from Venus in Frank Scully's *Behind the Flying Saucers* was factual, the recent *True* magazine exposé being the real fraud, for which the magazine soon would be sued (yet Scully's story and Adamski's were mutually exclusive in virtually all respects); and, finally, the reasons for the cryptic nature of Orthon's message: "national security was involved," and besides, "if it had been in English, it would have been written off as a fake."

Capping the mind-boggling afternoon, Adamski tried to convince me that during our interview he had used mental telepathy to anticipate some of my questions. I had sensed nothing from our conversation that suggested this, although the others present claimed they did. When I tried to pin Adamski down, asking him to read my mind as I concentrated on a particular thing, he evaded the issue, saying, "Telepathy cannot be accomplished by concentration." Instead, he offered as examples of his telepathic powers that I was very impressed by current scientific theories, that I wanted very much to believe his story but couldn't, that I had expected to find him uncooperative and had been pleasantly surprised to find him otherwise, and so on. Of course, all of this had been said or clearly implied during our chat. So while all Adamski's deductions were true, telepathy certainly wasn't required for him to arrive at them.

As darkness gathered outside the café, Adamski decided to close the interview. "When you are older," he said in a kindly tone, "you may learn the truth about the mission of the Space Brothers. It may be, but I hope not, that you will be too old a man, as alas I am, to do much about this."

Smiling benignly, he went on. "What I have told you and the others this afternoon is true. But who is it that asked in the poem, 'What is truth?' I don't remember. I am not a literary man. No matter. You must take not only my truth, but you must discover the truth for yourself. In that manner, you will truly believe, as I do."

All this sounded like tried and true mystical doubletalk to me, and I'm sure the shrewd contactee fully realized this. "If you don't believe in the spaceships and the Space Brothers," he added, "as I don't think you do, young man, wait until 1968 and you will find more understanding—or at the most until 1969."

As much as it embarrasses me to admit it today, despite the blatantly contradictory and often silly "wisdom" and alleged facts Adamski imparted that afternoon, despite the strong doubts I had when I went to see him, I nonetheless came away from the encounter not unfavorably impressed and well disposed toward him. Here's how I put it in my notes of our conversation:

> To sum up, Adamski strikes me as a very kind, intelligent, and sincere man. However, several of his theories are definitely "pseudo-scientific"

> or "crack-pot", and of course the facts he relates are still open to very serious doubt, especially as he and at least two of his six eyewitnesses [to his alleged meeting with Orthon] are not in full agreement as to how strong the evidence for the contact actually is, beyond Adamski's mere word on it. However, I do not feel Adamski's account is a "hoax", at least not in the usual sense of the word. If the account is untrue, Adamski is nevertheless sincere in relating it. This is a seeming contradiction, but actually it is a paradox. There are many possibilities. There is a very, very small possibility that Adamski's account is a deliberate and unscrupulous hoax; there is a much greater chance that it was a psychological or so-called "psychic" experience, in which case there are two possibilities: (1) This represents a normal operation of the mind, an operation that we do not understand; (2) Adamski is crazy. There is also a good chance that Adamski may in all good faith be lying in order to expound doctrines and ideas that he sincerely feels to be true, i.e., he feels that the contact with the space-man could have, or should have, happened just as he tells it; or that it will happen some day, and that he is therefore doing a service by preparing the world to accept saucers. (In this case, due to the many ways that the human mind can twist, it is not necessarily true that Adamski is aware that he is telling a lie.) There is a fourth and final possibility, and that is that Adamski's account is true; and after meeting Adamski, I would say that there is a very definite and real possibility that the incident really happened.

It wasn't long before I learned very much otherwise, and in my only major contribution to The Field as a Serious Ufologist, I exposed the truth in several articles in *Nexus* (later *Saucer News*), the magazine I launched six months after the Palomar Gardens interview. The first of these ran in the January 1955 issue, and in October 1957 I reprinted all of them in a special issue, easily available again for the first time in decades as an appendix to this book.

The appendix Tells All, but there are two elements of the story I want to emphasize as pivotal in changing my opinion of Adamski and, in retrospect, which contributed greatly to my shift in emphasis and interest from UFOs themselves to the people in The Field. The first of these was a letter Adamski wrote to Jerrold Baker on November 2, 1953, about six weeks *before* the interview at Palomar Gardens. In *Flying Saucers Have Landed*, Baker was credited with one of the saucer photos actually taken by Adamski, thus seeming to offer independent-witness confirmation of the Professor's claims. In his letter, Adamski made a sly but failed attempt to prevent Baker from blowing the whistle, writing his disenchanted protégé:

> Now you know the picture connected with your name [note the careful phrasing] is in the book, too—the one taken by the well with the Brownie. And with people knowing that you are interested in flying saucers as you have been, and buying the book as they are . . . you could do yourself a lot of good. For you have plenty of knowledge about these things [saucers], whereby you could give lectures in the evenings.
>
> There is a demand for this! You could support yourself by the picture in the book with your name [again, a careful choice of words]. Remember that you are as much publicized in the book as I am, as far as the picture is concerned. And having the knowledge you have of these things [saucers], you have your break right here.

Then there is the little matter of what German rocket scientist Dr. Walther Riedel discovered. At the time I spoke with him in December 1953, Riedel was a senior project engineer at North American Aviation and sympathetically disposed to the idea that flying saucers could well be ships from another planet. He even had made a short documentary film about saucers (which I was shown by its producer) and was associated with the Los Angeles–based UFO club Civilian Saucer Investigation (in April 1952 *Life* magazine had touted CSI as a serious, scientific outfit, apparently largely on the strength of this connection). Riedel told me he had microscopically examined the saucer photo used as the frontispiece in *Flying Saucers Have Landed* and discovered something both amusing and damning. On one of the three spherical landing "pods" of the craft, Riedel spied the "G.E." trademark of the General Electric Company, shedding new light on the Adamski story. This particular saucer landing gear was a 100-watt lightbulb, which certainly must have made night landings easier!

Adding insult to injury, the photograph in question was one that Adamski claimed had been enlarged eighty times by well-known Hollywood cinematographer Pevernell Marley (husband of actress Linda Darnell), leading to Marley's discovery of a spaceman peering through one of the portholes. While in California, I spoke with Marley about this. Not only had he not enlarged the photo and found a spaceman, he knew of no one who had.

After my exposé, Adamski was smart enough not to strike back. After all, he was much better known to flying saucer enthusiasts than I. By answering my points, he would only have given them—and me—more publicity than I ever could have generated on my own. The most he did was to accuse me of being "an agent of Wall Street." I took this as a disguised way of saying "agent of the Jewish conspiracy," and I think that's the way most of Adamski's followers understood the accusation.

I felt, and still do, that although Adamski's claims were absurd in many provable and almost-provable ways, and despite the anti-Semitic overtones of the "agent of Wall Street" slur, his "philosophy" was harmless, and that therefore he represented no threat to society and wasn't all that bad a guy. My rather base motivation for the exposé was that, if he could build his reputation on mythical interactions with spacemen, I had an equal right to build mine by exposing his con. One is as kosher as the other. Adamski was fair game, and I think I treated him fairly. If he were still with us, I suspect he would agree that I did.

Of course, there are many in The Field even today who believe Adamski really had the experiences he said he had, in some form or other. Among these is British ufological superstar Timothy Good, whom I first met at UFO '79, a special one-shot convention in San Diego. I had no idea who Good was or, of course, that he would become a big-league UFO writer.

As we chatted, the subject of Adamski came up, and Good asked for a copy of my special issue. I never got around to sending him one. I now wish I had done so, because he seems to be honest and really seeking The Truth, though more than a bit gullible. (To be fair, as he wrote me a while back, he's less gullible than he used to be. *Good* for him!)

HOLLYWOOD CONFIDENTIAL: SAUCERS, MY COUSIN BILL, and MORE

Augie Roberts and Dominic Lucchesi told me that one of the first people I should look up when I hit Los Angeles was Manon Darlaine. This elegant, vivacious French lady of eighty or so was a consultant to many movie studios on set design and decoration. She supposedly had lived a rather colorful life before settling in Hollywood, including some sort of shadowy involvement with French intelligence during one or the other or both world wars, depending on the teller and the telling. She also was well connected with practically everyone who was anyone on the L.A. saucer scene and, by correspondence, with other saucerers all over the country. She was an excellent source of gossip, rumor, innuendo, slander, and assorted inside scoop—the essential elements of the ufological subculture's lifeblood, perhaps more important to many saucerers than UFOs themselves.

When I telephoned Manon and told her what I was up to, she immediately insisted I come to breakfast at her Hollywood apartment the following morning. She said she would be delighted to fill me in on what was happening on the California saucer scene and help me avoid the many pitfalls and false trails that riddled that strange territory.

My next call was to a cousin of mine, actor William Talman, who then was just getting established in the movies. A few years later, he became a major television star, playing always thwarted District Attorney Hamilton Burger on the hit series *Perry Mason.* Although we had never met, he graciously invited me to his place for a bit of holiday cheer that same evening.

When I arrived, he was quite friendly—"Just call me Bill, Cousin Jim." After we'd gotten settled with our drinks, a bit of small talk and family chitchat ensued. Then Bill asked what brought me to California. As soon as I told him, I knew one drink was all I was going to get. I wouldn't say he hustled me out the door, but it came close to that. Maybe he was afraid flying saucers might be considered akin to communism by those then trying to root the Red Menace out of Hollywood, and so he feared consorting with me might get him blacklisted. Maybe he just thought I was a crackpot. Whatever his reasons, he was polite, but I was gone in short order, and there was no doubt he wasn't going to be giving me an insider's look at the movie business while I was in town.

Ironically, in early 1960, Bill's personal proclivities got him kicked off the *Perry Mason* show for a while. He was caught naked in a vice raid at a friend's home. It seems marijuana was present, but everyone except the unfortunate owner of the raided apartment got off on the drug possession charges. Their lawyers argued that, since all were nude, they had no means of possessing drugs. The judge agreed. Ah, California!

Some years later, another weed, tobacco, killed Bill Talman, who made a famous series of antismoking commercials as he was dying of lung cancer. These were quite moving, and I think they probably influenced many to quit smoking or not to start, but they were lost on me. I've been a smoker all my adult life and still am. I'm still involved in "ufoology," too. Maybe there's a moral here.

The next morning, following a wonderful breakfast, I lit up and leaned back to listen to Manon Darlaine's tales of the West Coast saucering scene. It quickly became obvious it was closer to a low-budget Saturday matinee science-fantasy serial with bad continuity than it was like anything to do with real science.

What Manon told me also crystallized something that had begun to form in the back of my mind after my interview with Adamski. The inner circle of California-based or -centered saucerdom was a small group of people, all of whom knew or were in fairly close contact with each other. Their major focus was on the truly far-out—contacts with benevolent Space Brothers, crashed saucers with dead little men from Venus aboard, disappearing saucerers (probably kidnapped by spacemen), ether ships from higher "vibration levels" or parallel universes rather than other planets of this one, all spiced with doses of California mysticism, hype, and hucksterism. While some, like Dr. Walther Riedel, precocious teenager Max Miller, and Ed Sullivan, head of Civilian Saucer Investigation, supposedly tried to study UFOs with the methods of science and critical thinking, the great majority of West Coast saucerers were far from scientific, more like Al Bender than Clyde Tombaugh.

The serious-minded inevitably found themselves entangled with the wacky, and so it continued as saucerdom developed from the scattered clubs of the early days and grew into today's national-global "ufological community." Back in 1953, I wasn't sure if this seemingly strange-bedfellows situation arose because everyone interested in UFOs, being a small but intense and busy bunch, just naturally drift together, like it or not, or if most of those who cultivate Serious Ufologist images and the contactee/abductee, crashed-saucer, and "4-D" types are brothers under the skin. Now, after nearly half a century of saucering, I think it's something of both, with the emphasis definitely on the latter.

The state of ufology in the early fifties and today is eerily similar. Consider "The World's First Flying Saucer Convention," held August 16–18, 1953, just four months before I arrived in California. It was sponsored by a nonprofit outfit called Flying Saucers International (FSI), which used the occasion to launch its new magazine *Saucers*, edited by FSI president, professional photographer, and Serious Ufologist Max Miller. Fifteen hundred people, including Manon Darlaine and some from as far away as London, packed the wonderful old and now long-gone Hollywood Hotel, and two thousand were turned away at the door.

There was a lobby display of well-wishing letters from such public figures as Vice President Richard Nixon (Boo!), the secretary of defense, and the mayor of Los Angeles, all of whom had been invited to the con but were "forced" to regret. Radio commentators Walter Winchell, Lowell Thomas, and Frank Edwards were invited, too, but none made it. A well-known science-fiction illustrator was there, with an exhibit of his SF-'zine cover art, as were Wendayne and Forrest Ackerman ("Mr. and Mrs. Science Fiction").

The main speakers included Arthur Joquel, author of the quite serious non-UFO book *The Challenge of Space,* who, likely much to his chagrin, shared the platform with George Adamski, Frank Scully, Silas Newton (the man behind Scully's crashed-saucer tales), and the cream of the crop of second-banana contactees at the time: Orfeo Angelucci, Truman Bethurum, and George Van Tassel. George Hunt Williamson couldn't make it, but sent word that he thought all the contactees had something wonderful to impart and urged them not to dispute their conflicting claims, but rather to focus on their shared message of brotherly love and the promise of a coming New Age guided by the wisdom of the Space Brothers. Orchestrating the event was principal program moderator Jeron King Criswell, well-known showman and author of the weekly syndicated column "Criswell Predicts."

Professional movie cameraman Jerome Welo presented a showing of the color film on which he supposedly had accidentally captured a flying saucer whizzing over Hollywood. Welo told the crowd he'd been testing his camera when the UFO flashed into and out of view. Welo offered his film to anyone willing to pay five thousand bucks. There were no takers.

The pioneering saucer gathering concluded on a note that will be all too familiar to those following ufological events in recent years. The assembled saucerers voted to petition President Eisenhower to release "all saucer data that would not jeopardize national security," and a letter was immediately dispatched to the White House. Another familiar note was sounded in the reply Flying Saucers International received from Brig. Gen. Joe W. Kelly, head of air force legislative liaison: "Your recent inquiry to the President of the United States has been referred to the Department of the Air Force for reply. I am sending you a report so that you will have a full picture of our activities in this matter to date."

Plus ça change, plus c'est la même chose. That morning at Manon's, however, all was new and fresh and somehow full of promise, even the baloney. By then, I knew much of what I was pursuing was just that, but I'd caught the saucer bug, and once bitten, there is no hope.

After telling me about the convention, Manon showed me a newspaper article from the month before; November 18, to be exact. Two local men, Karl Hunrath and Wilbur Wilkinson, had rented a light plane, allegedly to make contact with a saucer. They had taken off, headed east toward Arizona, and disappeared without a trace. It turned out that Hunrath had until recently been a member of Adamski's circle and Wilkinson was a close friend and fellow saucer enthusiast. According to Manon, Hunrath, an electrician, had built a machine he called Bosco (!), with which he intended to shoot down saucers. Oddly, this scheme seemed not to bother Adamski until Hunrath told him Bosco would indiscriminately bring down both saucers and American military aircraft. Adamski thought shooting down U.S. planes would be unpatriotic, said so in no uncertain terms, and banished Hunrath.

There might also have been another problem. It seems while still at Palomar Gardens, Hunrath had accidentally stumbled upon some of Adamski's equipment, including at least one model of a flying saucer. In embarrassment, Adamski claimed he'd built the model based on a photograph he'd taken of a real saucer.

As for why Hunrath and Wilkinson had disappeared, it seemed they had several good reasons to pull a vanishing act, reasons having nothing to do with saucers. I later learned that the FBI had decided they'd skipped across the border to Mexico. Not as exciting as being picked off in flight by a flying saucer. But then, what is?

Manon offered some other interesting disclosures about those close to Adamski. She'd recently visited George Hunt Williamson and his wife, Betty, in Prescott. While her husband was absent, Mrs. Williamson confided in Manon and another person that Adamski had told them before the meeting with Orthon that there would be a contact with a spaceman, this foreknowledge having been communicated to the Professor psychically. Yet Adamski told me and wrote in his book that there was no advance notice, that he only "hoped" for such a meeting.

For his part, "Dr." Williamson told Manon that his wife was herself from another planet, and that he was about to quit his job at the Prescott radio station to go on a lecture tour with the infamous fascist mystic William Dudley Pelley. A ferocious anti-Semite, Pelley had founded and led the pro-Nazi Silver Shirts before World War II and in 1942 began a fifteen-year prison sentence for sedition. When he was released after serving only seven years, he founded the racist occult group Soulcraft. I later learned that Williamson had worked for Pelley's Soulcraft Publications in Indiana before relocating to Arizona and hooking up with Adamski. Homegrown fascists, Space Brothers, and a spouse from space. Far out!

According to Manon, Jerrold Baker, the disenchanted nonphotographer of an Adamskian saucer, was now staying with Frank Scully and either writing about or doing research for Scully on the super-strong Venusian yarn. Without prompting from me, she went on to tell me the story of the falsely attributed photo, which Baker had admitted to her, thus corroborating what I'd heard from Al Bailey and Lyman Streeter.

Manon also offered some insights and advice concerning Adamski's imitators. Orfeo Angelucci, who claimed a long string of psychic contacts with space people beginning in 1946, seems to have been confined to a mental institution more than once. (Angelucci was on the East Coast while I was in California, but I met him several times in later years. He was a very amusing character, but definitely not normal, whatever that is.)

Then there was Truman Bethurum, who claimed some eleven actual contacts with not only spacemen but also one Aura Rhanes, a very sexy female saucer captain (latter named a corespondent when Bethurum's wife divorced him!). Manon said he was a total fraud not worth wasting time on. I decided to take her advice and gave Bethurum a pass on that trip, but met him in later years. Manon was right on target. Of course, if Aura had been with Bethurum, I might have taken him (and her) *very* seriously.

Finally, there was George Van Tassel, who was to play a large role in fifties and sixties saucerdom, hosting the (in)famous Interplanetary Spacecraft Conventions at his Giant Rock Airport in the desert near Yucca Valley, California. I was already doubtful about Van Tassel, as he had been highly recommended to me by Williamson, and Manon's comments convinced me I shouldn't waste any of my limited time trying to see him. It seemed that he and his followers sat around in a room hollowed out beneath Giant Rock (a huge, freestanding granite boulder) in some sort of mystic-circle séance arrangement, while Van Tassel contacted *his* spacemen via mental telepathy. So I decided to skip the Sage of Giant Rock, too, though in later years our paths would cross in interesting ways.

I left Manon Darlaine with my head spinning like an out-of-control flying saucer and a long list of people still to interview before I began my return journey to New Jersey. Manon had suggested it would be worthwhile to talk with Max Miller, so I called him from her place and arranged to meet him next.

Miller, with whom I eventually became friendly, was less than enthused about me that day. There was no doubt he considered me a presumptuous upstart, even though he was just a kid himself—a very bright kid, but a kid nonetheless. The second and third sentences out of his mouth were, "How is it you're going to write a book after only a couple of months' study of the saucers?" and "I've been at it for four years and still don't feel qualified to write one."

After I'd asked what I suppose he considered a few reasonably intelligent questions, Miller loosened up a bit. He gave me some background on Frank Scully and his connections with Silas Newton and Leo GeBauer, the two confidence men who'd given Scully the stories on which he had based his best-seller *Behind the Flying Saucers*. He considered the Scully affair to be a terrible hoax and a blow to the credibility of thoughtful saucer researchers. On the other hand, he stuck up for Orfeo Angelucci, who turned out to be a good friend of his. On everything else, Miller seemed very reasonable. In this, I suppose, he embodied ufology's split personality.

Over the next several days, my research continued to mirror this odd blend of sublime and ridiculous. In the sublime category was my interview with American Airlines captain Willis Sperry, who, along with the other two members of his flight crew, had a spectacular sighting three years before near Washington, D.C. A large, cigar-shaped something with an intense blue light on its nose (shades of Chiles and Whitted) had *circled* his airliner while it was cruising at three hundred miles an hour. The thing then hovered for a moment before whizzing off at very high speed. Later, Sperry learned another American Airlines pilot, flying further south, had seen something with the appearance of a meteor drop out of the sky in the vicinity of Sperry's plane, stop, change direction, and shoot away.

Despite the spectacular nature of his experience and its apparent confirmation by a fellow pilot, Sperry refused to jump to conclusions about what saucers were or where they were from. He thought the evidence was still too fragmentary. All he was sure of was that he definitely had seen a solid object.

In the realm of the ridiculous was Mikel Conrad, B-film actor and producer. In 1950 Conrad had made the first flying-saucer film, cleverly titled *The Flying Saucer*. I'd seen the picture, with its badly dubbed-in saucers, and hadn't been impressed. Neither had other moviegoers. The film became a near-instant flop. I went to see Conrad because in his book Frank Scully claimed the actor had shot some genuine footage of saucers which had been confiscated by the air force, with some of it later being returned and used in Conrad's movie.

Before Conrad would admit me to his office, I had to persuade him I wasn't a process server. It seems he was ducking a subpoena. Later he said he was just joking about this, but it was hard to tell when he was kidding and when he was not, as both he and the other man present, his cameraman partner, were well into a bottle of booze and kept working on it during the interview.

Anyway, Conrad claimed that in 1947, while shooting a picture in Alaska, he and his partner saw and filmed a flight of eight saucers, one of which landed. A humanoid spaceman of "frightening appearance" emerged and engaged Conrad in an inane conversation. Then the being reentered his ship and took off. The cameraman captured all of this on film. Then the air force grabbed the footage, eventually returning less than a third of it, which Conrad used in *The Flying Saucer.*

Conrad said he had "the most sensational film ever made" and he should have been able to "make a million from it." Alas, he hadn't because the nasty old government had taken the best parts away. So now no one believed him, and he refused to let anyone use his story unless he got "money, and lots of it. No petty cash like the big magazines have tried. It's a million or nothing—and while the government has my film, it'll be nothing."

I asked Conrad what he thought about Scully's story. He claimed to know the writer well, but said he thought Scully was a hoaxer. "I'm not, but he is. I'm the only man in the world with a genuine saucer film." Hmmm . . .

CRASHED SAUCERS, "LITTLE MEN," and CON MEN

When I interviewed Frank Scully at his home in Hollywood, sure enough, Jerrold Baker was there (this was our first meeting), as were two Catholic priests, who were showing Scully a Christmas film he was going to help them distribute. A curious gathering, to say the least.

Scully, a humorist and columnist for the show-business newspaper *Weekly Variety,* was the first author to claim the U.S. government had captured crashed saucers and the bodies of the "little men" who crewed them. The first of these had fallen to earth in March 1948, near Aztec, New Mexico. Sixteen three-foot-tall men "dressed in the manner of the 1890s" were aboard, killed and crisped to a nice chocolate brown shade by earth air rushing in through a broken porthole.

The writer had been given the story by longtime associate Silas Newton, allegedly a big-time oil man, inventor, and millionaire, and a colleague of his, "Dr." (another of those) Leo GeBauer, who supposedly was a "top magnetics" man involved in the recovery and study of the saucers. GeBauer ("Dr. Gee" in Scully's *Behind the Flying Saucers)* had pocketed various bits of Venusian technology for himself, and he and

Newton had adapted them for use in a "doodlebug," a gadget used to find oil, gas, water, gold, and other valuable natural resources (in fact, generally whatever the mark, uh, *customer* was looking for). They'd managed to peddle their doodlebug and interests in some of the vast oil finds that had been made with the device to Herman Flader, a wealthy and credulous Denver industrialist. The clever duo raked in more than two hundred thousand dollars for their efforts.

Naturally, Scully leaped at the opportunity for a major scoop, and a couple of times in the fall of 1949 and again in January 1950 he devoted his *Variety* column to the saucers and little men story. He soon had a book contract. In the space of six weeks, he knocked out a potboiler manuscript, and in September 1950 *Behind the Flying Saucers* was released, becoming the world's second saucer book. It quickly hit best-seller lists all over the country, generating tremendous controversy and making Scully a much-sought-after celebrity.

To make a very long story a lot shorter . . .

In no time at all, experts of all sorts were blasting the book for its scientific and other absurdities, not to mention Scully's awful writing. Of course, this didn't cut much into the book's soaring sales and may even have boosted them. Over the next couple of years, it sold over fifty thousand copies in hardcover and hundreds of thousands in paperback, with several foreign editions, magazine excerpts, and the like, adding nicely to Scully's royalties. (I hope this book does even half as well!)

Then the September 1952 *True* magazine hit the stands with a sensational article by investigative reporter J. P. Cahn. This exposed the whole wild story as a hoax perpetrated by Newton and GeBauer to promote their doodlebug and phony oil-strike schemes. Cahn, perhaps pulling a punch, concluded Scully, too, had been duped. About a month later, the two swindlers were brought up on fraud charges in Denver, where Newton lived in the fabulous Brown Place Hotel, when he wasn't hanging out in Hollywood golfing with and trying to con movie stars and other movielanders. When I went to see Scully that day in December 1953, the trial of Newton and his sidekick was well underway, making daily headlines in Colorado and quite a few in southern California, too.

Of course, the first thing I asked was what he thought of Cahn's charges. Scully emphatically declared he'd not been taken in. He then handed me a typewritten rebuttal to Cahn. Essentially, this accused the reporter of sour grapes. It alleged that Cahn had been thwarted when he approached Scully in the hope of building further upon the original story for a book or magazine article and then, failing in that, in an attempt to get Scully to give him an "I have been duped" story. So Cahn decided to do his own hoax story, which was "vicious and false"—and even worse before *True*'s editors "cleaned it up." I found it more than a little interesting that I'd gotten the same story, almost word for word, from George Adamski.

I'd read Cahn's article, and Scully's allegations definitely didn't ring true to me. By Scully's own admission, Cahn had spent some time investigating the case on his own before deciding to write his exposé. To my mind, he treated the material that way because no other treatment would work. The story Scully had depended upon surely was a hoax, as the criminal proceedings against Newton and GeBauer strongly suggested.

I told Scully as much, and he responded by defending Newton as a man of "high character." He also claimed Cahn's allegation that Leo GeBauer was the mysterious Dr. Gee of his book was totally false. Dr. Gee, Scully said, was a composite of eight scientists who gave him information. This he capped by alleging that Cahn somehow pressured the Denver district attorney into bringing the fraud charges and that, if the DA didn't have some "political reason" for pressing the case, it would have ended long ago with the exoneration of Newton and GeBauer. I got the very same line from Adamski.

Significantly, I thought, Scully said he didn't feel Cahn had libeled him. However, he *had* libeled Newton, and Scully claimed *True* would soon be sued by the great man for "a huge sum." This never happened, as Newton and GeBauer were convicted of fraud less than two weeks later, effectively validating Cahn's allegations.

Steering my host to a different issue, I asked him how he accounted for his little spacemen and Adamski's big ones looking so much like Earth people. After all, conditions on other planets were much different than those here. A practicing Catholic, he offered an argument I'd already heard from several saucerers, among them Adamski and Williamson: Since God made Earthmen in his own image, and since he also made the creatures on other planets, it follows that they look similar to us. "It would not be like God to make a monster. Besides, what does science *really* know about conditions on other planets?" (Scully didn't have much use for science.)

As I had already discovered, this connection with Christian theology was something a good number of saucer enthusiasts were making. Saucers were here to fulfill biblical prophecies, and in other ways they and their pilots supposedly supported and confirmed the Bible. A determinedly unchurched person, I've never found such arguments in the least convincing.

Scully did admit that the idea advanced by Adamski and others that there were spacemen walking the Earth unnoticed was "flawed." Nonetheless, and in spite of how it contradicted his own claims, he said he believed Adamski's story. "Anyway," he said, "I don't claim to know if spacemen walk the Earth. My book dealt only with dead ones. I have no knowledge of live ones."

As set down in my notes at the time, I left Scully with the following thoughts running through my mind:

> My impression of Scully after one short meeting, and after the things I have heard and read about him, is this: He was probably duped . . . and he probably knows it; he may even have known it at the time [he wrote his book], as he is a professional writer and probably not against making money, even on a hoax. He gives the appearance of being religious, but he does not seem like a kindly man or a truly religious man, and he therefore seems to be a hypocrite. Actually, I think he is "very much of this world," and perhaps he is not even a believer in saucers. I think, however, that after the controversy caused by his last book, and after the way he has been discredited, he will be very careful of his facts in his next saucer book [which both he and Manon Darlaine told me he was working on but which never saw print]. He probably won't write the truth in his next book, but I imagine he will be careful to use hoaxes that can't be easily checked upon.

PLANNED CONFUSION or PURE STUPIDITY?

On December 16 I conducted a very interesting and informative interview with two men who had been intimately and recently involved with the air force saucer investigation, Albert M. Chop and Edward J. Ruppelt. As far as I know, no one else ever interviewed them together.

From December 1951 through March 1953, Chop had been the civilian in charge of UFO information at the air force's Pentagon press desk and was the man Keyhoe quoted so freely in *Flying Saucers from Outer Space.* Ruppelt actually headed Project Blue Book, serving as the air force's Official Saucer Sleuth for two years until he left active duty in August 1953.

When I met with them, Chop was a public relations man for Douglas Aircraft and Ruppelt was an engineer at Northrop, another airplane company. Ruppelt had not yet begun writing about saucers. His first magazine article appeared the following year, and his famous insider account of his experiences as chief UFO hunter, *The Report on Unidentified Flying Objects*, wouldn't come out until 1956.

Meeting these two good friends together was particularly interesting and revealing. Chop believed that the saucers very likely were from outer space. Ruppelt did not. They had this difference of opinion despite both having had access to more or less the same UFO information as it came in while they were with the air force. Chop said he knew Keyhoe "pretty well" and liked him, and he thought that, "as long as you disregard Keyhoe's personal opinions," *Flying Saucers from Outer Space* was "one hundred percent factually correct." Ruppelt was less charitable, and agreed with me that "Keyhoe worded some of his material in such a way as to be technically accurate but still misleading."

I asked Chop about the January 26, 1953, letter reproduced on the back jacket of *Flying Saucers from Outer Space.* This was written on air force letterhead and signed by Chop. Characterized by Keyhoe in his book as "an official Air Force admission that the saucers came from space," the letter included the following dramatic paragraph:

> The Air Force and its investigative agency, Project Bluebook [actually, *Blue Book*], are aware of Major Keyhoe's conclusion that the flying saucers are from another planet. The Air Force has never denied that this possibility exists. Some of the personnel believe that there may be some strange natural phenomena completely unknown to us, but that if the apparently controlled maneuvers reported by many competent observers are correct, then the only remaining explanation is the interplanetary answer.

Chop said he asked Keyhoe about his "interpretation" of these words, and was told that "in the book it is *he* [Keyhoe] who calls this an official admission," not Chop, "so technically he is not in error, since it is his privilege to construe the letter as an official admission if he wants to." Chop seemed not to be disturbed by this self-serving rationalization of Keyhoe's, but he did give me a copy of a September 18, 1953, "To Whom It May Concern" letter he had written. It included this "clarification" of his position:

> Any opinions which Major Keyhoe attributes to the United States Air Force through me are expressions of my own personal opinions and do not reflect the official opinion of the United States Air Force and/or the Department of Defense.

When I looked up from reading the letter, a copy of which I still have, Ruppelt caught my eye, smiled wryly, and gave me a sly wink.

I then asked the two men about Scully and Adamski, and both laughed. Ruppelt said he considered Cahn's exposé of the Scully-Newton story "completely factual." He had spoken with Scully and got the "definite impression he doesn't believe his own material, but is getting a big kick out of the public's belief in it." Neither did he seem "really mad about Cahn's article, as he pretends to be." Chop noted that all of the "fifty or so people who claim to be in on contacts with spacemen are of questionable reputation, and they don't have any proof. Why don't the spacemen contact anyone reputable?" Good point.

This prompted Ruppelt to bring up a Robert Coe Gardner, who was lecturing in California and wowing his audiences with claims he had received secret information and previously unreleased photos of saucers from high-level government contacts, proving UFOs were from outer space. If possible, Ruppelt and Chop considered Gardner to be even lower than Scully and Adamski. Chop said he'd known Gardner for years, as they'd both grown up in Dayton, Ohio. It turns out that when confronted by the air force, Gardner admitted he'd clipped his "unreleased photos" from *newspapers!* The man had also once told Chop that Gen. Hoyt Vandenberg, former chief of staff of the air force, had told reporters off the record that the saucers were from space.

Both Chop and Ruppelt dismissed this claim as nonsense, but it did remind Ruppelt to tell me there was at least one air force general who firmly believed UFOs were interplanetary. He said it was this man's views that had shaped the very pro-saucer article "Have We Visitors from Space?" in the April 7, 1952, *Life*. Ruppelt wouldn't give me the general's name, but I later learned it was Brig. Gen. William Garland, a senior air force intelligence man. (The following month, I interviewed Garland by phone. He reminded me of the official negative air force view on saucers being interplanetary and, much to my disappointment, said "no comment" when I asked for his personal opinion. I took this to mean he did believe UFOs were from space, but didn't want to go out on a limb and say so.)

I asked the duo about Mikel Conrad's claims and the Bunch-McLean film. Chop emphatically denied the air force had ever confiscated anyone's film, including Conrad's, and said the Bunch-McLean film was too dark for anything of value to be seen. Ruppelt added that the air force had "thrown out" the original and additional copies of this film because it was "valueless." (Not quite confiscation, but . . .) This led to a discussion of saucer photos and films, during which Chop almost always was willing to come down on the side of the reality of saucers from space, whereas Ruppelt was not.

One case both agreed upon didn't involve photographs or movies. This was the famous Florida scoutmaster "saucer-attack" incident. On the night of August 19, 1952, West Palm Beach scoutmaster D. S. "Sonny" Desvergers was driving three boys home from a scout meeting, when something seemed to drop from the sky into a palmetto thicket just off the road. Desvergers went to investigate and found himself standing under a saucer hovering just above the ground. As he backed away, he claimed, a ball of red fire floated toward him out of the saucer's dome. It enveloped him and he passed out. When he came to, he made his way to the road, where the scouts and a couple of lawmen they'd summoned were waiting. It was discovered that the hair on one of Desvergers's arms had been singed, and there were tiny holes burned in his cap. The local sheriff's office contacted an air force unit at the West Palm Beach airport, and within twenty-four hours, Ruppelt and his deputy, Lt. Robert Olsson, were on their way by special plane to Florida, on the first of two investigative trips, the second taken largely because Olsson's girlfriend lived in the West Palm Beach area (your tax dollars at work—or play).

At first, the case looked good to Ruppelt, but he soon learned Desvergers "was of low character," and analysis of the man's hat strongly indicated it wasn't burned while it was on his head. Years later, I wondered why Ruppelt didn't tell me about the grass samples taken from the scene, on which only the roots had been scorched, a mystery he first made public in his 1956 book. On the other hand, my own 1954 interview with Desvergers seemed to confirm Ruppelt and Chop's assessment of him. By then he was telling of having fought with smelly aliens while teetering on the rim of the hovering saucer, and of having seen something else "too horrible" to talk about.

Finally, I asked Ruppelt and Chop to share their views on air force saucer policy. On this there was no disagreement: There was "no planned confusion" (Ruppelt). It was nothing but "pure stupidity" (Chop). They gave me a recent example. A couple of weeks before, the air force had announced it was going to set up special cameras in UFO-sighting hot spots to try to get photos of saucers. Soon after, the service released a "ho-hum" statement saying that practically all saucer reports had been solved and there was nothing to be concerned about.

Ruppelt and Chop added that Keyhoe was dead wrong about there being a difference of opinion in the top ranks of the air force about how much to tell the public about saucers (implying there was a Big Secret).

The real issue, they told me, was whether the air force should continue bothering with saucer reports or not, and this debate was still going on.

As I left Ruppelt and Chop, it seemed to me that their views of the official situation made sense. I also was struck by their completely different conclusions about UFOs, especially since they were based on essentially the same information, supposedly the best available. If these two smart and knowledgeable men could be so far apart, how likely was it that a solution to the riddle of the flying saucers was just around the corner and that I might be the one to discover it?

The STRANGE CASE of CSI

My last bit of investigation before leaving semi-sunny California was to look into the controversy surrounding Civilian Saucer Investigation (CSI), purportedly the first saucer club to pursue a serious, systematic, and scientific investigation of the UFO mystery. In late May 1951 Ed J. Sullivan, Werner Eichler, and Victor Black, all technical men in the aircraft industry, supposedly had spotted thirty or forty brightly glowing saucers that flew in a strange way and at great speed over Los Angeles. Impressed by what they had seen, Sullivan and Eichler got together with several of their colleagues, including Dr. Walther Riedel, and formed CSI, with Sullivan as president.

Riedel had told me quite a bit about CSI and its work, and I was quite impressed. Then I learned of an article Victor Black had published in the October 1952 *American Mercury* magazine. It was called "The Flying Saucer Hoax," and in it, Black claimed he and his two friends had made up their sighting as a joke. He wrote that when he realized the other two were going to treat it as real and try to make more than just a few friends believe it happened, he dropped out of the scheme. He also tore apart saucer believers in general and Sullivan in particular, asserting that Sullivan had organized CSI for profit and publicity. If those were Sullivan's aims, he'd certainly succeeded on the latter score, with the big story in *Life.* As for profit, I never learned anything that suggested CSI was any different than other saucer clubs back then (or now), running in the red or at best occasionally breaking even.

First I interviewed Eichler. He gave me an account of the May 1951 sighting and told me CSI would soon announce its conclusions about the saucers. The bottom line was that the saucers were from outer space. Concerning Black, he said the man wrote his article just to get publicity.

His charges were completely false, and the magazine had run some sort of retraction.

Then I went to see Black, who of course told a different story. He stuck to his claim that the sighting was a hoax ("It never happened!"), that Sullivan was only out to make a name and a buck for himself, and so on. He also alleged that *American Mercury* really didn't issue a retraction but, rather, that it simply published a statement making clear it did not intend in any way to impugn anyone's character. The magazine, he said, stuck by the substance of his article. (I never was able to check on this. Perhaps some ufological historian will take up the challenge.)

On to Ed Sullivan. He dismissed Black's charges, although he admitted they had "given CSI a black eye." His former friend, he said, had written his article just to make some much needed quick money, as his wife was about to give birth.

By then, I wasn't sure who I believed, so I turned the discussion to CSI's conclusions about saucers. Sullivan said the group's fourth and final bulletin would be out in a matter of days (it was) and would include CSI's findings. He said they'd analyzed about twelve hundred sightings, many of which they received through a by-then-ended cooperative arrangement with the air force. From reported "behavior and performance characteristics," CSI had decided the saucers existed and were not of earthly origin—but that there was "no tangible evidence that they were from outer space." Sullivan's personal opinion was that they were from space, but so far, the evidence for this was "only inferential."

He told me he felt CSI had done a great service in making it possible for people to report sightings without fear of ridicule and in convincing the general public to take UFOs seriously. He lamented the partially offsetting effects that Adamski and others on the "lunatic fringe" had produced, and half-jokingly said Max Miller's convention in August had set his work back "years."

Then he told me something Riedel had hinted at when I spoke with him. It seemed that all in CSI agreed they'd taken things as far as they could. The group's limited resources were not up to going on with saucer research, and they were looking for a scientific organization to take over their files and carry on.

As Justin Case later reported in my magazine *Saucer News*, it turns out that, due to some blundering, CSI had already missed an opportunity for its files to be used in a scientific UFO study at Ohio Northern University, something Sullivan failed to tell me. Finally, the case reports were turned over to a Michigan man who said he was going to organize a scientific investigation. This never happened, and in a few years the CSI files found their way to Donald Keyhoe's National Investigations Committee on Aerial Phenomena (NICAP), which was formed in 1956. Today, they are located in the musty Chicago file room of the revered-by-some J. Allen Hynek Center for UFO Studies (CUFOS).

Like so many who have come into ufology and stayed a while, making a big splash and occasionally a real contribution, Sullivan, Eichler, and their other CSI friends dropped out, never to be heard from again. If any are still around, I wonder what they think about saucers and ufology/ufoology now?

It is better to know some of the questions than all of the answers.
—James Thurber

After interviewing a few more saucer spotters and bidding Manon Darlaine farewell, I struck out for Farmington, New Mexico, where on March 17, 1950, a virtual armada of saucers had stayed over the town of three thousand long enough for a good percentage of the population to see them. I hoped to interview as many of these witnesses as possible to see how their versions compared.

Farmington is located in the far-northwest corner of New Mexico. It is only a few miles from Aztec, where the most famous of the Scully-Newton-GeBauer saucers supposedly touched down in March 1948, but so far as I know, no mishap befell any of the estimated five hundred or so disks that showed up almost exactly two years later (improved saucer-pilot training?).

My first interview after a very long drive from Los Angeles was with florist John Burrell, who told me that at about 11 A.M. on that fateful 1950 day, his attention was attracted to the saucers by a group of his friends on the street in front of his house just outside town. They were looking up at the sky and talking and pointing excitedly.

As soon as he realized this wasn't some kind of a gag, Burrell started scanning the sky himself, sighting three objects moving horizontally from south to north, then turning and reversing course. He estimated the saucers were several miles away and at an elevation of about forty-five degrees above the horizon, "metallic or silvery in color, and in a regularly spaced formation they held throughout" the sighting. As they flew, they fluttered or oscillated. Burrell at first thought they might be geese but changed his mind as he "realized each was tilting back and forth as a unit," with no sign of flapping wings.

He also concluded they were moving too fast to be birds, "perhaps faster than a jet." Burrell told me some of the other people thought the UFOs were wind-blown pieces of paper, but he didn't agree because of their tightly held formation, speed, and so on. His opinion was reinforced by another sighting he had about three that afternoon and another by his wife at about the same time. He saw a single saucer that "spiraled downwards, then went straight up and out of sight in a matter of seconds." In another part of town, Mrs. Burrell saw a whizzing cigar-shaped object. All these things Burrell suspected were "secret weapons" rather than ships from space.

From Burrell's home, I went downtown to the real estate and insurance office of John Eaton, who had been a B-29 tail gunner during World War II. Eaton didn't recall what time he saw the saucers (according to the local paper, it was between ten and eleven in the morning) or just how many UFOs there were, but "there were a lot of them, maybe a couple of dozen, perfect replicas of a dinner plate, even to the bottom ring, and silvery in color." He said several other people watched the saucers with him. Like Burrell, Eaton observed an oscillating motion as the things cavorted about at what he "guessed" was about fifteen thousand feet and "almost overhead, about seventy or eighty degrees above the horizon." He wasn't at all sure of the saucers' size, as "I really had no idea how far away they were." After performing for ten or fifteen minutes, they zipped off in pairs, disappearing "on the horizon."

Most amazing to Eaton was a "bright red saucer," which didn't come as close as the others and which he never saw at any great angle above the horizon. "This one looked just like it was painted red, and when the others paired off, it joined and went out of sight with them." He told me that his experience had made him greatly interested in saucers, which he had decided were "quite likely from outer space."

Robert Foutz, another real-estate man, told me he saw "eight to ten bright specks in the sky before noon that day." They were "zig-zagging around in the sky, and I watched them for about ten or fifteen minutes. They were small in size and round in shape." Foutz had no idea of their height or speed or what they were, but he was certain they weren't bits of paper or cotton fluff (a theory advanced by some).

After interviewing Foutz, I made my way to the Perry Smoak Garage and Chevrolet dealership. There I spoke with two employees, Marlo Webb and Robert Rhein, who spotted the saucers at the same time, which Rhein recalled as being about three in the afternoon.

Webb, a private pilot, said he saw "seven or eight white spots making erratic maneuvers at a high altitude." He watched them for about five minutes and could never make out their shape or get any good sense of their size. Although he told me he had no idea what he'd seen, he "didn't think they came from another planet."

Rhein said the "two dozen or so" objects he saw were solid, white, and "seemed to be spherical in shape." Whatever they were—he refused to hazard a guess—Rhein estimated they were at forty thousand feet and moving very fast. They weren't in formation but "moving more or less in the same direction." He didn't see them depart. After watching the UFOs zip around for ten or fifteen minutes, he looked away. When he tried to find them again, they were gone.

Pressed for time—I had a February 1 deadline to meet my coauthor, Ken Krippine, in Miami—I ended my investigation of the Farmington saucer swarm with the Webb-Rhein interview. If I'd had the time, I would have interviewed many more of the at least fifty to one hundred people who saw the saucers that wild St. Patrick's Day. One of these was the managing editor of the local paper, who, like Eaton, reported a red saucer among the garden-variety ones. These red-saucer sightings are significant because a short time after the morning show in Farmington ended and before any press reports had gone out, people in Tucumcari, another New Mexico town about 150 flying-saucer miles east-southeast of Farmington, spotted a flight of disks "playing in the sky and turning sideways," one of them red. This was just minutes after saucer sightings were made by twelve postal employees and apparently others in Las Vegas, about two-thirds of the way from Farmington to Tucumcari and almost exactly on a straight line between the two towns.

In Los Angeles, Ruppelt had told me he'd looked into the Farmington sighting while he was in charge of Blue Book. He claimed, as he later reported in his book, that a navy Skyhook research balloon had been tracked to the Farmington area the day of all the excitement. He speculated the balloon, huge and made of ultrathin plastic, had grown brittle in the extreme cold of the upper atmosphere and shattered into zillions of shiny pieces. These, he thought, flipped and floated in the sky over the little town, reflecting sunlight and scaring the rubes into thinking the Martians were coming.

After interviewing the people in Farmington and learning of the reports from other towns that included the same sort of performance and a bright red saucer, I thought—and still do—that Ruppelt was reaching for an easy "answer," debunking rather than really explaining. I'm not saying that what Farmingtonians saw that day was a fleet of ships from another world—a relief group dropping down from the Mother Ship of All Mother Ships and forming up over the Four Corners region before dispersing to their operational areas?—but whatever they were, I'm convinced they weren't bits and pieces of a burst balloon, cotton fluff, or wind-blown paper. The Farmington-area weather reports for March 17, 1950, say it wasn't at all windy.

RETURN of the "LITTLE MEN"

In his *Flying Saucers from Outer Space*, Donald Keyhoe had outlined an interesting "little men" story. That's little men as in little men aboard, found dead inside, seen with, emerging from, or scrambling aboard a flying saucer. Unlike other such tales, Keyhoe seemed to take this one pretty seriously. This was because it had been told by a well-respected, prominent business man, Joseph Rohrer, whom Keyhoe said was president of the Pikes Peak Broadcasting Company of Pueblo, Colorado. However, this was one more case in which the major (ret.) didn't check his facts well at all, apparently relying upon a single article in the *Pueblo Chieftan* newspaper.

On my way from Farmington to Pueblo, I phoned ahead to arrange an appointment with Rohrer and learned he and his company weren't located in Pueblo but in Colorado Springs, at the foot of majestic Pikes Peak. So I bypassed not-so-scenic Pueblo and pressed on to "the Springs" about forty miles further north and, appropriately enough, where there are no springs at all.

There I met with Rohrer at the famous and luxurious Broadmoor

Hotel, where we had lunch at lakeside. Rohrer, a very pleasant, jovial man, told me he never intended for his tale to be taken seriously. In June 1952, he'd made "about six" lectures on saucers. One of these, as Keyhoe reported, was at a chamber of commerce meeting in Pueblo. Rohrer showed me the notes he used for his lectures, which he insisted were "for entertainment only." There was some genuine saucer material, including two eyewitness sighting accounts, to which he'd added a phony saucer-and-little-men tale. Rohrer even used props, such as some powder that he told his listeners was the little men's food.

It was a great yarn. Much of it will sound very familiar to those following UFOdumb today. Rohrer claimed that seven flying disks had been bagged by the U.S. government, three of them "forced down" in Montana. One saucer operator had survived, a little man about three feet tall. He had been kept alive at a "secret, isolated site in California." Early attempts at communication had failed, but linguists had finally taught the spaceman how to read and write English. (I wonder if they served him strawberry ice cream while Tibetan music softly twanged? But I'm getting way ahead of my story.)

The downed saucers were giant rotating disks with stationary central crew cabins. Rohrer claimed to have been inside one: "It was one-hundred feet in diameter, eighteen feet thick, and put together in five sections. The sleeping quarters for the crew were tubes with caps on the ends." The rotating rings generated powerful magnetic fields, driving the saucers at tremendous speeds. Of course, the government was keeping everything secret to avoid panic.

Rohrer spun out his yarn as I looked over his notes, and he was very convincing. He told me he concluded each of his talks by telling his audience they "must choose which part of what I said was to be taken seriously," and at the end of every lecture but one, he had two men in white coats burst in and chase him around the room with butterfly nets. "The reason the *Chieftan* reported my chamber talk as factual," Rohrer laughed, "was because their reporter thought he had a hot scoop and rushed out of the room before I'd finished" and the men in white coats showed up.

It seems the paper later ran a retraction that didn't get picked up by the wire services, whereas the original story had. This may be why Keyhoe took the account seriously. During our brief June 1954 meeting, he said he realized his error "right after I okayed the book proofs, when it was too late to make changes." Yet, as far as I know, no correction was made in the numerous later printings and paperback editions of *Flying Saucers from Outer Space.*

Rohrer's little-men tall tale was pretty elaborate and very close to that told by Frank Scully in *Behind the Flying Saucers,* so I asked him where he got the idea. He first made the point that despite his humorous lectures, he genuinely believed "the interplanetary explanation is the only reasonable one for the saucer phenomenon." The little-men tales were another matter, however.

It turned out that Rohrer was well acquainted with George Koehler, who worked for Denver radio station KMYR and was a good friend of Scully's source, confidence/oil man Silas Newton. Koehler had helped Newton get his little-men story around, by spreading variations of it himself and arranging for Newton to give a controversial lecture to a Denver University general science class. It was through Koehler that Rohrer had been introduced to Newton, well before Scully's book was published. Both Newton and Koehler had regaled him with "hush-hush" information about captured saucers and dead little men from Venus. Rohrer believed not a word, but "got a kick out of it." Over the next couple of years, he had discussed Newton's stories with friends, eventually trying out his own version on them. This got him an invitation to give a talk on saucers before a "facts forum group," which led to his other talks. He was still being asked to give his lecture, but had decided to "stop adding to the confusion."

After lunching with Rohrer, I headed for Denver, arriving the afternoon of December 29, 1953. After checking into my hotel, I immediately telephoned KMYR and asked for George Koehler. F. W. Meyer, the president of the company that owned the station, took my call. He told me Koehler had "left for a job in San Francisco about the time Silas Newton got into his oil swindle difficulties." Meyer thought there was a definite connection, things having gotten "too hot in Denver." It seemed Meyer had bought some oil property through Newton and Koehler and felt he, too, had been swindled, though he couldn't prove it. Naturally, his views on the two men were hardly favorable. He was certain Newton and Koehler knew their little-men story wasn't true and claimed he never believed it, which made me wonder why he bought oil property from them.

After hanging up, I went down to the hotel lobby, where I spotted this headline on the front page of the *Denver Post:* "Doodle-bug Pair Guilty." Silas Newton and Leo GeBauer had been convicted of fraud in the oil-finder-gadget case! Hardly expecting to have any luck, I rushed to a public phone, called Newton, and asked for an interview. To my surprise, he was willing to see me that very evening. So as the rest of Denver was reading about Newton's fraud conviction, I was talking with him in the living room of his son's home. Even though he faced a possible thirty-year prison sentence, he was quite cheerful and a gracious host. It wasn't hard to see why people fell for his scams.

Once again, I heard the same story about J. P. Cahn's *True* exposé that I'd heard from Scully and Adamski (I wondered if all three weren't working from the same script). Newton added the specific figure of his soon-to-be-(but never)-filed libel suit against the magazine: $10 million. He also took a shot at Keyhoe, claiming the writer had come to Denver, offered him "a huge sum" for the little-men story, and when Newton refused, decided to "write it up as a hoax," just like Cahn, it seemed. Herman Flader, the victim of the swindle for which Newton had been convicted; saucer debunker Donald Menzel, who, Newton said, had completely distorted the facts about his Denver University lecture; and just about everyone else who dared to challenge the veracity of Newton and his friend Scully were denounced as opportunists, dissemblers, and conspiratorialists, perhaps in cahoots with the government.

I told Newton I was pretty well convinced the air force didn't have any captured saucers or bodies of little men. His response will seem all too familiar to today's saucer fiends: They are not held by the air force but by "another branch of the government which I am not at liberty to name. So it could very likely be that the air force knows nothing about them." According to Newton, there were two hangars at White Sands Proving Ground in New Mexico where the "fifteen or sixteen" saucers were kept. Virtually all of the disks were intact, having been controlled by a device that slowed their final descents so that they were at "magnetic zero" when they touched down. And on and on he went with a version of the tale he'd been telling for several years and which had given Scully a best-seller.

I asked about GeBauer being Dr. Gee, and got the "composite of eight scientists" story. I brought up Koehler and immediately was told he didn't leave town because of the fraud case. Returning to the Dr. Gee question, I pointed out that since the alleged eight scientists were not named in Scully's book and supposedly still could not be identified, all there was to go on was his and Scully's word. At that, and for the only time during our entire conversation, Newton became very annoyed (or, at least, convincingly faked annoyance), saying I was starting to sound like Cahn.

I could see I wasn't going to get anywhere with him on his own claims, so I asked about those of others, first bringing up what Rohrer told me about his lectures. Newton immediately said Rohrer was lying—that is, that Rohrer's little-men story was true. He said the same about another retracted saucer-landing tale, this one reported and later denied by Los Angeles businessman Ray Dimmick (whom I'd unsuccessfully tried to contact while I was in California).

Then I brought up Adamski. Newton said that while he didn't buy the Professor's mystical ideas or claims to have conversed with a Venusian, he *did* believe Adamski had met a spaceman and that his saucer photos were real. He said he and Scully told Adamski how to copyright his first three UFO pictures, which he claimed a "Hollywood trick photography expert" told him could only have been faked "at terrific cost and with studio equipment Adamski doesn't have." Since I knew otherwise, this convinced me Newton was lying.

As for the reality of the Adamski-Orthon encounter, it seemed Newton and Scully had gone to the meeting site just four days after the fact. There they found remains of strange footprints and plaster of Paris with which a cast of the prints supposedly had been made (Orthon's footprints included strange designs, which Adamski claimed experts were attempting to interpret).

It looked like Newton would back *any* claim that even remotely could be construed to lend support to his, even to the point of attempting to keep alive stories that had been retracted by those who had told them. Newton went on to confirm my suspicions by very solemnly telling as true the hoax story of the man from Venus who had made a gouge in a piece of steel with his thumb, a story which he said I could not reveal, implying it was a big secret known only to a few. His dramatically delivered closing line was, "And do you know that it took *seventeen hundred pounds* of pressure to reproduce that dent?" I stopped him there, thanked him for his time, and went out to my car.

As I drove away, I marveled at Newton's breezy nerve and style. There was no doubt in my mind that he was a confidence man through and through, and a very good one at that. It was quite likely that if I had talked with him before learning his background and doing my California investigations, I might well have been tempted to believe him. He told a great story—and with a straight face, too.

Over the next couple of days, I did some further checking on the Newton-Scully-GeBauer story. I met with Francis Broman, the Denver University science instructor before whose class Newton had lectured in

March 1950, providing the opening hook for Scully's book (Broman confirmed Menzel's account rather than Newton's). I also spoke with *Denver Post* reporter Thor Severson, who did the original story on Newton's Denver University lecture and the follow-up stories in which Newton was identified as the mysterious "scientist" who had given the talk. I wrapped things up with an afternoon of going through the *Post's* files on Newton's speech and trial.

My investigations left me with little doubt that Newton's saucers-and-little-men tale was a hoax perpetrated to help promote Newton and GeBauer's doodlebug confidence game. Yet even today, as with the Adamski saga, there are those who insist on believing otherwise, that some shadowy agency of the U.S. government still has Dr. Gee's saucers and little men stashed away in a secret facility. Newton, GeBauer, and Scully, you see, knew The Truth and were framed to keep it from being revealed.

The case has been the subject of a huge, self-published book by William Steinman and Wendelle Stevens and now forms the basis of an annual UFO festival in the tiny town of Aztec, New Mexico, à la the great Roswell fest held each July a couple hundred miles to the southeast (at least Aztec's is a benefit for the town library). A few years ago, Karl Pflock was shown something written by Newton in the early seventies, in which he claimed he'd been approached a second time by mysterious U.S. government agents soon after his fraud conviction and asked to stick by his hoax story. Recently, I learned that "Flying Saucer Physicist" and Roswell-crash booster Stanton Friedman is having second thoughts about the Aztec case, which he has long denounced as a hoax (perhaps because Roswell is crashing around him?).

Thus is confirmed another ufoological principle: No case ever is closed. Wait long enough, and what was thought dead and buried (pick your favorite case) will rise from the grave/Hangar 18/Area 51/a secret underground base, to walk among us again.

PURPLE COWS?

Heading eastward from Denver I rapidly crossed the Colorado plains and the seemingly endless flatness of Kansas to the Kansas City, Kansas/Missouri, area. My first interview there was with James Bachmeier, a Mid-Continent Airlines first officer who, along with Capt. Laurence Vinther, had one of the most speculated-about sightings of the early saucer era. This took place on January 20, 1951, over the Sioux City, Iowa, airport.

Vinther and Bachmeier were about to start their DC-3 down the runway for a trip to Omaha, Nebraska, when the airport tower asked them to check on a strange object air traffic controllers had seen hovering over the airport.

After they got airborne, the two pilots chased the object, which played cat and mouse with them, flew formation off one of their wingtips for a while, then streaked away into the night. All this was observed from the ground, visually and on radar. What made the case especially interesting was the UFO's shape. It looked more like a conventional airplane than a flying saucer. It had a cigar-shaped body and straight wings, but lacked both vertical and horizontal tail surfaces and any visible means of propulsion.

What the Sioux City UFO lacked, the saucer seen at close quarters by William Squires on August 27, 1952, near Pittsburgh, Kansas, had in abundance. Just at sunrise, Squires was driving to work, when he saw a classic saucer—like two oval dinner plates lip to lip—hovering about ten feet above a field and not far from the road. He told me he drove as close as he could, stopped, and started to get out of his car. Just as he did so, the saucer shot straight up and was out of sight in a few seconds (it was in view a total of about a minute).

Squires said he saw three or four windows, lit in changing shades of blue. Through these windows, he saw movement, shadowy forms he "thought were humans," and in a window at the front of the UFO he vaguely saw "a face looking out, but what sort of face, I couldn't be sure." Squires heard a sputtering noise coming from the saucer and saw "a great number of very small propellers" spaced very closely around the thing's perimeter. He figured these were used to "stabilize it and allow it to hover."

For some reason, at the time I was quite impressed with Squires's story. My notes say "he is no doubt telling the truth about his sighting, as he is a religious fanatic (though not of the 'saucer religion')," but rather a Jehovah's Witness. Why this impressed me, I now have no idea. *Propellers* on a ship from space? Maybe I was just tired.

On the other side of the Missouri River, I went to the Independence office of former president Harry S Truman, who had been out of the White House for only a few months. A couple of days before, I had called ahead for an appointment. Much to my surprise, Truman himself answered the phone. I was even more surprised when he agreed to meet with me after learning I wanted to interview him about UFOs. When I arrived, he greeted me personally and we went into his private office, just the two of us.

Rather nervous and not wanting to waste too much of such an important man's time, I got right to the point and asked him what he knew and thought about flying saucers. He grinned, chuckled, and quoted, "I've never seen a purple cow, I never hope to see one. . . ."

Seeing the startled-puzzled look on my face, Truman became more serious and rather kindly told me he'd never seen a saucer himself and "didn't know anything at all about such things." He added that he was sorry he couldn't give me any more help, but what he had told me was "the whole truth."

As nervous as I was, I didn't ask any follow-up questions. Instead, I just thanked the former president and left. Neither of us knew then that we'd meet again in the early 1960s, when, much to his delight, I'd put the saucer question to him once more, this time before dozens of newsmen.

TWO EXTREMES in CHICAGO

Having read statements he had made to the press concerning life on other worlds, I was very interested to talk with famed scientist Dr. Harold Urey, of the University of Chicago's Institute of Nuclear Studies. Urey was very gracious and seemed to take my questions and interest in saucers quite seriously.

While he believed Mars harbored plant life because of the seasonally changing features seen on that planet, he thought there was no animal life and, unlike Dr. Slipher, he felt the existence of canals had not been proven. He also was quite certain there was no life on Venus or any of the other planets of the solar system and said that, other than Earth, none of them had "a source of energy adequate to support the activity of intelligent beings as we know them."

So it was, he said, that if the saucers were spaceships, they would have to come from a planet of another star. Unfortunately, he said, "there is no known source of energy that would allow creatures from another solar system to travel to Earth, hence, I do not believe the flying saucers are spaceships." Instead, he thought, "they will turn out to be natural phenomena and/or hallucinations."

Urey's attitude was not at all dismissive, but was thoughtful and scientific in the best sense of the word. John Otto was another matter entirely. An extreme saucer enthusiast, he told me he'd had several sightings since his first in Alaska in August 1952, none of them the least remarkable, except in Otto's mind.

One of these was on the Arizona-California border, as he was driving to Los Angeles for Max Miller's 1953 flying saucer convention. Another apparently took place on the same trip, a few days earlier, near Warsaw, Indiana. As Otto was driving westward late on the afternoon of August 12, his "eye was attracted by a speck of light hovering in the sky at a great distance and at a great height. Suddenly, as I looked at it, it became brighter and larger. Then it faded out within a few seconds." Otto's explanation for the UFO's getting brighter and larger was that "I had noticed it, and it was responding to my attention by showing me its full size." I was tempted to ask him if he'd ever seen any purple cows, but I refrained.

The CLARKSBURG SAUCER SAGE

From Chicago, I swung southeastward across Indiana and Ohio. I was in a hurry to get to Clarksburg, West Virginia, for an interview with Gray Barker. From there I would head directly home to New Jersey and complete some additional interviews in the New York City area before going to Miami. There I was to hook up with Ken Krippine, discuss our book plans, and fly with him and Dick Weldy to Peru, beginning the adventure trip we'd contracted for.

At the time of our brief first meeting on January 8, 1954, Gray Barker had just started his motion-picture-booking business, then the only one in West Virginia and, eventually, the largest in the state, handling both indoor and drive-in theaters. Unusually tall, gangly, and awkward, Gray was living in a furnished room in someone's home. In contrast to the Barker of later years, he was rather shy, inhibited, and ill at ease with people, probably because of his then-repressed homosexuality.

Gray, who had been in The Field for a little over a year, was editor and publisher of the *Saucerian*, which seemed to me to be the best of the many saucer-enthusiast 'zines then being turned out. Of course, he also had been a key player in Al Bender's by-then-defunct International Flying Saucer Bureau, which was my main interest during this interview. He gave me copies of the first two issues of his magazine, and we talked briefly about saucers and saucer enthusiasts in general, and Bender and the IFSB in particular.

Augie Roberts and Dominic Lucchesi had filled Barker in about me, so he was a bit on guard, and I didn't learn anything new from him about the Bender Mystery, as he consistently and melodramatically called it. I had the sense he was holding back, wanting to hang onto the story for his own future writings rather than handing it to me for my book. I was right. Over the next couple of years, Gray exploited the strange business for all it was worth. He ran several pieces about it in his magazine and then devoted his first book to it. This was the classic *They Knew Too Much about Flying Saucers* (1956), which includes an account of our first meeting that is both hilarious and shockingly removed from the truth.

Despite Gray's professional jealousy and shyness, we hit it off well and agreed to stay in regular contact. It wasn't long before we were best friends, beginning years of ufological (actually, ufoological) fun and coconspiracy.

HOME AGAIN, BUT NOT for LONG

I arrived in Fort Lee on January 10, after two very busy, fascinating, and mostly very enjoyable months on the road. I didn't rest on my laurels, but continued doing saucer interviews, trying to get in as many as possible before driving to Florida.

One of the most interesting of these was with Hugo Gernsbach, generally acknowledged as the father of modern science fiction. The publisher of such pulp magazines as *Amazing Stories* and *Science-Fiction Plus*, Gernsbach had written in humorous but highly intelligent form an account of what life on Mars might be like, which bore little resemblance to the imaginings of one of his most famous authors, Edgar Rice Burroughs, creator of such beloved characters as John Carter of Mars and, of course, Tarzan. I thought Gernsbach's views might add an amusing touch to my book.

He was a vehement saucer skeptic. This wasn't surprising, as he was a friend of arch anti-saucerer Donald Menzel (who'd contributed stories to Gernsbach's magazines under various pseudonyms). "If the saucers are interplanetary," Gernsbach told me, "why is there no concrete evidence? Why do the things keep flying around indefinitely without landing? If they're from Mars [which he theorized was a dying planet], they surely would invade us and make Earth their new home."

He said he thought the saucers would eventually be explained as natural phenomena. This prompted me to ask him why he thought so many people were sure they were spaceships. His answer was interesting and, I think, perceptive: "People like to believe that they are interplanetary because the human mind has always enjoyed folklore—ghosts, fairies, etc.—and still does, in the form of flying saucers."

On January 20, I made a hurried trip to Washington, D.C., to get more saucer information at the Pentagon. This was when I learned the Project Blue Book material they'd freely shown me was no longer publicly available, thanks to Keyhoe, and that I wouldn't be allowed to visit Blue Book at Wright-Patterson Air Force Base in Ohio.

All was not lost, however, as I managed to get a telephone interview with physicist and cosmologist George Gamow, who then was a professor of physics at George Washington University. Interestingly, Gamow had no doubt there were planets orbiting other stars and that some of them harbored not only life but intelligent life. However, he was almost as skeptical about the flying saucers being from one of these worlds as was Menzel. In his view, what people were seeing were natural phenomena of various sorts.

As an example, Gamow told me of a sighting he and his wife had while on a road trip to Florida. "In front of our car, at some distance, we saw what looked like an elliptical balloonlike object. It was white and was moving horizontally and seemingly very fast through the clear, cloudless sky. Suddenly, it faded out, disappeared, then appeared again in another place."

Gamow stopped the car to observe the object more carefully. "It moved closer, and I could then see it was not a solid object, but a mass of white dots, which as they approached, resolved themselves into birds. They had appeared and disappeared according to how the sunlight happened to strike them. If they had not eventually come so close, my wife and I would never have discovered this and would have been sure we'd seen a real flying saucer. I suspect this is the sort of honest mistake many saucer sighters have made."

The INCREDIBLE COBWEB from OUTER SPACE

I arrived in Miami on February 1, the day, as agreed, Ken Krippine was to meet me. He didn't show up. I did connect with his partner, Dick Weldy, who was as much in the dark as I about Krippine's whereabouts.

While Weldy and I tried to sort out what was going on, I filled in the time by doing more saucer interviews. It was then that I first met William

Nash, a Pan American World Airways pilot who'd had a remarkable sighting off the coast of Virginia in July 1952, an experience that made him a true and very active saucer fiend. I also did my interview with Scoutmaster Sonny Desvergers and contacted a number of other interesting people. Among these was farmer Fred Brown, who had seen a saucer much like the one reported by Desvergers, but about a month later; Norman Bean, a pseudo-engineer and saucerer who'd invented a psychic machine that he claimed healed people at a distance; and Marine PFC Ralph Mayher, whom Nash had put me onto.

In late July 1952 Mayher had shot some movie film of a saucer. His superiors took the film to a local television station to have it developed, where it was processed by none other than Norman Bean. The Marine Corps allowed Mayher to talk about his experience, and stories appeared on local television and in the Miami papers. Soon after, the air force showed up, told the Marines they'd prefer Mayher clam up, and took custody of the film for analysis. Mayher never got his film back, and over the years his case has become one of the favorites of those who believe the government is covering up The Truth.

When I met with him, Mayher showed me still prints he'd made from the film, one of several consecutive frames and another a very large blowup of a single frame. In these, the saucer looked like an irregular, hazy, gaseous blob. However, Mayher also showed me some slides he'd made from his film, and I could see what looked like a solid form inside the hazy outline, a form which varied in shape from slide to slide, as did the surrounding haze.

It seemed to me that whatever Mayher had filmed, it most likely was some sort of odd natural phenomena. Even more odd, though, was the explanation offered in no uncertain terms by Donald Menzel. I somehow had learned that Menzel was in Miami, staying at the Harvard Club, and reached him by phone. During our chat, I asked him about the Mayher saucer movie. He said the UFO "probably was light reflecting from a nearby cobweb but appearing as if it were in the sky." When I told Menzel I thought this was absurd, he became very indignant and dogmatically insisted this was the answer. Later in the conversation, however, he said it might also have been an airplane! I couldn't believe I was hearing such unscientific and self-contradictory nonsense from a leading scientist.

(MIS)ADVENTURES with KEN

While I was chasing cobwebs that might have been airplanes, Dick Weldy had learned Krippine had gone right through Miami and on to Peru, apparently without attempting to contact either of us. We finally located him in Lima. I connected with him by phone, and it was obvious he was not as excited about our collaborative efforts as I was. Still, I was determined to keep things going. On March 2 I flew to Lima for the first of many times.

There, I met Krippine at his hotel. My diary summary tells the tale: "I immediately saw clearly what I had suspected for quite a while, that Krippine was considerably cooled off toward the idea of the saucer book and even in regard to having me around. This, as I later learned even more clearly, was because he no longer needed me for anything, whereas in New York, he had." I made the best of things, however, as I still wanted to make the promised (and paid for) jungle trip.

Krippine didn't see any more of me than he had to, but I made friends with associates of his and several others. After a short while, some of these people joined Krippine and me on a trip to Iquitos, in Peru's Amazon region, and from there by riverboat quite a distance down the Amazon River. After we returned to Lima, I occupied myself by pursuing local saucer stories and trying my best to learn as much as I could about Peru and its history.

Finally, the originally promised jungle expedition was mounted. I went by car with Krippine and others to a jungle town named Pucalpa, then on to a tiny village called Aguatilla, where Krippine and I had a very colorful falling out (the full, exciting story will be in our next book). I had deliberately taken absolutely no money on this trek, to force Krippine to pay for everything. So after we'd had things out, he generously gave me one hundred soles (about five dollars) to get back to Lima on. I rode across the Andes on a banana truck, almost drowned in a swiftly moving river because of my own stupidity, and eventually arrived in Lima alive and essentially well. Just call me Indiana Jim!

In late May, after many additional adventures, including some saucer-related ones that I will recount in chapter 6, I returned to Miami. From there I drove back to New Jersey, with a stop in Washington, D.C. There I had my meeting with Keyhoe and recontacted Clyde McLean, the young newspaper editor and UFO believer whom I had interviewed in Mississippi on the westbound leg of my saucer odyssey. McLean had recently taken a new job in the Washington area. I had hoped he might want to team up with me on my book, but he was too busy getting settled into his new position and home, so I decided to go ahead on my own.

As I rolled northward toward New Jersey, I pondered my future. I had become fascinated with Peru and was determined to go back, in pursuit of adventure and treasure, but saucers were in my blood, too, and they would not be denied. I was going to do my book, of course, but also wanted some way to be a regular and recognized player in The Field.

Somewhere on the road in Pennsylvania, I decided to start my own saucer magazine. If Gray Barker and Max Miller could do it, so could I.

The only way to get rid of a temptation is to yield to it.

—Oscar Wilde

Before doing anything else, I needed a decent place to live, something more spacious than the furnished room I'd been using. So it was that I rented my first apartment, still in dear old Fort Lee. This would give me the room I needed not only to live more comfortably, but also to crank out my new saucerzine and write my book.

While moving into my new digs, it occurred to me that to get people really involved and thus make them loyal, paying subscribers, I needed a UFO club for them to join, with my magazine as its Official Publication. I got in touch with Augie Roberts and Dom Lucchesi and invited them to participate in my new venture. Both jumped at the chance.

The COMING of S.A.U.C.E.R.S.

A few days later, Augie, Dom, and I gathered in the living room of my new place to scheme. I outlined what I had in mind, a saucer club with its own monthly magazine, which I hoped would be at least as good as Barker's *Saucerian,* not to mention at least marginally profitable.

We expended much time and energy on good-natured wrangling over the most important issue before us: What should we call our organization and magazine? I'd already decided the "initialism" for the club's name would be S.A.U.C.E.R.S., but what would it stand for? There were some pretty screwy ideas tossed around before we hit upon Saucer and Unexplained Celestial Events Research Society.

Augie was determined that our publication have a sophisticated and serious-sounding name with a scientific cachet. It was he who suggested *Nexus.* Of course, at the time we didn't tumble that the tag S.A.U.C.E.R.S. tended to offset the gravity of *Nexus,* but we were having fun. A year later, in implicit recognition of the true nature of my little periodical and my personal objectives and interests, I changed the name to *Saucer News.* The first issue under the new name was also the first bimonthly one (June–July 1955), a concession to the demands of my lengthy stays in Peru on what I hoped would be more lucrative business.

Although we didn't do much research, never formed a truly organized society, and didn't achieve a whole lot of fame, S.A.U.C.E.R.S. has been in continued existence longer than any other UFO group in the world—a distinction somewhat diminished by the fact that we have only two members, myself (still President and Supreme Commander) and Karl Pflock. My present newsletter, *Saucer Smear*—"Dedicated to the Highest Principles of Ufological Journalism"—is now the club's Official Publication and can trace its ancestry directly back to the first issue of *Nexus* (Karl's S.A.U.C.E.R.S. membership derives from his role as *Smear* Contributing Editor and Fifth Columnist, ex officio and all that).

Of course, in keeping with the golden rule (those who have the gold make the rules), I was elected S.A.U.C.E.R.S. president and *Nexus* editor by acclamation. I then dubbed Augie associate editor, and Dom, who was a fair if rather juvenile artist, art editor. My nonufological friend Richard Cohen allowed me to beef up our masthead by listing him as assistant associate editor, and while he contributed an occasional article, he came to serve mainly as the willing foil of some silly running jokes ("Member in Poor Standing: Richard Cohen, Edgewater, N.J.").

It was my evil plan that Augie and Dom would do most of the work (see "golden rule," above) while I served as idea man and chief pontificator. Of course, it didn't work out that way. Augie and Dom's enthusiasm waned quickly as they realized how much work was involved. After our third issue, I found it necessary to ease them out of any roles in which I had to depend upon them to apply any elbow grease or meet deadlines. They continued on the masthead and to be involved as contributors, mailing-party participants, and so on, but the real work of getting each issue out fell to me.

However, there was no lack of enthusiasm for and participation in our first twelve-page, mimeographed (ugh!) issue, which launched both magazine and club in July 1954 ("Book 1—Tome I"). Dom created the pulp-adventure-'zine cover and weird dedication page and contributed an article, "Entities from Lamuria" (yes, that's how we misspelled it). I wrote the lead editorial, the gossip column (cleverly called "Gossip Column"), a panning review of Williamson and Bailey's *The Saucers Speak,* and as (gasp!) "Joseph C. Ghoul," an article entitled "Why Don't the Saucers Land?" Augie weighed in with "Blues of a Saucer Addict, or What Saucers Have Done for Me," in which he lamented and extolled the tribulations and rewards of a life dedicated to saucering. Our initial mailing of about one hundred copies went out free to a list of saucer fans known to Roberts and Lucchesi, a few of my friends, many of the people I'd interviewed on my cross-country saucering trek, and as many of the Big Names in saucerdom whose addresses we could locate.

My opening editorial and the way I wrapped up the issue perfectly capture the tone and style of our maiden effort, a tone and style today's *Smear* readers will recognize in rough-edged youthful form (I'm sure there are even a few curmudgeons who will say nothing's changed in forty-seven years):

> GREETINGS FELLOW SAUCER FIENDS! Behold the first issue of a brand new Saucer Mag!
>
> Perhaps it is best if we start right off by stating the policy that will be persued [*sic*] by S.A.U.C.E.R.S. and by NEXUS, its official publication. We feel that flying saucers exist and are probably interplanetary, and we also feel that we are as serious-minded about the subject as anybody. However, we cannot persue [*sic*] our interest in saucers with a continued dead-pan expression, and for that reason NEXUS is particularly slanted for those who, like us, can get a laugh out of a rather serious subject.
>
> At times we will be poking fun at our fellow saucer-enthusiasts. Perhaps at times our humor will even be a little biting and sarcastic. How-

ever, it is not our intention to hurt anyone's feelings, and if we do so it will definitely not be on purpose.

[The Field can't say it wasn't forewarned!]

SUBSCRIPTIONS

Nexus will (we hope) be issued every month, and by simple arithmatic [*sic*] we therefore arrive at the conclusion that there should be twelve issues a year. For the privilege of receiving these twelve glorious issues, the cost to you will be only one dollar. (No stamps, foreign coins, or I.O.U.'s will be accepted; we are only interested in cold, hard cash.) Furthermore, your dollar will entitle you to a lifetime membership in S.A.U.C.E.R.S., and a beautifully printed membership card (not yet available). [So maybe Karl and I *aren't* the only members of S.A.U.C.E.R.S. after all!] If we think of any other fringe benefits later on, we will let you know. In the meanwhile, please send us your buck, huh? We don't want to have to keep sending you this lousy sheet for nothing.

CLUB OFFICIALS

Many high posts in S.A.U.C.E.R.S. are still open, such as regional directorships, area commanders, and what have you. (Any title you want, we've got.) Please write directly to the Editor about this if you are interested. In each issue after this one, a list of new club members and club officers will be given.

LETTERS TO THE EDITOR

If you are moved to comment on this Mag., either pro or con, please feel free to do so. Any tips, sightings, gossip, etc., will also be fully appreciated, and all personal mail will be answered promptly on genuine S.A.U.C.E.R.S. stationery. If and when you write, please indicate whether any portions of your letter may be reprinted in NEXUS, as we plan to start a Letters to the Editor column in the next issue. (If you indicate to us that your letter is not for public consumption, we guarantee that it will be kept in strictest confidence.) Our principal aim is to keep saucer news & rumors rolling in, so that we can rehash them and send them out again to all our subscribers. But the only way we can do this is through you, our loyal fans. So let's hear from you!

I closed the issue on this hand-signed note: "Well, that about winds up issue number one [actually, my review of *The Saucers Speak,* something of an afterthought, was appended behind this]. We'll be back again in thirty days or so with more news & views, including a Very Important Announcement." Establishing something of a *Nexus/Saucer News* tradition, in our August issue I informed our readers that "the Very Important Announcement promised in the July issue has been postponed until further notice." Obviously, like the nascent ufology of the 1950s, my little enterprise was a curious mix of serious purpose and silliness, with the proportions varying depending upon what was going on with saucers, reader comments and outrage, and, of course, my editorial whim.

The reaction to our first issue was gratifying and mostly very positive, with letters and dollars streaming in from such folks as Marilyn Feifer and Ted Bloecher (key members of New York's Civilian Saucer Intelligence, one of the earliest Serious Ufology groups), Al Bender, Desmond Leslie (George Adamski's coauthor), Clara L. John (publisher of the contactee newsletter *The Little Listening Post* and Adamski's ghostwriter/-editor), saucer spotters Bill Nash and John Otto, and Gray Barker. Our paid membership soared to nineteen, and I handed out grand titles with abandon, for example, making John Marana, a friend of mine, Supreme Commander of All Regions; Gray Barker, Supreme Commander of the Southeastern Region; and my dear friend and old family retainer Agatha Graits, Commander of the Miami, Florida, District. These and other appointments were announced in our August number. In the September issue, it was revealed that there had "been a vast shake-up in the S.A.U.C.E.R.S. hierarchy," with Marana being "deposed," and so on.

Despite such silly stuff, *Nexus/Saucer News* attracted great interest from saucer-scene VIPs across the spectrum of seriousness and belief. Many contributed long and sometimes important articles and in our pages participated in dialogues and debates about the issues and controversies of the day. A quick flip through the first four years' issues reveals contributions by and serious (and some not-so-serious) discussions involving all of the above, plus such luminaries as Aime Michel, Lex Mebane, Tom Comella (as Peter Kor), Frank Scully, Donald Keyhoe, Max Miller, Morris K. Jessup, Leonard Stringfield, Harold T. Wilkins, Justin Case, Lonzo Dove, Fred Broman, Meade Layne, Isabel Davis, Jerrold Baker, Frank Reid, the mysterious "Dr. D." (Leon Davidson, about whom much more later), I. Givva Damsky, and Richard "Dick" Hall, who was to become and remains today a leading and annoyingly pompous figure in The Field.

Nationally, there was a vacuum in ufology. (No snickering, please!) Saucer fans of all stripes needed a journal where they could read the latest sighting reports and insider dope, trumpet their views to their associates, and enjoy a chuckle or two. I stumbled right into that vacuum with *Nexus/Saucer News*. My little rag became ufology's publication of record, and we covered not only saucers but also a wide range of Fortean topics, events, and reports, from Florida's allegedly mysterious Coral Castle to fish falls in England. Writing in the Civilian Saucer Intelligence (CSI) of New York's newsletter (June 24, 1956), Lex Mebane called *Saucer News* "one of the most intelligent and enterprising of all saucer periodicals." By the end of 1956, our (mostly) paid circulation had grown to about two thousand and generally held between there and twenty-five hundred for most of the next fifteen years, with surges to greater heights during periods of great saucer excitement.

In December 1955 I launched my nonscheduled *Confidential Newsletter* (later, *Non-Scheduled Newsletter*): "information of a nature that is 'too hot to handle' in our regular editions of SAUCER NEWS" sent free of charge to saucerers on my comp and exchange lists and to those regular subscribers who paid a onetime fee of one dollar (I later added a "nonscheduled" one-buck subscription fee). Of course, the newsletter rarely carried any "confidential information that ordinarily never reaches the readers of saucer periodicals," but rather included pretty much the same sort of stuff I ran in *Saucer News,* albeit with a flair more like that of *Confidential* magazine. This gossip sheet is the true spiritual ancestor of today's eight-page *Saucer Smear,* which is both nonscheduled (but roughly monthly) and has only "nonsubscribers" (become one with a "love offering" made to James W. Moseley, PO Box 1709, Key West, FL 33041).

The contents of *Nexus/Saucer News* reflected what I've said about the serious and not-so-serious saucerers of those days generally getting along and considering themselves all members of one big (usually) happy family. We had our eccentric uncles, quite loony aunts, and naughty cousins, but we *were* family, after all, and we were on to something those of the mundane world didn't—and maybe couldn't—get. We were *certain* the answer to the flying saucer enigma was just around the corner, and each of us was playing a part in cracking the case.

This sense of affinity was reflected in the language used, with all and sundry employing terms like *saucerian, saucerer, saucering,* and *saucerzine,* which only a few years later became the stigmata of the "fringies" and characters like Barker and me. About the only really dirty word in The Field was *contactee,* and apart from the growing controversy over George Adamski, Scully, and their ilk, and the budding of UFO debunkery with Donald Menzel's first book, the choosing up of ufological sides really hadn't begun. Even the debate between the partisans on the contactee and little-men questions was mostly civil and often even friendly.

Despite the early 1950s being the Era of Ufological Sort-of-Good

Feeling, I managed to get some entertaining controversies going in our pages. Best remembered, I suppose, is the running verbal gun battle over Adamski, which engaged Desmond Leslie, Lonzo Dove, a peculiar character named Richard Ogden, numerous others, and me for some months. There was a continuing and escalating exchange of views leading up to my big exposé article in our January 1955 issue. Still more heated exchanges ensued, as more and more dirt surfaced, everything culminating in the special Adamski issue of October 1957. Then, of course, there was my "feud" with rival Gray Barker, the Earth Theory of saucer origins, and such. These I'll take up in due course, but first the Fate of my book.

REJECTION-SLIP BLUES

Augie Roberts led off the August 1954 issue of *Nexus* with a column in which he introduced the magazine's staff to our readers. With his typical enthusiasm, he wrote, "Last fall . . . [Jim Moseley] made a 10,000 mile trip [actually a little over half that] by car throughout the United States, gathering information for a forthcoming book on saucers which he expects to have published early next year." This revelation inspired me to see what I could do to make Augie's prediction come true.

On August 6 I went to Henry Holt and Company, Keyhoe's publisher, and learned to my surprise and joy that they were very interested in a book just along the lines I had in mind. However, they needed to see an outline and three sample chapters before making a decision. The editor at Holt told me any "long delay" in getting this material turned in might mean "a very long delay in publication."

So it was that for the next two weeks I devoted every spare moment to frantically grinding out the sample chapters and outline. On August 18 I delivered the result to Holt. Then began a period of anxious waiting, during which I spent most of my time working on the September issue of *Nexus*.

On August 27 (publishers moved *much* faster in those days) the verdict was in. It was negative. Undaunted, three days later I took the sample material to a literary agent, who on September 9 concurred with Holt, to my great discouragement.

I was then faced with a difficult choice. If I was to have any prospect of selling my book, I would have to devote virtually all of my time to that—revising, tweaking, lugging the manuscript from publisher to publisher, and so on. This would require abandoning *Nexus,* on which I had expended so much time and energy and which was a going, if not yet profitable, concern. Seeing the handwriting on the wall about my book —or, perhaps, convincing myself I did—I decided without too much disappointment to give it up, at least for the foreseeable future. As I noted in my 1954 diary summary, I thought it best "to stick to something I knew I could succeed with [!!], rather than take a chance and again be frustrated and disappointed." After all, "1954 did see me enter the field of writing for the public, even though on a very limited scale." And now, a mere forty-seven years later . . .

As it turned out, my travels and research didn't go for naught. I drew on what I had learned to fill many thrilling pages of *Nexus/Saucer News,* selected articles from which wound up in my first book *Jim Moseley's Book of Saucer News,* published by Gray Barker in 1967. Four years later, Barker, um, liberally interpreted much of my trip material as ghostwriter and publisher of my second book, *The Wright Field Story,* which in 1991 was further creatively corrupted by Timothy Green Beckley into the still-available *UFO Crash Secrets at Wright-Patterson Air Force Base.* Now Karl and I are drawing upon my musty notes for this volume, which I hope (no doubt in vain) will correct at least some of the misimpressions created by these earlier efforts. As, for example . . .

The "WRONG FIELD" STORY

While passing through Miami on my way home from Peru in May 1954, I met with George Wolfer, an extreme saucer enthusiast and wealthy Milwaukee businessman, owner of Lifetime Cookware Company. He told me of a woman, the wife of one of his company's Miami salesmen, who claimed firsthand knowledge that the U.S. government had captured flying saucers. In a telephone conversation he secretly recorded, Wolfer persuaded the lady to tell him what she knew. He played this tape for me, and I was impressed.

The woman claimed that sometime in the early fall of 1952, while she was a civilian employee at the Columbus Army Supply Depot in Ohio, she had seen several photos of a flying saucer. She said she had a high security clearance because of her duties as a night communications clerk handling classified messages. One evening, she wandered into the base photography shop, where she saw the photos. She said the shop manager told her he took the pictures of the saucer, which had come down somewhere north of the base. It looked, she said, "like a saucer should look." A few days later, the base was put under a "red and white alert." It seems it was feared the saucer people might attack because of the capture of one of their machines! Two weeks later, the alert was lifted, according to rumor, because investigations of the captured saucer proved there was nothing to fear.

Needless to say, the woman's story grabbed me. I tried to get her name and other information from Wolfer, but he refused. However, he did tell me enough to make successful sleuthing possible. In July, soon after getting out the flagship issue of *Nexus,* I flew to Milwaukee with my friend and S.A.U.C.E.R.S. member John Marana. There, under assumed names to avoid tipping off Wolfer, we began our snooping. Using the information I'd gleaned from Wolfer, I managed to wangle the names of three Miami salesmen out of someone at Lifetime Cookware headquarters, who, suspecting I was a competitor trying to hire away Lifetime staff, would tell me no more.

I told Marana to go back to New Jersey, and I boarded a plane for Miami. There after much cloak-and-dagger work, I finally located and met with the mystery lady, Vivian Walton. She told me a much more detailed story than the one she had related to Wolfer and identified the photographer as a Joe Hershey (I later learned his name actually was Sheehy). She said "Hershey" showed her a half dozen to a dozen photos of a saucer, taken from different angles. She thought the craft was about thirty feet in diameter and said it had a rim around its edge. She claimed to have learned from others such things as that the saucer's windows were made of some sort of one-way material, that the hull was composed of some supermetal "far superior to what we have," and that the machine had not crashed but "floated to the ground, as they usually did when they were temporarily out of or too far from the source of the magnetic power they run on." She also said "there were no humans or living beings of any kind found in this saucer," but she had heard the saucer men were "about five feet tall and a lot like us" and were from Mars or Venus. Supposedly, the saucer had been taken through her base to Wright-Patterson Air Force Base in Dayton—through "Wrong Field" (many saucerers wanted to believe Walton worked at Wright-Patterson, where Project Blue Book was located) to Wright Field.

Walton's story sounded very much like an adaptation of the Newton-GeBauer-Scully tale, and I did take note that the only saucer book the Waltons owned was Scully's *Behind the Flying Saucers.* Still, having gotten so far into the case, I was determined to pursue it as far as I possibly could.

Returning to New Jersey, I hopped into my trusty Hudson and headed for Columbus, Ohio, by way of Cincinnati, where I met with Leonard Stringfield for the first time. Stringfield, who died in 1994, was one of the nicest people in ufology. Inspired by a UFO sighting he had in 1945, nearly two years before Kenneth Arnold's report kicked off the Age of Saucers, he followed the UFO excitement closely. In early 1954 he formed Civilian Research, Interplanetary Flying Objects (CRIFO) and started publishing a monthly newsletter he later named *Orbit.* Over the years, he was a high-ranking official in both Keyhoe's NICAP and the Mutual UFO Network (MUFON), today the sole (barely) surviving major UFO-enthusiast membership group.

So Stringfield was one of the leading figures of Serious Ufology in the 1950s and 1960s, but he always struck me as more of an "I want to believer" and collector of saucer stories than as a careful investigator. This was reflected in the saucer work that occupied him from the late 1970s until his death: uncritically collecting and reporting mostly anonymous claims of flying saucer "crash/retrievals," saucers and alien bodies snatched up by the military and stashed and dissected at various secret facilities, including on the grounds of Wright-Patterson. He presented his first paper on the subject at the 1978 MUFON Symposium in Dayton —by interesting coincidence (?) a little more than two years before Charles Berlitz and Bill Moore published their *Roswell Incident.* His efforts began the process of luring Serious Ufologists back to crashed-saucer research, which in the wake of the Scully-Newton-GeBauer fiasco they wouldn't touch with a ten-light-year pole.

In his first book, the self-published *Inside Saucer Post . . . 3-0 Blue* (1957), Stringfield recalled our first meeting: "After several months of exchanging information by correspondence, Moseley visited my home in July of 1954, en route to Columbus where he said he was to check into a 'lead from a woman who worked with the army there, and who says that a captured saucer went through her base, on its way to Wright-Patterson.' " (Egads! Is it possible that I may have inspired Stringfield's interest in such stuff and thus unwittingly was a catalyst for the crashed-saucer madness of today?)

I went directly from Stringfield's place to Columbus. There, at the army supply depot, I interviewed Joe Sheehy and his boss, Clarence Thorne. Yes, they knew Vivian Walton. Yes, she'd worked there as a communications clerk on the night shift during 1952 and part of 1953, although she had handled nothing classified. When I asked about the saucer photos and attack alert, the men seemed both amused and concerned. There were no photos, Sheehy said. "I've never even seen a flying saucer, let alone photographed one!" There was no alert and no captured saucer taken through the base and on to Dayton. The story was just so much cracked crockery.

Thorne and Sheehy seemed genuinely amused by Walton's yarn, which they left no doubt they considered a pack of lies. Still and all, Thorne said he was going to report the matter to the CIA (!), which made me wonder if I might expect a knock on my door sometime soon (it never came). I suppose both Thorne's and my reactions were natural products of the McCarthyism and Cold War paranoia then epidemic in America. Everyone was jumpy and fearful of either the Red Menace or being denounced as part of it. Anyway, I left Columbus wondering who was telling the truth, and certain of only one thing: *Someone* definitely was lying.

Back in Fort Lee, I worked this minor saga into my book proposal as a featured item. When my ambitions were thwarted on that front, I decided to write it up as a long article in the September *Nexus,* where it appeared under the title "The Wright Field Story, or Who's Lying?" and touted as "concerning" the Very Important Announcement promised in the July issue. Here we see once again the blend of seriousness and irreverent nonsense that was and remains my hallmark and, to my mind, reflects the reality of ufology then and now. To an expression of my belief at the time that there *might* be something to Walton's story, I added some playful teasing to raise in my readers minds this question: Does Moseley possess The Answer to the saucer mystery?

"DR. D," the EARTH THEORY, and AIR FORCE AGENT MOSELEY

My "Wrong Field" article provoked a number of strong responses, the most important being from a scientist who at first preferred to remain anonymous and thus for some time was known to my readers as "Dr. D." This was Leon Davidson, an enigmatic character on the ufological stage. He had worked at Los Alamos on the atomic bomb project and had been a part of an informal group of scientists there, formed to study the weird green fireballs that had been seen zipping through the skies over atomic facilities and sensitive bases in New Mexico during the late forties and early fifties.

When Len Stringfield tipped me to Davidson, the scientist was living in the New York City area, so it was easy for me to interview him. This was the first time I'd heard a coherent, detailed theory that the saucers not only were from Earth but were secret American weapons, probably developed and flown by the U.S. Navy. Davidson claimed to base his beliefs on "classified documents and photographs made available to me because of my position" and his "careful study of saucer sightings according to area, showing a definite correlation between the location of military bases and the location, direction, and so on of saucer flights." He said this view was reinforced by "the air force's lack of alarm about saucers. This indicates clearly that our top military leaders are well aware of what the saucers are and why they can't be a menace to the United States."

Because Davidson was a high-powered scientist with an impressive background, I took his ideas seriously, and I quickly came to see sighting reports involving very humanlike saucer pilots as supportive of the Earth Theory, the idea that the saucers came from our planet, not outer space. I wrote an article for the October 1954 *Nexus* in which I told of my interview with Davidson, not identified by name, and related his ideas to reports of manlike saucer beings. In this piece, "The Flying Saucer Mystery—Solved," I brashly declared,

> I believe that we have here the key to the saucer riddle! Many times during the past few years "space-men" have supposedly been seen on the ground; but seldom have they been described as unusual in appearance except in regard to size, coloring, hair style, and the like. The conclusion is that these may not be space-men at all, but mere Earthlings testing secret devices. . . .
>
> It should be obvious from all I have said above that saucer researchers, no matter how hard they may wish for visitors from space, had better come back down to earth and consider the amazing work our own government has been doing since the end of World War Two! . . .
>
> The information I have discussed so far is a matter of public record. However, just before this issue of NEXUS went to press, I received irrefutable documented evidence which fully confirms these ideas. This information is due to a long-awaited leak from a high official source. It is now too late to assemble this startling data for this present issue, but it will be presented in full in the November issue.

Of course, there was no such evidence. My innately mischievous nature had gotten the best of me, and I'd backed myself into a corner. Naturally, I came clean. Well, not quite. Actually I penned this editorial for my November issue:

> I now owe my readers an apology. I must state that the documents referred to . . . [in my article] are no longer in my possession, and that I am not at liberty to make any further reference to them; nor am I permitted to elaborate as to why the information I promised you cannot be presented in this or any future issue. Suffice it to say that I simply am unable to publish this information, as much as I would like to.
>
> I would like to caution all flying saucer researchers to be extremely cautious in dealing with certain phases of the Saucer Mystery.

Whew! and thanks, Al Bender.

In spite of my budding Earth Theory heresy and in recognition of my contribution to ufological togetherness and the diligent research I was still pursuing—or maybe just because no one else wanted the job—I was elected president of Civilian Saucer Intelligence of New York in November 1954. This group was a quite serious bunch and was responsible for some very good research in the early years. At some point, my shifting views on saucers and various antics caused the earnest CSIers to regret putting me in charge. However, I don't recall ever being deposed or voted out of office. As I remember, CSI just stopped giving me things to do, and like an old soldier, I just faded away.

Meanwhile, Leon Davidson became a major *Nexus/Saucer News* contributor, writing as Dr. D until our June–July 1957 issue, when he finally "came out." All of his contributions were aimed at proving his U.S.-weapons version of the Earth Theory, and over time, his ideas grew more and more outlandish, and he abandoned his saucers-as-weapons idea and contended they were psychological warfare devices. He argued that Adamski wasn't a liar, but rather had been duped by the CIA in some sort of bizarre psywar experiment. When in 1964 New Mexico policeman Lonnie Zamora reported seeing a landed egg-shaped saucer with a strange "insignia" on its side, Davidson said this also was the work of the CIA. In fact, the insignia was a clever combination of the letters *C*, *I*, and *A*, which Davidson had unraveled.

The good doctor did make one major contribution to Serious Ufology. In October 1955 the air force had finally released *Project Blue Book Special Report No. 14,* the results of a statistical analysis of saucer reports done by the Battelle Memorial Institute under a contract with the air force UFO project. However, only a few copies were printed, and these were distributed only to air force public relations offices and not made available for purchase by the public. Instead, the air force widely distributed a press release that claimed the report proved saucers were bunk. The mainstream press bought the air force line almost without question, which I'm sure delighted the Pentagon and raised hopes in the air force that it might at last be able to dump its saucer responsibilities (no such luck).

Davidson smelled a rat. He camped in the air force's New York City PR office and studied the report closely. He found that the press release and supporting report conclusions were not backed up by the data and analysis. He revealed that "[u]nknown sightings constitute 33.3% of all the object sightings for which the reliability of the sighting is considered 'Excellent.' " He also pointed out that the chi-square test, a mathematical analysis done by Battelle, had shown that "there was very little probability that the Unknowns were the same as the Knowns. But they refused to admit that this meant that 'saucers' could be a real type of novel object."

Of course, Davidson was convinced *Special Report No. 14* was a clever ruse to keep America's saucer weapons under wraps. He badgered the air force into giving him permission to reprint the report, which he did in December 1956, including his own analysis of the data and conclusions.

Davidson's booklet was one of the first publications by others that *Saucer News* offered to its readers, a bargain at only a buck and a half. We also made free copies of the air force press release and attached report summary available "as a public service." Independent saucer researcher Justin Case and I studied the summary and presented its main points with our comments in the December–January 1955–56 *Saucer News*. Naturally, I concurred with Davidson's view on the origin of the saucers and asserted the air force report backed this up: "I am not suggesting that all saucer phenomena otherwise unidentified are necessarily U.S. devices. But I do insist that this new Air Force report makes it more clear than ever that the vast majority of recent and current sightings are of U.S. craft rather than space ships or aircraft of foreign origin."

Because of what Len Stringfield called my "big switch" on the origin of the saucers, some in The Field began to suspect I was some sort of air force disinformation agent. Still others came shockingly closer to the truth, writing me off, as Stringfield summarized, "as a sort of jester in the business."

I kept stirring the pot. In my December–January 1955–56 issue, I offered a $1,000 reward to "the first person who can furnish . . . [me] with concrete, material proof that flying saucers are visiting Earth from other planets." A few people responded, none with anything concrete or material, and my thousand bucks remained safe for me to waste on better things.

A few months later, I poured high-test saucer fuel on the smoldering controversy with "The Solution to the Flying Saucer Mystery," in the June–July 1956 *Saucer News*. I professed indignation about the charges that I was an agent of the air force and that my rescinded promise to publish "irrefutable documented evidence" proving the Earth Theory was an example of the disinformation I was spreading. I then declared, "I have therefore decided to take a chance—and a very big chance, I assure you—and publish *some* of the information I received back in 1954." So it was that the flying saucers as "radiation mops" tale was unleashed upon ufology.

I "revealed" that, unknown to the public, radioactive contamination of the earth's atmosphere had reached a very dangerous level due to atomic bomb and other, super-secret weapons work that got "decidedly out of hand." Disk- and cigar-shaped flying saucers were the ultrasecret means of decontamination and the reason for official silence on UFOs. Built and flown from a super-ultrasecret underground base in the American southwest, the saucers were powered by atomic engines that converted nuclear energy directly into electricity, which was used to produce "an entirely new and previously unknown type of propulsion." The deadly atmospheric radiation was converted by the saucers into electrical energy, which they released into the air, overloading it with electricity and causing abnormal weather all over the world. This project was run by a quasi-governmental group known to but a very few top-level officials, which I called The Organization.

I claimed I was "afraid I may be 'visited' [like Al Bender] once this article reaches print. Quite possibly this will be the last issue of SAUCER NEWS. . . ." However, I wrote, "I feel it is more important to get information I already have across to the public, than to 'play it safe,'" regretfully admitting that, with one important exception, my readers probably wouldn't believe me and would continue thinking all saucers were from space (which, I said, some might be). To these doubters I insisted, "I assure you that I do have proof, but it is of such a nature that I do not feel it advisable to identify it here." And the exception?: "the subscriber, whoever he is, who regularly reads this and other saucer periodicals to make sure that no one gets too close to The Answer."

Of course, the radiation-mop story was just a put-on. I'd borrowed one of many crackpot ideas cooked up by Dominic Lucchesi (one that I had half-believed for a while), implied it came to me from an Insider, and let my readers and ufological associates draw their own conclusions. Some agreed with Stringfield, many thought I had more nefarious purposes and masters.

One of these seemed to be Gray Barker. Publicly, he led the charge of those accusing me of being an agent of the air force, even reprinting a letter in the *Saucerian* from someone who'd checked and found there was or had been an air force lieutenant named James W. Moseley (I've never served in any branch of the military, though I have been an auxiliary cop). Privately, Gray and I were coconspirators, having fun with The Field while enhancing the circulation of our respective 'zines.

GRAY BARKER,...

By mid-1956, I realized that, while UFOs were a serious thing, my rather impatient, easily bored nature was not well suited to doing months or even years of detailed, painstaking work only inevitably to be frustrated when definitive answers remained out of reach. In short, I had discovered I wasn't cut out to be a Serious Ufologist, unless of course one was to count the work I did exposing Adamski and, as time went on, certain other fakers and frauds.

Which points up where my interest really was and remains: the people-and-personalities side of ufology. To me, this is much more entertaining (maybe even more important) than UFOs themselves, especially when I can stir things up a bit. Those drawn to saucers, believers and skeptics alike, always have been a remarkable bunch of characters. Many are highly credulous, easy targets for practical jokes and highly susceptible to kooky theories and tales of conspiracy, cover-up, and assorted weirdness. For better or worse, both Gray Barker and I quite happily took advantage of this, frequently as partners in crime. I leave it to others to ponder the whys behind our actions. Whatever the psychology involved, we truly enjoyed ourselves, and I have to admit my devilish adventures with Gray were some of the best times of my life.

Gray was reviled, laughed at, or ignored with difficulty by most Serious Ufologists but genuinely revered by hosts of Believers. He entered The Field in 1952, when along with zoologist Ivan T. Sanderson, he investigated the case of the Flatwoods Monster. This was the huge, smelly, green being that, aboard its flaming flying saucer, allegedly dropped from a September evening sky to land in Gray's home state of West Virginia; terrorized a few kids, a beautician, and a dog; and then disappeared in a cloud of vapor and curious confusion. As I've already mentioned, he—Gray, not the monster—was my good friend practically from the time we met in early 1954, during my cross-country saucer-chasing odyssey, until his untimely death in 1984 at the age of fifty-nine. He was a complex, private person, and I'm quite sure I knew him better than anyone else did during his adult years. He should have lived forever, but he didn't. I still miss him.

A lifelong West Virginian, Gray was the only member of his immediate family to go to college, Glenville State, where in 1947 he earned his degree, after which he taught high school English for a year or so before becoming an audiovisual equipment salesman. A couple of years later, he got into the film-booking business and, in time, did stints as a movie theater manager and owner, in addition to his saucer-related enterprises.

Gray was a child of real, grinding poverty. In the 1930s, when he was growing up on an isolated farm, his family was just getting electricity. The Barkers were very grateful to the New Deal for this and other conveniences they never dreamed of having. As the years went by and Gray became more successful, he set up a fancy office, hired a secretary, bought a new car and other luxuries, and eventually got so deep into debt that he went bankrupt. He just couldn't resist having the things that had been far beyond his and his family's means when he was a kid.

With his *Saucerian* magazine, started in September 1953 and eventually renamed the *Saucerian Bulletin,* Gray set a never-since-equaled (even by me) standard for ufological reporting—that is, the spinning of a saucer yarn in good, entertaining English that excited and titillated the reader. Throughout the 1950s and 1960s, he got a real kick out of saucers. He enjoyed putting together his magazine and writing and compiling many of the contactee and even more far-out books he published under his Saucerian Books/Press and New Age Books imprints. He also wrote about a dozen very humorous monographs, of which, as far as I know, I have the only existing copies. Like the so-called MJ-12 documents, some of these were "copy one of one" productions, while others were distributed to a tiny inner circle of friends. All offer wry and cutting commentary on ufology, ufologists, and life in general, marvelously written but, it seems, too pointed and unconventional for even such an iconoclast as Gray Barker to publish more widely.

As for Gray's general attitude toward UFOs, I understand it, yet it is hard to explain. In the early days, he appeared to take several of the better sensational cases quite seriously, and he seemed genuinely to believe that Al Bender somehow had stumbled onto the real nature and origin of flying saucers and been hushed up by government or alien agents. Or maybe he just enjoyed the somewhat childish pleasure of being a big wheel in Bender's tiny International Flying Saucer Bureau. Gray was IFSB chief investigator, and he and his fellow IFSB potentates would send formal, official-sounding memos back and forth to each other. Or maybe, when the hush-up of Bender came along, Gray simply sensed that a good story could come out of it. He always said I was too sensible or too serious (imagine that!) because I told him it was foolish to believe in an interplanetary invasion simply on the unsupported say-so of an obviously neurotic fellow like Al Bender. I insisted it was far more likely that Bender made the whole thing up as a dramatic excuse to bow out of the saucer game, for whatever personal reasons might have been driving him.

Later, and long before publishing Bender's own weirdly "evolved" version of his story as *Flying Saucers and the Three Men* (1962), Gray had given up any pretense of believing the tale. If he had ever had any serious belief in UFOs, the realization that Bender's story was a crock seemed to drive him into total disbelief. He thought of UFOs and ufology as he did motion pictures—make-believe, wonderment, entertainment, fantasy, fun and games. Yet, when I tried to pin him down, as I often did, asking if he didn't think at least some of the saucer phenomena might be real, he would say that, if there was anything to saucers, it was psychic, extradimensional, or something else rather esoteric, but definitely *not* interplanetary spaceships. He seemed quite serious, but who can say for certain?

In any event, Gray definitely disliked most Serious Ufologists, in particular Center for UFO Studies founder Dr. J. Allen Hynek and Jerome Clark, editor of the CUFOS magazine *International UFO Reporter*, both of whom he considered far too serious indeed. He absolutely hated Aerial Phenomena Research Organization Grande Dame Coral Lorenzen, and she reciprocated. There is a story that she told someone she didn't like Gray because he wore too much lipstick—which was nonsense, as he never used the stuff in any quantity. Obviously, this was a snide reference to his homosexuality, which was quite well known in ufology's Elite Inner Circle.

I don't know what, if anything, Gray may have done to repay Lorenzen's "compliment," but he did take advantage of his film-booking business to pull a priceless prank at the expense of the good Dr. Hynek. (I swear the following story is not merely shockingly close to the truth, but the shocking truth itself.) As most students of ufology will recall, Hynek served as technical advisor on Steven Spielberg's 1977 hit film, *Close Encounters of the Third Kind*. One of his minimal rewards was a few seconds on-screen in the movie. Gray carefully and professionally edited that tiny section of the film out of all the prints he handled before distributing them to his customers. Thus, at least in West Virginia, Hynek wound up on the cutting room floor.

...The THREE MEN,...

Perhaps Gray's high point in ufology came in 1956, when University Books published his only "real" book. Most of *They Knew Too Much about Flying Saucers* was devoted to a somewhat factual account of the Bender case and related alleged mysterious hush-ups. As will be remembered, Bender claimed to have been frightened into silence by three threatening visitors. These were the Three Men in Black, who have become a permanent part of saucer lore, ingrained forever in ufological consciousness by Barker and the later spooky embellishments of writer John Keel.

According to Bender's original story, his three visitors were menacing but definitely human. He told me and his IFSB cohorts he believed them to be agents of the U.S. government. As Gray exploited the story in his magazine, Bender's "three men in dark suits and homburgs" began to transmute into something decidedly more sinister, perhaps even beings from space, with weird countenances and peculiar ways of walking and talking. In his *They Knew Too Much about Flying Saucers,* he further cloaked the Three Men in sinister mystery and extended their operations overseas, with accounts of saucer researchers in Australia, New Zealand, and Canada being scared out of The Field by visits from one or more of them. Some shadowy agency, earthly or otherworldly, was seeking to put private saucer researchers out of business. Its agents seemed to have powers of knowledge and movement that were very much out of the ordinary, and they came from and disappeared into nowhere.

This sort of stuff was gobbled up by most saucer fiends, and those who could profit from it took full advantage. A major figure on the ufological-paranormal scene in those days was John "Long John" Nebel, a pioneer of talk radio and a somewhat skeptical version of today's Art Bell. His all-night show, *Long John Party Line,* began on New York City's WOR and, after many years there, moved to WNBC. Long John featured all the leading and many minor figures in saucerdom and other Fortean realms, whom he subjected to varying degrees of badgering and deference, depending on his mood and what he thought he could get away with (Long John wasn't a very nice guy). His listeners joined in via telephone. I made my first appearance in January 1958 and was on many times thereafter, usually talking about saucers.

Long John's normal format was a panel of four or five guests. One night in the late summer of 1959, August 22 to be exact, the panel in the WOR studio consisted of Gray Barker; Yonah Fortner, a Jewish scholar who wrote for *Saucer News* under the name Y. N. ibn A'haron; Ben

Isquith, a saucer skeptic and, according to the *New York Daily News* of August 24, 1959, "a programmer for computer machines"; and me. Shortly before the program went off the air at 5:30 A.M., Long John asked Barker his personal opinion about the alleged silencing of Al Bender and other saucerers who claimed to have been hushed up. Gray said he thought at least Bender was telling the truth, and he saw no reason to disbelieve the others.

Nebel then asked, "If these stories are true, do you think the . . . men in black are from this planet?" Gray replied to the effect that he believed they were, but that their peculiar dress and mannerisms were probably more frightening to Bender than the information they conveyed to him.

As Barker spoke, a phone rang in the studio's control room, plainly heard through a door that had been left open accidentally. At this point, Long John asked Gray, "Has anyone hushed *you* up?" Gray replied, "No." Nebel followed up with, "Did you mention in one of your recent magazine articles about the possibility of hushing Long John up? It was written in one of [Ray] Palmer's magazines that Long John will be hushed up. . . ."

At that point, music unaccountably started coming in from the control room and going out over the air. Nebel excitedly rushed out to talk with engineer Jack Keane, and a chill came over the studio. When Long John returned to us, he was very irritable and offered no explanation for what was going on.

The music continued for about ten minutes, while we milled around the studio in puzzlement. Then Long John went on the air, saying, "Due to circumstances beyond my control, we are going to enjoy more . . . music. . . . I'll be back with you a little later to say goodnight." Just before 5:30, he went back on and signed off with, "This is Long John again. I'm sorry that we ran into some difficulty, and I'll be back with you again tonight—I hope."

In my "confidential" *Non-Scheduled Newsletter* of September 1, I played the incident as a self-promoting hoax perpetrated by Gray Barker, using a confederate to phone WOR posing as someone from the Federal Communications Commission or the air force and ordering an end to the hush-up discussion. I wrote, "The fact that Barker will stoop to almost anything for publicity and profit has already been pretty well established. . . . Only time will tell whether this solution is the correct one, and whether the Long John program ever dares to discuss flying saucers again."

In fact, the self-promoting hoax was perpetrated by Long John himself with the connivance of engineer Jack Keane. It backfired, getting Nebel into serious trouble with WOR management, who knew nothing of his scam. He was ordered to have the same four guests back on a few nights later, discussing the same subjects, as a way of proving there had been no censorship or mysterious hush-up. During the breaks on this reprise show, Long John could barely contain his anger and was very nasty to all of us. The curse of the Three Men in Black strikes again!

...R. E. STRAITH, and ME

Gray was something of a drinker, some might say an alcoholic. In his prime, he would polish off about four quarts of beer in the course of an evening. When I visited him for a weekend, usually three or four times a year, he would go out of control, sometimes even drinking scotch with me. We would get pretty drunk together, and it was during one of these semi–lost weekends in 1957 that Gray and I perpetrated the infamous Straith-letter hoax. Until the MJ-12 papers surfaced in 1987, this stood as the most successful hoax in ufological history. The letter is still believed genuine by some, despite my front-page, lead-story confession in the January 10, 1985, *Saucer Smear* (published about a month after Gray's death) and the fact that within a couple of years of our little bit of trickery, several in saucerdom had looked into the case and publicly fingered Barker.

The real story is that one of Gray's young ufological friends had sent him a packet of official letterhead stationery, envelopes included, from several U.S. government agencies. This fellow, whose father was a quite senior State Department official, offered to pinch the paper for Gray, and of course, Barker couldn't resist. The next time I drove down from Fort Lee to visit Gray in Clarksburg, he and I decided we just *had* to do something fun with this windfall.

There was no advance planning of any kind. We made things up as we went along, emboldened by the evil of alcohol and fully enjoying the chance to throw long-term confusion into ufology. We wrote not one but seven naughty letters that December 1957 evening, each on the letterhead of a different agency.

One of these, on U.S. Information Agency stationery, went to Laura Mundo, a longtime fan and booster of George Adamski. Another, on a different organization's letterhead, went to APRO's Coral Lorenzen. Still another, signed by "A. G. Matthews, Chief, Liason [*sic*], Internal Affairs" (of what agency I don't recall and the surviving carbon doesn't reveal), went to Manon Darlaine, the Hollywood saucer enthusiast whom I had met in 1953. It thanked Darlaine for her "generous cooperation and employment of . . . [her] valuable time when Mr. Mosley [*sic*] visited you during his recent assignment to your region." The fourth went to someone in the inner circle of Civilian Saucer Intelligence of New York —probably Isabel Davis, Ted Bloecher, or Lex Mebane. One more was addressed to a semi-leading light in The Field whom I no longer recall. The sixth, on National War College letterhead, was addressed to my father, a retired U.S. Army general. It objected to his having indulged in extreme right-wing political activities while on a military pension, strongly implying he might lose the latter if he did not refrain from the former. The seventh was the Straith letter, addressed to the great Professor Adamski himself.

Gray and I jointly composed the missives. He knocked them out on his typewriter and signed them in my presence. On my return trip to Fort Lee, I passed through Washington, D.C., and mailed six of the seven. Having sobered up after our night of mischief, I wisely decided the one threatening my father was too hot to handle and threw it out. (A few years ago, I discovered a carbon copy resides in the Gray Barker archive at the Clarksburg-Harrison County Public Library. I must do something about that one of these days.)

Of the six letters I mailed, only one attained ufological immortality, that addressed to Adamski on U.S. Department of State letterhead and signed by "R. E. Straith." The signature block identified Straith as being with the department's Cultural Exchange Committee, which does not exist and never did. In essence, Straith wrote that some implicitly high-level people at State felt Adamski's claim to have met a spaceman on the California desert in 1952 was true. The letter (reproduced in facsimile in this book's appendix) read:

> My Dear Professor:
>
> For the time being, let us consider this a personal letter and not to be construed as an official communication of the Department. I speak on behalf of only a part of our people here in regard to the controversial matter of the UFO, but I might add that my group has been outspoken in its criticism of official policy.
>
> We have also criticized the self-assumed role of our Air Force in usurping the role of chief investigating agency on the UFO. Your own experience will lead you to know already that the Department has done its own research and has been able to arrive at a number of sound conclusions. It will no doubt please you to know that the Department has on file a great deal of confirmatory [*sic*] evidence bearing out your own claims, which, as both of us must realize, are controversial, and have been disputed generally.

> While certainly the Department cannot publicly confirm your experiences, it can, I believe, with propriety, encourage your work and your communication of what you sincerely believe should be told to our American public.
>
> In the event you are in Washington, I do hope that you will stop by for an informal talk. I expect to be away from Washington during most of February, but should return by the last week in that month.

Adamski reveled in this endorsement. He kept showing it around to bolster his claims. This precipitated FBI and State Department investigations and warnings from the G-Men to Adamski to stop using the letter to promote himself. He didn't.

Contrary to the wishful daydreams of some in ufology, the investigations were not pursued out of any fear that Adamski would prosper or that his nonsense had any basis in fact, but because of a quite reasonable concern about misuse of official stationery. After all, if Gray and I had been truly evil, we might have used the State Department letterhead in an attempt to touch off World War III.

The FBI visited Gray three times, scaring him half to death, while one of their agents dropped in on me once, in February 1959, asking what if anything I knew about Barker's unauthorized use of official stationery (of course, I knew nothing). The investigation sent Gray into a panic, and he smashed the incriminating typewriter to bits and buried the mangled parts in wet cement at a Clarksburg construction site. He was so paranoid about the matter that he refused to tell even me where this was. One has to wonder what Gray might have done if his visitors had borne any resemblance to those he'd conjured up out of Bender's tale!

Eventually, the investigations were dropped, either because no proof of who wrote the letter could be found, or because it was so obviously a harmless hoax, or because the father of the young man who supplied the official stationery quashed them. The one and only time I met our supplier, in the late 1960s, he claimed the latter was the case, which seems likely to me.

Gray and I never learned if Adamski ever believed the letter was genuine. Likely not, but then it really didn't matter one way or the other. It served his purposes quite nicely—in retrospect, my one real though slight regret about this affair.

Most of those in ufology who chose not to believe Adamski's Space Brother stories merely assumed the letter was a hoax and let it go at that. One went a bit further. Fifties UFO researcher Lonzo Dove wrote an accurate, detailed analysis of the letter in which he demonstrated it had been typed on Gray's typewriter. Dove made the mistake of submitting his article to me for publication in *Saucer News*. I refused to publish the piece (surprise), and Dove, who had written quite a bit for *SN*, never forgave me and never submitted another word for publication.

Of course, there were those who believed Adamski and still do. They assumed and still assume the letter was genuine. Their belief was bolstered when a number of them addressed certified mail to R. E. Straith at the State Department, all of which was signed for by the department mailroom, and when still others placed telephone calls to State and were told "Reynold is away from his desk right now" or "He's on leave." Thus, by what I call Saucer Logic, Straith had to exist and be a department official—perhaps downgraded, perhaps even being held incommunicado in some dreadful Foggy Bottom subbasement.

I didn't see any great harm in what Gray and I did, and still don't. However, I certainly understand why Serious Ufologists were offended. And Gray? He was only sorry the Feds had no sense of humor—and very glad they were unable to pin the caper on him.

Has this fellow no feeling of his business, that he sings at grave-making?
—William Shakespeare

After a year of publishing *Nexus* monthly while attempting to pursue what was becoming for me more interesting and potentially highly profitable business in Peru, I switched to a bimonthly schedule. The first such issue, June–July 1955, appeared under the new name *Saucer News*. Over the next four years, I was in Peru more and more frequently and staying longer each time, so with the June 1959 issue, *SN* went quarterly. Saucers were taking a definite backseat to treasure and adventure in exotic climes.

Still, things weren't exactly dull in saucerdom. There was a good deal of speculation and suspicion about where I was and what I was doing on my long trips out of the country. Of course, I deliberately cultivated this by keeping my exact whereabouts and activities semi-mysterious, now and then dropping hints and mentioning visits to Peru. There also was no lack of controversy and fun on other saucerian fronts, some of which I instigated and, as needed, helped keep stirred up.

NICAP FOLLIES

In the late summer of 1956, during a gathering of saucer enthusiasts hosted by George Adamski's original ghostwriter, Clara L. John, at the Washington, D.C., YMCA, UFO author Morris K. Jessup declared it was high time that a serious saucer research group be formed to coordinate UFO studies and get to the bottom of the mystery. One of those in attendance was somewhat flaky physicist T. Townsend Brown, who believed flying saucers were powered by antigravity engines and that he was closing in on the secret of such propulsion. Inspired by Jessup's idea, Brown and some associates filed incorporation papers for the National Investigations Committee on Aerial Phenomena. Thus was NICAP born, with Brown as director and a distinguished board that included the era's leading Serious Ufologist, Maj. Donald E. Keyhoe, USMC (ret.).

Saucerdom had high hopes for NICAP. In short order, though, the group was on the ropes, due to Brown's overambitious plans and bad management, not to mention a little funny business involving fat salaries for himself and a crony and some less than positive scientific fallout from Brown's antigravity theories. Keyhoe led a revolt of the board. Brown was forced to resign and Keyhoe was installed as the new director, promising to turn the organization around.

Before long, having fended off a contactee boarding party abetted by a fifth column in the person of soon-dismissed NICAP secretary Rose Hackett Campbell, Keyhoe had remade the organization in his image. In the pages of its always sporadically published newsletter, the *UFO Investigator,* and in various public pronouncements, NICAP endorsed Keyhoe's theory that not only were the saucers from outer space, but the U.S. Air Force knew it and was covering up this secret of the century.

While it put on a show of having investigating committees that looked into UFO sightings and did research, and while some of these committees and particular individual members did serious and sometimes important work, NICAP's obsession was Keyhoe's: through public pressure and congressional hearings, badger the air force to cough up The Truth. Virtually all NICAP's resources went into this effort, and while there were some small successes with members of Congress, until the mid-1960s when the air force established the Condon Committee to do a "scientific" study of UFOs, nothing really changed. Ironically, the Condon project, which came about at least in part through NICAP's efforts, ultimately led to the group's downfall.

Of course, I joined NICAP almost immediately after its founding, and of course, I and various *Saucer News* contributors just about as quickly began finding fault. At first, we were quite supportive of Keyhoe and what he was doing with NICAP. In fact, it was in an *SN* feature article by Morris Jessup that the story of the Keyhoe-led revolt and what was behind it were made public. But Keyhoe began his tenure promising to stick with previously announced plans for two regular periodicals (a thirty-two-page membership newsletter and a slick, serious 'zine for the general public), a "factual, scientific investigation, without bias or speculation," and so on, and then not delivering.

The controversy kept building. As it did, NICAP lurched along, barely staying solvent and issuing "personal appeal" after "personal appeal" from Keyhoe to the NICAP membership for contributions, advance *UFO Investigator* subscription renewals (for a newsletter that might or might not show up, and if it did, varying in size from issue to issue), and so on, all so "NICAP can continue its important work." Throughout, I always gave Keyhoe and his defenders a fair shake in my 'zine, even going along with the major's demands that his long, often nit-picky and obscure letters be published in their entirety. Still, he and his associates didn't appreciate my little crusade.

In the August–September 1958 *Saucer News*, Richard Cohen and I did an article called "The Rise and Fall of NICAP," in which we spelled out what we thought was going wrong and arched our editorial eyebrows over an announcement that, to raise funds, the organization would be selling "*all* the UFO books available" (emphasis added). This, we said, sounded as though "the once-proud NICAP" was "reduced to selling (and thus implicitly endorsing, whether they like it or not), books about contact claims." We also reported "a reliable rumor" that NICAP was about to fold up.

The saucers really hit the fan after that. The pro- and anti-NICAPers flooded us with letters. Keyhoe (politely) took us to task. Thus, during a generally slow time on the saucer-sighting front, *SN* remained interesting and lively. I'll admit my campaign was in part conducted for base motives, to needle Keyhoe and keep our subscribers interested and sending me money. However, although I strongly disagreed with the idea that the air force Knew All, I was sincere in my concern for NICAP. I hadn't yet given up hope for a solution to the UFO mystery or quite let go of the possibility that some saucers just might be from another planet, and other than Coral and Jim Lorenzen's Aerial Phenomena Research Organization, NICAP was the only game in town for believers and semi-believers like myself.

It was at about this time that Richard "Dick" Hall and I had a falling out. While a student at Tulane University, Hall had been an occasional contributor to *SN*, with letters and occasional articles, and had briefly published his own saucerzine, called *Satellite.* When he graduated, he moved to Washington and went to work as NICAP secretary, in charge of day-to-day operations. During the ten years he was with the organization, he was responsible for editing the newsletter and the famed *UFO Evidence*, a compilation of saucer-case data NICAP used to try to get Congress to *do something* about UFOs. During the past couple of decades, Hall, who fancies himself a high-powered intellectual, has come to be thought of by many—and certainly by himself—as ufology's elder statesman. Until recently, he wrote a stuffy and self-important monthly column for the *MUFON UFO Journal* in which he pontificated and passed judgment upon offerings in previous issues and the doings and what he sees as the failings of lesser ufological beings (he pointedly ignores me).

Sometime in 1958 or 1959, Hall and I had a telephone conversation concerning my "attacks" on NICAP. Almost before we began, he asked me if I was taping our chat. I truthfully told him I wasn't and that I didn't own a tape recorder (I still don't). He kept coming back to this, alleging he could hear clicks on the line and so on. I kept denying it. Finally, Hall practically shouted into the phone that I was lying, that he *knew* I was taping the call. I saw red, yelled "Paranoid!" into the phone, and slammed down the receiver. Things haven't been the same between the suspicious, ill-tempered, and very full of himself Dick Hall and me since. Meanwhile, my struggle to (heh, heh) reform NICAP continued into the middle 1960s, when . . . (To be continued.)

COMMIES *from* OUTER SPACE

Speaking of paranoia and seeing red, while Karl and I were combing through bound volumes of *Nexus/Saucer News* for material, he came upon something I'd completely and conveniently forgotten. Much to the embarrassment of this liberal Democrat and the amusement of my libertarian Republican coauthor, for a few months in 1954 and 1955, I suffered my very own ufological Red Scare.

Reading what I had written in *Nexus/ Saucer News*, I remembered with a start that for a brief time I had fallen under the influence of Charles Samwick, a retired army intelligence officer. Both a saucer fiend and very concerned about Communist subversion, Samwick was active in New York City–area saucering circles. Quite sincere and most convincing, he told me, as I wrote in the October 1954 *Nexus*, "the Communist Party has planted an agent in every civilian saucer club in the United States." I swallowed it, hammer, line, and sickle.

More shocking, and (blush) presaging what we were to hear in later years from arch anti-UFOlogist Philip J. Klass, I wrote and published this amazing editorial (*Saucer News*, June–July 1955):

On Communism and Saucers

> Although it is perhaps unwise to inject a political note into a flying saucer magazine, we feel obliged to point out to our readers certain dangers which, taken together, add up to a possible Communist menace to saucer enthusiasts.
>
> First, for several months we have had good reason to believe . . . that Communist agents have been planted in all of America's leading saucer groups, for information-gathering purposes. This in itself is not a startling fact, but it should serve as a note of caution to saucer researchers who in the course of their studies might unearth information of a technical military nature.
>
> Secondly, let us all give some very serious consideration to the many alleged space men being called to the public's attention—all of whom invariably tell us of the dangers of war and of the exploitation of atomic energy. No one desires peace any more sincerely than we do, but let us remember too that it is part of the Communist "peace line" to frighten the American people into ceasing our atomic experiments. It is quite possible that some of these "space men" are unwittingly playing into the hands of the Communists.
>
> Last but not least, let us not fall into the pitfall of condemning the Government of the United States just because the Air Force refuses to tell us all we would like to know about flying saucers.—I have been told that some of the remarks made at the Saucer Convention last March [the first Giant Rock event] came dangerously close to sedition!
>
> Even as ardently loyal saucer fans, we all can and should face the fact that there are more important and immediate problems in the world today. Whether the saucers are held to be from Space or Earth, it is quite obvious that they present no immediate threat to the safety of this Country; so there is nothing to worry about. Of course everyone would be happier if "officialdom" would be more generous with its

> information on saucers, but for the present we can only assume that there is a good and sufficient reason for the continuing scarcity of information from official sources.
>
> In making the above remarks, we are *not* referring to any particular individual or organization in the field of saucer research. We are merely observing that the saucerian field is alarmingly ripe for use in furthering Communist ends. Let each individual among us be on his guard that he does not fall into such a trap.

Egad! Could it be that Orthon was a Communist agent, maybe from the Red Planet—or at least the Kremlin—rather than Venus? Fortunately, I quickly recovered from this bout of anti-Communist mania. However, at least one other early saucering pioneer did not. This was Eliot Rockmore, a Brooklynite who served for a time as president of CSI of New York and published a saucer-reports 'zine called *Flying Saucer Review* (not to be confused with the later and famous British magazine of the same name). Poor Eliot seems to have been scared right out of saucer research by such notions. He did have other, personal difficulties that caused him to curtail his saucering activities now and again. However, I know he became very close to Samwick, and I'm quite sure he was persuaded by our mutual friend that saucer clubbing could abet the evil schemes of the Masters of Deceit. So it was that, during the summer of 1955, Rockmore left ufology forever.

FROM OUTER SPACE (?) to US

One of the Commie-dupe spacemen I would have had in mind had I known of him in mid-1955 was Howard Menger, unquestionably one of the most colorful characters of 1950s and 1960s saucerdom. This pleasant, rather handsome fellow went the contactees more than one better. He was a reincarnated Saturnian, and his second wife, Connie ("Marla"), was a reincarnated Venusian lass.

Menger came to the attention of the unsuspecting world in October 1956, when he was a guest of Long John Nebel's for the first of many times. Despite his outlandish claims, he projected a kind of naive sincerity (as he still does today) and so struck a very responsive cord with Long John's radio audience. Or maybe it was his titillating mix of sex, saucers, and pseudoscience that hooked them. Whatever it was, only a couple of days after his first wee-hours chat with Nebel, Menger hit national late-night television on the *Steve Allen Show*. Soon he was rivaling

Adamski in popularity, and in fact soon was known as "the East Coast Adamski."

Those who follow today's tales of people being repeatedly abducted by aliens from childhood on will find Menger's story oddly and intriguingly familiar. He claimed his contacts with space beings began at age ten, when a beautiful Venusian woman struck up a conversation with him in the woods near his home. Over the years, he continued having contacts, including a most peculiar one when he was in the army during World War II. While Menger was on leave in Juarez, Mexico, an Orthon-like spaceman with long hair invited him on a taxi ride, which to his later regret Menger refused.

After the war, he settled with his first and mere-earthling wife on a farm near High Bridge, New Jersey, where he went into business as a sign painter. Occasional contacts with the Space People continued, taking Menger's mind off his work—though some cynics suggested he combined his trade and saucering, making paintings of saucers, photographing them, and claiming he'd snapped real visiting spaceships.

In 1956 the frequency of Menger's contacts increased. Sometimes he merely saw humanlike beings who told him they were from other planets and imparted various morsels of Wisdom. Other times, he saw saucers as well, at two "field locations" in woods near his farm. The first time he took photos, they came out badly. He decided someone had tampered with them during processing. Thereafter, he used a Polaroid camera exclusively, so he could see the results immediately (hmmm . . .). Still, his photos continued to be poor. The spacemen told him this was a consequence of the "radiation field" surrounding their saucers. (At least there were no longer any negatives for anyone to check up on.)

According to the plan Menger's (literal!) Space Brothers revealed to him in 1946, the fantastically wonderful story about his contacts would have to be kept from the public until 1957. However, somehow (hmmm . . .) the story leaked out a few months ahead of time, and Menger started taking selected—i.e., easily misled—people with him on his contacts. Because of the saucers' radiation fields, the chosen few were never allowed to approach to within less than fifteen or twenty feet of the saucers and the beings who emerged from them. Oddly enough, these meetings always took place at night.

Gradually, things got even better. Menger took at least three trips into space. The first was "just" for a long-distance view of Earth. Then he was taken into orbit around the Moon and finally for a landing and guided lunar tour, during which he met some of the inhabitants (lunatics?).

And still better. It was at about this time Menger met "Marla Baxter" (Connie Weber), a beautiful Earth woman reincarnated from a past life on Venus. This encounter somehow lifted a "memory block" that had blotted out his remembrance of his own former incarnation on Saturn. It seems that during his days as a Saturnian, he had made a trip to Venus, where he met Marla for the first time. It turned out she was the sister of the Venusian beauty who had enthralled the ten-year-old Menger. It became plain, therefore, that in their earthly incarnations, Howard and Marla were a "natural couple," and Menger divorced his earthling wife and married his space soulmate.

Sometime in 1956 Menger began conducting evening sessions at his home, in which he instructed a small group of carefully selected followers in the teachings of his Space Brothers. After making big splashes on the Long John and Steve Allen shows, he made several lecture tours around the country and in fall 1958 sponsored a saucer convention on his farm, which brought out several hundred faithful and featured on-the-spot radio interviews by Long John.

One of those in attendance at the Menger con was Gray Barker, who knew a good commercial bet when he saw one. Marla/Connie had already told her side of the steamy story in *My Saturnian Lover*, published earlier that year by the vanity house Vantage Press. Gray persuaded Menger to crank out something for his somewhat more real Saucerian Books imprint. This was published with much fanfare in 1959 under the unforgettable title *From Outer Space to You*.

Barker claimed prepublication, special-discount ($3.50, one buck off) orders totaled three thousand. This seems to have been helped along by Gray's offer to include the names of the first one thousand lucky buyers on a special scroll that would, "if possible," be presented to the Space People. As the orders rolled in and sales surpassed one thousand, Gray amended the offer to include the name of *every* buyer on the scroll unless requested otherwise. (I have no idea what became of this scroll or if it ever existed at all.)

Another promotional gimmick in Barker's ingenious campaign was Menger's long-playing record (remember those?) called "Music from Another Planet," which was plugged on the back of the book jacket. The promo text told how Menger had received a telepathic message to drive to a certain mysterious house in the woods (Menger spent a lot of time in the woods, it seems). There he found a Saturnian playing exquisitely beautiful music on a Saturnian piano with weird symbols on its keys. Menger learned to play the tunes on his own mundane piano, and because the music was so popular with his friends and at his lectures, he agreed to record it and permit Barker to sell the records at $3.98 a pop. I've heard this far-out music in both recorded and live performances by Menger. All I can say is, Saturnians' taste must all be in their mouths.

What I found especially wonderful and telling about the success of Menger's book is that Barker made very clear in his promotional literature that he didn't believe a word of his author's story. On top of this, during the three years before the book's publication, I had run several articles in *Saucer News* in which Menger's spaceship and Space People photos had been shown to be fakes and his and Connie's claims had been ridiculed. When the book came out, I blasted it in a scathing review. Similarly devastating disclosures and commentary appeared in the CSI of New York and NICAP newsletters, as well as other saucerzines and mainstream publications.

Despite all this, Howard and Connie and their books and record were very popular and successful. Why? As I wrote in a review of one of Menger's New York City lectures (*SN*, December–January 1956–57), "With George Adamski now reported to be living in Mexico, the saucer-minded public in America apparently needs new saucer stories of a sensational nature to keep interest in the subject from fading. Mr. Menger has amply filled that need." He would continue to do so through the mid-1960s, when he changed his story dramatically.

WHATEVER HAPPENED to "DR." WILLIAMSON?

Another popular figure in the wilder precincts of saucerdom in the 1950s and early 1960s was the late non-Doctor George Hunt Williamson (also known as "Brother Philip" and "Michael D. M. d'Obrenovic"). It will be recalled that Williamson was one of the semiwitnesses to George Adamski's 1952 meeting with a Space Brother. For a time, Williamson was a key member of Adamski's inner circle, and in fact was the person who took the desert-meeting story to a Phoenix newspaper, leading to the feature article that gave Adamski's contactee fortunes a big boost.

Before long, however, in lectures, *The Saucers Speak!* and so on, Williamson began touting his alleged radio and psychic contacts with the Space People and other notions that made Adamski uncomfortable. Williamson had another liability in his close association with fascist mystic William Dudley Pelley. While Adamski quietly "admitted" psychic and telepathic abilities and communications with the Space Brothers, he played that angle down, and despite his own anti-Semitism, he certainly didn't want to be linked publicly with Pelley, even indirectly. The former would turn off "nuts-and-bolts" saucerers, and the latter hardly was compatible with the Space Brothers' cosmic sweetness and light message. These differences led "Professor" Adamski to banish "Doctor" Williamson.

On his own, Williamson continued to delve further into the paranormal, strongly influenced by the notions of Pelley and Meade Layne and his Borderland Sciences Research Associates. Before long, he hooked up with Dick Miller, another saucerer who claimed radio contact with space entities, and the two founded the Telonic Research Center, headquartered in Williamson's Prescott, Arizona, home. Both men were very popular at the early Giant Rock saucer conventions, where they wowed the sun-baked crowds with their tales of communications with the benevolent saucer people, but after about a year, they quarreled and the center was closed.

Moving right along, Williamson and his wife, Betty, recruited mystics Charles and Lillian Laughead, teenage contactee brothers Ray and John Stanford, and a couple of others and set out for Peru, establishing the Brotherhood of the Seven Rays in the Andean town of Moyobamba. From the mountain fastness, they began issuing bulletins to their followers in the United States, predicting all sorts of disasters, the end of the world, and so on, all of which was shockingly close to the messages Williamson claimed to have received from the Space People. The doctrines of the brotherhood also were liberally sprinkled with implicit anti-Semitism, anti-Catholicism (a bit dangerous in Catholic Peru), and Pelleyian paranoia about the evil influences of the International Bankers, all themes that would be featured in Williamson's later writings and pronouncements.

At some point during this mystical Peruvian idyll, Williamson's wife was killed in a highly suspicious accident, falling hundreds of feet to her death at the bottom of an Andean cliff. While the Peruvian authorities couldn't prove it, they strongly suspected Williamson of foul play, and they "suggested" it would be wise for him to leave the country with some dispatch. He took the hint and departed for home as soon as he and his brethren could pack up.

On his return, the good nondoctor began a series of lectures in the United States, Great Britain, and Japan, casting himself as a scientific adventurer and telling some very tall tales about his experiences, among them wild claims of amazing archaeological discoveries. I had spent a lot of time in Peru by then. I knew with certainty that at least two of Williamson's alleged discoveries actually had been found years before by other, real archaeologists. I also had visited and explored some of the places he claimed to have been the first "civilized or white man" to see—before Williamson and company ever set foot in the country.

Throughout the 1950s and into the early 1960s, I reported on Williamson's activities and wacky claims and notions in *Saucer News* and my *Confidential Newsletter*. There was little that he did that I let pass unremarked and, when justified, unexposed. For example, in the February–March 1959 *Saucer News*, Michael G. Mann and I reported on our exhaustive investigation of Williamson's claims of high academic achievement and anthropological and archaeological honors, all of which we proved were bogus.

I'm somewhat proud of my exposures of Williamson's scams and count them as my second (at least semi-)Important Contribution to Serious Ufology. Yet in his *UFO Encyclopedia* ufological historian Jerome Clark has characterized what I published as "what amounted to a vendetta against" Williamson. Perhaps Clark has been influenced by the thinking of his Center for UFO Studies colleague Prof. Michael Swords (who holds a *real*, earned doctorate). An Important Personage in ufology, Swords is a professor emeritus of natural sciences at Western Michigan University, a member of the boards of CUFOS and the Society of Scientific Exploration, and a leading advocate of the extraterrestrial hypothesis—the view that the best explanation for UFOs is that they come from another planet.

Swords also has a soft spot in his, uh, heart for contactees, notably George Hunt Williamson. In his article "UFOs and the Amish" (!) in the September–October 1993 issue of the *International UFO Reporter* (the CUFOS 'zine edited by Jerome Clark), he wrote, "Williamson was basically an honest man. . . . I am led to conclude that he actually believed all the stuff—the wild, amazing, impossible-to-believe stuff—that he wrote about. . . . Williamson is not easy to explain and cannot be deposited into some conveniently labeled box." Here we see The Problem of Ufology nicely boxed up, personified and in black and white.

ONE of OUR AGENTS IS MISSING

I've mentioned that there were those who wondered what I was doing when I was somewhat mysteriously out of the country for two to five months at a time. Was I *really* in Peru? What was I *really* up to? Others thought it pretty amazing that I could publish a bimonthly/quarterly magazine from New Jersey when I was thousands of miles away in South America. At last at least partial answers to these burning questions can be revealed (the rest of the story will have to wait for our next book).

The answer to the magazine-publishing mystery is easy: barely. I had friends who picked up the mail from the *Saucer News* post office box and sent the current issue to new paid subscribers. Other than that, everything would pile up until I returned, which explains why I so frequently had to apologize for issues being late.

There was one thing that didn't pile up while I was gone: cash. During my absences, the ratio of cash to checks and money orders sent in by new and renewing subscribers decreased dramatically. Could it be that my friends pocketed most of the currency? Like the answer to the UFO mystery, the answer to this one has to be shocking—but at this late date must remain speculative.

The answer to where I was and what I was doing there is a bit more complicated and takes a bit more telling, although one Richard Ogden thought he figured it out. A hard-core Adamski-ite, so hard-core that he was almost but not quite an embarrassment to the Professor, Ogden decided I never was in Peru. He checked the Lima phone book and found I wasn't in it. This was because, although I had an office and residence in Peru's capital, in those days, it took a year or two to get a telephone. (When I left for the last time in 1961, I sold my phone and phone line for almost five hundred dollars.)

Then Ogden checked with the U.S. Passport Office, asking if I had a passport, and so on. They, of course, told him such information was confidential, which in his mind proved I was some sort of government agent (the poor guy eventually wound up in a mental institution).

Continuing his sleuthing, Ogden also checked with the American embassy in Lima. Most in-country Americans registered there so they could be contacted or helped in times of emergency. The embassy had no record of me. I had decided that, because of the nature of my activities, it would be wiser not to register.

Capping his "discoveries," Ogden learned there was or had been an active-duty air force officer named James W. Moseley. For him, all of this added up to my being a secret air force agent, one of whose jobs was to sow disinformation and discord in the ranks of saucerdom. Of course, Ogden did his best to spread this delusion far and wide, and some saucer fiends fell for it. Perhaps the fact that Gray Barker claimed to believe it and he and I pretended to feud over it helped this along.

THE LOST CITY and a COUPLE of HOT SAUCERS

In truth, I *was* in Peru during most of my extended absences from New Jersey and, to me at least, what I was up to was far more interesting than ufological cloak and daggering. I was seeking fame and fortune, pursuing treasure, adventure, and comely Latin señoritas. While I was at it, I did keep my ear to the ground for and looked into saucer-sighting reports, and even made one myself.

As will be remembered, during my first trip to Peru in the spring of 1954, my association with Ken Krippine ended in a blowup in the jungle followed by my rather harrowing trip back to Lima. I was determined to make the best of things, and while considering what to do next, I met a fascinating adventurer named Andy Rost. A Dutch seaman who was fluent in English and Spanish, Rost had jumped ship, probably not for the first time, and was hanging out in Lima. He claimed his father had been a Communist and a member of the anti-Nazi underground in Holland during World War II. Rost said, as a child, he had helped his father's organization blow up Nazis and do other exciting and dangerous things.

My first adventure with Rost was an unsuccessful gold-panning trek into the jungle. To make the trip worthwhile—I probably had in mind the prospect of free publicity for the saucer book I still was planning to write—we claimed to have found a "lost city," an important Inca ruin. We were in league with François Guzman, one of the top reporters on *Ultima Hora*, the leading Lima tabloid. Guzman was so "flexible" he would have made an excellent press secretary for Bill Clinton, and he got our story on the front page. On a subsequent trip to Peru, I came across a very small wire service item in English, simply saying that two American explorers had found a lost city in the Marañón River area, where Rost and I had been on our gold-panning trip. For a moment this really excited me, then I realized this was a belated report of our tale. I had been taken in by my own hoax!

Another of our stunts, with similar motivations, also made front-page news in *Ultima Hora*, twice. Rost and I drove around the desert near Trujillo and later near Lima till we found suitably isolated spots. Our plan was to pour gasoline on the ground in a good-sized circle, touch it off, take photos of the result, and claim it was caused by a landed saucer. Our first several (!) tries fizzled because we didn't have enough gas. The fourth or fifth time it finally worked, but I came close to being burned by the saucer myself.

On the morning of May 9, 1954, Rost, a tourist guide named Oscar, and I drove out of Lima in Oscar's vehicle. As I noted in my diary, "we started to work about 11, but [yet again!] we didn't have enough gasoline along to finish the job. . . . So . . . over Oscar's protests regarding his time, car, etc., we returned to the edge of Lima and dropped Andy off there, so that he could go to another appointment. We bought 12 more gallons of gas, and returned to the spot of the burning." As I was about to touch off the gasoline, the wind shifted. If Oscar hadn't shouted a warning, I might have wound up in the photos as a charred alien body. When the fire was out, Oscar and I took photographs (see the photo section). We then headed back to Lima to get ready for the second part of the scheme.

The next day, Rost and I hired a small plane and flew out over the desert, where I took photos of a large, lone, roughly circular and dome-shaped bush. Of course, this was the landed saucer before it took off, leaving its mark behind. Guzman managed to make two exciting stories out of this burning-and-bush foolishness, and I wound up doing at least one radio interview in Lima as a result.

My saucering activities in Peru weren't limited to pranks. I also pursued some serious research for my book. I collected numerous seemingly legitimate sighting reports from Peruvians and Americans visiting and resident in the country. A couple of these were very good sightings by airline pilots, but the best was the Case of the Smoking Saucer.

As a result of my hoax-generated notoriety, I met Pedro Bardi, an agricultural engineer. He told me that on July 19, 1952, while on a farm in the Madre de Dios region of central Peru, he and others saw an unusual saucer. This took place in the late afternoon while he and his companions were talking with associates in Lima by radio. Suddenly, the radio went dead, and looking out the window of the farmhouse, all saw a round object flying past at high speed. Bardi estimated its altitude at one hundred meters (325 feet) and size as "a little smaller than a DC-3" (sixty-five feet long, ninety-five-foot wingspan). The saucer "made a buzzing sound as it went by" and left a white "vapor trail" behind, which was visible for twenty minutes after the object rushed out of sight.

Four minutes later, Domingo Troncosco, a customs administrator at Puerto Maldonado, saw an object of similar size but cigar-shaped (a disk seen edge-on?). The object was flying "quite low and fast" and left a dense smoke trail in its wake. Troncosco, who was in the process of photographing his children when he spotted the UFO, quickly snapped a remarkable photo (see the photo section of this book), and I obtained a print from him. If Bardi and Troncosco saw the same object, and it seems likely they did, the thing was really moving, covering the seventy-four miles between the two sighting points at 1,117 miles an hour.

I found both Bardi and Troncosco highly credible, and unlike what one would expect in the Peru of those days, neither of them sought to make a *centavo* on their stories, which Troncosco certainly could have. I ran the photo and story in the April 1955 *Nexus* and later passed everything along to NICAP, which ran the photo with an article in the August–September 1957 *UFO Investigator.* The photo has since appeared in many books and other publications, including *Look* magazine's special UFO issue (1967). Yet, as far as I know, no one has ever followed up, and the case remains unsolved. So what was the smoking cigar/disk and where did it come from? Permit me to eliminate one answer some readers may have thought of: Andy Rost and I had nothing to do with it.

"NOT ENOUGH GHOSTS"

Another person I got to know on my first trip was a rather well-connected and licensed Peruvian tour guide named, believe it or not, Robert Kennedy. He eventually turned out to be my most reliable Peruvian associate, and we pursued some very interesting, exciting, and semiprofitable ventures together. A native of Arequipa, Peru's second-largest city, Kennedy was quite knowledgeable about archaeology and both the Spanish colonial period, which included a number of wars and "lost treasures," and the Inca and pre-Inca eras, involving pre-Columbian burial grounds, artifacts, and much gold. It was Kennedy who told me the story and made the introductions that led to my first great treasure dig, which began in early 1955, during my second trip to Peru.

By this time I had acquired a metal detector and brought it in from the States. I gradually learned it wasn't of much use. All it could do was indicate a metal object if it were within about two feet of the ground's surface, and then only if the surrounding earth were absolutely neutral. But just having a metal detector made people think I was some sort of scientist or engineer, which along with Kennedy's wide-ranging contacts, helped open many doors.

Lima was full of haunted houses and ghost stories, and Kennedy, Rost, and I went around listening to these tales, more than a few of which involved buried treasure. We never found any ghosts or treasure, but I did have, for example, the pleasure of digging up one man's pigpen, only to find a lot of subsurface water. The only metal object we ever found using my detector was an old, rusty buried shovel. I could see the whole approach was a farce, but it was *fun.*

Then Kennedy put me onto the Quishuarani Treasure. This involved an alleged heap of gold statues and such, including a solid gold Virgin Mary, supposedly stolen from churches by the Jesuits when in the eighteenth century the order was kicked out of Peru and several other South American countries. Kennedy introduced me to members of a family who lived in a rural valley near his hometown. This poor family had heard that a huge cache of the Jesuit loot had been buried in their valley and had sent one of their number to Spain to do research. He brought back a copy of a document that described the location of the treasure, which of course they no longer had when I showed up. However, "all the important information" had been committed to memory. Based on this, the family had bought the land where the treasure supposedly was located, and solely for this reason.

Kennedy and I found a fellow with a much better metal detector than mine, and he got a very strong reading near the little river that ran through the property. The treasure supposedly was in a place below the riverbed, which should have given us a clue that whatever the guy had picked up, it wasn't anything artificial. However, with the glitter of gold dazzling us, we weren't thinking too clearly.

So began a project lasting about eight months and costing me nearly five thousand dollars. When I wasn't in Peru, Andy Rost ran things for me, at least until he got drunk one night and emptied his pistol through the door of the home of one of our workers. Rost quit after this, leaving a young Peruvian and a drunken Swiss mining engineer in charge.

When we got down below the level of the river, the hole kept filling up with water (surprise!), so we had to use a gasoline-powered pump to keep it dry. Since this was all in an underground room we had built, there was a slight problem with carbon monoxide. The workers complained of headaches—fortunately none of them died!—and at one point they all went out on strike. After that, we improved the ventilation, and the job went on and on and on.

Then, at last, we found the treasure! It was an underground stream with large associated natural deposits of iron oxide (rust!), just the kind of thing that would produce a strong metal-detector reading. So ended my first major treasure-hunting venture.

All was not lost, however. In highly fictionalized form I wrote up the fiasco for *Fate* magazine, the "true tales of the strange and the unknown" pulp magazine founded by Ray Palmer and Curtis Fuller. Called "Curse of the Quishuarani Treasure," this article was at first rejected with a note saying, "Not enough ghosts." I added an absurd number of ghosts and sent it back. They bought and ran it in their May 1957 issue ("The Peruvians said the treasure was jinxed by 'el diablo'—and an earthquake almost proved it").

"ONE WEEK"

After the Rost-rust disaster, it dawned on me that it was more practical to zero in on pre-Columbian burial grounds and find *something*, no matter how small, than to go for the big treasures with solid gold virgins, which were not likely to exist, at least where I was digging. So in 1956 Kennedy, Isabel Martinez—a lovely bar girl who had become my mistress—and I went to a very well known burial ground right next to the Pan American Highway. This was about fifty miles north of Lima, where the Chancay civilization once flourished. There were countless thousands of tombs in the area, and it was obvious it would take the little band of grave robbers who lived there many years to clean them out, though by now they probably are all gone.

When I was there, tourists would drive up from Lima and buy directly from the diggers. On any given weekend afternoon, there were many cars and quite a crowd, a regular pre-Columbian flea market. Of course, all of it was highly illegal, but so far as I know, the authorities never cracked down. This likely was because they were bought off, probably for very little, as not much gold or anything else of great monetary value was ever found in the area.

On our first expedition to Chancay, we hired two men. Each would dig into one grave in the course of a day, for a wage amounting to about one American dollar. One of these guys insisted that they found gold in about 50 percent of their graves, and so by excavating two at a time, I was sure to find treasure. Sure! I thought, but it actually turned out that way. The pottery we found was crude and not worth keeping, even for archaeological reasons, but in one of our first two graves, we found a small, low-karat gold feather, which had been attached to a typical Chancay wooden burial mask. At the time, I figured it to be worth about ten dollars, but many years later, when I donated it to the, believe it or not, Graves Museum in Dania, Florida (near Fort Lauderdale), it was appraised at over a thousand, based on age, rarity, and so on. So here we have still another clue as to how naive I was.

However, I did learn something from my early experiences at Chancay: stick to graves. By 1957, when I was at my peak as a ghoul, or, more accurately, ghoulmeister, I had diggers up and down the Peruvian coast collecting antiques for me, and I was running digs of my own in several places, buying other items from jewelry stores, and so on. I had a nice two-room apartment and office in a new building in the heart of downtown Lima (sixty American dollars a month), a Land Rover, and a driver-helper for Kennedy, who couldn't drive.

Kennedy had a *compadre* on the docks at Callao, Lima's port, who for certain considerations could send out two small crates of anything every few weeks. The total cost to me, including those certain considerations, came to under one hundred dollars a shipment. This was an essential connection. While it was legal to collect and own antiquities in Peru (technically, some sort of official permission was required to dig, but this was more often honored in the breach), it was a major crime to ship such artifacts out of the country.

Once my loot was out of the country, I had a partner in New York who could receive the items quite legally, as there were not yet any laws on the books prohibiting importation of ancient artifacts into the United States (ah, the good old days). For a cut, this fellow then sold the items to dealers, collectors, and museums. It was a very nice business while it lasted, although in the long run I essentially broke even. (Since breaking even is the way almost all my business ventures have worked out, "Break Even" has become my unofficial business motto.)

My greatest triumph as a master grave robber also came in 1957. Kennedy put me in touch with one Edmundo Auriche, one of several brothers who owned a very famous ranch near Chiclayo, on the northern coast. Called Baton Grande, this was a huge eighteenth-century Spanish land grant of some eighty thousand hectares (more than three hundred square miles). It was inhabited by just a few Indian families, the men of which worked for the Auriche brothers as diggers, whenever the brothers were so moved.

The area was one of light jungle and warm, moist climate. It had been the center of a pre-Inca civilization called Chimu, which peaked around 1400 C.E. and was still viable when the Spanish arrived in the early sixteenth century. So-called contact tombs have been found, containing bright-colored Spanish glass, presumably traded for gold.

In the 1930s the Auriche brothers' father literally had stumbled upon one or more gold objects. Soon, other gold artifacts were found, and the word began circulating in Chiclayo, where certain government higher-ups took an interest. Eventually, the president of Peru, a General Benevidas, issued an executive decree under which 150 or so soldiers were sent to a Chimu burial site on Baton Grande. There they dug for several months, sending out what I was told was "an endless stream" of large bags filled with metal objects. None of this ever showed up on the antiques market (surprise), which suggests to me that most if not all of it was melted down, following the barbaric lead of the Spaniards during *La Conquesta.*

After the death of their father, the Auriche brothers dug sporadically, with varying success. Kennedy and I worked mostly with Edmundo, with whom we sat down and agreed that for an "entrance fee" of about five hundred dollars I would be allowed to hire men and dig. Then we agreed on how whatever was found would be divided, but I stupidly didn't insist on putting this in writing. I will never forget how during this negotiation Edmundo said simply, "One week," meaning we'd find gold in one week. I decided that if it were that easy, he'd have long since found it himself.

Kennedy, Isabel, and I set up a tent camp on the site, with the diggers sleeping on the ground around our two tents and eating the beans and rice we'd brought in for them. Edmundo stayed in his house in nearby Chiclayo, visiting the dig during daylight hours and only infrequently.

Then we set to work. The first couple of days we found absolutely nothing, not even bones. On Edmundo's advice, we brought in a *brujo*, a male witch, who stayed up all night with several of the workers, chanting and drinking some evil brew to increase his psychic powers. The next morning, he told us where to dig. We dug. Once again, we found absolutely nothing. So much for psychic powers!

Finally, our chief digger came to us with a tip. He said that in one group of tombs nearby, where they had dug a few years before, they had been in such a hurry that one rich tomb might have been overlooked. Gold had been found nearby, and the diggers' superstition was that rich tombs came in pairs (husband and wife, perhaps?).

This made sense to me, so we put our crew of about twenty men to work on the tomb suggested by the chief digger. It took about three days to get to the level of the body, between twenty and thirty feet down. On Saturday of our first week's digging, we were very near the body, but knocked off work on Sunday as usual, in deference to local custom. The following Monday was a long day of discovery, and we took out well over a hundred pounds of copper tools and other copper objects, about thirty decent pieces of pottery, and about nine pounds of gold artifacts. According to our deal, Edmundo kept the pottery, and I bought the gold objects from him at an agreed-upon price.

Then various things began to go wrong, almost like in the movies. Kennedy and I spotted Edmundo pocketing small pieces of gold instead of putting them with the rest, to be inventoried later. At the end of the day, we had about 750 grams of copper, bone, and gold balls piled up. As usual, Edmundo returned to town for the night, foolishly leaving the loot behind, wrapped up and carefully sealed. Kennedy and I estimated the weight of the gold Edmundo had stolen, opened the package, removed the estimated quantity, and replaced it with dirt. We then resealed the package and gave it to Edmundo the next day.

We never heard a word from him about this little payback. However, Isabel overheard Kennedy and me talking in English about Edmundo's perfidy. Her English was such that she thought it was she we didn't trust. She got drunk that night and declared she was going into town and turn us all in. Nothing I could say would persuade her she was wrong, and she even drunkenly said she probably wouldn't get to town anyway, because I'd shoot her with my *pistola.* To reassure her, I unloaded my handgun in front of her and told her to go into town if she really wanted to. She set off on foot into the pitch darkness, but soon was back, saying she'd go to the authorities in the morning. Then she and I went to bed. Magically, by morning Isabel forgot all about turning us in.

Over the next couple of years, we continued to dig in Baton Grande, but never matched our initial success, which had come as Edmundo predicted, a week to the day after we had begun digging. I wrote an article about our first find, not quite as fictionalized as my *Fate* piece on the Quishuarani "treasure." This appeared in the June 1964 *Argosy* men's magazine luridly entitled "Inca Treasure—by the Ton!" The cover teaser shouted, "New Treasure Find: Mounds of Inca Gold!" and the article lead-in read, "There is a fortune to be made in Peru—if you're willing to risk the dangers of being buried alive, shot by claim jumpers or spending a long stretch in a smelly jail as a smuggler." The piece included several of my photographs of the dig and the artifacts we unearthed (see the photo section). To my chagrin, as all my photos were in black and white, the article also included a patently phony color shot of "me" examining "Inca Gold!" artifacts that looked like they had been won at Coney Island, on a beach near which the photo had been taken—shockingly far from the truth.

The PLAIN TRUTH ABOUT NAZCA

Of course, Kennedy and I, often with Isabel, had many more adventures. Perhaps those of greatest interest to saucer fiends involved the Nazca Valley and the famed Plains of Nazca.

In 1954, back when Andy Rost, Oscar, and I were driving around on what were then the outskirts of Lima looking for a place to stage our gas-fired saucer landing hoax, Oscar's sharp and experienced eye spotted something of much greater interest. This was a strange, faint, arrow-straight line running away from the dirt road we were on, down to the end of a narrow little valley. If one wasn't looking for it or didn't know what to look for, it would be passed by, completely unnoticed.

Oscar stopped the car, and told us our discovery was just like the mysterious lines on the Plains of Nazca, which I had not yet seen. With amazing stupidity, we didn't bother to note the location or take photographs, and today the site probably is covered by an apartment complex, as Lima has grown tremendously in recent years. We never bothered to report our find to any authority (or even François Guzman), so to this day, no one realizes that the Nazca Lines are not confined to the well-known area where they "belong," hundreds of miles from Lima.

Oscar explained that the famed lines are located on the Plains of Nazca, an immense, flat expanse of parched desert near the southern coast of Peru. They occupy an area of at least forty square miles, and were created by the pre-Inca Nazca people (ca. 200 B.C.E.–600 C.E.). They received very little attention until the 1940s, when a German American amateur archaeologist began what became a lifelong study of them. Maria Reiche, who died in 1998 at the age of ninety-five, roamed the plains with a Jeep and a ten-foot stepladder, painstakingly mapping the lines and the huge animal figures associated with them.

Reiche's work was not generally known in the United States until an article I did appeared in the October 1955 *Fate* ("Peruvian Desert Map for Saucers?"). I use *did* advisedly, as Maria Reiche's words comprised about 90 percent of the text, like the greatly enhanced aerial photo that accompanied it, stolen directly from an uncopyrighted pamphlet self-published by Reiche in Peru. Later, because of the lines' superficial resemblance to a giant airport, Erich von Däniken and others popularized them with the highly speculative notion that they were intended to be seen and used by flying saucer crews as a landing field.

In fact, the lines are an important engineering feat only because of their great length and remarkable straightness over distances of up to several miles. Many run almost parallel to each other, and in a few cases, up to a dozen intersect at small artificial mounds.

The large animal figures are very similar to designs on ancient Nazca pottery still found in tombs in the valleys near this coastal desert. These figures and the lines themselves were made quite simply by clearing away the reddish topsoil of the desert, exposing the white sand beneath. Since there is virtually no rain in the area, these markings have remained nearly intact for hundreds of years.

There is no question about who made the lines and figures and how they were done. The only real mystery is why, making it easy for von Däniken and others—like Yours Truly—to peddle their ancient astronauts, saucer landing field nonsense. Since the Nazca and other ancient peoples of the region had no written language, we'll never know the "why" for certain. However, Reiche and other serious investigators have suggested an astronomical explanation, and this is most likely correct. The lines appear to have been an attempt to correlate the positions of the most prominent stars and planets. Over the centuries, the apparent positions of all these bodies have shifted, probably accounting for many of the lines being nearly but not quite parallel.

One of the persistent legends about the lines is that they can be seen only from the air. While it's true they can be seen in their entirety only from the sky or, these days, from space, Reiche observed virtually the entire area a bit at a time from her ten-foot ladder, and large portions easily can be surveyed from the surrounding low hills. As I've noted, the photo Reiche used in her pamphlet was greatly enhanced, so the lines could be seen clearly. Nazca's artificial markings are very faint and, like the line Kennedy, Oscar, and I found and lost, quite difficult to see from the air except under the best atmospheric conditions. One would think saucer pilots would have demanded—and made possible—something much more reliable to home in on.

Our discovery of the "stray" line and Oscar's account of Reiche's work piqued my interest in Nazca, and the next year I secured written legal permission (!) from the Ica Museum, which controls archaeological matters in the Nazca region, to dig in that district, including not only the plains but the tomb-crowded Nazca Valley nearby. I'm all but certain I'm the only amateur archaeologist who ever received such permission, and the arrangement was that half of what we found was to go to the museum. This little detail I evaded by adhering to Peruvian tradition, buying off the man the museum sent to keep an eye on us.

Kennedy, our "watchdog," and I went to the plains and, with a small crew, dug on the lines for only a couple of days, focusing on the little mounds at the major intersections and finding nothing. The workers quickly got bored and told us the mounds were earth that had never been moved before, so we were wasting our time. Retrospectively, I find this hard to believe. Consider how difficult it is to get all the dirt back into a hole you've dug, especially one into which you've put something.

Anyway, it was clear the odds were against finding anything valuable on the plains, so we moved into the valley, which in those days held many rich and unopened tombs. We took out some very valuable Nazca pottery, which at its best is as smooth and beautiful as recent European ceramics. At least we met our expenses, once again living up to the break-even principle.

UNMASKED!

Sometime in 1958 I bought a fabulous gold Chimu burial mask from one of the Auriche brothers. I offered it to Mujica Gallo, a very well known and wealthy Peruvian collector of pre-Columbian antiquities. A measure of Gallo's power and influence is that he personally had written the Peruvian antiquities law of that era, which made private collections of pre-Columbian artifacts in Peru legal while continuing the ban on digging for and exporting such items. Since Gallo was the biggest private collector in all Peru, this might be seen as a bit self-serving on his part, but as he had the ear of President Manuel Prado, no one complained.

When Gallo refused to offer what I considered a fair price for the mask, I stupidly reminded him that "there's always the international market." This was a bad move that likely contributed to the troubles that lay just ahead.

The mask went to New York and was sold by my partner through several middlemen, one of whom arranged for it to appear in *Life* magazine, hoping this would enhance its resale value. Unfortunately, the Spanish-language edition of *Life* was read all over South America, where in June 1959 everyone—including Gallo, all the Peruvian government bigwigs, and I—saw two spectacular color photos of the mask, front and side views, and read:

> The almond eyes had been staring up into the darkness of a tomb ever since the golden mask had been put there, almost a thousand years ago [the Chimu civilization isn't nearly that old], to adorn the corpse of a

> Peruvian dignitary. But a few months ago the sanctity of the tomb was shattered when explorers in search of art treasures broke into the ancient burial site in Lambayeque (near Baton Grande—Ed.), and brought the startling face to light.
>
> The mask, . . . was made by a craftsman highly skilled in the goldsmith's art. He had beaten the metal into a smooth sheet, one-eighth of an inch thick, and then carefully hammered out the stylized features of slanting eyes, broad nose, tight lips and giant-lobed ears. To further embellish the gleaming metal, he partially covered the mask with paint and darkened it with an array of dangling gold ornaments.
>
> Because of its unusual size—12 by 19½ inches—its fine state of preservation and its extreme rarity (only two other large masks are known to date), this is one of the most important new finds of pre-Columbian art. Now on view at the D'Arcy Galleries in New York, it is valued at $25,000.

Needless to say, the *Life* feature came as quite a surprise, but at first it didn't occur to me it might spell trouble for me and my grave-robbing enterprises. My name wasn't associated with the matter (yet), and the initial reaction seemed limited to indignant items in the Lima papers. Then came attempts by the Peruvian national police and Interpol to find out who had exported the mask. Finally, about a year later, my name came out.

I never spent more than one or two nights in jail. I was fortunate in my choice of attorneys, at different times one of the deputy ministers of justice and the secretary to the minister of justice. That is, both my lawyers worked for the ministry that brought charges against me. In the States, this would have been a clear conflict of interest, but Peru was and probably remains more casual about such things.

Nonetheless, I was up against something very serious. I had legally become a permanent resident of Peru. This meant I was subject to prosecution under Peruvian law, whereas if I'd been a student or tourist, I would simply have been kicked out, like George Hunt Williamson. The charge against me was *delito contra el patrimonio nacional*—high crimes against the nation, just one step short of treason. If convicted, I could have spent seven years in one of Peru's delightful prisons. Moreover, under Peruvian law, a criminal case is never closed until the Supreme Court has reviewed it, and, as in the United States, the Supreme Court hears very few cases. Thus, even if I'd been found innocent by a lower court, the possibility my case could be reopened would always be hanging over me. Some say the system is based on the idea that everybody can't be bought off, so if someone's really guilty, eventually there will be a conviction.

The handwriting was on the wall. My grave-robbing days were over. In early 1961, while my attorneys and some well-distributed "considerations" continued to hold off my prosecution, I sold the Land Rover and all my other in-country assets. These included a house in Lima I'd bought as an investment. Kennedy put me in touch with a friend of his, the director of the American Express office in Lima, who wanted to buy the property as a wedding present for his son. Sadly, this young man and his bride were killed in a plane crash returning from their honeymoon. Word got around that I was under pressure to leave the country, so offers from subsequent prospective buyers dropped off precipitously, and I finally had to sell the place at a big loss.

At least I managed to get out of the country in one piece, and I returned to the wilds of New Jersey and Manhattan somewhat wiser if not any materially richer for the experience. But, oh, what fun it had been!

The 1960s: Swamp Gas and High Hopes

Part 2

Conform and be dull. —J. Frank Dobie

The absurd is the essential concept and the first truth.

—Albert Camus

As what were to become the far-out 1960s rolled in, ufology was all but becalmed by an extended slump in both the number and sensational content of saucer-sighting reports and a consequent drastic decline in public interest. The major UFO organizations, NICAP and APRO, struggled to maintain their memberships, keep the dues money flowing, and stay afloat. There were definite signs that flying saucers and saucer mania might have gone out with the fifties. No one had the slightest inkling a saucering boom was just around the corner.

Despite the ufological doldrums, hard-core *Saucer News* readers remained loyal. Our circulation held steady at about twenty-five hundred, and the 'zine ran only a little rather than a lot in the red. This may be because I did everything I could to keep things interesting. Major Keyhoe obliged by continuing his role as high-profile foil for my NICAP needling campaign, and Gray Barker did his best to help things along with creative antics and holding up his side of our mock feud. It wasn't that Gray and I felt we had some sort of duty to stir the ufological pot when things got dull, but for better or worse, this turned out to be one of our recurring contributions to the ufoological side of The Field. Naturally, ufoology did its part by spawning more than a few way-out characters, all of whom became grist for the *Saucer News* gossip and controversy mill.

VENUSIAN DOG HAIR and a PRINCE of a FELLOW

In the fall of 1958, one Douglas Hancock appeared on the New York saucering scene. During his nationwide travels as a member of the U.S. Army Band, he had met and fallen under the spell of contactees Buck Nelson and Lee Childers.

Nelson, an Ozark Mountains farmer from Mountain View, Missouri, claimed to have been visited in April 1955 by Little Bucky of Venus and his Venusian dog, Big Bo. Nelson and *his* dog, Teddy, then joined Little Bucky and three-hundred-(Earth?)-pound Big Bo on a saucer trip to the Moon, Venus, and Mars. They witnessed many marvels and, on Venus, learned the inhabitants practiced racial segregation, oddly enough, an endorsement of Buck's own preference. All of this Nelson recounted in his self-published book *My Trip to Mars, the Moon, and Venus* (1956).

The space-faring farmer became a regular at contactee gatherings of the fifties and early sixties, including those he held on his farm. For one of these, a two-day affair he held in 1959, Nelson ordered nine thousand hot dogs, but only three hundred people showed up (I'll bet Big Bo put on a lot of weight eating the leftovers). At another event in 1964 Nelson showed slides that included a blurred photo of a humanlike spaceman, a clearly focused picture of himself, a shot of Big Bo, and another of Buck's small dog Teddy. By amazing coincidence, the blurred spaceman and the focused Nelson bore an amazing resemblance to each other, as did Big Bo and Teddy.

Nelson wasn't much more subtle about hair. During his public appearances, he not only told his story and sold his book, but also peddled with some success physical proof of his adventures: packets of Venusian dog hair, plucked, of course, from the friendly and generous Big Bo. When it was pointed out that the alleged otherworldly fur was identical to earthly canine hair, Nelson countered, "Wal, course 'tis. Dawgs is dawgs. Don't matter what planet they're from." The same is true of suckers like Douglas Hancock.

Which brings me back to New York, 1958. Soon after he arrived in town, Hancock introduced himself to William Woods, who headed up a saucer club called the Bureau of UFO Research and Analysis (BUFORA, not to be confused with the British outfit with the same initials). Hancock joined the group, and in short order, he convinced his fellow BUFORAians they should sponsor a lecture by Lee Childers, a Detroit baker and contactee. (Why Buck Nelson was slighted, I don't know. Maybe he and Teddy were between planets, or perhaps his and his Venusians' racist notions made the New Yorkers uncomfortable.)

Woods and BUFORA arranged for Childers to hold a press conference and appear on Long John Nebel's radio show in early December. At the press conference, Childers and two female associates, Beth Docker and Fannie Lowrey, unveiled a rejuvenation machine, which had recalled Childers from the dead not once but three times—all three after he had been killed by the Men in Black, who had machine-gunned, poisoned, and crushed him (all death records were destroyed, and the coroner's memory of making out the death certificates was deleted by the Space People).

From this triumph, it was on to the Long John show, where, just before going on the air, Childers predicted that a fleet of flying saucers would swoop down and rebroadcast the program worldwide. He also revealed he wasn't a mere earthling contactee. No, he was Prince Neosom of the planet Tythan, located 8.5 light-years from Earth. It seems he had taken over the body of a stillborn child. This was witnessed by an elderly physician, who of course would not remember the event because Neosom's people had wiped out his memory of it.

As we've seen, Long John had a keen sense of showmanship that made him more than a little accommodating to phonies and crackpots—as long as they were clever and entertaining. He didn't find Neosom and his two-woman entourage to be either. Then there was the little matter of the saucer fleet, which failed to appear on cue. After a few minutes on the air, Nebel ordered the trio to leave the WOR studio.

Neosom-Childers was undaunted and over the next few days made the rounds of New York saucerdom, telling his tale and adding ever wilder embellishments. On the other hand, Neosom-Childers's sponsors were nonplused. They thought they were getting a contactee and wound up with royalty from a never-before-heard-of planet. Somewhere between Detroit and the Big Apple, an amazing transformation had taken place.

Perhaps Childers had read too many comic books during the trip east. According to a letter written to BUFORA chairman Woods by a Michigan saucerer and received after the prince had returned to the Motor City, Childers's

> wife has proven to members of the Detroit UFO Group that much, if not all, of Lee's claims originated in comic or science fiction books. Before one local group, Lee claimed to have made a trip to the Moon, Mars, and Venus, all three within ten minutes time, right before their eyes. Each time he acted as though he had passed out for a few minutes and that was his trip! His mother says Lee has always been a problem child. He has left his wife with five children, one of whom is very ill.

In short order, Childers made Beth Docker his wife, bestowing upon her the title and name Princess Negonna.

All this was too much for New York saucerer and parapsychology buff Jonas Kover, who decided to take matters into his own hands. He sent a telegram to Douglas Hancock. Signed "Mission for Space Unification," this read in part: "Congratulations. You search reality. Neosom no longer Prince. King. . . . [F]ather gone to higher karma. We contact Tythan via pre-audio-electrolysis. Hail the King. . . ."

Hancock immediately phoned Prince Neosom and read him the wire. *King* Neosom informed poor Hancock that he already had heard the sad-joyful news from his home planet, expressing surprise that the Mission for Space Unification had taken so long to send its congratulatory message. Hancock then set about calling everyone he knew to pass on the wonderful tidings. Before long, Neosom's followers were delighting in their comic-book prince's elevation to comic-book king.

All but Douglas Hancock, that is. In January 1959, still a member of the army band, he was placed under observation in the psychiatric ward of a Long Island hospital. Some months later, he was released and given a "Section Eight" (mental instability) discharge from the army. In 1963 he committed suicide.

Michael Mann amusingly exposed this amazing tragicomedy of errors and fools in a March 1960 *Saucer News* article. Meanwhile, King Neosom and his queen bravely carried on. I met them at my first Giant Rock Interplanetary Spacecraft Convention, the seventh such annual event, in May 1960. They were wandering about suffering from a lack of attention, probably because, the year before, Giant Rock airport proprietor and convention sponsor George Van Tassel had denounced Neosom as a phony. (Why? Well, he had bad teeth—the Space People have perfect teeth—and drove a broken-down van—when on Earth, Space People always drive Cadillacs.) It turned out the royal couple hadn't seen Mann's article, so I showed it to them. It was quite amusing to watch the shock that came over Neosom as he read, gradually changing his comments from "How interesting" to "Someone is going to be sued for this!" No one ever was.

Despite the bad blood between Van Tasell and Neosom, the princely alien and his consort kept showing up at the Giant Rock affairs. In a July 1963 *Argosy* magazine article, Los Angeles saucerer Max Miller recounted events at the 1962 gathering, including this revealing anecdote:

> A gentle, near-sighted and elderly lady, carrying an armload of flying-saucer books and magazines, asked the prince about the mysterious light observed on the previous evening.
>
> "That was a spaceship the princess and I had called down," he announced casually. Someone then inquired as to the sparks that had fallen from it. "They were scout ships," Prince Neosom rejoined. "Two of them went north and three others took off southwest."
>
> As Prince Neosom wandered toward his group of followers, a young engineer admitted to the elderly woman that he and some friends had sent up the flare the previous evening. They had attached a delayed-action fuse, and released it at dusk.
>
> "Why do you lie like that?" the little woman demanded. "I *know* it was a space ship. You must be working for the government and the dark forces!"

Once again we see there is no claim too wild, no story too silly not to find some adherents in saucerdom's Land of I Want to Believe. However, saucer fiends do get bored, and after a while, the Prince/King and Princess/Queen of Tythan faded away, perhaps light-years away, back to their home world—or maybe just back to Detroit.

A LITTLE TOO MUCH OFF the TOP

Another character who livened things up during the doldrums of the early sixties was Andy "The Mystic Barber" Sinatra, whose antics I gave a lot of play in the pages of *Saucer News,* much to the chagrin of Serious Ufologists. Sinatra, an Italian immigrant who didn't speak English (or Italian) very well, was a Brooklyn barber, but his far more important—and amusing—calling was as a prophet and seer enlightened by his psychic contacts with space beings. Andy's act was partly put on to gain attention, but he seemed genuinely to believe he was in mental contact with entities from other worlds. He claimed to have made several astral voyages to the Moon and the center of Earth, during which his wife, Giovannina, communicated with him psychically. Both Sinatras wore (and sold) bizarre metallic headbands—"psychic machines," to keep malevolent Space People from reading their thoughts (there are Bad Guys everywhere). As I wrote in the June 1960 *Saucer News*, the Mystic Barber's "contribution to the field of saucer research can best be measured in the light of his most recent prediction—that the world would come to an end during the week of May 10th."

But Andy kept on trying. On February 4, 1962, a date which various astrologers—and Andy—predicted would see various disasters visited upon Earth due to a unique planetary conjunction, Sinatra staged a one-man demonstration and mystical ceremony in front of the United Nations building in Manhattan. Well, it wasn't quite a one-man affair. I was there in my capacity as *Saucer News* photojournalist, and Andy had with him his "army of invisible Martians." It seems the Martians had warned that if the peoples of the world did not unite within ninety days, "terrible destructive forces" would be unleashed, possibly leading to the toppling of the UN edifice itself (gasp!). Decked out in his seer's outfit, complete with a ridiculous metal beanie topped with what looked like a small Bazooka tube, Andy conducted his peculiar ritual as a group of bemused tourists and a cop looked on and I snapped photos (see the photo section). Obviously Andy's mumbo-jumbo worked. The UN complex still stands today, and Andy became the first saucer personality to get his picture on the cover of *Saucer News* twice.

The high point of Andy's ufological-mystical career was an appearance on Johnny Carson's *Tonight Show*. Cruelly, they refused to pay him the one hundred dollars he'd been promised, claiming he was incoherent. Poor Andy eventually died of cancer, which the Space People were either unwilling or unable to cure.

The GREAT GIANT ROCK CON(S)

Beginning in 1954 and continuing for a couple of decades until marauding bikers scared off far more gentle saucerers and ruined the scene forever, contactee and channeler of alien wisdom George Van Tassel held annual Interplanetary Spacecraft Conventions at his Giant Rock Airport, located on a large expanse of Mojave Desert land he leased from the federal government. I covered these events in *Saucer News* through articles contributed by participants like Frank Scully, and in May 1960 I finally attended one myself.

Gray Barker and I flew from Pittsburgh to Los Angeles, rented a car, and drove to the Rock, a seven-story, freestanding granite boulder situated in a starkly beautiful area a few miles north of the little town of Yucca Valley. Gray and I set up a table to peddle his *Saucerian Bulletin*, my *Saucer News*, and books published by Gray's Saucerian Press. About two thousand or so contactee faithful turned out for the con, some even flying in aboard private planes (to my knowledge, none arrived by saucer). It was a far smaller crowd than the ten thousand who attended Van Tassel's first affair in 1954, but a good bit larger than the one in 1959.

Given my exposé of Adamski and well-known general disdain for other contactees, I expected to be treated as something of a social outcast, but to my surprise, nearly everyone was quite friendly. *Saucer News* sold briskly, and Van Tassel was most cordial. He even invited me to address the throng of saucerers from the high speakers' platform erected in front of the looming Rock. I took the opportunity to stress that I had always been willing to print articles of rebuttal written by anyone who had been "attacked" in *Saucer News*, pointing out that if some of them had chosen not to take me up on this, it was their fault, not mine. The few in the crowd who were listening to me, rather than scanning the skies for Venusian scout ships, seemed pleased by this.

Various other speakers droned on all day Saturday and Sunday, and as most of them didn't seem to have anything startling to reveal, I confess I paid very little attention. Instead, I spent most of the weekend mingling with the crowd, taking photos and conducting interviews. Among the speakers were Truman Bethurum (who'd done better than most contactees by making the close acquaintance of lovely Clarionite Capt. Aura Rhanes), Dan Fry (who in 1950 had been whisked from New Mexico's White Sands Proving Ground to New York City and back aboard a remote-controlled flying saucer), and Orfeo Angelucci (whose contacts with space beings were psychic rather than physical).

Contrary to my assessment of a few years before, perhaps the most interesting contactee present was Van Tassel himself, who told me his organization had no financial problems, which was why he allowed conventioneers to attend, camp, park, and the like, at no charge. The circulation of his publication was steadily increasing, and donations continued to be "most generous."

A mile or so from Giant Rock itself, on the ranch property where Van Tassel and his family lived, my genial host had recently completed a strange domed building built with no nails or other metal of any kind. He told me this had been paid for with $42,000 donated by his followers. (It was rumored that a good bit of the cash actually found its way into George's pocket, but this was never proven.) When everything was completed—it never was—the big dome would house an "integratron" (later, the building itself somehow became the Integratron). This was a rejuvenation machine, the design for which had, of course, been given to Van Tassel by the Space People (among them Ashtar, who has remained a hearty regular in the realm of space-being channeling). Also to be included, George told me, was something called a "bi-polar magnetic detector," which would create a "zero time factor." This and other gadgets would make it possible for people to walk into the Integratron for a few seconds and come out rejuvenated.

Van Tassel added that there would be an "automatic adjustment factor," which I decided definitely would be needed. I couldn't imagine anyone wanting to walk into the place an old man and come out as a child, infant, or fetus. But it turns out I misunderstood Integratronic rejuvenation, which only works at the cellular level. Thus a "rejuvenee" wouldn't show any outward physical change, while his internal workings would be renewed: Do the Integratron and be and feel but not look younger. Whee! (I think.)

Apparently Van Tassel never took advantage of his own creation, as he died in 1978, a matter of days short of his sixty-eighth birthday. The Integratron is still going strong, though, and its current owners continue to tout its rejuvenating powers, offering healthful "sound baths" and the like.

Another Big Name at the convention who seemed not to be having any financial difficulties was Gabriel Green, founder and president of the Amalgamated Flying Saucer Clubs of America. In his thirties, Green was the author of a weird political platform, which he called "Prior Choice Economics." He claimed his plan would cure all the ills of the world, including eliminating the need for money. Green, a pleasant fellow who died in September 2001 at the age of seventy-six, seemed somewhat discouraged when I spoke with him, reporting he was not making much progress with his economic program. He admitted that he would have to fold up unless he could reach "the masses," a prediction almost borne out by his abortive campaign as "the flying saucer candidate" for president later that year. He seems to have done a bit better reaching the voters with his message over the next two years, as he got 171,000 votes in a 1962 race for one of California's U.S. Senate seats. Maybe Prior

Choice Economics was responsible, but more likely it was the endorsement Green got from Nobel Prize winner Linus Pauling.

Despite his lack of political progress when I met him in 1960, Green did seem to be doing quite well with regard to money, which he was so anxious to eliminate. He had big plans for a huge saucer convention in Los Angeles that August (where he announced his presidential candidacy). There were rumors abounding about who his financial backers might be, and Serious Ufologists were both up in arms about Green's impact on the image of ufology and deeply chagrined that a guy like him seemed to be able to attract major funding, while they could barely keep their doors open. These days, Green would have been denounced as a government disinformation agent in the service of the Great UFO Cover-Up.

Under the magic spell of the California desert and the great Rock, even a hardened cynic like myself began wondering if—Prior Choice Economics aside—"nothing is impossible," as the contactees claimed. At least two thought-provoking events occurred that weirdly enjoyable weekend. I offer them here as part of the record and nothing more.

The first took place early on Saturday evening, at the book stand Gray Barker and I had set up just a few feet from the Rock. A group of friends had gathered around the table to talk with Gray, when suddenly it was noticed that several drops of blood had fallen on the books and the ground nearby. No strangers had passed, and no one there was bleeding. A medical laboratory technician attending the convention analyzed the drops and said they were human menstrual blood, which often is associated with the occult. Needless to say, there was much consternation and speculation about this affair during the rest of the convention.

The second peculiar happening I learned about from a young and very serious-minded engineer later that same evening. We were sitting together with several others in the room under the Rock where Van Tassel held his séances, during which contact was made with the Space People. This fellow told me he wasn't a saucer believer, but had come to Giant Rock out of curiosity. At roughly the same time as the blood incident, he had been standing in the shade of the Rock talking with a character who was telling him about the occult, auras, and electromagnetic fields surrounding the human body. This man was demonstrating some point or other by making a circle with his finger in the palm of the engineer's hand. Suddenly, and for no apparent reason—and this was well after the heat of the day had ended—the engineer had fainted, as if he had been "magnetically short-circuited," as he put it. This was a man who insisted he had never studied or believed in the occult, and had never before fainted. He seemed to me genuinely and very emotionally upset by what had happened and his inability to think of any rational explanation.

As should be obvious, for me the most interesting thing about the convention was the wild cross-section of people. For every serious person, there were perhaps ten True Believers of all types and descriptions. I doubt if any two people in the whole assemblage could have been found to agree entirely on any issue. Yet there was a prevailing tolerance, as strangers went around introducing themselves to each other and trying to outdo everyone else in spouting their own views and theories.

For instance, there was a "faithist" named Zenon Rosiechi, who came out to the desert in a battered old car covered with signs proclaiming the virtues of the mystical Oahspe Bible. He handed out two tracts, one of which he warned must be read with the proper frame of mind, or else the reader would suffer dire consequences. (I never found out what the proper frame of mind was, so I guess I'm doomed.) Then there was the gentleman who stopped me as he drove by to advise that the contactees were not in touch with Space Brothers at all, but with "familiar spirits." As he drove off, he was muttering something about the devil. For my part, I wondered what sort of bottle he was getting *his* spirits from.

A somewhat more comprehensible character was Ted Wentworth, who exhibited examples of his "precipitated art." He claimed that as he did his drawings, his hand was guided "electronically" by unseen space beings. Second-tier contactee Dana Howard, author of several saucer-contact books, enthusiastically endorsed Wentworth's work. She told me he was illustrating one of her books before he or anyone else had read the manuscript. According to her, this proved he really was in contact with the Space People, even though some of his drawings didn't correspond with any of her books. This, she said, meant they were intended for her future writings! It seemed more likely to me that her new books would be written to fit Wentworth's illustrations.

Another Hollywood denizen whom I found considerably more interesting than Wentworth was a lovely young blonde named Daryle Neiman, a model and, of course, contactee. She told me that in 1952 she and a group of friends had met a spacewoman named Soloma. Decked out in a white robe, Soloma discoursed at some length about interplanetary life and philosophy and then suddenly disappeared. However, Daryle stayed in "mental contact" with her, had seen saucers on various occasions, and once saw a space animal named Mika, which she described as appearing like a cross between a rabbit and a cat. While Daryle's tale was no more convincing than the others told at Giant Rock (actually, even less so), there was something (!) about Daryle that filled me with the Will to Believe.

A high point of the weekend came late on Saturday afternoon, when then very popular psychic Mark Probert went into one of his famous trances, during which he always managed to contact one or more of the sixteen "controls" or dead entities who composed what Probert called his Inner Circle. Probert's wife, Irene, seemed to have an uncanny knowledge of which member of the Circle would be heard from each time. In this case, just before the séance began, she said, "Now, *if* the Yada di Shi'ite comes through, he will speak first in his native language and then in English." (The Yada supposedly was an Asian ruler who died five hundred thousand years ago.) Sure enough, the Yada *did* come through, and he spent his first few minutes with us spouting some unintelligible gibberish. He then switched to something resembling English. The translation thus offered was disappointing, both because it contained nothing interesting and, mainly, because the Yada had such a terrible accent it was difficult to understand anything he said. After five hundred thousand years of astral living, he should have been able to do a better job. But I suppose the Yada was lucky to be speaking in any language, even poorly, after having been dead for so long.

The Probert-Yada show was entertaining, but for the true saucer fans, the most exciting event of the con took place after dark on Saturday night. There was a real, honest-to-goodness sighting. Of course, what was sighted wasn't an actual saucer, except in the eyes and hearts of a few diehards who believed everything they saw in the sky had to be a spaceship. Even Van Tassel told the crowd that what they had seen wasn't a saucer. The object, visible for several minutes, appeared to be a balloon with red flares attached—and that's exactly what it was. Investigation revealed that a group of hoaxers had sent up a government surplus balloon with flares dangling from it. But a fake sighting is better than none, and even the Serious Ufologists ran around in controlled excitement, watching the balloon through binoculars until it disappeared.

Before this thrilling event, Van Tassel had primed the crowd by predicting a real flying saucer might actually land at Giant Rock at noon on Sunday, this in accord with some sort of cyclical theory of saucer activity. Exactly one year before, at the 1959 convention, someone had photographed a saucer hovering over the area (although apparently no one but the photographer saw it), so Van Tassel said he expected a return visit. Of course, there was no landing at noon that Sunday, much to everyone's disappointment. However, right at noon, a flight of jet fighters from a nearby base roared overhead. Naturally, the Hard Core claimed the jets had frightened off the approaching saucer.

I'd had such a great time in 1960, I went back to Giant Rock the following year, when the convention was held in October. This time, I was disappointed. The crowd was much smaller than the year before, and the sense of wacky fun was all but missing. I took this to be yet another reflection of the saucering doldrums of those days.

Still, once again Van Tassel permitted me to ascend the golden stairway and address the assembled masses (I sold a few *Saucer News* subscriptions), and there were a few other interesting happenings. One of these was Truman Bethurum's wedding. Apparently, after being named a corespondent in divorce proceedings brought by the contactee's first wife, the very beautiful Capt. Aura Rhanes had split for Clarion, leaving poor Truman without either a wife or an interplanetary girlfriend.

Then the not-so-beautiful Alvira Roberts entered his life. They were married on the Giant Rock speakers' platform by an elderly preacher called up from the audience. The old man forgot most of his lines, but apparently covered the legal essentials and pronounced Truman and Alvira man and wife. Immediately after the ceremony, Bethurum returned to selling his books and pamphlets, pursuing his first love—money.

Another of the old contactee guard present was Dan Fry, who gave a long, rambling astronomical discourse, during which he said almost nothing about his claimed contacts with the Space People. This may have been because his claims weren't particularly interesting, which makes what I consider to be his greatest achievement all the more remarkable. Soon after he became a regular on the contactee circuit, Fry founded Understanding, a nationwide network of small occult/saucer study groups. By 1961 he had about fifteen hundred members in fifty or so "cells," most headed by middle-aged ladies. Touring across the county from cell to cell, lecturing along the way, Fry could always find "understanding" and a warm bed each night.

Orfeo Angelucci was back that year, too. One of the earliest and, for a time, most popular contactees, he was a genuinely likable fellow. He claimed to have seen his first saucer in 1946 and to have had remarkably beautiful "dreams" and psychic contacts with the Space People, who told him of an impending world war that would be followed by an idyllic "New Age of Earth." He told of this in two books, *The Secret of the Saucers* (1955) and *Son of the Sun* (1959), and uncounted lectures. When I read *The Secret,* I took Angelucci for a nervous, sensitive sort, possibly prone to hallucinations. When I finally met him, it turned out he was a hard-core Italian wino, a wild and crazy guy who was a lot of fun to be with.

Oddly enough, one of Angelucci's good friends was serious saucerer Max Miller, of *Saucers* and World's First Flying Saucer Convention fame. On one occasion, the three of us went out drinking—or rather, Orfeo and I drank, while Max sipped soft drinks. Angelucci got quite drunk and I, moderately so. Max kept after his friend to tell "the sheep story," but Orfeo repeatedly begged off, though I had the definite feeling he would give in eventually. And he did. It seemed that, quite a few years before, he and a group of drinking buddies (presumably Earthmen) lived near a sheep farm. When they got really crocked, they would sneak down to the farm and "fool around" with the sheep. After rather circumspectly telling of these bestial adventures, Orfeo suddenly laughed and burst out, "Me, *I* always made sure I got hold of a female sheep, but some of those other guys would fuck *anything*."

The considerably less savory George Hunt Williamson also was on the 1961 program. He had just returned from a trip to Japan, where he was described in print by a leading Japanese saucer researcher as "the baby-faced quasi-anthropologist who put flying saucers on a paying basis." At Giant Rock, Williamson assumed his usual persona of dignified scientist who just happened to believe in saucers. He wowed the credulous crowd, but (surprise!) not me.

I remember the best speaker that year as being the Rev. Frank Stranges, who was and remains a real professional at crowd pleasing. Frank, a quite charming and amusing rogue, is still going strong today despite certain difficulties with the law—among them a 1963 California conviction for running a diploma mill (doctorates of divinity for twenty-five bucks) and a later arrest and conviction having to do with drug smuggling (Frank claimed he was an innocent victim, and he was later pardoned). He is an evangelical preacher who combines his teaching of

Christian scripture with books, lectures, and movies on UFOs—inspired, Frank says, by a meeting he allegedly had in the Pentagon with a Venusian named Valiant Thor, whose purpose on Earth was "to help mankind return to the Lord." The author of such ufoological masterpieces as *Flying Saucerama* (1959), *My Friend Beyond Earth* (1960), and *The Stranger at the Pentagon* (1967), Stranges is the chaplain of a national police officers' association and recently told me he has been appointed some kind of judge by the Immigration and Naturalization Service. I have my doubts about the latter, but then maybe I'm lacking in faith. After all, according to information he provided Ronald Story for *The Encyclopedia of UFOs* (1980), Frank is "a Ph.D. in psychology, a Th.D., D.D., B.Th., B.C. Ed., L.l.D [*sic*], Doctor of Humanities, and Grand Evangelist of the Sovereign Order of Alfred the Great." He also claimed to have attended "colleges in the United States, doing further study at the Graduate Theological Seminary, Macau, Asia; Hong Kong; and at the Society of St. Luke the Physician, London, England . . . also a Ph.D. from the National Institute of Criminology, Washington."

Frank is always looking out for his fellow man, as Gray Barker and I discovered during the 1970 Giant Rock convention. One morning Barker and I were rather late getting to the Rock from our motel in Yucca Valley, Gray having imbibed heavily the night before. As I pulled up and parked our car, I spotted Stranges and another man loading books into a station wagon—Gray's books, which we had left on his vendor table overnight. Gray was in no condition to be concerned, so I leaped into action. "What the hell are you doing, Frank?" I asked gently. "Those are Barker's books!" Without skipping a beat Stranges replied with a broad smile, "Oh, I know, Jim, I know. I was just putting them in my car for safekeeping." I thanked him for his concern and pointed out that, as Gray was now on the scene, this was no longer necessary. The Reverend and his acolyte quickly returned the merchandise to the table and even more quickly fled the area.

Returning to Giant Rock 1961, while there was no saucer sighting that year, there was an exciting display of aerobatics by top stunt flyer Cliff Winters (far more entertaining than a balloon and flares). However, much to my disappointment, another daring performance in which I was to take part was canceled. A certain Professor Ne-Leh, who billed himself as an "illusionist, mentalist, prestidigitationist [*sic*] and hypnotismist [double *sic*]," was to have driven an automobile across the desert while blindfolded. The professor had agreed to allow me to ride along to make sure he didn't peek. I had pictured myself speeding across the sands, possibly begging Ne-Leh to *Please!* peek just once, as our car headed straight for a yawning abyss. Alas, this was not to be, leaving me saying sadly to myself, "Wait till next year!"

Which is as good a slogan as any for Giant Rock and perhaps ufology and ufoology in general. In any case, I always found the gatherings at the Rock to be mostly innocent fun, with a good time had by all. The speakers and crowds were mainly harmless crackpots, hoaxers, faddists, and True Believers, with a sprinkling of serious saucer researchers and interested skeptics thrown in for good measure. This is why I've never agreed with Serious Ufologists and Oh So Serious Skeptics that such gatherings and those who peddle their wares and nostrums there should be discouraged. Life without sideshows—caveat emptor!—would be far less fun.

SUNDRY UFOOLOGICAL ODDITIES, MR. ALEXANDER, and the RETURN of AL BENDER

In January 1960 Gray Barker announced in the *Saucerian Bulletin* that he and about twenty others had been invited by the Space Brothers to take a saucer ride to an island off the coast of Brazil. The invitation came via George Marlo, a St. Louis saucer researcher–contactee who claimed regular communications with the Space People. Among those who, in addition to Barker, had accepted the invitation was Dr. Leon LeVan, then a member of the NICAP Board of Governors (what I wouldn't have given to be a fly on the wall when Donald Keyhoe and Richard Hall got wind of this!).

Then Long John Nebel got into the act. One night soon after Gray's announcement, famed comedian Jackie Gleason came on the air and offered Barker a $10,000-to-$500 bet that the saucer jaunt wouldn't take place. Gray wisely refused Gleason's proposal. At the last minute, the trip was canceled, when a "Mr. Z," allegedly a government agent, warned the Space Brothers to call it off.

A few months later, Howard Menger took advantage of a guest spot with Long John to begin backing away from the claims made in his Barker-published 1959 book *From Outer Space to You.* He said if he could write the book again, he would do it differently, because he wasn't really sure whether the events he described actually happened "the way I related them at the time. I may have been hoaxed or hypnotized, but I was and am sincere."

In the fall of 1963 rumors were circulating about Menger and a convention he might be planning. In mid-October, in the midst of this, I got a call from Howard and we set up a meeting, which rambled on for hours. It seemed Menger was working at an undisclosed location in the Pennsylvania mountains, where he was developing the X-4 Electro-Craft, a four-foot, radio-controlled saucer, powered by a new principle he invented, employing "free electrons under extreme pressure, used together with certain rare metals which have a high valence."

Plans were afoot for a private demonstration of the X-4 for the benefit of "scientists and a high-ranking military observer"—and me, if I wanted to attend. After this, and allowing enough time for a publicity buildup, the convention would be held, probably in the spring of 1964, as Menger was short of funds (he'd given up his sign-painting business to devote full time to the X-4). The convention's purpose would be to unveil the X-4 publicly and "prove there are people like us on other planets, far more advanced than us, scientifically, spiritually, and biologically." When I asked Howard about his own account of contact with the Space Brothers, he was reluctant to talk about it, saying only that he "was misinformed at the time as to the origin of the people I was meeting."

There never was a private X-4 demonstration, and the convention didn't come off, but Howard kept trying to get backers for his Electro-Craft. In 1964 he wrote a couple of articles for *Saucer News* boosting the project and offering to sell sets of plans for $100 to those who promised to build working saucers from them. Then, after a few people sent him their money, Howard declared that, as the inventor, he had a right to keep his plans secret. For some reason, the flow of cash dried up after this.

About the same time, Howard and his space soulmate, Connie, moved to Florida. From there, Menger circulated a strange letter, in which he revealed what he said was the truth behind his own alleged encounters with the Space People. After he sent some of his UFO photographs to the Pentagon, a supersecret government agency that "knew extraterrestrials were visiting earth" asked him to help in an important experiment. A true patriot, Howard agreed, and according to his letter the scheme involved "a spacecraft landing in an obscure town, and some alien creatures disembarking, giving messages of good will by a local yokel [Menger] acting as 'contactee.' . . . This would be one way of getting an index of human reaction." In the same letter, Menger asserted

From Outer Space to You was "fact/fiction" and wrote that after his story was "widely publicized and the experiment was considered finished, I completely withdrew from all activities in saucer research. . . . I had completed my mission. I wanted peace."

But things change. A couple of years later, Howard wrote to Gray Barker, saying he was hard at work on a new book, in which he would reveal the full story of the government-sponsored hoax. As with so many things promised in The Field, the book never appeared, and, as we shall see, Howard and Connie Menger never really quite got out of saucering. Oh, yes, and the X-4 is still with us—and still not flying.

Then there were the mysterious Better Book League and the famed Rissler Observatory in Philadelphia. The league surfaced in saucerdom in 1964 when Jim Wales, an associate of Detroit contactee fan and writer Laura Mundo, got several phone calls from a league representative. This person offered Wales money to take Mundo's book *Flying Saucers and the Father's Plan* off the market. Wales and Mundo were convinced this was an attempt to muzzle Mundo, perpetrated by the Space People or the Silence Group (the fifties-sixties name for the government insiders covering up The Truth about the saucers).

Gray Barker also reported getting similar calls from the league, as did other saucerers. For a short while, there was quite a bit of worried (hopeful?) whispering in ufoology, and then the league seemed to fade away. In fact, Gray Barker just got bored. He'd cooked up the Better Book League to amuse himself and, quite possibly, to give a boost to sales of his Saucerian Books titles. Apparently he was only mildly successful at the former and not as much so as he'd hoped with the latter.

About the same time as the Better Book League allegedly was striking terror into his heart, Gray began hearing from Erwin Vertlieb and Norman Shreibstein, who wrote on the very impressive Rissler Observatory letterhead and seemed to be genuine scientists, Shreibstein being the observatory director. Then the two began telling Gray and me of weird experiences in which they supposedly were being approached by Men in Black and warned away from saucering, and so on, à la Al Bender.

In early 1965 I drove to Philadelphia to look into the story and give a talk to a UFO interest group with which the two men were affiliated. It turned out Vertlieb and Shreibstein were just bright teenagers with overactive imaginations, which extended to their observatory. This marvel of science and its telescope were housed in the *basement* of the Shreibstein family home! I refrained from telling the kids what I thought, gave my talk to their little circle of saucer fiends, and headed back to New Jersey. Before long, Vertlieb found better things to do with his time (girls?), but Shreibstein became one of the (much) lesser players in Barker's sideshow, hanging around The Field into the early seventies.

The Rissler Observatory boys weren't the only ones being visited by Men in Black in those days. They—or at least one of Them, maybe—contacted me in early 1963. I received a telephone call from a man who identified himself only as Alexander. He said he was most anxious to meet me, inviting me to join him for dinner at New York's Dixie Hotel that night.

When I arrived, Alexander, a dark-olive-skinned, middle-aged man of fairly heavy build and medium height, was already eating with two companions, who identified themselves as Margot Dunmier and Robert Baldwin. Neither of these two would say much about themselves, and Dunmier in particular was rather unusual and dressed in very old-fashioned clothes.

Alexander, who had an odd, impossible-to-place foreign accent, wasn't much more forthcoming. He refused to say where he was born, offering only that it was a country I'd never heard of. He never quite claimed he was from another planet, but did say he traveled all over the world without a passport, had met everyone in saucer research, and had read "absolutely everything available on the subject." He also said he was interested in psychic phenomena and claimed to have extrasensory powers—though he declined to demonstrate them.

His pitch to me was that he had unlimited funds from some unspecified source and wanted to finance me on a series of saucer lectures around the world (MIB reverse psychology?). I met with him again the following evening, but he never got down to details on the lecture tour. Our dinner companion was a rather attractive young woman whom he introduced as his secretary, and this time Alexander did some very bad card tricks to prove his psychic powers. He did the tricks so poorly that I got the impression that what he actually wanted was to *disprove* his claims. Alexander closed this odd meeting by telling me he had to depart the next day on a brief trip to Washington, D.C. (ah, ha!), and that he would be in touch as soon as he returned.

I never heard from or saw Alexander again, but I did learn he had met with at least two other saucerers while in New York, who were as puzzled by him as I was. Then in June, I attended a theatrical party, completely unconnected with saucers, and ran into the woman Alexander had introduced as his secretary. We had a long talk, during which she claimed she had met Alexander only a day or two before he had contacted me. He had promised her employment, bonded her at his own expense, begun a passport application for her, showed her an office in Manhattan that he supposedly had rented, and then left for Washington. She, too, never heard from him again.

A month later, I received a letter from George Marlo, the St. Louis contactee who had tried to set up the saucer ride to Brazil for Barker and others. Alexander had paid visits to Marlo and other St. Louis saucer enthusiasts. He then disappeared from that city as quickly as he had from New York. Marlo was convinced, he said, that Alexander was a spaceman, adding,

> I am finished with radio and T.V. appearances about UFO's [*sic*]. I will talk on other subjects, but this one is too dangerous for me. Since talking to Alexander, *I know better now*. . . . I won't give out any information to the public that could and would cause panic. I can't give you any further details at this time, but may someday. Alexander wanted me to be a leader when they land the circular flying machines here on Earth. They have other means of coming here too, or so he stated. . . . Part of his plan was to confuse you. . . . *I found myself talking to the air three times when he was with me.* He would disappear into thin air on certain occasions when other people were around.

While I found the Alexander affair quite puzzling and to some degree still do, I semi-seriously wonder if it wasn't more than just coincidental that the activities of this MIB-like character followed closely on the heels of Gray Barker's publication of Al Bender's *Flying Saucers and the Three Men* in late 1962. Gray had done a big build-up to publication, with mysterious delays, tales of menacing strangers, and the like, and had immediately followed Bender's book with *Bender Mystery Confirmed* (1962), a compilation of screwy letters from Bender believers. Then, with both books on the market for only a few months, Alexander materialized out of the blue or from the depths of space—or from Barker's mischievous imagination, with a little help from George Marlo.

This would have been just like Gray—even hoaxing me, his best friend—and it certainly tied in with the wildly embellished version of Bender's story as told in . . . *The Three Men* with much editorial "help" from

Barker, and which bore little resemblance to what Bender had told me and others back in 1953. The Three Men in Black no longer were merely intimidating agents of the U.S. government. Now they were beings from the planet Kazik (the *z* is silent), who floated about a foot off the floor of Bender's room and stared at him with glowing eyes. They also gave him a piece of metal, by means of which he could contact them if he held it tightly in one hand, turned on his radio, and repeated the word *Kazik* (silent *z*). This he did two days after the MIB's first visit, and it got him astrally transported to Antarctica, where the Space People had a secret base. On a second such visit, he was ministered to by "three beautiful women dressed in tight white uniforms," who stripped him bare and massaged him with a strange liquid ("every part of my body without exception"). And so on and on and on—silent-Z-grade, soft-porn science fiction.

So who was Alexander? Was he just a well-heeled screwball or . . . ? I doubt we'll ever know. However, we do know that Al Bender sank back into obscurity about a year after the small splash made by his book and not long after his second *Saucer News*–sponsored lecture in New York City. It was then that he and his new bride packed up and moved out of ufology and off to California, where they still live today.

SHOCKINGLY CLOSE to SERIOUS

The foregoing is but a small sample of the sort of wacky things that were going on in saucerdom in the early sixties, much to the chagrin of Serious Ufologists. But there were some serious things happening, too, both in my activities and in The Field in general.

In early 1961, after seven years of publishing *Saucer News* from my Fort Lee apartment, I opened a small *Saucer News* office in New York City at 303 Fifth Avenue. I operated from this building, in offices of varying size, for most of the rest of the sixties. As we shall see, this turned out to be fortuitous.

That fall, I launched the *Saucer News* Discussion and Lecture Committee. This began with small gatherings at the office and talks given by myself and other *Saucer News* associates. Before long, we changed venue to various larger halls, with most of the events being held in the Woodstock and Diplomat hotels, which were almost directly across from each other on West Forty-third Street. Over the years, presentations by some of the Big Names and many of the Not-So-Big Names in ufology, Fortean studies, and related fields were sponsored by the committee. Among them were John Fuller, Ivan Sanderson, Long John Nebel, John Keel, James "The Amazing/Amusing" Randi, Gray Barker, and of course Al Bender. Most of these events were well attended and some even showed a small profit.

The following year, 1962, I finally realized my long-standing ambition to become the first civilian saucer researcher to visit Project Blue Book headquarters at Wright-Patterson Air Force Base, near Dayton, Ohio. Well, not quite. I didn't know it at the time, but highly respected ufologist Walter Webb (of Betty and Barney Hill abduction fame) had been permitted to visit in 1956, so I was number two, a sort of ufological Buzz Aldrin.

Anyway, my trip resulted from one of my periodic and always turned-down requests to the air force's Pentagon press desk. Much to my surprise, in early 1962 I received a letter that authorized me to be given an unclassified briefing and shown unclassified UFO reports at Wright-Patterson. So it was that in late March, then Blue Book head Lt. Col. Robert Friend picked me up at my motel near the base and drove me to the inner sanctum of air force saucer investigation. I've been told that Friend, who is black, really didn't want the Blue Book job, but accepted the assignment when he was told it was the only way he would be promoted to full colonel. I don't know if this is true, but however he wound up running Blue Book, Friend lived up to his name, and I spent a very pleasant and interesting day with him. I came away very impressed with the efforts of the colonel and his minuscule staff. It was obvious they didn't have the resources or top-level support they needed to do a worthwhile, objective job, but it seemed to me they were doing their level best with what they had.

I'd like to be able to tell about the strange little man, with fur all over his face, whom I passed in the hall near Colonel Friend's office; or about the huge saucer-shaped canopy beside the Blue Book building, surrounded by armed guards; or the odd way the good colonel winced when I mentioned the name Albert K. Bender. Unfortunately, none of these things happened, and in fact, most of what I learned is not of much interest today (those who care will find a long, detailed article in the September 1962 *Saucer News*).

However, I did see one strange thing. There was a large blackboard on the wall of Friend's office, and it had some very peculiar, squiggly writing on it, with this notice in large block letters: DO NOT ERASE. I asked Friend about it, and as nearly as I can recall he said it was a motto or saying in ancient Syrian, which he had copied from a book. It was something as commonplace as "Never put off until tomorrow what you can do today." He said he had left it up on the blackboard for about a week just to elicit questions like mine.

Maybe this was true, maybe not. It struck me that putting mottoes in strange languages on the blackboard of an office devoted to serious intelligence work was rather peculiar. Was it alien writing the Blue Book team was trying to decipher? I didn't think so then, and I certainly don't today. It happens that on the day I visited Blue Book, there was a military coup in Syria. Maybe there was a connection and Friend was just pulling my leg. Whatever the real truth was, this was as close as I came to anything really weird or exciting during my memorable visit to the "(W)right Field."

It will be remembered that in 1954, I abandoned the extraterrestrial hypothesis for the origin of UFOs, taking up what I called the Earth Theory: Saucers were supersecret machines built by the American and Soviet governments. Although I abandoned the rather silly "radiation-mop saucers" notion soon after I published it, and although the Earth Theory made me very unpopular with ufologists, Serious and Not So Serious, I genuinely believed the Earth Theory was the best explanation for reports of "nuts and bolts" UFOs.

However, from 1957 on, as the U.S. and Russian space programs got well underway and the rockets and other technology involved and their capabilities showed not the slightest resemblance to flying saucers and their amazing performance, I changed my mind. In an editorial in the June 1962 *Saucer News,* I announced I had "returned to . . . [my] original feeling that the saucer phenomenon is still a mystery and that the extraterrestrial solution is the most likely one." I went on to say I felt "very strongly that there is as yet no *proof* of extraterrestrial visitations" and made clear that my offer of a few years before to pay $1,000 "to anyone who can prove that saucers come from other planets" still stood. Until such proof was brought forward, I wrote, I would "hold to . . . [my] present belief that the saucer mystery is no closer to a general solution . . . than it was in 1947 when Arnold made his famous sighting." I also hopefully suggested that as space and the "unknown areas of our own planet" were explored, "by process of elimination, Mankind will at least learn more and more about where saucers do *not* come from; and perhaps before too long, we will find out where they do come from."

So it was that I moved back closer to the mainstream of ufology, unwittingly helping to set the stage for my next Great Ufological Role: Expert.

Don't look back. Something may be gaining on you.

—Satchel Paige

Public interest in UFOs always rises and falls with the number of saucer sightings and the level and tone of media coverage. The latter tends to be driven by dramatic cases and waves of reports. In the early sixties, not much was going on, and at least in the United States, saucers were out of sight and thus mostly out of the minds of the media and general public.

Still, things weren't entirely dead, especially outside the United States. For example, in 1962 there was an extended and major sightings flap involving virtually every country in South America. I covered this extensively in *Saucer News.* In 1965 this coverage was mentioned in a letter of (gasp!) praise from none other than Jerome Clark, today the leading historian of ufology and an editor of what it's fair to say is *the* journal of Serious Ufology, the *International UFO Reporter,* better known as *IUR*. At the time he wrote, Jerry was new on the saucering scene. He was in college, which he freely admits he attended for five years without earning a degree, adding rather cryptically that he "got caught up in the madness of the sixties." Whatever that may mean, it's obvious he was thinking at least semi-clearly when he penned the following (*Saucer News*, June 1965):

> Let me say that I think *Saucer News* is getting better and better all the time, and it is unquestionably one of the very best publications in the field today. Apparently you have decided to remove the aura of mystery from yourself, which is fine; and Richard E. Wallace's [Eugene Steinberg's] nauseating book reviews appear to be the only throwback to the days when you thrived on personal bickering and controversy. Personally, I think *Saucer News* is well worth the price just for its coverage of recent UFO and Fortean incidents alone. I refer specifically to your attention, two or three years ago, to the South American flap of 1962. To my knowledge, this was the only complete reporting of that wave in any American saucer zine. Good luck and keep up the excellent work.

Like myself, Clark has held a variety of different views about the nature and origins of UFOs. I liked his 4-D thinking of the late 1970s—when he also took fairies seriously—better than his current return to "nuts and bolts." But who knows? He may come around again. As many in The Field know, over the years, Jerry and I have clashed frequently, mainly because I rather unkindly enjoy pushing his buttons to bring out the worst in him—a quick temper and harshly opinionated views. However, I *do* respect him as a Leading Authority, and there is no question he has made many important contributions to ufology. Moreover, he always spells my name correctly in his encyclopedias!

As for *my* elevation to Expert, lightning didn't strike until 1966. But as someone once said, luck is what happens to those who are prepared for it, and I was pursuing a number of different things that, as it turned out, helped set the stage. As I've already mentioned, this included opening a *Saucer News* office in Manhattan and a (sincere) recantation of my heretical Earth Theory and (sincere) return to the Outer Space Theory (about which I later got even more specific, declaring [sincerely] in the September 1964 *Saucer News* that "the saucers are probably extraterrestrial, probably from Mars, and probably piloted by humanoids, i.e., 'little men' "). I also began more actively seeking speaking engagements outside saucering circles and appearances on radio and television.

WHERE WERE YOU in '62?

In April 1962 I returned to the Princeton University campus for the first time since dropping out twelve years before. Somehow I'd managed to arrange with Dr. Earl Douglass, a Presbyterian minister on the university staff and a member of the NICAP board (!), to get me an invitation to speak before Cap and Gown, one of the school's eating clubs (fraternities). I don't remember anything about what I said, but letters from Douglass and Cap and Gown president J. A. Tellefsen Jr. published in *Saucer News* offer two slightly different and telling slants on the impression I made. First Dr. Douglass: "You gave us all a pleasant and profitable evening . . . last week. As I told you and told the students, it was an excellently presented resume of what has been taking place in the sky in recent years—and in very ancient times as well. . . ." Now Tellefsen: "Not only on behalf of myself, but also on behalf of almost everyone else who was present, I would like to thank you ever so much for taking the time to come down here to talk to us—sharing your enthusiasm with us and letting us know a little bit more about the mystical subject of flying saucers. All those to whom I spoke afterwards agreed that your talk had been quite something. . . ."

Later the same month, I went on a "personal appearance tour" in Clarksburg, West Virginia, arranged by Gray Barker. The main event was being a "special guest" on a children's television show, my first time on TV. I have nothing in my memory, diary, or files about how I was received, but I'm sure I wowed the kids. Four months later, continuing my meteoric rise on the boob tube, I hit the big time as a guest on the national daytime television quiz show *Play Your Hunch.* I have no idea how I did, but it *was* national television.

Princeton, a West Virginia kiddie program, and a game show. For some reason, this combination strikes me as a nearly perfect metaphor for ufology.

And then I got married. That summer I had met Sandy Swendsin (sometimes Stevens), and was smitten. On September 15, with the mayor of Fort Lee officiating and a few close friends looking on, we were married in a private ceremony. Our honeymoon was a two-month road trip to Mexico, during which we made a stop in Clarksburg so I could introduce Sandy to Gray. By amazing coincidence, Harry Truman was in town at the same time, lending his support to the campaign of the Democratic candidate for governor.

Gray saw a newspaper notice that the former president was staying at the Stonewall Jackson Hotel, then the best in town, and would be holding a press conference there at such-and-such a time on October 5. Gray and I decided to see if we could crash the conference. I had a phony press card, certifying me as a correspondent of the Accredited Press (a couple of years later, I almost bought the outfit that sold these fake credentials). Gray brought along a movie camera on a heavy tripod, but for some unfathomable reason of his own, he deliberately loaded no film in it.

We went to the hotel, and those being the days before the Kennedy and King assassinations, my "AP" card and Gray's camera got us into the press hospitality room. To our delight, there was a free, pour-your-own bar, which we took full advantage of. The genuine reporters were quite friendly, but I sensed at least some of them thought—but didn't really care—that we were not of their brotherhood. ("Accredited Press? Never heard of you." "Oh, uh, we're a small independent outfit based in New Jersey. How about a drink?")

After a half hour or so of gratis boozing and avoiding exposure and expulsion, Gray and I were relieved when a minion came into the room and announced, "The president will see you now." We filed into a hall where thirty to fifty people were already gathered, with Truman at a podium up front. The former president didn't make a statement, but immediately invited questions. After he answered a few, he said something very close to: "Everywhere I go, people ask the same questions, and I get tired of answering them. Doesn't anyone here have an *interesting* question?" This seemed to take everyone by surprise, so Truman repeated his invitation.

That was my cue, and emboldened by the free liquor, I stood and said something like: "Mr. Truman, several years ago I met you briefly in your office in Independence, and asked you about flying saucers. Your answer indicated that you don't take the matter too seriously. My question to you now is, has anything happened since then to cause you to change your mind?"

Truman grinned broadly, obviously pleased to have a chance for a little comic relief, and after a couple of seconds of stunned silence, everyone else in the room roared with laughter. The former president politely fielded my question with a skillfully nonresponsive answer. I tried again with a slightly rephrased version. He responded with a slightly rephrased version of his first answer. I tried once more with the same result, and not wanting to overdo it, said, "Thank you" and sat down. This definitely was the high point of the press conference, and I'm glad to have given Truman something "interesting" to have a bit of fun with.

Afterward, he and I shook hands as Barker snapped a not very good but nonetheless Historic Photo (see the photo section).

JUST CALL ME UFOLOGY'S RUPERT MURDOCH

During this period, I began acquiring other UFO publications that were in financial trouble or whose owners found the ego boost of being editor-publishers no longer outweighed the drudgery. These included the *Interplanetary Intelligence Report,* published by young Oklahoma City saucerer Hayden Hewes; the *Interplanetary News Service,* edited by even younger saucer fiend Timothy Green Beckley; and the *UFO Reporter,* cranked out by *Saucer News* staffer Gene Steinberg. Given the saucering slump, there were numerous opportunities, and I hoped this would be a cheap, quick way to raise my circulation and thus my advertising rates. I also thought that, in the event of a new burst of saucer excitement, it might put me in a position to upgrade *Saucer News* from fanzine to professional periodical.

It didn't always work out quite that way. What one of these mergers usually meant was that I got little or nothing more than a subscriber list and the privilege of fulfilling mostly soon-to-expire subscriptions with copies of my magazine. A good many subscribers thus acquired already were *Saucer News* readers, so I gained very little in the way of new paying customers.

The deal with Hewes was the worst. Hewes, who made something of a ufological name for himself in the 1970s, was always bragging about his rag having thousands of subscribers. I bought him out expecting a mini-bonanza. When his list arrived, in the form of a box of a few hundred index cards, I discovered that, literally, all but ten of the subscriptions expired with the newsletter's next issue!

One acquisition that turned out very much better was that of Gray Barker's *Saucerian Bulletin* in early 1963, for five hundred dollars down and five hundred more later (I'm not sure if I ever paid the second installment). Gray had tired of the grind associated with cranking out a regularly scheduled periodical, which meant the *Bulletin* had become quite irregular. He was going through a bit of an upheaval in his personal life and was in something of a financial bind. Also, he'd found that his real interest lay in saucer and New Age book publishing, at which he had been fairly successful. To give him a hand and at the same time dramatically increase my circulation—from about twenty-five hundred to in excess of four thousand—I bought him out. As part of the deal, Gray became a *Saucer News* associate editor.

Of course, in keeping with saucerdom's expectations, we put a slightly different public spin on things. Here's how I announced our deal in the June 1963 *Saucer News*, the first combined issue of two of The Field's most august publications:

> Readers of SAUCER NEWS will recall the long-standing feud between your Editor and Gray Barker, editor of "The Saucerian Bulletin." Recently, we [that is, editorial *we*] had occasion to drop by the office of Mr. Barker in Clarksburg, West Virginia. A serious conversation was entered into between the two editors, and we became convinced of the reality of some of the [saucer-related] persecutions which Mr. Barker has, for many months, been loudly proclaiming in his zine and elsewhere. . . .
>
> Taking cognizance of the situation existing in Clarksburg, we made to Mr. Barker a most generous offer, whereby we would combine his magazine with ours. Barker agreed to our terms, and the merger was formalized in a legal document dated February 24th, 1963.

Well, this *was* shockingly close to the truth.

PUTTERING AROUND WAITING *for* SOMETHING to HAPPEN

As saucering continued to languish, I stepped up my involvement in a variety of other endeavors. Among these were a number of complex enterprises in which I worked with and covered most of the expenses of Yonah Fortner, also known as Yonah ibn A'haron. These involved ancient manuscripts and further Peruvian treasure hunting, with Yonah and others in Peru, while I stayed safely in the States. Nothing much came of any of this, but recalling it gives me an opportunity to acknowledge Fortner, who unfortunately is now a figure little known in ufology. In the early days of *Saucer News,* he wrote a very scholarly but dreadfully obscure series of articles called "Extraterrestrialism as an Historical Doctrine." His thesis was that the god of the Old Testament was a space being, and it depended upon controversial interpretations of certain key words in the Bible. In a very real sense, it could be said that Yonah pioneered the ancient astronauts idea later so profitably exploited by Erich von Däniken.

Sadly, Yonah has been crippled all his life by polio, and his physical condition has gotten worse as he has grown older. However, as with many in ufology, his greatest handicap was psychological. In his saucering days, his personality and attitude were such that he rarely got along with anyone. Today he lives in quiet obscurity in California, and we rarely are in touch.

While Yonah and I were trying to pick up again where I had left off in South America, I decided to take a crack at turning my earlier Peruvian adventures into a book, which I thought (and still think) could be commercially successful. I worked at this in fits and starts until well into 1963, compiling notes and such, but, all that's come of this effort (so far) is chapter 6 of this book and my highly fictionalized article in the June 1964 *Argosy* magazine. I placed the latter with the help of publicist Sanford "Sandy" Teller, who was in Long John Nebel's circle of hangers-on. I later offered *Argosy* a UFO article, which was rejected, and even tried to peddle some of my more ghoulish grave-robbing photos to the *National Enquirer*. No luck there, either.

I did better with Long John—for a while. I was on his show fairly regularly, both as a guest and as a member of his panel of "experts," including two appearances with George Adamski. The first of these was in May 1962, the second in March 1963. During one or the other of these, Adamski asserted there were twelve inhabited planets in our solar system. I asked how he knew this. He quite gravely replied, "Because, like three and seven, twelve is a mystical number."

A bit later—or maybe during the other program—I put another question to the Professor, which he answered as I knew he would. "George," I asked, "how much is two plus two?" Without skipping a beat and with a straight face, he responded, "It is five—four plus the unit of energy necessary to make the addition. But it can be four, five, or six depending upon the circumstances."

On these programs, Adamski and I went round and round about these and other issues, but despite this and, far more significantly, my 1950s exposé articles, he always was unfailingly pleasant, at least in his direct dealings with me. Following my wedding, I received a congratulatory letter from him, in which he wrote, "I wish there were more people like you, who come out into the open instead of hiding behind the written word. I believe that the debate you and I had on Long John's radio program was the finest get-together that anyone could have. We let the public be the judge. But there are some people who wouldn't do anything like that, even if they were given the privilege. . . . I respect you far more than you perhaps realize. . . ." Somehow, I think he was quite sincere in this, if only in the "I meant it at the time" sense.

In November 1963 Long John had me on as his sole guest for the entire five-hour show. The topic wasn't saucers but my Peruvian adventures, and it was a big hit. As a result, I met Sandy Teller and we succeeded in selling the article to *Argosy*. Long John was delighted—until he began getting criticism from museums, professional archaeologists, and other such stuffy people. All of a sudden, and quite typically, his whole opinion of the show flip-flopped, as did his opinion of me, and it was quite a while before he invited me back again.

This was a setback, but it was somewhat made up for by the fact that the publicity generated by the show and my article got me on national television again, this time on the quiz show *To Tell the Truth*. I wasn't briefed on the rules of the game, so, believe it or not, I managed to embarrass myself by actually trying to give complete, honest answers to the quiz panel's questions instead of trying to quasi-truthfully mislead them, as I was supposed to do. I'm told this segment is included in a worst- or funniest-ever TV shows videotape anthology, making it one of my greatest showbiz triumphs.

I also was becoming a semiregular on a New Jersey college radio show and the very popular *Contact*, a call-in program hosted by Bob Kennedy (he called himself "The Other Bob Kennedy") on Boston's WBZ. In February 1964, when I went to Boston for one of these appearances, I arranged for an interview with Harvard astronomer-astrophysicist and arch UFO skeptic Donald Menzel, whose second anti-saucer book, *The World of Flying Saucers*, written with (Mrs.) Lyle G. Boyd, recently had been published and unfavorably reviewed in *Saucer News*.

The brief encounter took place in Menzel's office at the Harvard Observatory in Cambridge. While I had spoken with him by telephone many years before in connection with the Ralph Mayher "cobweb"-saucer film, this was our first face-to-face meeting. Menzel was reasonably cordial, but tended to answer specific questions in generalities. At the time, I had the definite impression he didn't write his anti-saucer books for profit, fame, or prestige; that his private war against flying saucers was a vendetta carried on for very personal reasons having much more to do with his ego and personality quirks than objective science—and certainly nothing to do with a secret role as a crashed-saucer cover-up insider (more on this when we get to the 1980s). I still believe this to be true.

I suggested to Menzel that he try to catch me on the Bob Kennedy show that night. He said he "might" listen. As it turned out, Menzel not only listened, he was the most persistent of many callers, grabbing about ten minutes of airtime out of the hour and a half program. He was quite emphatic in expressing his negative opinions of saucers and saucer sighters, but when cornered in debate, he resorted to generalities, just as he had done during our interview. A curious and difficult man, was Donald Menzel.

Meanwhile, I had become a father. My daughter, Elizabeth Barber "Betty" Moseley, was born on October 6, 1963. Everything about Sandy's pregnancy and the birth was quite routine, despite a voodoo doll being sent to us, ostensibly by George Adamski! I never believed Adamski was responsible, and before long my old "friend" Richard Ogden—the fellow who thought he'd proved I'd never been to Peru—confessed.

Perhaps the doll had a quite different and entirely unintended effect. For some reason I still don't understand, and despite my general dislike of police, in September 1963 I joined the Fort Lee, New Jersey, police reserve. The reserve and civil defense organizations were combined into the same outfit, and I eventually rose to acting sergeant and assistant deputy director of civil defense, gold badge and all. Wisely, the real police did not allow us to have guns, but I had fun anyway. Among other things, my duties included badgering building superintendents to join us and inspecting the stores of survival rations stocked in areas of apartment complexes designated as fallout shelters. More daunting was what the reserve was supposed to do in the event of nuclear attack: guard the New Jersey end of the George Washington Bridge and prevent citizens of Manhattan from invading Fort Lee. I remember our director telling us, "Yes, you do that. As for myself, I'll be on my way upstate."

SAUCER STIRRINGS

Things began to look up in 1964, at least in ufology. I can't say the same for my marriage. Despite the birth of our daughter, efforts to work together on *Saucer News* and the S.A.U.C.E.R.S. monthly lecture series, and an active, shared social life that, among other things, included throwing numerous large parties with such honored guests as Tiny ("Tiptoe Through the Tulips") Tim, Sandy and I, to put it mildly, weren't getting along. Perhaps it was the curse of Ogden's voodoo doll or another sent from Chicago by a neurotic female *Saucer News* subscriber, but more likely it was mutual immaturity. After much quarreling and a brief separation, we were divorced in early 1965, and I eventually won custody of Betty, who joined me on many of my saucering and other travels, and for a while was the *Saucer News* "staff artist."

But, as I was saying, things ufological began looking up again in 1964. Appropriately enough, this began in New Mexico. Late on the afternoon of April 24, 1964, Socorro town cop Lonnie Zamora reported spotting a strange, landed egg-shaped machine—even, he thought, maybe, glimpsing two members of its crew.

While chasing a speeder on the south side of town, Zamora heard a terrific roar and saw a strange flame descending from the sky. Thinking a dynamite shack in the area might have blown up, he dropped the traffic chase and headed his cruiser in the direction of the shack, in an isolated area of high-desert scrubland. Topping a rise, Zamora was shocked to see the weird craft and, maybe, the little men, whom he thought might have seen him, too.

Within a few seconds, the thing took off with a roar, a jet of flame spewing from beneath it. As it rose slowly and noisily, Zamora thought it might blow up, and he dove for cover behind his car. Then the flame abruptly cut off, the roar stopped, and the UFO headed south, rapidly picking up speed and slowly gaining altitude.

Zamora radioed for help. Then he walked down into the shallow arroyo where the saucer had been. There he found "pad" prints and scorched earth and bushes, some of the latter still smoldering. Before long, the state police, FBI, and army were on the scene, with the press not far behind. Soon the story was on the national news wires, and the air force's Project Blue Book had investigators on the way, as did both NICAP and APRO.

Poor Zamora, who seemed to me a simple, honest, small-town sort of guy trying to make sense out of a weird, frightening experience, was overwhelmed and became the target of much ridicule. The wags really picked on him after an amusing exchange with a television news reporter. Asked, "Were you in a state of shock?" a very nervous Zamora replied, "No. I was in the state of New Mexico."

The skeptics went after him, too, of course. Donald Menzel attacked the case in much the same way he did the Mayher film, in which, according to him, the saucer was light reflected by a cobweb or, if not, was an airplane. He first asserted Zamora saw a mini-tornado known as a dust devil, then switched to the notion that he had been the victim of a prank by vengeful teenagers (or maybe it was both). Phil Klass, who arrived on the scene a couple of years after the fact, came up with the silliest skeptical "explanation": Zamora was part of a hoax by Socorro's mayor, who owned the land on which the saucer had touched down. This, said Klass, was part of a clever scheme to boost tourism—a scheme that worked so well Socorro has hardly changed in almost forty years.

Zamora's sighting really caught the attention of the media, and, apparently because of all the publicity, the air force went so far as to send its scientific consultant, astronomer J. Allen Hynek, to Socorro. He was stumped. So was Project Blue Book head Maj. Hector Quintanilla, who saw his job as explaining away every UFO sighting, no matter what, and keeping things quiet for the air force. Both concluded Zamora had seen something very real. Quintanilla thought it was some sort of secret experimental aircraft, even though exhaustive inquiries turned up nothing. Hynek, though he was careful in what he said publicly, was inclined to wonder if it wasn't something from another planet. In my opinion, this was the case that started moving him away from staunch skepticism to belief that UFOs were real, anomalous phenomena of some kind.

This seems to be a good place to reveal that Hynek, who died in 1986, was and remains my ufological "father figure." He was a solid scientist who, in my opinion, genuinely and honestly sought the truth about UFOs and related phenomena. When, after about twenty years as a skeptical scientific front man for the air force, he could clearly see that some UFO events really were unexplainable, he resigned as an air force consultant and, a few years later, formed his own pro-UFO organization, the Center for UFO Studies, which still exists today. Later, concluding that saucers don't fit properly into science's present conception of the universe, he reluctantly but fearlessly plunged into 4-D thinking, as many others, including myself, have done (way to go, Allen!).

These two moves showed great intellectual courage, for which I believe Hynek should be remembered fondly and with respect by all ufologists. He was keenly aware that the UFO mystery would not be solved during his lifetime, something he expressed to me more than once, but he kept plugging away. In the process, he more than replaced Donald Keyhoe as ufology's number one spokesperson. I didn't know him as well as I would have liked, and I was deeply saddened by his death from a brain tumor. Ufology has had no one like him since and is much poorer for it.

SAUCER SWARMINGS

Anyway, whatever and whoever it was that scared the wits out of Lonnie Zamora, his experience marked the beginning of what turned out to be the most exciting and tumultuous years in the history of saucerdom. Throughout the rest of 1964 and the first half of 1965, there was a slow but steady buildup of sighting reports. In July 1965 a full-blown, nationwide wave of sightings began, and it continued until mid-1967. This generated the first serious and continuing interest in UFOs by the mainstream press since the early 1950s, much of it highly critical of the air force, and ultimately it led to the (in)famous University of Colorado UFO study, better know as the Condon Committee.

Of course, *Saucer News* gleefully covered all this, and I and several of my associates were in increasingly greater demand for radio interviews and the like. In September 1964, I made my first guest appearance on James "The Amazing/Amusing" Randi's all-night radio talk show, which was in direct competition with Long John Nebel's new one. That summer, Long John had left WOR for WNBC and more money, and Randi, a professional magician with an interest in UFOs and Fortean phenomena, had taken over the old "Party Line" slot.

At the time, Randi was relatively open-minded about saucers and other weirdness. We became friends, and I was a regular on his show until he was somewhat mysteriously fired in January 1966. As time passed, Randi's cautious open-mindedness dissolved, and eventually he went well beyond thoughtful skepticism and off the deep end into dogmatic debunkery. His "colorful" statements about spoon-bending psychic Uri Geller led to costly legal battles and have generated much controversy. Because of what I consider to be Randi's hypocrisy, arrogance, and philosophical extremism, I eventually became disillusioned with him, ending what had been an interesting friendship.

Throughout the mid-sixties, though, Randi and I were on quite good terms. As the saucer excitement continued to build, we did our best to entertain and enlighten New York–area night owls with all the latest reports, and Randi was a featured speaker in the S.A.U.C.E.R.S. monthly lecture series and, later, at the greatest indoor saucer convention ever held (coming up in our next exciting chapter).

The night of the great Northeast blackout, November 9, 1965, Gray Barker and I went above and beyond the call of saucerian duty to help Randi out. For many hours, beginning in the early evening and lasting well into the wee hours of the next day, most of the northeastern United States and parts of Canada were without electricity, and everything came to a screeching halt, à la *The Day the Earth Stood Still.* There were several UFO-sighting reports that night, including one of a saucer over New York City and another of a huge globe of fire, seen expanding and rising into the sky near Syracuse, just above some major high-voltage power lines. So, of course, there were those who said UFOs were responsible for the big blackout; and, of course, *Saucer News* (March 1966) got in on the act with an article about freeloading, power-sucking saucers.

When the lights went out, Barker and I were in my Fort Lee apartment, where we had the weird experience of watching the New York television channels fade away, one by one, while the Philadelphia channels began coming in clearly for the first time ever. Outside my windows, Manhattan, just across the Hudson River, was totally dark. Needless to say, Gray and I had to get out and see what was going on.

After midnight, when the traffic situation had eased, we made an expedition to Times Square. Along the way, we saw and heard about thousands of people sleeping in the subways, bus terminals, and every available building lobby. To our amazement, on my car radio we also heard Randi broadcasting from WOR, using electricity from a small generator running on gasoline donated by a New Jersey listener. We made our way to 1440 Broadway, and in the dim light of countless matches, trudged up flight after flight of stairs to the WOR studios on the twenty-fourth floor. There we joined Randi in spouting forth over the air to all who had battery power. Whatever else might be said about me, no one can say I wasn't determined to be in showbiz!

In the months leading up to the blackout, Americans were being thrilled and chilled almost daily by exciting reports of remarkable and very close UFO encounters. One of these took place during the wee hours of September 3, 1965, near Exeter, New Hampshire, where a teenager and two policemen were buzzed several times by a huge, low-flying UFO, scaring one cop so badly he almost drew his service revolver and took a shot at the thing. *Saturday Review* columnist John Fuller, a self-described saucer skeptic, decided to look into this case firsthand, after which he wrote a not-so-skeptical column that drew the attention of a book publisher. This got him a contract to do a book about the case, *Incident at Exeter: The Story of Unidentified Flying Objects Over America Today* (1966).

Fuller went back to New Hampshire to do research for his book, and while he was there, a series of articles in the *Boston Traveler* revealed the very strange story of Barney and Betty Hill, a Portsmouth, New Hampshire, couple who, while undergoing hypnotherapy, supposedly discovered that a UFO sighting they had four years before was more than just a sighting. The Hills, it seemed, had been captured by the crew of the saucer, taken aboard, and physically examined. Betty Hill claimed to have had a very interesting, possibly telepathic discourse with one of the spacemen, whom she took to be the leader of the expedition. Until being hypnotized by psychiatrist Benjamin Simon (who was not a UFO believer and, unlike today's abductologists, wasn't looking for anything like what he found), the Hills' memories of their kidnapping were blocked by amnesia. Fuller met with the Hills, was impressed, and this led to another book, *The Interrupted Journey: Two Lost Hours "Aboard a Flying Saucer"* (1966). Riding on the wave of saucer sightings and swelling public interest, and boosted by excerpts run in *Look* magazine, both of Fuller's books were best-sellers and added fuel to the saucerian fire.

But what really fueled the frenzy—and, appropriately enough, my elevation to Expert—was swamp gas.

DESTINY

Ironically, I emerged as a UFO Expert a matter of days after being summarily expelled from NICAP. On March 16, 1966, I received a vitriolic letter from Donald Keyhoe effectively charging me with anti-NICAP subversion. Keyhoe cited an article by Yonah Fortner attacking NICAP that had appeared in *Saucer News*, with an editorial disclaimer, almost a year before (June 1965), but it was obvious his main concern was the Resolution for a Better NICAP that Gene Steinberg, I, and several others had put together. Published in the March 1966 *Saucer News* and signed by twenty-one leading (or, at least, known) ufologists, all NICAP members, it listed several criticisms of Keyhoe's organization and proposed some reasonable solutions for them.

I admit I saw the resolution in part as another way to needle Keyhoe and Richard Hall, generate controversy, and keep the ufological pot stirred. However, all who signed the resolution, including me, were quite sincere in our criticisms and the hope that they and our proposed changes would really lead to a better NICAP. Of course, Keyhoe and Hall didn't see it that way.

Oddly (or perhaps not), I was the only resolution signer to be cast into outer darkness. All others had their annual memberships renewed, and one even received an honorary (free) membership. Of course, I was crushed. Then, less than a week later, saucers were sighted over Dexter and Hillsdale, Michigan, and my tears turned to smiles.

Actually beginning in Wisconsin on the night of March 14 (the day Keyhoe penned his banishment letter to me), the flap swept eastward into Michigan over the next several days, culminating in sightings in Dexter and nearby Hillsdale on the nights of the twentieth and twenty-first. In Dexter, a police car was buzzed and farmer Frank Mannor and his son Ronald said they encountered a silent, football-shaped something "about the length of a car" hovering low over a swamp. It was "grayish-yellow, like coral rock, and pitted. There seemed to be a kind of fog underneath it," and it sported pulsing blue and white lights. As the Mannors ran through the swamp toward the object, the lights went out, the saucer disappeared, and for a few seconds the two heard a kind of "whoofing sound, like one of those new police sirens, kind of like shooting a bullet through a canyon." The next night, almost ninety coeds and others at a Hillsdale College dormitory watched a UFO hover and do maneuvers over a marsh, on and off for several hours. The saucer was described as football-shaped, and college officials backed up the students' stories against air force claims that what they, the Mannors, and others reported were just misidentifications of natural phenomena.

The national publicity surrounding these interesting but not particularly spectacular sightings compelled the air force to at least appear to be taking the matter seriously. Allen Hynek was thrown into the breach. He and a group of air force investigators flew to Michigan, traipsed through the swamps, and interviewed witnesses. Then, at a hastily called press conference at the Detroit Press Club on March 25, the largest in club history, Hynek made one of the most famous and fateful pronouncements in the annals of ufology: swamp gas did it. Noting that "a dismal swamp is a most unlikely place for a visit from outer space," Hynek said "rotty vegetation" produces swamp gas that "can be trapped by ice and winter conditions" and suddenly released when the ground thaws. "The gas makes popping noises" and can glow.

Hynek tempered this with careful qualifications, but all the press and public saw in the official release he handed out were the words *swamp gas.*

Ridicule and outrage followed, and three days later two Michigan congressmen, Democrat Weston Vivian and Republican Minority Leader Gerald Ford, called for congressional hearings. Ford wrote a letter to the House Armed Services Committee, enclosing several newspaper articles criticizing the air force investigation of the Michigan and Exeter, New Hampshire, sightings and saying "the American public deserves a better explanation than that thus far given by the Air Force." The swamp gas definitely had hit the fan, and a week later, for the first time ever, there was an open congressional hearing on flying saucers. Where NICAP had failed, the saucers (or something) and bad spin management had succeeded.

Meanwhile, back in New York City, all the major national news organizations were rushing around trying to find an instant saucer expert to interview and quote. Mine was the only listing in the Manhattan phone book under "Saucers" (for *Saucer News*), so everyone came to me. (Remember this when you see an expert—on anything—quoted in the papers or on television.) Of course, I didn't know anything more about the ins and outs of the Michigan and New Hampshire cases or the scientific merits of Hynek's notions than did the reporters who interviewed me—but I *did* know saucers and those who chased them. Instantly, I was an Expert.

For weeks, I was on radio and television or doing some other sort of personal appearance or interview almost daily. Once again, I was a semi-regular on Long John's program, almost as if my defection to Randi had never happened, despite having been told by Sandy Teller that anyone who went on Randi's show even once would never be granted an audience with Long John. *Sic tyrannis fundid,* or whatever.

I didn't do these appearances just for the ego trip. I always got the *Saucer News* address announced as often as possible, which translated directly into "money mail," new subscriptions and sales of saucer books and other items. My circulation had been slowly increasing since Zamora's sighting, and was at about five thousand when the swamp gas ignited. Before long, it was in excess of eight thousand, and in the first six months of 1966, I grossed $10,000 in the mail-order business. For the first time since 1953, saucering was profitable.

Then I got a call from the American Program Bureau in Boston.

We are all in the gutter, but some of us are looking at the stars.
—Oscar Wilde

For anyone who didn't live through it, it is hard to imagine just how widespread and intense saucer excitement was during the mid- and late 1960s. There really hasn't been anything like it before or since. The Roswell and abductions manias of recent years don't even come close. It seemed like saucers were on *everyone's* mind, not just those of "the usual suspects."

A VERY DIFFERENT KIND of FLAP

Before the sixties, saucer flaps stirred up a lot of public and media interest, but it didn't last long. Scientific interest during these periods, at least as publicly expressed, was minimal and dismissive. Military and other government interest was along the lines of "Maybe the Russians have something new and dangerous" or "Maybe the saucers are from space and possibly hostile." When it (probably) was decided neither was the case, the official approach became almost entirely one of explaining everything away. Saucers weren't considered a danger, but saucermania was. The Russians might be able to exploit it for psychological warfare and other evilness.

For some reason, things were different in the 1960s. Several scientists, like James McDonald, Allen Hynek, Thornton Page, and even Carl Sagan, treated the subject very seriously, publicly as well as privately. McDonald and Hynek succeeded in getting the prestigious American Institute of Aeronautics and Astronautics to set up a committee to study UFOs. For the first time since the 1952 *Life* magazine article "Have We Visitors from Space?" the mainstream press published numerous articles and editorials that answered the question "Yes!" and severely criticized the air force for its handling of UFOs. There was even a series of "objective" UFO articles in *Science and Mechanics* magazine, and for the first time, major publishers began turning out mass-market 'zines devoted exclusively to saucers. Of course, Hollywood and television got into the act, and one result was *The Invaders*, a briefly very popular ABC-TV series starring Roy Thinnes (about whom more later).

All this was great for me and others in saucerdom. As I've already mentioned, *Saucer News* circulation quickly went up about 60 percent, to over eight thousand. Memberships in saucer clubs like APRO and NICAP took off, too, with NICAP doubling its numbers to eleven thousand. The crowds at George Van Tassel's Giant Rock conventions were much better than they had been in years, and even Gabriel Green's Amalgamated Flying Saucers Clubs of America (advertised in *Saucer News*) claimed almost four thousand members.

But all this wasn't so great for the Pentagon. Hynek, who for some time had been trying to get the air force to do a genuinely scientific study of UFOs, finally was able to persuade the right people to establish a panel of scientists, including Carl Sagan, to review the situation and make recommendations. Known as the O'Brien Committee, this group decided there might be something of scientific value in studying UFOs, and it recommended the air force contract with a number of universities to do the work. The powers that be tried to ignore this.

Then the swamp gas bubbled up out of the Michigan bogs, and the Armed Services Committee of the U.S. House of Representatives held the open hearing demanded by Rep. Gerald Ford. During this event, the

O'Brien group's findings and recommendations were (oops!) mentioned by Secretary of the Air Force Harold Brown. Members of the committee jumped at the chance to publicly endorse something positive, and the air force was all but ordered by the congressmen to get on with it.

My guess is that at first air force leaders were very unhappy about this, but before long, it dawned on them it was a golden opportunity, a chance to get the whole flying saucer mess off their hands. They could turn the research over to a bunch of university eggheads, and whatever came of that wouldn't be the Pentagon's fault. Better yet, it probably would lead to a way for the air force to hand the UFO project over to some other government agency, or maybe even close it down altogether.

Before long, a $313,000 air force contract (eventually increased to $500,000) was given to the University of Colorado, and in October 1966, famed and rather controversial physicist Edward U. Condon and his group of a dozen or so scientists started work. Everyone in saucerdom on all sides of the UFO issue were optimistic that the "Condon Committee" would finally get to the bottom of things, or at least come up with some good ideas about how to do so. Practically every saucer group rushed to help, with sighting reports, field investigations, advice (lots of advice), and so on. Of course, this included S.A.U.C.E.R.S. On October 10, 1966, I wrote to Condon and offered our Expert assistance. I advised that my group had "voluminous files containing important information on UFO sightings and landings going back many years" and extended our "full cooperation" and "the use of all facilities" to Condon and his team.

Things definitely were looking up for saucerdom.

LET'S HEAR IT *for* DRUNKEN ENGINEERS

Actually, they had been looking up for me personally for several months. Remember that call I got from the American Program Bureau in the spring of 1966? The bureau, a leading lecture-booking agency, was in desperate need of a UFO Expert for an upcoming meeting of the Engineering Society of Detroit. The bureau's Expert, none other than Maj. Donald Keyhoe, had demanded too large a fee, and they had to come up with someone to replace him. On the recommendation of another APB lecturer, radio host Bob Kennedy, the bureau called me. Of course, I jumped at the chance, and they took me without an audition or anything else other than Kennedy's endorsement.

So it was that on May 20, 1966, I made my maiden voyage as a saucer lecturer in what purports to be the real world. I was nervous and my talk was ludicrous, especially for an engineering group, but it turned out that practically all of them were drunk and just out for a good time. They loved my talk. A society official wrote a glowing letter to Bob Walker, head of the APB: "Jim Moseley's recent appearance before the Engineering Society left our audience spinning [it was the booze, Bob]. He did an excellent job not only on the platform but before radio and t.v. microphones here in the metropolitan area. We would certainly endorse Mr. Moseley as a regular speaker in your stable. . . ."

I was launched.

ENLIGHTENMENT on the CHEAP

Over the next eight years, I lectured on more than one hundred college campuses and at a few other events, one of these a fashion show somewhere in Massachusetts. The small audience watched the models strut their stuff. Then, as a bonus, they got about a half-hour of me. I'm not sure if I was even advertised as being part of the show, but it was clear from the puzzled faces before me that the ladies didn't quite know how to take what they were hearing or why they were hearing it.

While my expertise and brilliant speaking style were keys to my success, it was even more important that I was a cheap date. Keyhoe, who was the leading ufological public figure at the time, was getting something like $750 a lecture. I usually got $400 (of which the APB took 30 percent) and covered my own expenses. Since college lecture committees were always trying to save money, I had a big edge, even though I was essentially an unknown, at least compared to Keyhoe. UFOs were a very hot topic, and what really mattered was to land a speaker who could give an entertaining pitch about the subject, regardless of actual substance. If he came at a discount price, so much the better.

I recall that I once went on a series of three or four lectures in the space of a very few days, all of which had originally been booked for Keyhoe. The APB told the colleges the major was ill, when in fact, apparently, the bureau and Keyhoe had had a falling out over his refusal to lower his fee. Whatever the actual reason, I benefited and the schools saved money.

Some time later, a college cheaper or poorer than most didn't want to foot the bill for having me speak in person. So for $100, net, I gave my talk by phone from New York. I could hear what was being said in the auditorium, and the audience could hear me, piped from the phone to the loudspeakers in the hall. A very odd experience.

There were others. On one occasion, I arrived somewhere in the Bible Belt to speak at a small fundamentalist religious school. I flew in at night in a downpour. The college people picked me up at the airport, and when we arrived on the campus, for some reason we had to traverse a few yards of very muddy ground. It was cold, the rain was sluicing down, and I was quickly approaching miserable. All of a sudden, I stepped into a water-filled hole several inches deep. I couldn't help blurting out, "Jesus Christ!" Then, in an ill-considered attempt to recover the situation with a bit of humor, I sang out, "Praise the Lord!"

On another occasion, I was introduced by a professor of physics, who was the chairman of the faculty hospitality committee or some such, and thus stuck with the job. He was a stuffy sort and left no doubt he most definitely didn't approve of me or my topic. When I stepped up to the podium, I received a rousing, standing ovation, much to the very obvious chagrin of Prof. Stuffed Shirt, who remained on the stage during my presentation. Throughout my talk, I was interrupted by enthusiastic applause. I was puzzled but delighted. Professor Shirt was puzzled and steaming. When it came time for him to thank me for my "most 'interesting' lecture," it was all he could do to contain his near apoplexy. Following the program, several students told me that, while they really did enjoy my speech, the superenthusiasm of the crowd and, in fact, my invitation to speak, extended by a student committee, were intended mainly to needle the very unpopular Professor Shirt. Oh, well, as long as I was of service to a Good Cause . . .

Then there was the great Flying Sausages Incident. This took place in February 1967, when I was in Atlanta to lecture at Georgia Tech. In those days, Lester Maddox was governor of the Peach State. Maddox was the notorious segregationist who had been elected on the strength of the publicity he garnered chasing civil-rights activists from his restaurant, threatening to beat them with an ax handle.

Once a month, Governor Maddox set a day during which he would meet and greet the masses under the dome of the state capitol. It happened that the day for February fell when I was in Atlanta, so I joined the crowd. Despite our vast political differences, I wanted to get a picture with the governor. I had to stand in a queue, which, curiously enough, was comprised mostly of black schoolchildren. When my turn came, I showed Maddox a copy of *Saucer News* and told him it was about flying saucers. He, attempting to be genial, said something like, "Oh, yes. I've always been interested in sausages." Obviously, he had misunderstood me. I started to explain. Then I realized it really didn't make any difference, and that the man might be so ignorant as to have never heard of flying saucers. So I had a friend snap a photo of the governor, *"Sausage" News,* and me, and we went on our way. The Historic Photograph is included in the photo section.

SPICING THINGS UP with the LOST CREEK SAUCER

All in all, although I wasn't particularly enthusiastic about lecturing—I wasn't yet the ham that I am today—I had a generally good time on the circuit. Besides making a small profit on the lectures themselves—at least most of the time—I garnered a lot of publicity and quite a few paying subscriptions to *Saucer News,* as well as establishing many good media contacts around the country.

My standard, hour-long presentation was for the most part based on topics I picked up out of *Flying Saucers: Serious Business* (1966), a hot-selling book by nationally popular radio broadcaster and saucer enthusiast Frank Edwards. I began with possible saucers in ancient history, such as Ezekiel and the wheel, touched on some of the wilder stories from the coast-to-coast mysterious airships flap of 1897, mentioned the so-called foo fighters reported by pilots during World War II, and then introduced the Age of Flying Saucers with the Kenneth Arnold and Thomas Mantell stories. Next was the big 1952 Washington saucer-invasion case, followed by the 1957 flap and its possible connection with the launch of *Sputnik I,* and then the recent swamp gas events, emphasizing Hynek's statements about them. I closed with some musings about possible UFO origins (with not a word about the Earth Theory) and rounded out the hour with about twenty minutes of questions and answers.

If I do say so myself, it was a good summary presentation of saucer history and events, and given the high level of public interest at the time, it was all anyone really needed for success. Still, I wished for something a bit more exciting. In late summer 1966 my wish was granted: a new motion picture of a flying saucer.

Here's how I reported this spectacular development in *Saucer News* (winter 1966–67):

> For the first time in our nearly thirteen years of publication, we have been able to obtain an apparently genuine movie film of a flying saucer. The film, taken with a Bolex camera in 16 mm. color, was made on the afternoon of July 23rd, in a rural area called Lost Creek, located near Clarksburg, West Virginia. The photographer has asked to remain anonymous. At the time of the sighting, he and an employee named John Sheets were driving through Lost Creek in a Chevrolet pick-up truck, on their way to photograph a little league baseball game, as a favor to a mutual friend.
>
> As they were driving along a lonely stretch of road, a strange object began following the truck at very low altitude. The camera was not loaded, and by the time Sheets' boss loaded it, the object was gone. They stopped the vehicle and waited for several minutes, apparently with some sort of premonition that the object would return. Eventually it did, and several feet of film were shot. During the filming, the object was again at very low altitude. Sheets says that it looked to be about ten feet in diameter, though to us it appears to be smaller. Trees visible in the background can be used as reference points; and a photographic expert in Clarksburg has declared that the object is at least twelve feet in diameter in his opinion.
>
> In the course of the filming, the photographer kept shifting his camera from the sky to the ground, apparently thinking that the object was going to land. According to Sheets, it did not land, but shot off again, at high speed, making a strange humming sound. Afterwards Sheets was ill for two days, either from the excitement or from some after-effect of the close sighting.
>
> Mr. Sheets, a young man in his early twenties, had worked for saucer researcher Gray Barker part-time several years ago, and knowing Barker's interest in UFOs, he brought the undeveloped film to him. Barker cooperated with SAUCER NEWS in developing the film and making an extra copy. The latter was sent to us several weeks ago by Barker. . . .

In addition to showing the film on New York–area television and at one of the *Saucer News* monthly lectures, I incorporated it and the story behind it into my American Program Bureau talk. This got some very interesting reactions from the college audiences, which usually included many townspeople, who, as a goodwill gesture, were invited to attend free. There always would be some quiet laughter, but many people took the film seriously, some gravely speculating that the saucer's jerky flight might be due to its being powered by Earth's magnetic field. Generally, those predisposed to think it genuine thought it genuine, and vice versa.

The skeptics were right. The only true elements of the story were the date, location, and the involvement of John Sheets and Gray Barker. I had decided I needed a "prop" for my lectures, and Barker agreed that, if I footed the bill, we would do a brief saucer-sighting movie, complete with accompanying story. We made the film from my car. I drove, while Barker filmed out the window from the front passenger seat. Sheets, a friend of Gray's, perched on the car roof, with a model saucer dangling off the end of a fishing pole. The complexity of the motion of the car and of the model, which bounced around like crazy, made it very difficult to tell how big the saucer was, or how far away. Befitting my bargain lecture fee, this was a very cheap production, just one roll of film, slightly edited by Barker, a silver-painted plaster saucer model, and a little gas. (For those who might be interested, the actual Lost Creek saucer—shockingly closer to ten inches than ten feet in diameter—is on display as part of the Gray Barker Collection at the Clarksburg-Harrison County Public Library in Clarksburg, West Virginia.)

I once attempted to get on Johnny Carson's *Tonight Show* with the Lost Creek film. I managed to make it as far as a viewing for the show's writers, who watched in bemused silence, thanked me for my time, and sent me on my way. But as I made no attempt to protect any ownership rights in the film, and as Gray Barker peddled copies of it in a package with two other somewhat questionable saucer films, it wasn't long before it was showing up in many places. Not long ago, I chanced upon a rather terrible UFO documentary on television. In the background behind the credits at the beginning and end of the program was the Lost Creek saucer bobbing around semi-mysteriously. When I saw this, I burst out laughing. Here was my very crude hoax film in a supposedly serious presentation, quite a clue as to the level of authenticity of the rest of the program.

The FLYING SAUCER PHYSICIST

One of today's leading saucerers who got started in The Field during the sixties UFO excitement was Stanton T. Friedman. Stan once billed himself as "The Flying Saucer Physicist" and still makes a point of underscoring what seem to me to be his professional insecurities by making sure "Nuclear Physicist" always appears after his name. Before swamp gas raised saucers to new heights, Stan had been interested in UFOs but not active as a ufologist, reading all the books, joining APRO and NICAP, and exchanging correspondence with Keyhoe, the Lorenzens, and others, while earning his living in the defense industry as, in his words, "an itinerant nuclear physicist."

One ufological Big Name whom Friedman got to know was Frank Edwards, who sent him a copy of *Flying Saucers: Serious Business* right after it was published. By Stan's own account, this led him to give his first saucer lecture—an interesting coincidence, given the important role Edwards's book played in my lectures. Before too long, Stan was on the college circuit. Today he is a full-time UFO lecturer and researcher, found at practically every UFO gathering in North America and many abroad, and still beloved by college students.

I think Stan semisecretly yearns to be considered Hynek's successor as ufology's leading statesman. However, he lacks a Ph.D. and has never held an academic or research position of the sort required to gain a real-science stature anything like that enjoyed by Hynek. He also comes across as too glib and too hucksterish, while at the same time exuding evangelical true believerism, nothing at all like Hynek's low-key, tweedy-academic style.

I know I'm not alone in being unable to figure out how much of his ufological spiel Stan really believes and how much he "believes" because it's necessary for his saucering career—or even if he knows the difference himself. These days, his mainstays are the alleged Roswell saucer crash and MJ-12, the supersecret outfit supposedly behind the big saucer cover-up, or as Stan calls it, The Cosmic Watergate. Thank the space gods that's no longer the title of Friedman's standard lecture. Still, his basic pitch remains the same. While Stan is an excellent professional speaker, like any aging comedian, he *really* needs some new material.

Back in the sixties, though, Friedman was just starting out, a fresh new face and voice on the scene, and he was very aggressive in pursuing bookings. For example, several of the colleges at which I spoke told me they had received calls from Stan, *after* I was already booked, trying to get them to switch to him. It goes without saying this was dirty pool and shows what kind of a guy Friedman is—or perhaps *was*, as these days he seems not a bad guy at all, and we get along okay.

Such was the cutthroat competition in those heady days, and while there were others out pounding the ufological podium, Friedman and I were the top bananas for quite a while. Eventually, and to be honest, justifiably, Stan began bagging more and more of the college dates, and I fewer and fewer. This, combined with just plain being tired of it all, finally led me to quit the American Program Bureau in 1974. Of course, I haven't entirely given up lecturing, but now give my "True Experiences of a Skeptical Believer" talk only when I feel like it and as much for my own amusement as that of my audiences.

"MIDDLE UFOLOGY"

In 1964, a couple of years before my elevation to Expert and ufological lion of the college lecture circuit, three saucer fiends got together in Cleveland, Ohio, and formed a group they called the Congress of Scientific Ufologists. The perpetrators were two Clevelanders, the late Al Manak and Rick Hilberg, who's still active in ufology, and Atlanta saucerer Al Greenfield, who all but dropped out of The Field years ago and now writes on considerably more esoteric subjects. Hilberg, Manak, and Greenfield were concerned that the only ongoing public saucer gatherings were dominated by contactees. They also felt the major national saucer groups, particularly NICAP, were too narrowly conservative in their approach to saucers. They concluded a middle ground was needed. So it was that the movement we somewhat pompously labeled Middle Ufology was born.

The three conspirators decided the congress would stage an annual convention, like their group, grandly called a congress. This would feature public sessions, at which prominent saucerers would speak, and smaller closed sessions restricted to selected UFO researchers, where it was intended that serious saucer research would be conducted and discussed. A small governing body called the Permanent Organizing Committee was set up, and I was an original member. From 1964 through 1970 the congress was headed by Manak. I succeeded him as Permanent Chairman in 1971, and I'm still at it—Permanent Chairman for Life, no doubt.

After a few years, we realized the name Congress of Scientific Ufologists was far too pretentious, so we changed it to the more modest National UFO Conference (NUFOC). Under this title and my permanent chairmanship, the NUFOC continues today, still staging what is the longest continuing series of annual UFO conventions in the world, perhaps even the galaxy. I have spoken at every one except the 1970 event, when the time-honored earthly pursuit of filthy lucre prevented it. After the 1960s NUFOC gave up any pretense of doing research, and putting on an annual convention somewhere in the United States became and continues to be our sole purpose. Each year between 150 and 400 devoted saucerers continue to turn out.

The first congress, held in Cleveland in June 1964, drew some three hundred saucer fiends. The principal speakers were the late Earl Neff, for many years a leading Ohio ufologist, and myself. The following two years, *Saucer News* was a cosponsor, and in 1967, at the height of the Great UFO Excitement, the gathering was staged in New York City, with me as local chairman. This turned out to be the largest indoor saucer convention ever held, and, except for one of the earliest Giant Rock events, held outdoors, was the largest saucercon ever staged, period.

The GREAT CON

Planning for the Fourth Congress of Scientific Ufologists, the first held outside Ohio, and New York City's first-ever flying saucer convention, began almost a year in advance. I hoped to make the event both memorable and profitable. At least I succeeded with the former.

Over the long weekend of June 22–25, more than eight thousand people showed up at what was then the Commodore Hotel to hobnob with and listen to talks by a lineup of luminaries that, among others, included James Randi, Howard Menger, Gray Barker, John Keel, Frank Stranges, Ivan Sanderson, Long John Nebel, Paris Flammonde, and television star Roy Thinnes. I'd also hoped to include Barney and Betty Hill; Dan Fry; Frank Edwards, best-selling UFO-book author; Ray Palmer, a cofounder of *Fate* magazine and in 1967 editor and publisher of *Flying Saucers*; and Kenneth Arnold, the Man Who Started It All (I'd set the convention dates to coincide with the twentieth anniversary of his June 24, 1947, sighting). But this was not to be.

I never found out exactly why the Hills turned down my invitation, but I suspect NICAP talked them out of participating. Donald Keyhoe and Richard Hall went out of their way to condemn the convention in advance because a couple of contactees were on the program and, of course, NICAP-expellee Moseley was the organizer. Unfortunately for Keyhoe and his toady, many NICAPers attended, some attempting to get in free with their NICAP membership cards, and George Earley, an engineer who headed the Connecticut NICAP affiliate, covered the con for the *Hartford Courant* and gave me many photos he took of the weekend's events to run in *Saucer News*.

Dan Fry had given me an oral commitment that seemed good right up until the last minute, but he failed to show. Maybe he found one of his Understanding ladies more, shall we say, in need than our con goers.

Edwards had agreed to participate very early on, but Lyle Stuart, his publisher, talked him out of it. Stuart felt the atmosphere would be too crackpot for Edwards's image. Stuart even threatened to sue me if I didn't remove Edwards's name from my original promotional flyer, which of course I did, reprinting five thousand of them. By chilling coincidence, Edwards died the weekend of the congress, on June 24 at that. Imagine the results for ufology if he had dropped dead on the convention stage!

As for Palmer and Arnold, well, Palmer was a very nice guy, and he had agreed to speak for little or no money. He was going to drive all the way from his home in Wisconsin (for semi-mysterious reasons he never flew). Arnold, on the other hand, was a money-grubber. He wanted first-class airfare to and from *Australia* for himself and his wife. It seems he intended to move there, but hadn't yet done so—and never did. I can't explain the logic other than that Arnold was after a large chunk of fast dollars. It would have come to about $4,000, so I turned him down, and he never forgave me for it. Palmer had been a close friend of Arnold's since 1947, and when he heard how much Arnold was asking for, he, too, suddenly decided he wanted real money, which I was unwilling to cough up. So Palmer didn't come either.

Ten years later at a Chicago convention sponsored by *Fate,* I saw Arnold in the mingling room. We had not had any contact since 1967, and I had never met him in the flesh. Realizing this might be my only opportunity to meet this legendary figure, I went up to him, introduced myself, and held out my hand. He pointedly turned and walked away. This made me more determined than ever. I took several more passes at him, and finally, either I got him cornered or he gave up. He reluctantly shook hands, but as far as I can recall, said not a word.

Back to 1967. As curtain time approached, things grew more and more hectic. Among other things, I cut an LP record (remember those?) with Long John Nebel, specifically to be sold at the con. I was given a good price for the expenses involved, but when it was too late for me to do anything about it, Long John insisted that only his name appear on the album jacket. Dear old Long John!

I also had allowed Gray Barker to talk me into doing my first book, *Jim Moseley's Book of Saucer News.* This was an anthology of what I considered to be the best articles from the first fourteen years of my magazine. In the midst of everything else, I managed to find time to pull this together, and Barker published it just before the convention, where I believe it sold rather well. Unlike a later publishing collaboration with Gray, I'm proud of this one. Today, it is a rare collector's item.

In early June, as the countdown continued, I held a memorable precon party in my Manhattan apartment, to which I had moved from New Jersey a few months before. Such legendary saucerers as Augie Roberts, Max Miller, Ivan Sanderson, and John Keel, as well as many lesser lights, were there, and we partied all night.

A weird highlight (?) of this event involved the resident of an apartment a block or two away. For some time, I had noticed with amusement that this guy had huge, varicolored lights on his balcony, blinking on and off all night almost nightly. Well, that night or, rather, the following dawn I found out who my "neighbor" was. Annoyed by my guests' continuing and obvious curiosity, he went to the roof of his building and pointed—but didn't fire—a rifle at us. It was then that I saw it was famed jazz musician Charlie Mingus. What a night!

A week before the Big Day, I checked into the Commodore, not because I feared Mingus might start shooting, but so I could stay on top of things. While I was at the hotel, I let Howard Menger and his wife, Connie, stay in my apartment. I don't recall for certain why this was, but I suspect the Mengers were broke. I was glad to help them because I thought Howard, whom I'd brought out of semiretirement to speak at the con, would be a draw, which he was. Unfortunately, his speech turned out to be a disappointment, very brief and with next to nothing about any of his alleged experiences as a contactee/patriotic phony contactee/saucer inventor/and so on.

The glorious 1967 congress was the first such conclave I had ever hosted myself. I had a lot of groupies and volunteers but no experienced people working with me. I did a lot of things right, but as usual in my life, did enough wrong to make up for it. Though we had a full house of about two thousand for each of the four public sessions, and although I sold a lot of books and gross receipts were quite substantial, I barely broke even.

Thousands of dollars slipped through my hands in ways I could do little or nothing about. There were reliable rumors of evil hangers-on stealing books from the vending tables, but the worst problem was control of access to the lecture hall during the opening session. There were seven entrances to the ballroom, spaced several yards apart. As I recall, we charged two dollars a person, and there were no advance ticket sales. So I put three trusted people, with starting change, at three of the entrances and blocked the other four doors with chairs. Then I was off to attend to other matters. When I returned, the crowd was pouring through all seven entrances, four of which were unmanned. It turned out the hotel management had removed the chairs, as it was a violation of the fire code to block any of the doors.

So there I stood, helpless, as dozens and dozens of eager, freeloading saucer fiends rushed past me through the unguarded portals. Not that this surprised me. As honest as I consider myself to be, if I saw three pay-as-you-go doors and four free ones, I might well choose a free one, as most people did in this case. I'll never know how much I lost on that one, but I straightened things out during the remaining sessions.

I cannot exaggerate what a media event the convention was. I was in league with the New York Convention Bureau, which helped enormously. Other than sports and a show or two on Broadway, mine was *the* event of the weekend in the Big Apple. I couldn't expect the hotel staff to give all the details to people calling in, so I set up a room where an ever-changing group of volunteers manned phones and gave out convention information to press and public, referring to a large blackboard set up at the front of the room for all to see. The only trouble was, to keep the volunteers happy, I agreed to have an unlimited tab charged to the room. So these guys ran through at least a couple of hundred bucks in beer, snacks, and who knows what else in the course of a weekend.

Once underway, we had saturation press coverage from all the local and some national media. There were no fewer than fifty reporters and press representatives covering the convention at least part of the time, including people from the United Nations, Radio Free Europe, the Library of Congress, the Associated Press, and *Look* and *Time* magazines. One afternoon, I was sitting in a quiet corner talking to the man from *Time*, trying to sound as sane and sensible as possible. Suddenly my former *Saucer News* cohort Dominick Lucchesi appeared. Dom had a somewhat sadistic sense of humor, and much to my chagrin, he sat down with us. Immediately, he began telling one of his favorite absurd tales, something to do with a mysterious "black box" left on Earth by the Space People. I don't recall the details, but the story was patent nonsense, and I saw the reporter react negatively. I closely perused the following week's issue of *Time* but, oddly enough, found not a single word about the convention.

Of course, Lucchesi wasn't the only strange bird at the congress. Another, much more attractive than Dom, was Barbara Hudson. Barbara was a comely young black woman with such claims to ufological fame as spending a night with George Adamski—she said they just talked, which I believe—and, when she was a child, having seen a saucer land in Central Park (!).

Barbara also claimed that for years she had been shadowed by a mysterious group which she cleverly and creatively called "The Group." This outfit of about four or five included both Earth and Space People. Barbara had ridden in their car and been shown marvelous gadgets from other worlds. When she changed residences, The Group quickly found her again each time. They didn't seem to threaten her, but instead sought to give her enlightenment about interplanetary matters.

According to Barbara, The Group was very interested in my convention. After some prodding, she "admitted" she had been sent to keep an eye on things. Thus began a very interesting and fun relationship that lasted several years.

Some of the speakers who did show up were entertaining in more ways than one—for example, our star, Roy Thinnes, the male lead in the very popular television series *The Invaders,* featuring evil aliens secretly on Earth who flew saucers curiously similar to those made popular by George Adamski's photographs. Thinnes claimed to have had a number of UFO sightings himself and, if I recall correctly, even to have seen Space People walking the streets of Hollywood (sounds plausible to me!). Recently a semi-regular on *The X-Files,* playing a benevolent alien with miraculous healing powers, Thinnes agreed to appear at my con for no fee, "just" all expenses for himself, his wife, and his mother-in-law, who was his agent. Despite the extra expense involved, I readily agreed, knowing he would bring in not only saucer fiends but many more paying customers from the much larger audience of science-fiction fans.

However, things did not go well. Thinnes was supposed to make a short speech at each of the four sessions, Friday evening, Saturday afternoon and evening, and Sunday. He gave a rather uninspiring talk at the Friday session and then allegedly came down with "the runs," which those who had been involved with convention operations ever after called The Roy Thinnes Disease.

Thus, our headliner appeared only once. On Saturday, I found out at the last minute that he was indisposed and realized I would have a hopping mad audience on my hands. Just before the session was to begin, with no featured celebrity or substitute in sight, I ran into a then well known New York–area contactee, Alex McNeil. I knew he was a good speaker, so I asked if he'd like to fill in, which he did, gratis.

I'll never forget McNeil's performance. He was spellbinding. After I introduced him, he got up and started yelling, "I've seen them! They are real! They come here from other planets!" He had the audience in the palm of his hand in moments, gave a very good talk, stuck to the time limit, and in every way acted like a pro. I really should have slipped him some cash.

As for Thinnes, all we got from him was his one lackluster talk, and I never really got to meet him. The closest I came was as we—Thinnes, some of my groupies, and I—were running down a hotel hall to escape a gang of *his* groupies. Thinnes asked, "Does anybody have a cigarette?" I slipped him one, he thanked me, and that was that.

One of the minor highlights of the convention was the presence of Dr. Edward Condon, whom I had invited to attend the convention in my letter of a few months before, offering assistance to his UFO study. In response, Colorado UFO project coordinator Robert Low wrote (*Saucer News*, spring 1967), "I will certainly see that your invitation to Dr. Condon to attend the Convention in June is brought to his personal attention. If he is unable to make it, and he is terribly busy, so that the chances are not too good, would any of the others of our investigating group be welcome?" Of course, I immediately assured Low that anyone associated with the project definitely would be welcome.

Apparently, Condon adjusted his schedule so he could make it to the con as an "observer." When it was confirmed he was in the audience—he was attempting to keep a low profile—I embarrassed him by insisting from the podium that he stand and take a bow. This he very reluctantly did, to scattered applause, scattered boos, and scattered indifference. Later, his being in attendance would be cited as an example of how he focused on the kookier side of saucerdom at the expense of the serious stuff.

I tried to use advance appearances by a couple of speakers to boost the convention. One of these was Gray Barker. I arranged for him to appear on the *Alan Burke Show*, a local television talk program. Burke had a confrontational on-air style, but off the air he was a very nice fellow. He did his best to help me publicize the con by having several of our speakers on his show over a number of days.

When Burke asked Barker where and when the convention was to be held, Gray slowed down his spiel and groped through all of his pockets for the piece of paper on which he'd written the details. I don't think he ever found his crib sheet, but he faked the pitch fairly well, probably bringing in a few people who might otherwise have done something else that weekend.

Less successful, to say the least, was Fortean writer John Keel, who had burst onto the saucer scene just over a year before, but who already was a solidly established professional writer, with credits as a globe-trotting reporter and television scriptwriter. His first book, *Jadoo* (1957), offered up his adventures in the Far East, including what he thought might have been a yeti (abominable snowman) sighting. When he appeared at the 1967 convention, he was specializing in "creature" sightings, which were being reported in increasing numbers all over the United States. Of course, this included West Virginia's famed Mothman, a strange being Keel was to immortalize in his *Mothman Prophecies* (1975). Before long, he would establish himself as one of the leading lights of 4-D saucering, and it was he who would coin the term *MIB*, for the notorious Men in Black invented by Gray Barker with inspiration supplied by poor Al Bender.

It seems to me that Keel has had a chip on his shoulder about me almost from our first meeting in the sixties. One issue, I suppose, is that he knew Gray Barker and I were not entirely serious about saucers—but, then, neither was he. Still, we managed to get along after a fashion, and he contributed some interesting articles and very strange and usually very funny letters to *Saucer News*. But he and I haven't spoken for several years, ever since a fateful telephone conversation in which I "accused" him of being a ufologist as well as a Fortean (horrors!). Enraged, he apparently smashed his phone against the wall, ending our conversation with quite a flourish.

Today semiretired, Keel is a unique thinker and a very good writer, whose musings, for better or worse, have added a great deal to saucer lore over the years. However, I've seen him give lectures in which he generalized and theorized in a most unscientific way. I wish he'd exercised similar imagination—or even just stuck to the script—when, on June 23, he appeared on the *Today* show in my place.

Unfortunately, I was too busy to make it myself, so I recommended Keel. I thought he, as a rising young author, would be eternally grateful for such a break, getting on one of the most-watched national television programs. Instead, he was seriously ticked off about having to get up so early! Those who saw the show told me Keel (in my opinion deliberately) said not a word about the convention.

Another of my unintended Keel-related gaffes was presenting him with the Ufologist of the Year Award (then called the Robert Loftin Memorial Award). This was the first time the Congress of Scientific Ufologists/National UFO Conference had bestowed such an honor, and I thought Keel would be very pleased. However, when I added the presentation to my introduction of his talk, it threw him off completely. Apparently, he is a somewhat nervous public speaker, and he literally didn't know what to say.

Some of Keel's MIB or Barker's Men in Black or certain equally semimysterious someones seem to have been lurking around the Commodore during the convention. (We know they weren't from Barbara Hudson's Group, as she had me covered.) Several con goers told me they had been watched or followed on the lower levels of the hotel by men who looked and acted like official military or civilian investigators. They seemed to be working out of a room near the hotel's coffee shop, to which there was easy access from both the lower-level hall and, by tunnel, nearby Grand Central Station.

One day I was rushing up the front steps of the Commodore, when a hanger-on with me said something like, "There's two of those guys I've been telling you about!" I looked where he was pointing and saw two well-dressed, professional-looking young men hurrying in the opposite direction toward the lower level. I was very curious indeed, but there simply was no time to check them out. After the convention wound up, I asked the hotel management about the men and the rumors. Of course, they claimed to know nothing. The impression I got was that the hotel security people had allowed "the MIB" to set up phone-tapping equipment during the con. Of course, by the time I inquired, it was too late to learn anything. That's the way it always is with the MIB.

Despite all the snafus, evil-MIB-doings, and the like, the Fourth Congress of Scientific Ufologists was a big success. The public was entertained, Middle Ufology got some serious and semi-serious press coverage, and in the closed sessions, attended by about one hundred registered delegates from seventeen states, the Distinct of Columbia, Canada, and Great Britain, some important work got done. Oddly enough—or perhaps not—other than the appointment of a committee to choose the site of the 1968 convention, I remember only two of these great accomplishments. The first of these was passage of a motion—neither sponsored nor endorsed by *Saucer News* or me—calling upon NICAP to reinstate my membership, a flattering but futile gesture (later, the semi-mysterious National Committee for the Restoration of James W. Moseley's Membership in NICAP was formed, with similar results). The other major action was the defeat of a motion condemning the Condon Committee, which was embroiled in the early stages of the controversy that would soon explode around it. It seemed to me then that such a condemnation was premature and, less seriously, sticking by Condon would generate internal controversy in saucerdom, keeping the ufological pot boiling.

My only real regret is that the con wasn't a financial success. (If only I had four more ticket takers for that first session!) At least it lived up to the goal, intended or not, of all my business endeavors over the years, saucerian, grave robbing, real estate, you name it: break even. And in keeping with so much else about the convention, even the money side of things wrapped up in a peculiar fashion.

On Sunday night, the convention over, I had (as it turned out) about $16,000 in small bills that had to be counted, sorted, and taken to my bank the next day. This is quite a job for one person, so a trusted advisor (whose name is lost in the mists of memory), Barbara Hudson (whom I barely knew, but sensed wasn't interested in money), and I spent about three hours carefully counting and recounting the loot.

Monday at about noon, I went to my bank alone. This was Bankers Trust on Wall Street, hardly a hick institution. Yet when I walked up to a teller with a carrying case full of cash and handed her a deposit slip with the totals, she flipped out and hit the panic button! Guards rushed over, and I found myself having to explain that I wasn't there to rob the place but to make a fairly substantial deposit. They and a bank vice president who took charge of the situation remained suspicious and at first refused to accept the money. Then I agreed to accept *their* count, even if it differed from mine. So they took my deposit, to be counted at their convenience, and I left under the still wary eyes of the guards. Later, my bank statement showed their count matched ours exactly.

So it was that the Great Con of 1967 passed into ufological history. As it turned out, this was to be the height of my saucering career. Exactly ten years before, in 1957, my discovery of the gold treasure at Baton Grande marked the height of my grave-robbing career. Coincidence? *Hardly!*

The MORNING AFTER

Perhaps oddly, it was in the wake of this huge success that I began to consider scaling back my involvement in saucering. In part, I suppose, this was due to my near-total exhaustion. I was so wrung out and there was so much yet to do in the way of postconvention "clean up," that the first after-con issue of *Saucer News* was mailed more than a month late.

As odd as it may seem, another factor was the phenomenal growth of *Saucer News.* During the buildup to the con, our circulation had soared to more than ten thousand, jumping about 25 percent in a few months. Was this because *Saucer News* was *the* source for UFO information, or perhaps because my magazine was such a slick, professional production (which it was getting to be)? No. What did it was a couple of appearances I made on a television show for kiddies.

A very nice fellow named Terry Bennett had a popular daily show on New York City's WOR-TV. He was a puppeteer-ventriloquist, and his dummy was his cohost. It was the usual silly kid program—fortunately, without a studio audience—but Bennett always had a serious or purportedly serious guest on each day. I was one of the latter. When I appeared, Bennett very generously plugged, over and over, the *Saucer News* address and subscription price, which was two dollars a year (four issues).

As a result of this wonderful free advertising, I received a couple of thousand new subscriptions—from elementary school kids. Of course, very few renewed. This, plus the rapid collapse of general interest in saucers when the Condon Committee issued its report, drove me back down to between two and three thousand subscribers in a couple of years. I sometimes wonder how many of my youthful readers were corrupted by my influence, continuing to scan the skies for UFOs as they grew up.

Back on Earth, not only had our circulation soared, at least temporarily, but I had expanded the magazine itself. We were averaging between thirty and forty pages an issue, and the "Special Convention Issue/ Collector's Edition" (summer 1967) weighed in with fifty-six pages and a heavy coated-stock, four-color cover. I had a substantial number of paying advertisers, and I had been approached by a number of magazine publishers and distributors who were interested in adding *Saucer News* to their list of titles. I was on the threshold of having what I *thought* I had wanted all along, a successful professional magazine.

Then there was the overhead. In order to keep up with success, I had to hire several people to work in my New York office. The wages of friends and friends of friends who went on my payroll and the related bookkeeping and tax paperwork this brought on ate up my profits, and as the bloom went off the ufological rose, this cut even deeper, and I slipped into the red.

One of those who helped this slide along was a teenaged Timothy Green Beckley, who doubled as managing editor and advertising manager. Tim was and is quite a character. I finally had to fire him after he took one four-hour lunch break too many. Since then, he's made names for himself in saucerdom ("Mr. UFO") and soft- and hard-core porn ("Mr. Creepo"). Over the years Tim has peddled, in his various books and magazines, every outrageous point of view imaginable about UFOs and kindred subjects, even though he believes very little of it himself. I once asked him how he could push New Age "sweetness and light" and porn to different audiences at the same time. He immediately replied, "I give them what they want." Tim makes no pretensions, and doesn't have a vicious bone in his body. I consider him to be an honest businessman and a good friend.

Beckley stuck with saucering, but I was a victim of my own success and, in all honesty, innate laziness. Suddenly I was faced with a lot more work and very little more fun. Keeping up the pace just didn't seem worth it anymore.

Oh, yes, then there was the little matter of the sudden availability of a very large chunk of money. In late January 1968 the last of my trust fund's two trustees died, and the corpus of the trust, over a million dollars, soon would be mine to do with as I wished. Let's see . . . Should I invest it in *Saucer News*? Should I set up a UFO research fund? Or how about real estate, apartment buildings and such? . . .

In February 1968 I sold *Saucer News* to Gray Barker. Gray became editor in chief, and I continued on the masthead as editor. This mostly meant that Gray wrote lengthy, wacky articles and letters to the editor and put my name on them. He managed to keep the magazine going for five more irregularly published issues, the last of them (vol. 17, no. 1, whole no. 75) appearing in spring 1970. After seventeen years, the second oldest continuously published periodical in saucerdom was dead—or so it seemed.

Meanwhile, I wasn't quite out of saucering, which is like malaria: once it's in your blood, you never quite shake it. I continued to attend and speak at National UFO Conferences and to accept (fewer and fewer) American Program Bureau engagements. Because I really enjoyed my role as impresario, I also kept the S.A.U.C.E.R.S. monthly lecture series going for another couple of years. As UFO talks were bringing in fewer and fewer paying customers, I added other topics, ranging from the conspiracy behind the assassination of John F. Kennedy (which really bombed) through witchcraft to "frozen death" (cryogenic preservation of cadavers in anticipation of life-restoring medical breakthroughs). Most of these events lost money, and so the last of them—fittingly, on frozen death—was held on January 30, 1970, with a huge crowd of eighteen in attendance.

While I was winding down my saucering activities and dreaming and scheming like Donald Trump, a storm broke over the Condon Committee. It's a long and complicated story that has been told very well by others, among them Prof. David Jacobs (*The UFO Controversy in America,* 1975) and Jerome Clark (*The UFO Encyclopedia,* 2d ed., 1998), so I won't bog down this exciting narrative with the details. Suffice to say that internal intrigues, staff firings, and some sensational disclosures in mid-1968, and Condon's own public statements (not to mention his appearance at my convention) combined to create a cloud of serious doubt over the work of the University of Colorado project. UFO groups like NICAP, which had been cooperating with the investigation, publicly broke with Condon, and John Fuller blasted the project in "Flying Saucer Fiasco," a widely read *Look* magazine article (May 14, 1968).

Right in the middle of all this, I was told Dr. Condon was very interested in attending the 1968 National UFO Conference, which was scheduled for Cleveland on June 21–23. According to my diary entry for June 5, 1968,

> I phoned Dr. Condon of the Colorado University UFO investigation this P.M. from the office, and learned that he is definitely coming to the Cleveland Con., and also, surprisingly enough, that he is attracted to,

> and apparently a believer in, the wilder or "fringe" areas of UFO research, i.e., he appears to be genuinely interested in saucer conventions, and thinks that we know something he'd like to find out.

However, despite his emphatic "I'll be there" to me, Condon didn't show up, although about seven hundred others did, and passed a pro-Condon resolution, too.

Still very curious about what Condon had told me, I arranged to interview him when I was in Colorado in early October. Quoting again from my diary (October 3, 1968):

> [I was] up at 9 A.M., to check out of the hotel and get over to Dr. Condon's office at the U. of Colorado, nearby, at about 10. He kept me waiting a few minutes, which did not bother me, but then he kept the interview down to a little over an hour, and said he was busy for lunch and thereafter. He was very guarded in the way he talked, and was polite but not at all cordial or frank in any way. He admitted that he does not trust anyone, including me. Apparently my having engineered the pro-Condon resolution at the Cleveland Convention made no favorable impression on him at all, so my whole long-drawn-out strategy of buttering him up and possibly getting off-the-record information, has fallen through. . . .

I guess for a simple, straightforward saucerer, I was (am?) more of a schemer than I realized! Be that as it may, there's something a little strange about Condon's attitude flip-flop. I'm not suggesting anything nefarious, but it seems to me this is something a Serious Ufologist should look into. Maybe Condon's personal papers hold the answer. It could be he had simply decided to keep his head down until his report, about to be reviewed by a special committee of the National Academy of Sciences, was released. Or perhaps he was onto the Secret of the Saucers, which he was honor-bound not to reveal. If only he had come to Cleveland . . .

In January 1969 the huge report of the Condon Committee (*Scientific Study of Unidentified Flying Objects*) was made public. Those who took time to comb through the report's hundreds of pages—I didn't, but many others have—discovered that a third (!) of the cases investigated remained unexplained, and at least one of these—the McMinnville, Oregon, photo case of May 1950—seemed to have involved a real classic flying saucer. Yet Condon's conclusions and recommendations that led off the report were strongly negative and included these words, which came to frame the media's and the public's impression of the study's results and UFOs in general:

> . . . [T]he emphasis of this study has been on attempting to learn from UFO reports anything that could be considered as adding to scientific knowledge. Our general conclusion is that nothing has come from the study of UFOs in the past 21 years that has added to scientific knowledge. Careful consideration of the record as it is available to us leads us to conclude that further extensive study of UFOs probably cannot be justified in the expectation that science will be advanced thereby.

Saucer fiends like to quote the above words and, justifiably, contrast them with the evidence in the report. Doing so makes one wonder if Condon had read the results of his team's work before sitting down to write. On the other hand, there are these words from the same "Conclusions and Recommendations" section of the report, usually ignored by anti-Condon partisans:

> Scientists are no respecters of authority. Our conclusion that the study of UFO reports is not likely to advance science will not be uncritically accepted by them. Nor should it be, nor do we wish it to be. . . . Our hope is that the details of this report will help other scientists in seeing what the problems are and the difficulties of coping with them.
>
> If they agree with our conclusions, they will turn their valuable attention and talents elsewhere. If they disagree it will be because our report has helped them reach a clear picture of wherein existing studies are faulty or incomplete and thereby will have stimulated ideas for more accurate studies. If they do get such ideas and formulate them clearly, we have no doubt that support will be forthcoming to carry on with such clearly-defined, specific studies. We think that such ideas for work should be supported. . . .
>
> Therefore, we think that all of the agencies of the federal government, and the private foundations as well, ought to be willing to consider UFO research proposals along with the others submitted to them on an open-minded, unprejudiced basis. While we do not think at present that anything worthwhile is likely to come of such research[,] each individual case ought to be considered on its own merits.

Of course, a case can be made that this was just protective cover—wink, wink—and even a subtle warning—wink, wink—to scientists concerned about university tenure and research grants in more conventional areas of science. I'm not sure about this, one way or the other. Whatever really was the case, when the report came out, skeptics rejoiced. Believers fumed. The air force began making plans to shut down Project Blue Book (which it did in December 1969). Public interest in UFOs evaporated almost overnight, and with it went the flow of subscription and dues money on which NICAP and other groups relied and which had fueled publication of UFO books and magazines. NICAP, the largest of the UFO groups, had defined itself in terms of government cover-up and demands for disclosure and an objective investigation. When the Condon report hit, Keyhoe's group seemed no longer to have any purpose for existing. People reasoned that it had gotten what it wanted, the answers were in, and that was that.

The ufological Dark Age was upon us.

For the rest of 1969 and on into 1970, I continued to putter around the fringes of what was left of saucerdom. Gray Barker, Barbara Hudson, and I took in the 1970 Giant Rock affair, a mere ghost of the past. Once again I let Gray talk me into another book—this time by doing all the work himself as my ghostwriter. This was *The Wright Field Story* (1971), an absurdly fictionalized version of my great saucer odyssey of 1953–54 (compare it with the 1950s chapters of this book). As *UFO Crash Secrets at Wright-Patterson Air Force Base* (1991), an even more absurd "updated" version cranked out by Tim Beckley, it is still available to the gullible (autographed copies direct from me, "the author," discounted one dollar). I was never proud of this book, and it's so shockingly *far* from the truth that I literally have never even *read* all of it and probably never will.

For better or worse, in late October 1970 Barker began to peddle *The Wright Field Story* on a prepublication basis. Meanwhile, I was wrapping up my ufological affairs once and for all, or so I thought. The heading on my diary for October 31, 1970 (Halloween!), says it all: "Last day of N.Y.C. office. Am out of the UFO field except for the phony book due out soon through Gray."

But the Space People had other ideas.

Till their own dreams at length deceive 'em,
And oft repeating, they believe 'em.
—Matthew Prior

The nature of things is in the habit of concealing itself.

—Heraclitus

As decades often have a way of doing, the sixties lingered well into the 1970s, not really ending until Richard Nixon finally got the message and resigned his presidency in August 1974. At first, unlike flower power, drugs, love-ins, and the war in Vietnam, it seemed saucers and saucerdom had been left behind, Condon's report a stake through their hearts. At first.

I spent the early seventies engaged mostly in pursing opportunities in real estate (New Jersey apartment buildings), profit in the stock market (in the long run, about breaking even), and limited involvement in the legal sale of pre-Columbian antiquities in the United States, for James Randi, among others. I also hoped to return to Peru for one last treasure hunt, at a certain location I knew about from the old days, but unfortunately this never worked out.

Another of my ventures was a hippie band called, you guessed it, The Flying Saucer. In spring of 1972, I became their booking agent. Neither the band nor I made a dime from the half dozen or so gigs I got them. They always were "auditioning," receiving only tips, if anything. Unlike their namesakes, the Saucer was extremely loud, but that's about all the guys had going for them. It wasn't enough.

When I wasn't cleaning up with these various entrepreneurial undertakings, I traveled, very often with my young daughter, Betty, and frequently including Barbara Hudson. In early 1971 one of my trips took me to a Kentucky Fried Chicken corporate convention in Las Vegas. There I met Colonel Sanders and his wife, a Historic Event made possible because I knew a fellow named Bob Golka, who had dated the Sanderses' daughter, known as the Chicken Queen even though she was a vegetarian. Golka was something of a mad scientist who had spent years investigating ball lightning at his lab in Massachusetts. Eventually, he claimed success in creating it artificially, although I don't know if this was ever verified by real scientists.

A true celebrity I came to know slightly during this period was boxer Muhammad Ali, whom I met for the first time in early December 1970. This was in New York's Central Park, where he went to train around dawn each day. About a week earlier, the newspapers reported Ali had seen a UFO hovering over the park (no, Barbara Hudson wasn't involved), so I thought I would try to talk with him about it. From what he said, the UFO almost certainly was a street light seen through early morning haze or fog. Of course, neither I nor anyone else had the nerve to tell him that!

Obviously, I never quite lost the old saucering bug. I continued as a regular at the annual National UFO Conference gatherings. I also stayed in regular touch with Gray Barker, visiting in Clarksburg and going to various saucer events with him. With the burden of publishing *Saucer News* lifted, saucering was fun again, a diverting hobby, except for the occasional and increasingly rare American Program Bureau lecture. Some of this fun took place at events sponsored by APRO.

SEX and SAUCERS

Coral and Jim Lorenzen's Aerial Phenomena Research Organization, the first major saucering club (founded in January 1952), actually came through the ufological holocaust in reasonably good shape. While Coral—who definitely ran the APRO show—shared the Keyhoe-NICAP suspicions about government cover-up of The Truth, she always was quite outspoken against the NICAP strategy of lobbying for congressional hearings and making a devil of the air force. She thought UFO clubs should devote their limited resources to investigating and publishing information about UFO reports and educating the public about the evidence and The Meaning of It All. This, she thought, not Washington politics, ultimately would crack the Secret of the Saucers.

The Lorenzens and APRO differed from Keyhoe and NICAP in another important way. While they, too, staunchly opposed contactees, they were quite open-minded about stories of "little men," saucer landings, alleged physical evidence, and other more interesting things. APRO's charter declared the group's purpose to be "to promote the eventual enlightenment of the people of the world in regard to the truth of the saucer phenomena—that they are in fact interplanetary vehicles," and said, "Contact with the beings operating them shall be strived [*sic*] for." Still, even the Lorenzens sometimes pulled their punches when it came to really far-out reports, such as the 1957 sex-in-a-saucer case of Brazilian farmer Antonio Villas-Boas. While Coral and Jim privately were fascinated with and convinced of the reality of Villas-Boas's claim to have been forced to have sex (twice!) with a sultry, seductive Space Sister, it was a long while before they went public with it. In general, though, APRO was much more willing than NICAP to stick its neck out.

Both these stances served APRO well when the saucer excitement of the sixties imploded. While membership and subscription revenues dropped off, they held up better than NICAP's, and in fact, many NICAPers jumped ship and joined APRO when things turned bad. So it was that, despite a severely crippling mass defection in mid-1969 (stay tuned), APRO became the mainstay of American ufology through the Dark Days of the early 1970s.

None of this is to say there was any love lost between Coral Lorenzen and me. Coral was opinionated, prejudiced, and just not a very nice person—but she *was* a hoot to drink with, and once matched me martini for martini, though she claimed she only got drunk at saucercons. It is amazing to me that Coral was the head of a major UFO organization for such a long time (maybe it was her capacity for martinis that made the difference). As for Jim, I met him only once, and he seemed quite nice, a fact others have confirmed to me.

Coral pretty much ignored me and my saucering activities throughout most of her lifetime, but back in the 1950s, I subscribed to two press-clipping services, one U.S. and the other international, the latter including coverage of England, France, and Spain. Thus I received more original material on the wild 1954 French little-men and saucer-landing flap than anyone else, at least in American ufology. I used what I wanted in *Saucer News* and then sent the clippings on to APRO.

As far as I know, the Lorenzens had no other access to these news accounts, and I mailed them big batches over a period of a few years. Coral never thanked me or even acknowledged receipt of this material, but it seems obvious that she used my clips as important sources for the *A.P.R.O. Bulletin* and her several quite successful books.

Well, actually, it may be only shockingly close to true that Coral never thanked me. I met her just a couple of times, at saucercons in the seventies, and I remember once asking her about the clippings. She merely said, "Oh, I thought we *did* thank you for that," or something to that effect. Was that a thank you, or at least shockingly close to one?

I think it unlikely this exchange took place the first time Coral and I met, this in January 1971 at an APRO convention in Baltimore, which I attended with Gray Barker. Allen Hynek was one of the featured speakers, and Gray and I somehow had persuaded him to meet with us privately after his talk, which he gave during the last, "secret" session of the con. Not being among Coral's favored few, Gray and I were excluded from this session. Naturally, having had a "few" drinks, we tried to crash it. This led to a very loud argument with a couple of APRO minions, who were guarding the meeting room door. In short order, Coral joined the fray and things got very nasty. I decided not to risk putting Hynek off by continuing the argument and persuaded Gray that discretion was the better part of valor.

We retreated and waited for Hynek across the hotel lobby—in the bar, of course. When the good doctor emerged from the meeting room, he was surrounded by fans, whom we had to escape if we were to have any privacy for our talk. I think it was I who suggested we go off the premises.

I didn't know the area, but was aware there were a couple of bars within a block of the hotel. It was a somewhat seedy neighborhood, and the place we went to turned out to be a B-girl joint, with loud music and all the other usual charms of such an establishment. The three of us went to a corner table, hoping not to be noticed and where Gray and I could hear Hynek, who spoke very softly.

Unfortunately, business was slow. As we talked, Hynek smoked his ever-present pipe, and I was somewhat horribly embarrassed when one of the girls sauntered over and, when she couldn't get our attention, sat down in Hynek's lap. I immediately wondered how on earth he, or we, would deal with this, but thanks to Hynek, it all turned out well.

There was no scene, no indignant outcry from the distinguished astronomer-ufologist. Hynek just kept puffing on his pipe and talking quietly, as if nothing unusual were going on. The woman finally shot him a puzzled and shocked look—as if to say, "My God! Are you *dead*?"—and flounced away in a huff.

Sex and saucers!

REVOLT in the HEARTLAND

Although I can't prove it, the NICAPers who joined APRO in 1969 seem to have been fifth columnists (not to be confused with my Esteemed Coauthor, who is *Saucer Smear's* Fifth Columnist). If they didn't start out that way, they soon became such. In May 1969, a large contingent of APROians, the majority former NICAPers, walked out of APRO and formed the Midwest (soon Mutual) UFO Network under the leadership of Walter Andrus, upon whom they bestowed the glorious title International Director. One of the few Serious Ufologists to claim a UFO sighting—a formation of four oddly behaving silver disks over downtown Phoenix in 1948—Andrus had been an APRO field investigator for about five years and was some sort of regional leader in Illinois at the time of the Great Defection.

Various unresolved grievances and doctrinal differences were cited as reasons for the revolt, but I think it had more to do with personality conflicts, old organizational animosities, and personal ambition than anything ufologically noble. I doubt many old NICAPers were comfortable under the leadership of Coral Lorenzen, whom many considered the wicked witch of the west (APRO was headquartered in Tucson, Arizona). On top of that, based on my experience with Andrus over the years, I'd say he probably really lusted to be *the* big fish in organized ufology's small pond, a role he delighted in for more than three decades before stepping down from the MUFON throne in July 2000.

Outwardly an affable doofus, Walt is a shrewd character. He ruled MUFON with an iron hand, even, I'm told, deftly fending off a number of coup attempts over the years. He personally picked all the state directors and many of the lesser officials, and he kept a close eye on who was applying for and admitted to membership. Me, for instance. I first tried to join MUFON in 1974, only to be turned down by Walt on the unanimous recommendation of the MUFON board. Later, Lucius Farish, one of the board members and a longtime Arkansas ufologist, told me he, at least, felt rumors of my involvement in hoaxes, my phony feud with Barker, and other "fun and games" disqualified me from membership. Some years later, Walt relented, and as I will reveal in due course, I rose to great MUFONic heights.

It wasn't long after the MUFONite exodus from APRO that most former NICAP leading and lesser lights had affiliated with MUFON. However, ufology was still in the doldrums, with no dramatic new sightings or other developments to capture the public imagination and keep all but truly hard-core saucerers actively involved in The Field. So, while MUFON was well organized and definitely Serious, it had little to do but collect dues and send its monthly journal, *Skylook*—now, redundantly, the *MUFON UFO Journal*—to its membership, which had settled at but a few hundred, as had APRO's.

Then the Claw Men landed.

THEM AIN'T NO CRAWDADS, CALVIN!

At about nine on the evening of October 11, 1973, Mississippi shipyard workers Charles Hickson and Calvin Parker were fishing from a pier on the banks of the Pascagoula River. Little did they know, or so they later claimed, that someone or something was fishing for *them.*

Alerted by what he described as a "zipping sound," Hickson spotted a large (the size varied in Hickson and Parker's tellings), domed, football-shaped object dropping down from the night sky. The UFO, with two windows and bright blue lights, descended until it was hovering about two feet above a level area thirty to forty yards behind the two fishermen.

As the two men watched, a hatch opened and three weird, identical beings about five feet tall floated out and toward Hickson and Parker. In *UFO Contact at Pascagoula,* a book he coauthored in 1983, Hickson described the robotlike things this way:

> The head seemed to come directly to the shoulders, no neck, and something resembling a nose came out to a point about two inches long. On each side of the head, about where the ears would be was something similar to a nose. Directly under the nose was a slit resembling a mouth. The arms were something like human arms, but long in proportion to the body; the hands resembled a mitten, there was a thumb attached [he originally compared them to crab or lobster claws]. The legs

> remained together and the feet looked something like elephant's feet. The entire body was wrinkled and had a greyish color. There could have been eyes, but the area above the nose was so wrinkled I couldn't tell.

Two of these Claw Men grabbed Hickson by the arms, and he felt a stinging sensation where a claw clamped down on his left arm, after which he became numb and paralyzed, but still remained conscious. Parker had fainted dead away, and the third being held his limp body. According to Hickson, the whole party then floated into the saucer, where his and, probably, Parker's bodies were examined by a football-sized floating mechanical eye. Afterward, the two hapless good ol' boys were floated back to the dock and unceremoniously dumped (Earth seems to be a catch-and-release area). Their captors then quickly whooshed back to their craft and zipped off into the night sky. As they did so, a telepathic message was beamed to Hickson: "We are peaceful. We meant you no harm."

After debating what to do while Hickson knocked back a few slugs of whiskey, the two men wound up at the Jackson County Sheriff's office, where they told their story and insisted they wanted no publicity. The next day at work in the Walker Shipyard, Hickson received a call from the sheriff, who demanded that he and Parker come to his office immediately. It was full of reporters who insisted on interviewing them.

The story hit the national news wires, and the next day Pascagoula was alive with reporters from all over the country. Two ufologists also showed up, Dr. Hynek and James Harder, an engineering professor at the University of California and an APRO consultant. Hynek, no longer an air force UFO consultant and now firmly convinced that UFOs were something real and important, was there on his own, on behalf of what he came to call his "invisible college," scientists, engineers, and other technical people with whom he was quietly studying UFO reports. Harder was representing APRO. After interviewing Hickson and Parker and some unsuccessful attempts by Harder to hypnotize them, the two ufologists held a joint press conference. Both said they were convinced of the men's sincerity. It wasn't quite a ringing endorsement of their story, but that's how the press played it. Subsequent investigations by UFO skeptic Phil Klass and others raised many reasonable doubts about this case. But that was quite a bit later. The Great Flap of 1973–74 was on.

SOMETHING DIFFERENT

Saucers were back—and often up close, too close for comfort. Over the next few months, there were many bizarre landing and creature reports, and just a week after the Claw Men pinched Hickson and Parker, an Ohio Army National Guard helicopter crew claimed to have had a spectacular near-collision with a huge UFO in the night sky near Mansfield, Ohio. This wayward hot-rod saucer and the Claw Men really captured the public imagination and I think fairly can be said to characterize the flap, especially the Mississippi weirdness.

I had the sense that there was something different about this return of the saucers. Proportionately, there were many more reports of landings, strange beings, and very close encounters than in past flaps (in the United States, at least). Oh, yes, and the U.S. Air Force was missing in action. Having closed down Project Blue Book in December 1969, it stayed out of the fray. All investigations and pronouncements, pro- and anti-UFO, were made by private groups and individuals, and I'll bet that, in base officer's clubs all over the world, a lot of top air force people were drinking toasts to their good luck.

There was joy in saucerdom, too. APRO's membership surged, almost getting back to where it was during the Good Old Days of the pre-Condon-report sixties, and the Lorenzens' conventions were very popular and, I assume, financially successful. Upstart MUFON really boomed, growing by leaps and bounds and drawing a lot of interested volunteers from scientific and technical ranks, all this giving it the boost it needed to establish itself as the number-one UFO club. Even NICAP experienced a minor lift, although not anything like those of the other clubs.

In general, the public and media attitude seemed to be much more receptive to saucer reports than at any time before. The same was true of the inevitably renewed claims that the government knew The Truth but was concealing it. This probably had something to do with the Watergate scandal and revelations about the Vietnam War that were then current and on everyone's minds and lips. If that kind of thing was going on, why not a saucer cover-up? Whatever the reasons, there appeared to be a much broader constituency for saucer tales than ever before.

In late 1973 there was a development that suggested ufology *might* be growing up. Allen Hynek and Chicago businessman and longtime saucerer Sherman Larsen launched the Center for UFO Studies, the first real attempt to set up a private research group genuinely dedicated to scientific investigations and study of UFOs. Hynek and Larsen's organization wasn't a saucer club and, for a while, wasn't open to general membership. Participation was restricted to scientists and other professionals who donated their time and expertise, Hynek's invisible college. This wouldn't last—though CUFOS has—but it was a wonderful idea.

The flap also brought to the fore a "new Menzel": Philip J. Klass. Trained as an electrical engineer, Klass was an award-winning senior editor of the prestigious magazine *Aviation Week and Space Technology*. He had first become interested in UFOs in 1966, when almost by chance he picked up and read John Fuller's *Incident at Exeter*. Based on what Fuller wrote and his own study of another classic tome, NICAP's *UFO Evidence* (1964), Phil at first was convinced people were seeing something truly anomalous—but nothing from outer space. Because so many of the sightings reported by Fuller had occurred over or very near high-tension power lines, Phil concluded UFOs were ball lightning and free-floating plasma discharges. He first mentioned this idea in 1966, in an *Aviation Week* article, and then expanded on it in his first UFO book, *UFOs Identified* (1968), in which he also outlined his doubts about some of saucerdom's leading figures and their thinking. This was the early "kinder, gentler" Phil Klass, but it wasn't long before we got a taste of the arch-debunker whom for decades all Serious and Not-So-Serious Ufologists have loved to hate.

When Phil's ball lightning and plasma UFOs quickly were shot down by top scientists—including the Condon Committee—his attitudes hardened, and he mounted a major attack on his leading critic, highly respected atmospheric physicist James McDonald, who was the most vocal and vigorous scientific UFO proponent of the time (Hynek hadn't yet come all the way out of the closet). Phil tried to prove McDonald had misused Office of Naval Research (ONR) grant funds for his UFO investigations, sending a blizzard of letters to the navy and fellow journalists demanding action. This went on for a year and a half before a navy audit completely exonerated McDonald. Despite this, the physicist never again received any ONR research grants, probably because the bureaucrats were afraid Klass might stir up more trouble, perhaps even using the pages of the influential *Aviation Week* to do so.

By 1973 Phil was a confirmed "no-prisoners" UFO skeptic and had all but taken over from Menzel as Debunker Numero Uno. On October 23 of that year he told a United Press reporter that "there simply is not a shred of physical evidence [for UFOs] after more than 25 years of sightings. Quite literally. Not a shred, in any of tens of thousands of UFO sightings that have been reported, that you could take before the National Academy of Sciences and ask: 'Have you ever seen its like on Earth?' " The title of his second UFO book, published in 1974, summed up his certainty on the subject: *UFOs Explained.*

In the years since, Phil has written four more anti-UFO tomes and founded and led the Committee for the Scientific Investigation of Claims of the Paranormal's dreaded UFO Subcommittee (now, I believe, just a subcommittee of one: Phil). In recent years he has written and published the informative and amusing bimonthly *Skeptics UFO Newsletter* (*SUN*), done in the same eight-page format as my *Saucer Smear* but (usually) more dignified. When pressed, most leading ufologists will admit that, unlike so many other debunkers, Phil really knows the subject and the people involved in it, and he's even welcomed or at least pleasantly tolerated at major UFO gatherings, in his words, as "the skunk at the garden party."

Because Phil and I are friends, and because we agree on many things ufological, there are those in saucerdom who consider me a "Klass Klone." Nothing could be further from the truth. We have had and continue to have intense doctrinal and factual disagreements, and there are things about Phil's "style," like his attack on McDonald, that I do not admire or agree with. Nevertheless, unlike most other ufologists, I *do* believe Phil is sincere in his views and that even with his excesses, his work ultimately is beneficial to The Field. Every religion needs a devil. Phil is ufology's. I don't know anyone capable of even coming close to replacing him.

TO MAT or DEMAT, THAT IS the QUESTION

Also mixed into the new saucer stew were several way-out takes on the nature and origin of UFOs, which, given a tuck here and there, finally led me to my semi-serious 4-D Theory. Back in the 1940s, Meade Layne and his Borderland Sciences Research Associates pushed the idea that the saucers were "ether ships" and their occupants "etherians" from a vibrational plane (whatever that means) different from ours. They could "mat" and "demat," that is, materialize and dematerialize, enter and depart our vibrational plane by lowering and raising their vibes (or whatever). When saucers "just appeared!" and "just disappeared!" they were bipping back and forth between their parallel, alternative universe (or wherever) and ours. This notion didn't catch on except in the most far-out fringes of saucerdom, but it was always there in one form or another, hanging around waiting for someone to notice.

Then, in the 1960s, John Keel came along with his idea that UFOs and UFO beings were "ultraterrestrial," hailing from the "superspectrum," all of which he semi-admitted was not much more than Layne's notions dressed up in different terms. Keel's ultraterrestrials—and these included the MIB—were malevolent, were toying with us, were certainly *sort of* real, but not in the "nuts and bolts" sense.

About the same time, Jacques Vallée, a close associate of Allen Hynek, began advancing similar views. He threw out all sorts of theories, one of them being that via the myths, rumors, and beliefs it generated, the UFO phenomenon is "a regulator of man's development," employed by some superintelligence beyond our understanding. Unlike Keel, Vallée didn't seem to be sure if this intelligence was benign or evil. Maybe it was a little of both. Writer Brad Steiger, on the other hand, took a New Age take on things, sweetness and light. The saucer beings definitely were here to help us, non- or semi-material versions of the Space Brothers of the 1950s.

Then there was the really far-out "New Wave" idea that the saucers were psychic projections willed into existence by the human mind, either individually or by humankind's collective unconscious. Better yet, this wasn't limited to conjuring up a few saucers and little men. There was no such thing as objective reality. What we called reality was just a product of mind, and the universe or any part of it we'd like could be rebuilt, wiped out, spiffed up, just by wishing it. Subjective ufology. Whee!

Even in mainstream ufology, many found ideas like these attractive. Decades had gone by since Kenneth Arnold's sighting, and no saucer from another planet had landed on the White House lawn. Maybe it was time to consider other explanations. Jerome Clark bought into some version of 4-D for a while, although, now safely back in nuts-and-bolts land, he's reluctant to admit it. Allen Hynek also opened up to 4-D thinking, but with the careful, thoughtful approach of a scientist considering still not quite settled hypotheses. The old saucers-from-space idea was slipping, and things were getting wild. Whee!

But nuts and bolts are tough.

"ANY DAY NOW" and the CRASHED SAUCER COMEBACK

For some reason, the flap of 1973–74 brought an almost euphoric sense of optimism to the ranks of saucerers. New revelations were just around the corner—not from the Space People, but from the U.S. government. Early in 1974, in their book *Beyond Earth: Man's Contact With UFOs,* Ralph (who had covered the Claw Men case for *Cosmopolitan*!) and Judy Blum boldly declared, "We predict that by 1975 the government will release definite proof that extraterrestrials are watching us."

A few months later, on August 25, that paragon of responsible journalism the *National Tattler* ran an interview with APRO's Jim (not Coral) Lorenzen, in which he claimed, "A program has been undertaken that will over the next few months make it obvious that the government has reversed its position . . . [and] will release all its information [on UFOs] within the next three years." This would be done so officialdom "won't be left with a red face, again lessening government credibility," and to avoid panic, the shocking truth would be made known "little by little."

Then there was somebody named Robert Berry, head of something called the Twentieth Century UFO Bureau, who was quoted in the Canadian tabloid *Midnight* (October 25, 1975): "The government will tell us what's been going on, in a series of television documentaries over a period of months. . . . The entire story is slated to be disclosed by the 200th anniversary of independence on July 4, 1976."

Of course, these and other such predictions fizzled, but the idea that Something Big was coming didn't die—or rather, become dormant—until late 1977, when newly elected President Jimmy Carter failed to tear away the cloak of secrecy as saucer fiends had hoped he would. During the 1976 campaign Carter had revealed he'd seen a saucer (years later shown to have been Venus), so saucerers thought one of the first things he would do after being sworn in was demand to know and then make public The Truth. As it turned out, it was only after a major newsmagazine repeated a version of one of the "any day now" predictions that the White House asked NASA to check things out. Of course, NASA punted, and that was the end of that (for a while).

One of those making predictions of coming disclosures was a character named Robert Carr, a retired University of South Florida professor of mass communications and NICAP's southern director. During a press conference on October 15, 1974, Carr went everyone else one better. He opened by saying, "Five weeks ago I heard from the highest authority in

Washington that before Christmas the whole UFO cover-up will be ended. There will be public admission that UFOs always have been real, and that for the past twenty-five years the United States government and the Air Force have known they were piloted by humanlike beings." Carr then went on to claim certain knowledge that two saucers had been captured in 1948 near Aztec and Farmington, New Mexico. These and twelve alien bodies found aboard were stashed in, yes, Hangar 18 at Wright-Patterson Air Force Base, Ohio.

Of course, this was just an embellished version of the Scully-Newton yarn from 1950, but practically everyone outside of saucerdom didn't know or had long since forgotten that tale, and Carr's story made a big though brief splash. Even some people inside The Field wondered if there wasn't something to it, and consideration of crashed saucer retrieval stories began to regain respectability. Looking back, it seems to me this may have been a reaction to the 4-D weirdness that was going around. Even those, like Jerry Clark, who were drawn to 4-D were uneasy about it. The prospect of physical proof of flying saucers being hardware from Out There was a lifeline back to 3-D reality for them.

Then one of the grand old men of The Field who had continued to be active but out of the limelight staged a comeback. In 1977 Leonard Stringfield's *Situation Red: The UFO Siege* was published. One of the accounts in Len's book was that of a "Fritz Werner," who claimed to have been in on a saucers-and-bodies retrieval near Kingman, Arizona, in 1953. Werner's story, too, had all sorts of telltale similarities to the original Aztec hoax, but Len didn't seem to notice. Unlike Carr, whom most Serious Ufologists considered at least a bit suspect, Stringfield was highly respected, so the Werner account was taken seriously.

This was only the beginning. Len Stringfield would soon start unveiling many more saucer "crash/retrieval" stories. Maybe I should have told him about this one (diary entry, December 22, 1975): "I received a letter today from someone who claims that years ago, as a member of [I didn't have this "quite" right] the National Security Council, he learned of the existence of a captured UFO and a dead 'little man.' This sort of rumor was common when I first got interested in UFOs in 1953 and thereafter, but this is the first I've heard of captured little men in recent years. The letter sounded unusually sane, and maybe I'll eventually learn something. I answered the man tonight. . . ."

Len and all ufology would find out about this character and his story soon enough. Most of us wish we never had.

We are all born mad. Some remain so.

—Samuel Beckett

The saucers—crashed and otherwise—and Len Stringfield weren't the only ufological comebacks of the mid-1970s. In 1976, to the chagrin of more than a few Serious Ufologists, I returned to saucer publishing.

In mid-February, I mailed the first issue of what evolved into today's *Saucer Smear* to about one hundred friends and saucerers whose addresses I still had from the old days. This two-pager—the second page a letter from John Keel mailed from "The Bermuda Triangle" and signed "A Former Friend"—was the *Saucer News Non-Scheduled Newsletter,* vol. 23, no. 16 ("Official Publication of the Saucer and Unexplained Celestial Events Research Society"), merging *Saucer News* and its "news too hot to handle" companion into a single scandal sheet. Six years had passed since the last issue of the old *Saucer News* had been published, vol. 17, no. 1, so in a bow of sorts to consistency (and confusion), and assuming one volume per year, I began anew with volume 23 (I'm not at liberty to reveal why the first issue in the volume was numbered 16).

The given reason—excuse—for this lapse of semisanity was to announce and begin promotion of the thirteenth annual National UFO Conference, but I threatened to continue cranking the thing out: "This then, is the 'long-awaited' (by whom?) first issue in a new series of nonscheduled newsletters, to be published *free* as frequently as apathy drives us to it. At times we will be serious, at times we will attempt to be facetious, and at times we will not be certain whether we are being serious *or* facetious, and you will have to make up your own minds." As the three hundred or so loyal *Smear* nonsubscribers (admitted readers) and many more haters (closet readers) know, I made good on these threats (except the "free" part: love offerings now gleefully accepted). I have continued to publish approximately once a month ever since, very early on settling into the eight-page format I'm using today. (Shameless solicitation of new nonsubscribers: *Saucer Smear*, PO Box 1709, Key West, FL 33041-1709. Make love offerings payable to James W. Moseley.)

"WHAT'S in a NAME?"

While I settled on my newsletter's size after just a few issues, its name took quite a bit longer to fall into place. It will be recalled that I'd sold *Saucer News*, S.A.U.C.E.R.S., and everything associated with them to Gray Barker in early 1968, and he continued erratic publication of *Saucer News* and its supplemental newsletter for a couple of years after that. Of course, Gray strenuously objected (wink, wink) to my presumptuous reappropriation of the *Saucer News* name, and so on. So my second issue (March 15, 1976) carried both Gray's fulminating letter of pseudo-objections and this title banner:

THIS NEWSLETTER IS *NOT* to BE CONFUSED with *SAUCER NEWS*

I called the succeeding issue *Saucer Muse*, the next, ("This Is a Magazine to Inform You About") *New Saucers*, and so on through such semi-amusing gems as *Saucer Gnus*, *Saucre News*, *Saucer Stews* ("For the Ufological Gourmet"), *Saucer Leer*, *Saucer Gear* ("Dedicated to All of the 'Nuts and Bolts' Theorists"), *Saucer Crud*, and *Saucer Stud*. At last, with the July

15, 1981, issue (vol. 28, no. 7), *Saucer Smear*, a name I'd first used six months before, became our Glorious Name for Life, capturing the true essence of our motto: "Dedicated to the Highest Principles of Ufological Journalism." I *definitely* was back into ufoology (*not* a typo).

SAUCER SCOOP(ERS) HAPPENING

The timing of my comeback couldn't have been better. A week after I mailed my first issue, I read about now (in)famous ufologist-abductionist Budd Hopkins's first case. Rather than a UFO abduction, it was, amazingly, a throwback to the good old days of saucering: a landing or near-landing complete with little men doing incongruously ordinary things. According to an article by Hopkins in the March 1, 1976, *Village Voice* (on the stands February 25), this took place in North Bergen, New Jersey, at a spot barely a mile from where I was then living in Fairview (and about the same distance from Times Square!). I drove past it almost daily in connection with business at an apartment building I owned in nearby Guttenberg. Of course, I immediately began poking around.

The witness was seventy-two-year-old North Bergen resident George O'Barski. He was co-owner of a liquor store in Manhattan's Greenwich Village, across the street from Budd Hopkins's residence. I telephoned O'Barski a couple of days after I read Hopkins's article, and he said he'd have to "clear it with Budd" before we could meet in person. Hopkins, an artist whom I'd never heard of before, was one of O'Barski's regular customers. In November 1975, when the store owner learned Hopkins was interested in UFOs because of a sighting he'd had himself in 1964, he told the artist what he supposedly witnessed in the wee hours of a January 1975 morning, likely but not certainly the twelfth. Prior to this, O'Barski had told only his son, who'd advised him to keep quiet about what he claimed to have seen. The next day, Hopkins contacted well-known ufologist Ted Bloecher, one of the founders of the old Civilian Saucer Intelligence of New York, of which I briefly was president in 1954. Bloecher and Hopkins then launched an investigation, the results of which Hopkins wrote up for the *Voice*.

Apparently O'Barski got Hopkins's okay to see me, because we got together on February 29, a couple of days after our telephone conversation. He seemed like the least imaginative guy one could imagine—old, an immigrant from eastern Europe, not too bright, low-key, not obviously eccentric in any way, and a teetotaler—and although his story was wild, he seemed to believe it and still be frightened as he recalled it. Of course, by the time I met with O'Barski, he already had received a great deal of publicity in newspapers and on television in the New York City area and was under Hopkins's control. So we really can't be certain how much to trust his story. Although I can't prove it, if any of it was made up or, more likely, embellished, I would bet Hopkins was responsible in some way.

Anyway, O'Barski told me he'd left his store about 1 A.M., and at about 2 A.M., as he was driving home through North Hudson Park in North Bergen, heavy static began crackling on his car radio. Then he spotted a lighted, egg- or domed-saucer-shaped object gliding down through the trees. At first, it hovered about ten feet above an open expanse of grass and not more than sixty feet from the right side of the road O'Barski was on. It was making a sound "like a refrigerator that's starting up." Within seconds, a ladder of some kind dropped down from the side of the UFO facing O'Barski, a door opened above it, and about a dozen uniformed figures about three and a half feet tall quickly descended to the ground, "like kids coming down a fire escape. . . . They looked like little kids in snowsuits." The saucer then slowly settled to the ground or to a point just above it.

O'Barski kept his car moving slowly as he watched, but the little men (or "kids") paid no attention to him. Each of them carried a large spoon-like tool and a little bag with a handle. "They were working like little beavers, you know?" and seemed to be digging up soil and grass samples. "It was three minutes and they must've scooted up. As I say, they got out before it landed, got filled up, and by the time it landed, they got back in, right? And they took off. It was that quick. I hear this droning, you know? And I notice this thing . . . it just took off . . . and there was no propellers on it, or nothing! It just seemed to float, but boy! It went just like that! . . . And all I know is to get the hell out of that park. I was goddamn scared."

O'Barski claimed he went back the next day, "Because I didn't believe it looking at them. . . . I thought I was dreaming. So I went back there and there were all these little holes in the ground. They were about four, five inches wide, maybe six deep. I even felt the holes, right? Because I didn't believe it looking at them. Well, then I was even more scared, you know?" According to Hopkins and Bloecher (*Proceedings of the 1976 CUFOS Conference*), in November 1975 they found "12 to 15 small triangular spots in thick, untrampled turf where the sod, roots and all, was missing. Each spot was slightly depressed, exactly what one would expect after ten months; while rain had gradually refilled the holes, the roots still had not grown back into the spots." (*Only* little spacemen could have made these, right?)

Hopkins and Bloecher began looking for corroborating witnesses and found an all-night doorman at the Stonehenge, a thirty-story, circular (!) apartment building about one thousand feet from the alleged landing site. The man claimed to have seen the landing and that, as the UFO was passing overhead, some sort of projectile (which never was found) had broken the plate-glass window in the building's foyer.

After interviewing O'Barski, I visited the Stonehenge and learned that not quite six weeks before and almost exactly a year after O'Barski's sighting, there supposedly was another landing at the same place in the park, this witnessed by several Stonehenge employees. I also learned that almost all the staff and many residents claimed to have made unusual sightings in recent months, all this during a period when, in the wake of Hopkins's article about O'Barski, the local papers and television news shows were filled with stories of saucer sightings in the same general area.

But I had an exclusive. Supposedly, on at least three nights in February 1976, members of the Stonehenge night staff had seen a mysterious figure wandering in the area of North Hudson Park nearest their building. I interviewed these witnesses, one of whom described the figure as about five feet tall, wearing a helmet with a light mounted on it, like a miner's helmet. This mystery being avoided streetlights, walked in a robotlike manner, and was constantly bending down in an awkward way, apparently to pick things up from the ground. The face was invisible because of darkness, and the figure seemed to look up at the sky a lot. Because the being wasn't on Stonehenge property, the three employees just stayed inside the building's foyer and watched him make his rounds. The police were not called, either because of the New York City area's infamous mind-your-own-business rule or, perhaps, because the figure was a figment of overactive imaginations. Whatever was going on, if anything, it quietly set the stage for the far from quiet culminating affair of the Great Stonehenge Mini-Flap of 1975–76.

This was a "media event" for which I was not responsible, but which I helped facilitate. In early March, I got a call from Tim Beckley. He told me of an impending visit to New York by Warren Freiberg, then a well-known Chicago radio personality who had interviewed me years before, and his wife, Libby, a trance medium. Beckley said that, at midnight on March 6, he and Harold Salkin, a New Age writer and publicist of sorts, were going to stage a "happening" at the O'Barski landing site in North Hudson Park, complete with an attempt by the Freibergs to communicate psychically with the Space People. Since my Fairview apartment was close to the park, Beckley and Salkin wanted to use it for a prehappening press conference the same evening. Of course, I couldn't resist, and thus it was that I had my first "delightful" contact with Budd Hopkins.

On March 6, I drove to midtown Manhattan to pick up Beckley, Salkin, and the Freibergs, then headed back to my place in Fairview, with a carload of Beckley and Salkin's friends following. We arrived about eight-thirty, and the press started showing up an hour later. As a courtesy, I decided to phone Budd Hopkins and invite him to join us. This was the first he'd heard of the event, and he was furious—at me. I tried to explain I was by no means the organizer, but Hopkins wasn't listening. He *demanded* that I kick Beckley and everyone else out of my apartment, and if I didn't, he would see to it that I never published anything again, anywhere, period. He meant it.

I was absolutely stunned by this threat, and I have never forgotten or forgiven Hopkins for it. I suppose this outburst was an example of his artistic temperament, which doesn't belong in science, even a semi-science like ufology. I will admit Hopkins is a better artist than he is a scientific ufologist-abductionist, although I'm not favorably impressed with him in either regard. We've had little contact over the years since our first contact that strange night in 1976, and I think we both like it that way (I know I do). However, a bit over twenty years later, at the 1996 National UFO Conference, we came shockingly close to making up. One evening in the convention hotel's cocktail lounge, at the urging of Jerry Clark, Hopkins came up to me where I was sitting at the bar with my Esteemed Coauthor (remember, Karl?). As I reported in *Saucer Smear,* he "was gentlemanly enough to shake hands with your editor, with an offer to 'bury the hatchet' regarding our well-known posture of not speaking to each other at all. Thus, in the interests of détente, we will not review *Witnessed* [Hopkins's then-recently published book] herein." Me hold a grudge? Of course not.

But that was in 1996. In 1976, following the press conference, our jolly crew piled into several cars and drove to North Hudson Park, ahead of the midnight happening hour announced in the local newspapers. We were met not only by more media people, but by a mob of about five hundred mostly Hispanic teenagers out for a Saturday night good time. In spite of the taunting, somewhat hostile crowd, the Freibergs bravely trudged out to the landing site. There we formed a circle around them, chanting at their request, "Alpha! Omega!" From the surrounding mob there arose the rival chant, "Frisbee! Frisbee!"—and other inharmonious phrases.

The noise level grew, and the crowd closed in around us. Then (whew!) everyone's attention suddenly was diverted by the distant sight of someone decked out in a tinfoil outfit, trotting along carrying a flare. Our fickle "fans" rushed over to investigate, and some of us took the opportunity to head quickly in the opposite direction and regroup in the foyer of the Stonehenge.

Unfortunately, the Freibergs didn't follow us, but instead ran to one of our cars. Having lost the "spaceman" in the darkness, the crowd started looking around for more fun, spotted the Freibergs, swarmed over, and began pounding on and rocking the car. Somehow, Warren managed to drive safely out of the mess, and a short time later showed up at the Stonehenge, where one of the staff allowed us to go up on the roof. There, high in the cold air and a bit nearer outer space, the Freibergs finally held a rather pathetic séance in which an entity named Colderin (what?) allegedly came through. Through Libby Freiberg, he revealed that his people, the Grapalins, were here to encourage us to save our environment—thus the digging in the park the year before (of course!). He also promised that the Grapalins would return on July 4 and hover over Times Square, apparently in honor of the bicentennial of the Declaration of Independence. (They didn't make it.)

I wonder what George O'Barski—or for that matter, his little men—made of that weird night? Too bad Budd missed all the fun. Or was that him in the tinfoil? . . .

A FATEFUL 3½-D INTERLUDE

On the weekend of June 24–26, 1977, exactly ten years after my still-record-holding New York saucercon, *Fate* magazine staged the First International UFO Congress, again keying on the anniversary of Kenneth Arnold's Sacred Sighting. This event—by its name clearly intended to be the first of many such, but, alas, fated to be the only one—was held at Chicago's Pick-Congress Hotel. It was far better organized and far more sedate (yawn) than mine. However, the attendance didn't come close, and my record held.

I arrived the day before the convention, and was somewhat surprised to find one of my former S.A.U.C.E.R.S. lecture series speakers on the airport bus with me. As we crawled through downtown traffic, Stella Lansing, psychic UFO photographer, was using her ever-present movie camera to take shots of neon lights along the way. I wondered if these lights would later appear as UFOs in some production of Lansing's—a mystery, like the Saucer Mystery itself, not yet cleared up.

ugust C. Roberts, ca. 1961. Augie, "the Flying aucer Photographer," introduced me to saucerlom and was a cofounder of *Saucer News. (Saucer News)*

Dominick (aka Dominic) C. Lucchesi (right) and I, ca. 1955, conducting highly scientific ESP experiments. Dom joined Augie Roberts and me in founding *Saucer News. (Saucer News)*

oseph Barbieri, Connecticut saucerer, points to a ole made in a New Haven, Connecticut., signboard 1953 by a mysterious flying object—a true FO. This case was my first in-depth saucer invesgation. *(August C. Roberts/Saucer News/Tom Benson)*

The semi-mysterious "Dr. D" and Albert K. Bender at a party in my New Jersey apartment, ca. 1964. In 1953 Bender's claim to have been hushed up by three mysterious Men in Black launched one of the most enduring ufological myths. And Dr. D? Well . . . See chap. 5. *(James W. Moseley)*

In 1950 Maj. Donald E. Keyhoe, USMC (ret.) told the world flying saucers were real and from outer space. He was Serious Ufology's top spokesperson during the 1950s and 1960s. *(Saucer News/Tom Benson)*

Keyhoe and I didn't see eye to eye, but here som one or something (a MIB?) seems to be eyeing hi secretly—or maybe Keyhoe was just doing som saucer snooping the old-fashioned way. *(Micha G.Mann/Saucer News)*

Georgia farmer Ralph Horton shows me the "flying saucer" that landed in his yard in July 1952, suspiciously like the one that crashed near Roswell, New Mexico, in 1947. If I'd only know this at the time! *(James W. Moseley/Saucer News)*

"Professor" George Adamski—*the* flying sauc contactee—with a portrait of Orthon, the Venusia Space Brother he claimed to have met on the Ca fornia desert in November 1952. *(Timothy Gree Beckley/James W. Moseley)*

Doctor" George Hunt Williamson (aka Michel 'Obrenovic and Brother Philip), one of the wit-esses to George Adamski's alleged 1952 "desert ontact" with a spaceman and a highly controver-ial figure in 1950s saucerdom. *(Saucer News/Tom enson)*

Gray Barker, ca. 1967. Barker was one of the leading figures of early saucerdom, one of ufology's most controversial characters, and my best friend. *(Tom Benson)*

ray Barker impersonates the famed Flatwoods onster of West Virginia, very near the scene of e bizarre 1952 encounter. Note scratches, nich may (or may not) have been made by the onster. See chapter 5. *(James W. Moseley)*

I am caught in the act of perpetrating another exciting issue of *Saucer News*, ca. 1955. *(James W. Moseley)*

Hot on the trail of ancient treasure and saucers in Peru, 1954. See chapter 6. *(James W. Moseley)*

Adventurer and writer Ken Krippine and frier somewhere in Peru, 1954. Krippine and I were write a UFO book together, but we had a fallir out in the Amazonian wilds. *(James W. Moseley)*

Loot! Some of the treasure from my most successful Peruvian grave robbery. *(James W. Mosele*

Vith great difficulty, I "discovered" a saucer landng site on the Peruvian desert, 1954. *(James W. Moseley)*

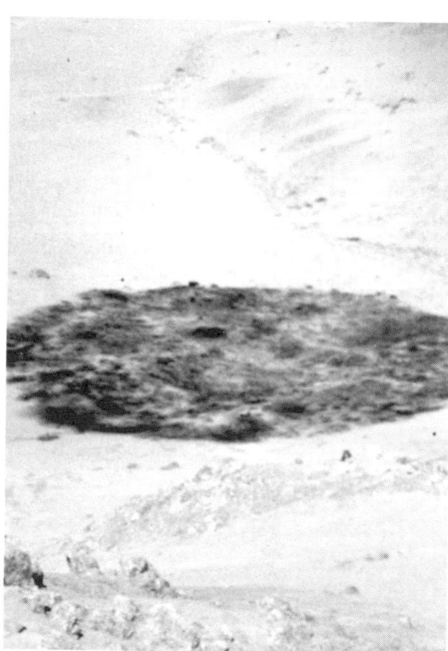

The mysterious Peruvian saucer-landing site seen from a nearby hill. This incident made the front page of Lima's most popular tabloid—twice. *(James W. Moseley)*

ot the UFO that scorched the Peruvian desert. his famous photo was taken by a Peruvian cusms inspector in 1952. I obtained it from him r my book that never was, later publishing it in *ucer News*. *(Domingo Troncosco/Saucer News)*

With keen marketing instinct, Gray Barker donned a space helmet for a 1956 television appearance promoting his new book *They Knew Too Much about Flying Saucers*. *(August C. Roberts/Saucer News/Tom Benson)*

Saucer contactee Howard Menger, the "East Coast Adamski," working on a test model of his X-4 Electro-Craft, 1964. Among many other things, Menger claimed to be a Saturnian reborn as an earthman. See chapters 6 and 7. *(Saucer News/Tom Benson)*

Connie Menger ("Marla Baxter"), second wi and space soulmate of Howard, ca. 1957. Conni claimed to be a reborn Venusian. *(August Roberts/Saucer News)*

Giant Rock, 1960. From 1954 through 1974, this California Mojave Desert monolith was the focal poi of contactee George Van Tassel's annual Interplanetary Spacecraft Convention at his Giant Rock Airpo *(James W. Moseley)*

rincess Negonna and Prince Neosom (Beth Dock-
r Childers and Lee Childers) of distant planet
ythan at the 1960 Giant Rock convention. Space
eople or . . . ? See chapter 7. *(James W. Moseley)*

Gentle but earthy contactee Orfeo Angelucci at Giant Rock, 1961. *(James W. Moseley)*

regale the assembled saucer fiends at the 1960 Giant Rock convention as host and contactee George
an Tassel looks on. *(James W. Moseley)*

George Van Tassel's Integratron, near Giant Rock, 1960. Van Tassel built the rejuvenation device wit wisdom channeled from the Space People and $42,000 in donations—but did all of the money go int the Integratron? *(James W. Moseley)*

Contactee Dan Fry (right) and unknown admirer, presumably from this planet, at the foot of Giant Rock, 1960. Fry's occult/saucer study society Understanding was very popular with lonely middle-aged ladies, as was Fry. *(James W. Moseley/Saucer News)*

I seek interplanetary enlightenment with Dary Neiman, a Hollywood model, contactee, and frien of space animals, Giant Rock, 1960. *(James W. Mosele*

Serious Ufologist Max Miller and semi-serious political candidate Gabriel Green, founder and president of the Amalgamated Flying Saucer Clubs of America, at Giant Rock, 1960. (*James W. Moseley*)

Contactee Truman Bethurum and his second wife, Alvira, outside the Giant Rock Airport Café just after their marriage at Van Tassel's 1961 convention. Bethurum's first wife divorced him when she thought he'd gotten too chummy with Aura Rhanes of the planet Clarion. (*James W. Moseley/Saucer News*)

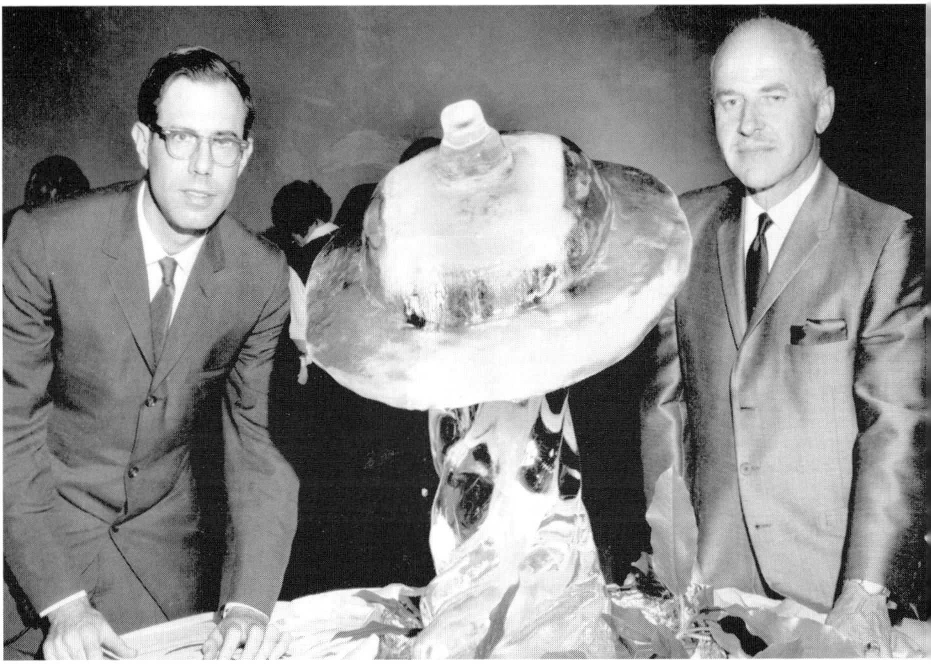

At a meeting of the Detroit Engineering Society, May 1966, with a society official and a saucer from a very cold planet. This was my first speaking engagement booked by the American Program Bureau. *(Ange Baune/James W. Moseley)*

Andy "The Mystic Barber" Sinatra single-handedly saves UN headquarters from being toppled by "terrible destructive forces," February 1962. See chapter 7. *(James W. Moseley/Saucer News)*

I share the latest *Saucer News* with famed talk-radio pioneer Long John Nebel, 1964. I was a regular on Nebel's program in the 1950s and 1960s. *(Sam Vandivert/Saucer News)*

I corrupt the kiddies with saucer lore on Terry Bennett's New York City television program, 1967. My several appearances with Bennett drove *Saucer News* circulation to over ten thousand—for a while. *(August C. Roberts/Saucer News)*

In my semi-humble opinion, astronomer Dr. J. Allen Hynek was the greatest of Serious Ufologists. *(John P. Timmerman/Center for UFO Studies)*

Ray Palmer, cofounder of *Fate* magazine and major booster of the Man Who Started it All, Kenneth Arnold, October 1965. *(James W. Moseley)*

Roy Thinnes, star of the saucers-and-evil-aliens television show *The Invaders*, addresses the first session of the 1967 National UFO Conference in New York City. The look in his eyes suggests he already was coming down with The Roy Thinnes Disease. See chapter 9. *(James W. Moseley/Saucer News)*

Famed Fortean writer John Keel and I at NUFOC 1967. Keel was a new superstar on the saucering front and, having only recently met, we were still on good terms. *(George Earley/Saucer News/Tom Benson)*

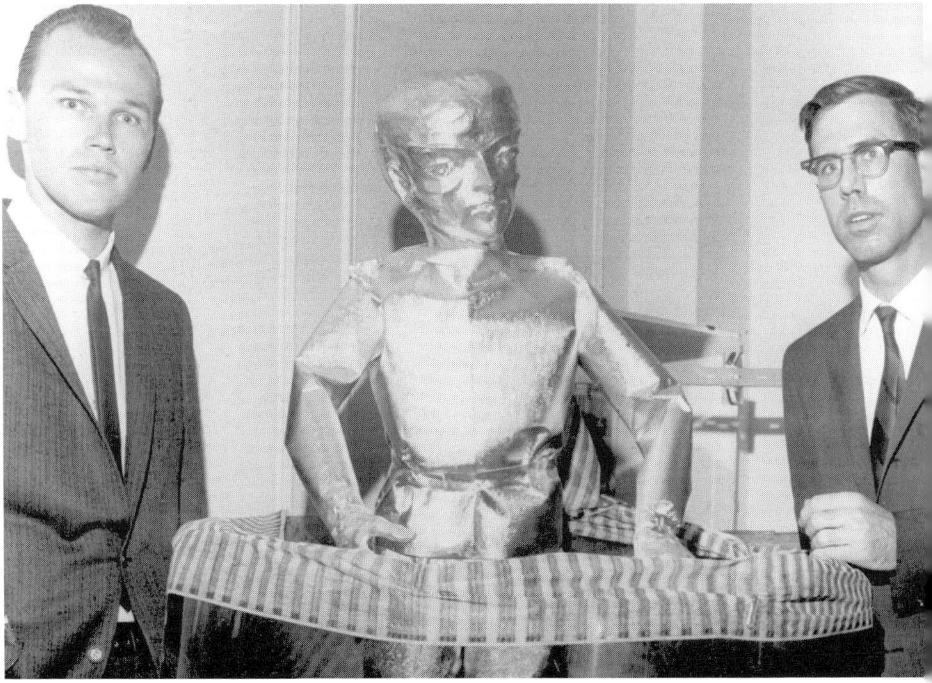

Serious Ufologist Max Miller, a being from a planet other than ours, and I, NUFOC 1967. *(August C. Roberts / James W. Moseley)*

One of Harvard astronomer and arch UFO debunker Donald Menzel's many far-out paintings of mythical Martians. Inscribed to me, this hangs in *Saucer Smear* Headquarters. *(James W. Moseley/Saucer Smear)*

Shaking hands with Harry S Truman, Clarksburg, West Virginia, October 1962, after asking him his views on flying saucers at a press conference. A mysterious energy field seems to have blurred the image—or maybe it was just Gray Barker's shaky hands. See chapters 4 and 8. *(Gray Barker/James W. Moseley)*

Sharing *"Sausage" News* with Georgia Governor Lester Maddox, February 1967. See chapter 9. *(James W. Moseley)*

Hamming it up with novelty-pop falsetto favorite Tiny Tim at a party in my New Jersey apartment, 1964. *(James W. Moseley)*

Encounter with The Greatest. I (far right) along with (from left) publicist-saucerer Harold Salkin, Timothy Green "Mr. UFO" Beckley, and Paul Karasik of unknown rock band the Flying Saucer visit with boxer Muhammad Ali in the early 1970s. *(James W. Moseley)*

At the eighteenth annual National UFO Conference, Green Bay, Wisconsin, 1981 (left to right): Gray Barker, "Flying Saucer Physicist" Stanton Friedman, NUFOC cofounder Rick Hilberg, myself, and Mutual UFO Network founder and now retired Maximum Leader Walt Andrus. *(James W. Moseley)*

Quoting from *Saucer Smear* (December 15, 1981): "Gray Barker [in hat], shown with several close relatives, standing in front of the recently remodeled Manor House of his luxurious country estate near Sutton, West Virginia," November 1981. *(James W. Moseley/Saucer Smear)*

From left: Saucerdom's Great Satan Philip J. Klass, astronomer and UFO semi-skeptic Carl Sagan, and Committee for the Scientific Investigation of Claims of the Paranormal Chairman Paul Kurtz at CSICOP conference, Los Angeles, April 1987. Have they just gotten wind of the upcoming MJ-12 documents announcement at NUFOC 1987? *(James W. Moseley)*

The MJ-12 documents unveiled, 1987 NUFOC, Burbank, California (from left): William L. Moore and his confederates Jamie Shandera and Stan Friedman. See chapter 13. *(James W. Moseley)*

Ed and Frances Walters wow the crowd at NUFO(1990, Miami Beach, with tales of their late-1980 UFO-photo-and-encounter fest in Gulf Breeze. Se chapter 15. *(James W. Moseley/Saucer Smear)*

Dr. Bruce Maccabee, leading Serious Ufologist and "Mr. Ed" Walters supporter, tickles the ivories at the 1999 MUFON International Symposium in Arlington, Virginia, proving that as a ufologist he makes a great piano player. *(James W. Moseley)*

Standing in for Walt Andrus, I encounter th semi-mysterious and definitely amusing Ladonia Texas, alien skeleton at NUFOC 2000, Corpu Christi, Texas. See chapter 17. *(James W. Moseley*

The next morning, by sheer accident I stumbled into the convention press conference. Thinking quickly, I whipped out my Accredited Press card, which has never failed me, allowing me to interview Harry Truman, Vivian Leigh, and Jane Russell, among others. It worked again at the *Fate* affair, and I was issued full press credentials.

Then it was on to the mingling room, where I had my previously described Historic Handshake with Kenneth Arnold. There I was very cordially greeted by everyone but Arnold and, somewhat to my surprise, treated as something of an elder statesman, which was both flattering and somehow oddly poignant.

The convention banquet Saturday night featured Dr. Hynek as the after-dinner speaker. Hynek's speaking style was not thrilling, and his voice was very soft. In order to hear him at all, people were afraid to cough or move their chairs, and except for Hynek's near whisper, the banquet room was all but silent. At some point, he made a routine remark about psychic phenomena. His words immediately were punctuated by a huge crash of flying, breaking crockery in the kitchen, shattering the silence and provoking gales of laughter.

Following the dinner, I ran into Coral Lorenzen in the hotel bar, our first meeting since our heated encounter in Baltimore. She was sitting alone at a small table, accompanied only by a six-inch-high papier-mâché star with her name on it, which identified her as one of the convention speakers. Oddly, her husband, Jim, was sitting at another table nearby, accompanied by *his* star. (I leave it to the reader to speculate on The Meaning of this.)

I sat down with Coral, who out of the blue described herself as "looking pretty good for an old broad" (which, I guess, was true), and we began discussing ufological theories over a martini or three or four. By then, I had slid ufologically leftward from my previously held conservative nuts-and-bolts, saucers-from-space view, and was espousing a 3½-D theory, somewhat similar to what my coauthor adheres to now. Essentially, the idea is that whoever is flying the saucers has technology so far advanced from ours that they can do things that seem magical or paranormal to us, but which actually are based upon scientific principles as yet not discovered or fully understood by mere earthlings. Coral was arguing vehemently against this when Hynek walked in and joined us.

Hynek had just finished delivering a pro-3½-D lecture, so he was loaded for bear. He jumped in on my side of the debate, and before long, I simply settled back and listened. I was pleased and gratified that Hynek agreed with the fundamentals of my not very original idea. As I thought about it, I realized that the majority of the convention speakers seemed to be on the same wavelength, too—and that only a few years before most of them would have argued just as vigorously against it as Coral was. For better or worse, Serious Ufology was a-changing.

The MAN WHO CAME to DINNER

One of the most controversial characters to come onto the saucering scene in the 1970s was W. Todd Zechel, alias Ted Zachary, alias Ted Zilch, alias Todd Zilcovich, alias et al. It was he who wrote to me in December 1975 claiming he knew of a saucer that had crashed on the Mexican side of the border near Del Rio, Texas, sometime in 1950 (or 1948 or, maybe, 1954). It seems he was told this by a fellow soldier when he was stationed in Korea as a member of the U.S. Army Security Agency, a communications eavesdropping outfit linked to the (shudder!) National Security Agency (not the National Security Council, as I'd recorded in my normally infallible diary). Supposedly, American military forces retrieved not only the saucer from Mexico, but also the body of its alien pilot.

Before long, Zechel, as Ted Zilch, was a regular contributor of letters, commentary, and (frequently scatological) humor to my newsletter. More important, and (I think) in his real name, he actively courted Serious Ufologists, wowing them with his crashed-saucer story and his claims of ten years inside the intelligence community, working for NSA and another, unnamed "civilian intelligence agency." Zechel had a gift of gab and a way of presenting himself as someone in the know that really appealed to saucerers. Of course, it didn't hurt that he seemed to be someone from the "inside" who was hot on the trail of the Holy Grail: physical proof of interplanetary flying saucers.

Sometime in 1976, Zechel was named director of research for Ground Saucer Watch (GSW), a private Arizona saucer-investigations group, whose director, Bill Spaulding, specialized in (allegedly) highly sophisticated analysis of UFO photos. Imagine my surprise—and that of Serious Ufologists—when later the same year Zechel, with Spaulding's okay, appointed me GSW's New Jersey director. Zechel acknowledged that I might take this honor less than seriously, noting that "Ground Saucer Watch understands that your current publication is satirical in nature" and allowing that "we enjoy jokes about ourselves as we do about others." The seriousness of my approach to GSW duties is revealed by the title I entered on my membership card: Grand Dragon.

Spurred on by their dynamic director of research, in 1977 GSW filed a Freedom of Information Act lawsuit against the CIA, demanding release of UFO documents. While this was pending, Zechel, a California ufologist named Brad Sparks, and Peter Gersten, the attorney who had brought the suit on behalf of GSW, formed a group called Citizens for UFO Secrecy (CAUS). Oddly enough, when the GSW suit brought the release of several hundred pages of CIA documents in 1978, CAUS took the credit.

In July 1978, a few months before the release of the CIA documents, Len Stringfield issued the first of his series of saucer crash/retrieval reports. This, like all his others, was a compilation of mostly anonymous claims, which made these sometimes very interesting and entertaining stories useless as proof of anything—which Len readily admitted to me and others. One of the stories in Len's first report and included in his next one, which appeared in early 1980, was Zechel's Del Rio tale. Zechel was praised and named. None of his witnesses were.

Mr. Z had been embraced with great, almost unquestioning enthusiasm by Serious Ufologists, some of whom could hardly contain themselves in their praise. For example, in an article in the August 1978 *UFO Report*, Jerry Clark, then an editor of *Fate*, burbled, "At this moment in history, it's distinctly possible that Todd Zechel is ufology's major figure." Later, when Phil Klass had the audacity to call the Major Figure's claims and character into question, Clark wrote Klass to say he'd gotten to know Zechel very well and that he was a person of "uncompromising integrity."

Too bad none of the Big Names in The Field were reading my newsletter, or, if they were, were too blinded by dreams of the Holy Grail soon to be handed them by Zechel to believe what they read.

Okay, okay, I confess. I, too, was at least semi-blinded by Zechel's stories—not to mention the prospect of making a buck if they proved true or at least marketable. Zechel wanted to make a film based on his investigations and failing or in conjunction with that, to write a book, the working (*sic*)/promotional title of which was *Under Intelligence Control*. So in April 1977 I agreed to see what I could do about coming up with a movie deal through my limited New York showbiz contacts. Before long, Zechel had signed me up for five years as exclusive agent for his ufological and related writings.

Here, as published in the September 25, 1977, *Saucer Smear* (as *Saucer Hughes*), is how this venture unfolded:

> Now, finally, must be told the intriguing tale of Todd Zechel, alias Ted Zilch, alias Todd Zilchovich, etc., etc. Alas, dear non-subscribers, he is

not a figment of your Editor's over-active imagination, but a real-life personage, in spite of rumors to the contrary.

T.Z., as we will call him here (to protect his non-identity), arrived on the New York scene in early May, with a fat contract (thanks to us) from a totally unknown movie outfit called Scotia-American. Scotia was contemplating a UFO documentary movie, and T.Z. was hired to do the Research. T.Z.'s specialty was crashed disc stories from former military personnel—in line with the theme of Frank Scully's 1950 classic, "Behind the Flying Saucers". But the Research dragged along, Scotia became impatient to get on with the movie, and within about a month they decided they had no further use for his talents. Apparently the film will be based on some of the better-known recent UFO tales, rather than on T.Z.'s sensational but unproven material.

Even so, everything should have turned out fine, because T.Z. had an agreement with Scotia that he could use his material for a book if they didn't want to use it. All he needed was a Pad to freeload in while the book took shape. At this point, last June, your Editor (unwisely, as it turns out) stepped forward and volunteered to let T.Z. spend a few weeks in our humble N.J. headquarters, getting together a few chapters and an outline for a publisher to look at.

The weeks rolled on, and although T.Z. was a pleasant house guest, he became more notable for his devotion to TV sports than for his dedication to the written word. Most of his Research is done by telephone—and this also became a problem. Just a teeny weeny problem at first, but a much larger one later on. Perhaps T.Z. is a follower of the legendary Carlos Allende, who claims to know the secret of how the U.S. Navy once made a ship invisible [the so-called Philadelphia Experiment]. In any case, T.Z. managed somehow to make a key phone bill invisible for several weeks. When it finally came to our attention anyhow (as the Phone Co. was threatening to cut off service!), we learned to our horror that the bill was a hefty, incredible *$735* for one month! About one third of this outrage was for calls to a single California researcher. (You know who you are B.S.! [Zechel's CAUS partner, Brad Sparks]) In all, T.Z.'s three month Visitation with us set your naive Editor back almost $2,000—and not all the bills are in yet! [When they finally were, the total came to over $3,000.]

Upon becoming aware of the $735 bill, we invited T.Z. to move on to greener pastures elsewhere [I gave him twenty-four hours to move out], even though he still had not written enough chapters to show a publisher [actually, he'd not written a word]. He has now apparently returned to his native Wisconsin to re-group his forces, or whatever. We still hope to help T.Z. with his book, and thus to eventually help ourselves to repayment plus some of the royalties. [*Under Intelligence Control* has retained its Exciting "working" title all these many years, but has yet to be written.] But no one short of our ideal, the late Howard Hughes, could afford T.Z. as a house guest! His telephonic zeal is reminiscent of some unfortunate people's devotion to Heroin. . . .

Note that I made this story public in September 1977; yet a year later Stringfield still was taking Zechel's stories seriously, and Clark was calling him "ufology's major figure." Then Phil Klass issued the first of several white papers on Zechel and sent it to the Leading Lights of ufology. For one thing, this paper showed I wasn't the first to have been financially taken in by Zechel. It also revealed what the CAUS-meister had been doing during the ten years he supposedly was an intelligence man. He spent three of them in the army, with the Army Security Agency. After he was discharged, he worked for six years in a Wisconsin factory as a carpenter and a fireman. Then he'd moved on to bigger and better things in Milwaukee, where he managed a sex shop/pornographic bookstore. I'm sure at least the last job was a cover for intelligence work.

Klass's exposé provoked Clark's vigorous defense of Zechel as a man of "uncompromising integrity" and a thank-you from Bill Spaulding. It also launched a major feud, with a blizzard of white papers and accusations and counteraccusations and threats of legal action spewing forth from Zechel and Klass and a spirited defense of Zechel being mounted by some of Ufology's Finest.

Then Zechel moved into Jerry Clark's house. It wasn't long before the name W. Todd Zechel disappeared from the vocabulary of Serious Ufology. In keeping with ufology's approach to embarrassments in recent years, it suddenly was as if Zechel had never existed.

In late summer 1979 I received a letter from the Former Major Figure, which I ran in my September 10 issue (*More Saucer Tit*):

> I'm . . . concerned over the fact that my personality has become a bigger issue than UFOs and my research thereof. Therefore, as I told you over the phone, I have decided to withdraw from active participation in organized Ufology, and will from this point on conduct my work as quietly and with as much dignity as possible.
>
> Accordingly, I have tendered by resignation as Director of CAUS and as Director of Research for GSW. Whatever role I play in these organizations in the future will be as a private individual contributing funds, information, and other forms of support to worthy projects. . . .
>
> Unlike Nixon, I don't expect my resignations will protect me from further abuse. No, you will still have Todd Zechel to kick around—and I'm sure you will avail yourself of every opportunity. I merely want to

> ensure that when I'm being kicked, deservedly or not, that innocent people aren't harmed by the blows. . . .

Todd Zechel, noble to the end. Well, not quite . . .

In July 1993, after almost fourteen years of ufological silence, Zechel returned to the saucering scene with a report called "The Fund for CIA Research? Or Who's Disinforming Whom?" This was published by the mysterious Associated Investigators Group (undoubtedly just Zechel and a typewriter), and it attacked the Fund for UFO Research, run by Richard Hall and others, as a CIA front. Soon after, my Esteemed Coauthor published an article in the November–December 1993 *UFO* magazine, "I Was a Ufologist for the CIA—Not!" in which he told the story of his volunteer work with NICAP while he was employed as a CIA intelligence officer. This included mention of Zechel's 1978 claim in *Just CAUS*, the newsletter of Citizens Against UFO Secrecy, that NICAP had been destroyed by CIA agents in its midst, naming Karl and subtly hinting he somehow was involved in this evil scheme.

This provoked another AIG report and much associated ranting and raving from Zechel, who seemed to be attempting to move back into ufology as a crusading investigative reporter. Then he faded away yet again, only to resurface once more in 2000 with some weird letters and postcards to me and similarly strange missives to Karl, complete with demands for apologies and threats of legal action. I spoke with Zechel on the telephone a couple of times, and learned that he'd had a "mild stroke" about four years before, and was on disability and living with his father in beautiful Prairie du Sac, Wisconsin. By the end of the year, after a few further fulminations, he was gone again, though recently I heard he'd surfaced yet again, this time on the dreaded Internet.

I almost—*almost*—feel sorry for Zechel.

ANOTHER CRACKPOT in the UFOLOGICAL PANTRY

Then there was Ray Stanford, whom it will be recalled was, with his brother, a member of "Dr." George Hunt Williamson's entourage in Peru back in the fifties. As teenagers, Ray and his sibling claimed to be contactees and even wrote a pamphlet about their alleged experiences. In the 1960s Ray founded a supposedly rigorously scientific saucer research outfit called Project Starlight International. As a NICAP representative he'd also investigated the 1964 Lonnie Zamora landing case in New Mexico and written a book about it called *Socorro "Saucer" in a Pentagon Pantry* (1976).

The night of December 7–8, 1977, I was on the Long John Nebel show with Stanford, who was the main guest, plugging his book. Our host was Candy Jones, Long John's wife. Long John was suffering from colon cancer (he died in 1978), so Candy was more and more often handling the program solo.

In keeping with the scientific tone of his book, Stanford's commentary was low-key and sober for the first couple of hours. Then we got off onto the subject of psychic Uri Geller, with whom Stanford had spent quite a bit of time. Stanford became increasingly agitated as he told wilder and wilder stories about Geller's powers, ending with a really weird one about Geller having teleported Stanford's car—with Stanford in it—over a distance of several miles.

At about 3:30 in the morning, Candy began to take calls from listeners. One caller asked about contactee Herbert Schirmer, the Nebraska policeman whose life had been ruined by a 1967 UFO experience. In answer, Stanford boldly stated that Schirmer was a "pathological liar," and relentlessly proceeded to elaborate in considerable detail. Regardless of the merits of the Schirmer case, this was an incredible violation of radio and television taboos by a guest who supposedly knew better.

At the next commercial break, Candy explained to Stanford the station policy of sending a written apology to anyone who might have been slandered on the air. Stanford responded by stating angrily that he was leaving, whereupon he got his belongings together and stalked out of the studio. As he passed the control room, he grabbed and attempted to rip up the standard release form he had signed before the program. A brief wrestling match ensued between Stanford and the show's engineer, the torn form was recovered, and Stanford was escorted from the building.

At least good old Ray livened up what otherwise would have been a routine UFO talk show (yawn)—just as Len Stringfield, APRO, and a few others were beginning to do for ufology at large (so to speak).

From the sublime to the ridiculous is but a step.

—Napoleon I

The seventies were a time of dramatic transition in America. Ufology, too, went through a metamorphosis. The decade began, like, a downer. Then with the 1973–74 flap, it blossomed into, like, a supercool upper. Then it began to seem, like, a bad trip, you know? In the process, The Field was, like, transformed. Like, wow!

Terrifying abductions replaced chance and fleeting encounters with little spacemen. Crashed saucers and dead aliens grabbed by nasty, secretive military men overshadowed sightings of silvery disks zipping through the blue. Sliced and diced cow carcasses shoved aside accounts of animals temporarily frightened by the "vibes" of passing saucers. Was this just a reflection of post-Vietnam, post-Watergate fears and cynicism? I think this was at least part of it. Whatever the reason(s), a "subculture" characterized by hopeful excitement, anticipation, and fun was taking on a grim cast. Like, wow.

SNATCHED

Even after the 1961 Betty and Barney Hill case had been warily accepted by most Serious Ufologists—including my coauthor but not I—as probably being a real UFO abduction, The Field remained pretty skittish about such cases. Then Hickson and Parker got pinched and eyeballed, their story blessed by Hynek and Harder, and—presto—abductions by saucer beings became respectable, or at least giving them serious consideration did. Of course, if we really are being visited by aliens from space, then it's entirely reasonable that, at some point, our visitors would want to take a good close look at a few of us. Still, I was surprised by the enthusiasm with which The Field latched onto abductions after decades of dismissing contactees and even far more believable claims of very close encounters with spacemen. I suppose I shouldn't have been surprised. After all, abductions are much more exciting than fleeting lights in the sky, especially after fruitlessly chasing the latter year after year after year.

While Hickson and Parker's story was being debated and pondered, Ohio schoolteacher and amateur astronomer Marjorie Fish was working quietly on something very interesting. In 1974 she revealed the results of several years of research on a star map that Betty Hill said she had been shown while aboard the UFO in which she and Barney had been held. Supposedly, the map displayed her captors' trade routes and journeys of exploration as lines connecting twelve stars, and, following a suggestion made by her psychiatrist while she was under hypnosis, Betty made a posthypnotic sketch of the map as she remembered it. In 1966 this was reproduced in *Interrupted Journey*, John Fuller's book about the Hills' experience. Fish saw it there and decided to see if she could figure out which stars were involved and perhaps even discover where the spacefaring kidnappers came from.

In an article in the Fortean magazine *Pursuit* (January 1974) and a few months later in a lecture at the 1974 MUFON symposium, Fish presented her findings. She claimed to have identified all the key stars on the map and said it seemed likely that one of the two most prominent objects, the stars Zeta 1 and Zeta 2 Reticuli, was the home sun of the Hills' "hosts." Walter Webb, an astronomer and the first and primary investigator of the Hill case, endorsed Fish's findings, as did Flying Saucer Physicist Stan Friedman, who flat out and enthusiastically claimed that we now *knew* where at least some of the saucer pilots came from.

The December 1974 issue of *Astronomy* magazine carried a very serious feature on the star map by its editor, astronomer Terence

Dickinson. This ignited a storm of controversy. During the year that followed, the magazine was filled with dueling letters from supporters of Fish's work and detractors like Carl Sagan, who argued—I think persuasively, while my coauthor does not—that the pattern Fish claimed to have found could easily be the product of chance. Inside ufology, Fish's conclusions were embraced as proof—or shockingly close to it—that saucers were from another planet and at least one abduction was a real outer-space snatch. Whee!

Then, in October 1975, the Hills' story was dramatically presented as an NBC-TV movie, *The UFO Incident,* starring James Earl Jones and Estelle Parsons. About two weeks later, on November 5, 1975—and entirely by coincidence, of course—Travis Walton, a young Arizona woodsman, disappeared after being blasted by a saucer's not-quite-death ray, supposedly in full view of the six other men on his forestry crew.

After a frantic search directed by the local sheriff and five days of tremendous media attention—newspaper, television, and radio reporters swarmed into Arizona literally from all over the world—Walton was back, unceremoniously dumped from a saucer onto a mountain highway not far from where he'd been zapped and snatched. In short order he was taken out of circulation again, this time of his own free will and by APRO and the *National Enquirer,* America's top supermarket tabloid, which had acquired at least semi-exclusive rights to his story. At the time, the *Enquirer* had a standing offer of $100,000 for proof of extraterrestrial visitation and a $5,000 prize for best UFO case of the year, both as determined by a panel of prominent ufologists.

APRO sent in James Harder and another of its consultants, University of Wyoming psychologist Leo Sprinkle. Hynek was there for CUFOS. (All three were on the *Enquirer*'s UFO panel.) Bill Spaulding's GSW was first on the scene, but seems to have referred Walton to a quack for a physical exam and so put itself out of the running. It wasn't long before GSW denounced the incident as a hoax. (Maybe they should have called in their New Jersey Grand Dragon.)

Walton's story had everything. The "victim" had been blasted by a saucer's ray gun. Unconscious, he was taken aboard the saucer and, maybe, whisked to a mother ship. There, still on board the capture saucer, he awakened to find himself surrounded by a group of big-headed, big-eyed, "fetus-like" aliens (with important physical characteristics amazingly like those of the aliens depicted in *The UFO Incident*). Heroically, Walton battled these creatures and then attempted to escape—by trying to fly the saucer himself!

As he was fiddling with the saucer controls, Walton was confronted by a tall blond man in a spacesuit, complete with fifties-TV-style fishbowl helmet. The man had long hair very much in the earthly seventies fashion (hmmm . . .). This semi-updated Space Brother silently escorted Walton out of the saucer, whereupon the earthling discovered he was inside a huge hangar, where he saw several saucers as he and the Space Brother passed through to another room.

In this room, two more Space Brothers and a Space Sister were waiting, all blond(e)s but not wearing helmets. This trio required Walton to lie on a table, a mask was placed over his nose and mouth, and once again he went out like a light. The next thing he knew, he was sprawled on the highway beneath a hovering saucer, which silently poofed off into the night sky. Getting his bearings, he discovered he was not far from the little town of Heber, where he went to a phone booth and called his brother-in-law. Back home, he "learned" he'd been gone for five days, a period he claimed was virtually a total blank to him.

Adding to the apparent credibility of the story, the six men who were with Walton when he was zapped by the saucer had been given lie-detector tests by an Arizona State Police examiner, and five "passed," with the other producing inconclusive results. Walton had been interviewed by three psychiatrists, APRO consultants, who pronounced him sane and truthful. Once again, Harder and Hynek, backed up by Sprinkle, endorsed an abductee's sincerity, lending their professional credibility to Walton's story. Of course, all this was touted enthusiastically by APRO's Jim and Coral Lorenzen. Then, a couple of months later, it was announced Walton had passed a lie-detector test himself, with flying colors.

Despite all this, MUFON and NICAP were quite skeptical of Walton's story. MUFON leader Walt Andrus said he didn't think there was enough information to conclude anything one way or the other and expressed concern about "inconsistent factors." NICAP made clear it was leaning toward a hoax explanation. Jim and Coral Lorenzen of APRO told anyone and everyone that it was a real abduction, maybe even the most significant case in UFO history (there are lots of those).

In its July 6, 1976, edition, the *National Enquirer* announced its 1975 Best UFO Case of the Year: the Walton abduction. Walton and his woodcutter friends split $5,000. Three years later, Walton would publish a book, *The Walton Experience,* and in 1996, a movie based on it, *Fire in the Sky,* would appear, along with an updated, expanded, and retitled-to-match version of Walton's book. Who says saucering doesn't pay?

While all the excitement was going on in the months after Walton's alleged abduction, Phil Klass had been conducting his own quiet investigation. A few days after the *Enquirer* announcement, his findings were headlined in the *Arizona Republic*, the state's largest newspaper. It's a complicated story, and I'm not sure I agree with everything Phil concluded, but the bottom line is that (surprise) he decided the incident was a hoax (I agree). One of his key discoveries was that soon after Walton returned, APRO and the *National Enquirer* had arranged for him to be given a lie-detector test. He flunked, badly. The examiner said Walton engaged in "gross deception." APRO and the tabloid had hushed up this, ahem, unfortunate outcome. When Klass discovered this and asked Jim Lorenzen if Walton had taken any other test but the one he supposedly passed, Lorenzen unwisely and emphatically denied it.

MUFON and GSW published Klass's findings in full, and NICAP ran highlights in its newsletter. The Lorenzens and APRO stuck to their guns and scrambled to justify their deception. They claimed the first exam was badly constructed, Walton was too emotionally disturbed at the time for a valid test, the examiner was hostile to Walton, and so on, and so forth. However, this didn't go down well, even with many hard-core saucer fiends, and I think this was the beginning of the end for APRO, though it hung on for several more years.

Still, the case had taken hold of the imaginations of even those saucerers who were concerned about the actions of the APRO leadership. It was real for those who wanted it to be so, and it didn't hurt that Allen Hynek and his Center for UFO Studies backed it. As the good doctor put it when he and Walton appeared together on the ABC-TV talk show *Good Night America* in late 1976, "It fits a pattern, see. If this were the only case on record, then I would have to say, well, I couldn't possibly believe it. But at the Center for UFO Studies now we have some two dozen similar abduction cases currently being studied. *Something is going on!*"

What was going on more than anything else was that saucerdom was buying into abductions. Budd Hopkins had moved on from O'Barski's little men with shovels to investigations of claims by people who thought they might have been snatched. He used hypnosis to probe (and, I believe, add to) their unconsciousness memories, even though he was not a licensed hypnotist. Ray Fowler, a Massachusetts ufologist and long-time NICAPer, got caught up in the still-continuing saga of Betty Andreasson, who believed she'd been abducted by a gang of short, big-headed, big-eyed, gray-skinned aliens led by a character named Quazgaa. Fowler's first of several books on the case, *The Andreasson Affair*, appeared in 1979, and he now thinks he himself is an abductee!

CRASHED

At the same time The Field was getting caught up in abductions, crashed and retrieved saucers began to fall into place, too. Len Stringfield, who had reopened that forbidden door in 1977 with his *Situation Red: The UFO Siege*, began hearing from numerous informants, most of whom, as I've already noted, insisted on anonymity. Len began collecting these stories, and delivered a paper at the 1978 MUFON symposium, held that year in Dayton, Ohio, just a stone's throw from Hangar 18. He called it "Retrievals of the Third Kind: A Case Study of Alleged UFOs and Occupants in Military Custody" (shudder!).

This was to become the first in a series of seven self-published "status reports" Len was to issue over the next sixteen years under the overall title *The UFO Crash/Retrieval Syndrome.* More than any other single ufologist, Stringfield was responsible for restoring credibility to the notion that saucers from space had crashed and, along with the bodies of their crews—and maybe even a survivor or two—had been scooped up and secreted away by the U.S. government. In this way, he laid the groundwork for the (ugh!) Curse of Roswell.

Stan Friedman and previously unknown but soon to be very (in)famous researcher William L. Moore had already joined forces to look into Roswell, based on two interviews Friedman had done in 1973 and early 1978, in which he had been told about what seemed to be the same saucer crash in New Mexico during the summer of 1947. The latter interview was with Jesse A. Marcel Sr., who had been the base intelligence officer at Roswell Army Air Field at the time. Stringfield interviewed Marcel a couple of months after Friedman did and named him in his second status report. Marcel was involved in retrieving something that, in 1947, the army first said was a flying saucer and then quickly changed its story, saying it was a case of mistaken identity. What Marcel had hauled in from the high desert was a weather balloon and its radar target, a story ufologists accepted for more than thirty years.

More—much more—on this later.

I can't think of a better way to convey the flavor and feel of saucerdom's take on crashed and retrieved nuts and bolts (and bones)—then and now—than to quote at some length from Stringfield's introduction to his *Status Report II: New Sources, New Data* (January 1980):

> Since Dayton, new informants continue to emerge; people, like my earlier firsthand contacts, who want no open, active part in UFO research.

Independent from each other, they, ever so cautiously, share sensitive information about their alleged roles in a retrieval operation, or claim to have been in an authoritative position to have seen the deceased humanoid entities under a variety of "need to know" circumstances. . . .

. . . The more I probed into old and new leads the deeper I became enmeshed in an inconsistent world of real people on one end; and on the other, the unreal tales they told.

Just as unreal, or so it seems, were some of my own experiences during these probes. One, no longer hushed incident, was my close encounter with a "phantom" force at the Dayton symposium. There, before going on stage my life was twice threatened. On both occasions word came through an intermediary, once by phone at 4:30 a.m. on July 29 [the day Stringfield spoke]; the other by physical confrontation just moments before my address. Uninformed of the threats, I spoke for nearly 2 hours [yawn . . .]. However, the moment I finished I was suddenly whisked off stage by three armed plainclothesmen with walkie talkies, escorted to the Stouffer Hotel, where I held a prearranged press conference, then again escorted to my room which, not of my choosing, was in the process of being changed with a lady tenant on the far end of the hotel. I was advised not to reveal my room number to anyone and not to leave its premises. In effect, until dinnertime I was detained, incommunicado. I missed everyone I had arranged to see, including a medical person with information.

A real threat or a scare tactic? To this day it is unclear if I was being protected from a lunatic adversary, or, if the whole episode was a ploy to deflect potential informants in the audience from reaching me. I had indications beforehand, while preparing my "Retrieval" paper that someone connected with the C.I.A. was concerned about some of my sensitive material and how far I might go with it. He advised that the use of some data in my possession could be risky and for my own safety I "should always stay in crowds." . . .

Whatever the intent of my would-be-assailant or of the Intelligence Community, my role and objectives in research have since changed. To me, the key to truth lies in what we may call the UFO crash/retrieval syndrome. Lights in the sky, close encounters of all kinds, and even the grotesquerie of abduction cases have all lost priority. Time, with its influx of new data from new and old reliable sources, now affirms my belief that beyond my fingertips and perhaps forever unreachable, is the evidence extraordinaire—the alien cadavers and the craft. . . .

. . . The whole story of my experience in this endeavor may never be told, mainly because of the sensitivity of some of the names, places, and subject matter. . . . I know, firsthand, that my continued quest for UFO crash/retrieval information is a venture that can be as risky and frustrating as it is rewarding.

What a delicious thrill such thoughts and words give to the true saucer fiend! We're on to The Truth, and the government will stop at nothing (well, almost nothing) to prevent us from getting The Proof and revealing it to the world. This is Roswell and the hidden subtext of ufology in a nutshell. I know. I used to feel the same way (shudder!).

Unfortunately—or maybe not for those who prefer the delights of mystery and intrigue to those of solving a case—almost nothing Len published was useful in getting any real answers to anything. Many of the stories he was told surely were tall tales. In fact, I know for certain that some were. Charles Wilhelm, for a while during the seventies a Big Name in Ohio saucerdom, told me he was Stringfield's sole source for a couple of his better published stories. It seems he did this as a way to test Len's care in evaluating the accounts he was given before going public with them. I don't know if Wilhelm was disappointed in the outcome of this little experiment or not.

MUTILATED

Len Stringfield may have decided that abductions should take a backseat to crashed saucers and alien bodies stashed in military refrigerators. Others in The Field did not. The two "phenomena" peacefully coexisted and somehow actually complemented each other, as they still do, even though "abductology" largely has shifted into the world of 4-D and beyond. Most ufologists did tend to specialize in one or the other or in some more conservative aspect of saucering, each a happy big frog in his or her own little pond. One who didn't was Linda Moulton Howe, the Animal Mutilations Queen, sometimes irreverently called Linda Moldy Cowe (not by me, of course).

Linda, a former Miss Idaho and still quite attractive and dynamic, got into saucering via the animal mutilation craze that swept the country beginning with the not-so-mysterious 1967 death of a Colorado horse named Lady—better known to saucerers as Snippy (was this bogus name a subtle joke?). I've met and talked with Linda several times, and find her quite delightful. She's also a very good speaker who knows how to involve and hold a crowd. However, she may well be the most credulous of all Serious Ufologists and seems to have no problem at all accommodating many mutually contradictory ideas. In her career, she has covered the ufological waterfront, and claims to have established links between animal mutilations, UFO landings, little-men sightings, and even abductions. She also has been an important second-string player in the crashed-saucer saga (including as a booster of the seemingly immortal Aztec case). Somehow, she's managed to bring all these things together in a way that make her and her many fans happy, and I think she genuinely believes what she says and writes, at least at the time she says and writes it.

But it was "mutes" that got her started. Throughout the seventies, there were several waves of mute reports from the Midwest, the southwest (mostly New Mexico and southern Colorado), and the South, with many cases involving sightings of UFOs, strange people or beings, and spooky black helicopters. Cows, horses, other farm animals, dogs, cats, even buffalo were found dead, supposedly with various parts—usually including the genitals and other unmentionables—cut away with "laser-like precision." Reportedly conspicuous by their absence were blood and, usually, the tracks of the perpetrators.

Howe and a Texan named Tom Adams (who coined the term *mutes*) became the principal proponents of the mute-UFO connection, and when the major UFO groups were choosing up sides on the issue, Howe and Adams became MUFON's top "mutologists" and spokesbeings. Walt Andrus had bought into the idea of mutes being UFO related almost immediately, as did the Lorenzens and APRO. NICAP rejected the idea. So did CUFOS. Kevin Randle, then a rising star in ufology and an APRO field investigator, conducted his own independent investigation and concluded there was nothing to the mute craze, except that it was just that, a craze. (What did the Lorenzens say when you told them that, Kevin?)

Thanks largely to Adams's and Howe's efforts, not incidentally including *Strange Harvest*, a 1980 television special Howe produced for a Denver station, the idea of evil, sneaky, slicing-and-dicing aliens became a fixture of ufological lore as the seventies segued into the eighties. It would gradually grow to encompass strange, paranoid tales of earthlings being tossed into the alien stew pot.

As for me, I like my beef well done, preferably in a nice meatloaf.

The 1980s:
Cosmic Babblegate
PART 4
Truth exists, only falsehood has to be invented.
—Georges Braque

What a man would like to be true, that he more readily believes.

—Francis Bacon

Ufology always has been cursed by an overabundance of those—believers and skeptics alike—who take *themselves* far too seriously. As the eighties dawned, an added downer was the shift of The Field's focus to the Dark Side—abductions, supersecret government crashed-saucer cabals, mutes, and even covert official human cooperation with the aliens to the extreme detriment of ordinary earthlings. Saucering wasn't nearly as hopeful and certainly not as much fun as it once was.

Of course, there's a bright side to everything, even the Dark Side, and as always, I found it in the antics and foibles of my fellow saucerers. Also as always, I was attacked for this. In early 1980 I had been catching more than the usual flack, so on a flight (airliner, not saucer) between New York and Phoenix I penned this editorial for the April 10 *Saucer Smear* (as *Saucer Stool*):

In effect, a number of people have expressed the feeling that we make Ufology "look bad" by our presentation of feuds, hoaxes, obviously absurd viewpoints, and other Negative material. We are not, we are told, properly backing the Ufological Team. We are demeaning the Field in the eyes of the General Public by "washing our dirty linen in public", rather than doing our bit to wield this unwieldy group of saucerers into something resembling a United Front. Above all, we give too much Space & attention to the ravings of the super-critics. . . .

Quite naturally, we plead guilty to all of the above charges. We feel that there are already enough journals that *advocate* UFOs, and even a couple of journals devoted basically to an "anti" position. Nothing is needed *less* than still another zine purporting to prove, re-prove, and super-prove the existence of UFOs!

Has it occurred to anyone that, if truly mysterious flying saucers really do exist, they will continue to do so in spite of the howls of the skeptics, and if they don't, no amount of Unity among the Believers will bring them into being?

Our purposes in "Saucer Stool" (not necessarily in order of importance) are:

—To satisfy our own over-inflated ego. (Why should we be any more modest than the astoundingly egocentric clubheads and skeptics?)

—To help deflate *other* egos.

—To amuse. (Ha!)

—To inform.

—To entertain, if possible.

—To cause our little band of loyal non-subscribers to think along new lines, to consider new ideas, and above all, just *to think* rather than *to advocate.*

In our opinion, the "science" of Ufology is at present slightly less advanced than was astronomy in the depths of the Middle Ages! But there *is* hope. Apparently a real phenomenon, whatever it may ultimately turn out to be, *is* behind these weird sightings, landings, etc. As the years go by, the educational level of the loudest voices on both sides of the argument is increasing—slowly but perceptibly. Some day, if we all live long enough, the mystery will be solved, or will solve itself.

Meanwhile, our peculiar fascination remains in the far-out, fascinating personalities who have been attracted to both sides of the argument. We do not mean to laugh unkindly at anyone, but rather to chronicle, in our pseudo-humble way, a unique sociological phenomenon of our times.

Increasingly, it appears there may even be a relationship between the personalities of the researchers and the phenomenon itself. Perhaps saucers are neither 3D or 4D, but, as we suggested semi-facetiously

> some time ago, *3½ D* or thereabouts. As "Professor" Adamski used to say, "Time Will Tell".
>
> Meanwhile, if we *must* have a serious message, it would be: Don't take yourselves too damn seriously! Don't be dogmatic! Hopefully, even the saucer entities (if any) have a sense of humor.

Recalling what I wrote in my prologue to this book, I see my views on UFOs and ufology haven't changed much in the past couple of decades, that they've just been somewhat refined, if that's the correct word. My most Important Insight remains exactly the same: Unless ufology learns to laugh at itself, it never will be taken seriously.

There's certainly no shortage of things to laugh about. The eighties offered up some doozies, and in this and the next couple of chapters, I'll share some of my favorites. Roswell (eek!) is the first that comes to mind.

BETTER CHECK OUR WARRANTY, ZORT

In the late 1970s, Len Stringfield got ufology to start taking crashed and retrieved saucers and dead little men seriously again. My ufological motto is, *Consider* everything, *believe* nothing. So I was willing to consider the possibility that saucers had crashed and that they and the bodies of their crews had been secretly grabbed and stashed away by elements of the U.S. government. However, there is a limit. Len soon had several dozen tales of separate incidents. If one accepted these tales, then in the late 1940s and early 1950s saucers were dropping out of the air like flies. I couldn't swallow that. After all, if the saucer beings were smart enough to travel safely through space over distances of billions and billions of miles, how likely was it that they'd be dumb enough to crash by the dozens once they got here? Were their saucers built by the lowest bidder? I had the same problem with the stories of Silas Newton and his cronies thirty years before.

But there was one story that seemed like it might have something to it: Roswell. Today, this is the one UFO case practically everyone, no matter how interested in UFOs, has heard about. Most know the basic story. In the summer of 1947, just a couple of weeks after Kenneth Arnold's sighting report kicked off the first flying saucer flap, a saucer supposedly crashed near the southeastern New Mexico town of Roswell, where there was a major army air forces base. This base was the home of the 509th Bomb Group, then the only operational atomic bomb outfit in the world (a point mentioned ad nauseam by pro-Roswellians). When the rancher who found some of the saucer-crash debris showed up in town and reported it to the local sheriff, the base was informed, and intelligence officer Maj. Jesse Marcel was sent out to the boondocks to check things out.

Marcel came back with a couple of boxes full of odd junk, and a few hours later the base issued a press announcement saying one of the mysterious flying disks had been captured. Of course, this instantly became a major news story all over the world—until, a few hours later, higher army headquarters said a mistake had been made. What had been found was nothing more than a weather balloon and the radar target it had carried aloft (like the one "captured" by Georgia farmer Ralph Horton five years later).

After this deflation, the story was dropped and forgotten for many years, except as an example of jumping to conclusions. Ufological pioneer Ted Bloecher included it under the heading "Hoaxes and Mistakes" in his classic *Report on the UFO Wave of 1947* (1967), confirming this as the accepted wisdom in saucerdom.

Then, in February 1978, Stanton Friedman met the long-retired Jesse Marcel in Louisiana. The story he heard from Marcel seemed to tie in to one he'd been told five years before, and he was inspired to re-inflate Roswell. He began mentioning the case in his talks around the country and asking people to come forward with anything they might know. Following a lecture in Minnesota, Friedman heard yet another seemingly related account—this one including the bodies of dead saucer beings!—and soon after, he had a research partner, Minnesota high school English teacher William L. Moore, who had a long-standing interest in UFOs. Friedman and Moore dug into newspaper morgues and other archives and interviewed dozens of people who claimed knowledge of the big crash and its aftermath. It wasn't long before they were convinced there was more to Roswell than a weather balloon and a beat-up radar target. They were sure the army really had bagged a flying saucer and the bodies of its crew back in 1947. Of course, the next step was a book.

Moore, who had coauthored the best-selling *Philadelphia Experiment* with Charles "Bermuda Triangle" Berlitz in 1979, persuaded Friedman that they'd have a better chance for a sale and big money if they teamed with Berlitz to do the book. Somehow, Friedman didn't get on *The Roswell Incident* (1980) as coauthor, only receiving minimal credit for his research and some share of the royalties. This didn't exactly enhance

Moore-Friedman relations, although they continued to work together for several years.

The Roswell Incident did well commercially and still is in print as a paperback, but it didn't really catch fire in saucerdom when it first came out. I remember reading it and thinking to myself, "Is this all there is?" and saying as much when Berlitz and I appeared together on the Candy Jones talk-radio show shortly after the book was published. The information about the Roswell case itself was sketchy and somewhat contradictory, and fully half the rather small volume was filler—UFO history and, worst of all, a notorious April Fool hoax photo of a captured spaceman presented as something real and mysterious. While many saucer fiends wanted to Believe, most couldn't quite bring themselves to swallow the Roswell story—yet.

Still, the efforts of Moore, Friedman, and Stringfield did have The Field buzzing and debating, much of it in the pages of my newsletter, and none of the three gave up his quest. Throughout the early 1980s, all of them presented papers on their latest findings at MUFON symposiums and on the lecture circuit—Friedman in particular, who began referring to the crash cover-up and related nefarious government activities as the (ugh!) Cosmic Watergate. All of this had the effect of lifting the stigma from crashed-saucer tales, which grew more and more popular into the mid-1980s, if not yet topping the charts. Then MJ-12 was exposed.

SO, IKE, WHAT DID YOU KNOW, and WHEN DID YOU KNOW IT?

In late 1984 an envelope with an Albuquerque postmark showed up in the mailbox of movie and television producer Jamie Shandera, a semi-mysterious associate of Bill Moore and Stan Friedman. Inside was an exposed roll of 35 mm film. When this was developed, a Great New Discovery was revealed: a supposedly Top Secret 1952 briefing paper prepared for an old friend of my father, then President-elect Dwight Eisenhower. The very mysterious organization that prepared it was the now notorious Majestic-12 Group, MJ-12 for short.

According to this document, which told of the Roswell saucer crash and another about three years later south of the Texas border in Mexico, MJ-12 had been "established by special classified executive order of President Truman on 24 September, 1947, upon recommendation by [presidential science advisor] Dr. Vannevar Bush and Secretary [of Defense]

James Forrestal." The briefing paper listed the (of course) twelve members of MJ-12. First Director of Central Intelligence Roscoe Hillenkoetter, who later served on the NICAP board (hmmm . . .) was MJ-1. Another member (MJ-?) was famed UFO debunker Donald Menzel (double hmmm . . .). All twelve were conveniently dead. Also included as an attachment was a "go ahead" memo addressed to Forrestal and signed by President Truman (wish I'd known about this when I interviewed Truman in the 1950s and 1960s!).

Supposedly, over the next two and a half years, Moore, Friedman, and Shandera closely studied the briefing document and attached memo and did hundreds of hours of research trying to confirm their authenticity. Then, in the spring of 1987, in anticipation of public release of the MJ-12 papers at that year's National UFO Conference scheduled for June 12–14 in Burbank, California, Moore and Friedman began a publicity buildup they hoped would draw big media interest. In connection with this, Moore, who was the local NUFOC host, mailed me, as national chairman of NUFOC, a completely clean and uncensored copy of the papers and discussed them with me by telephone. A few days later I flew to California from Key West (where I had relocated in late 1983), primed and ready for the convention and the big unveiling.

From the beginning, I had very serious doubts about the stuff, among other things because of internal flaws and inconsistencies and one (at least to me) glaring problem that I'm now certain was both a clever "authenticating" ploy and joke. Of course, the Believers, especially those with a stake in the papers, were not so critical. Neither, it seems, was at least one skeptic. Phil Klass contacted the FBI after the documents were made public, urging an investigation into the possible unauthorized release of highly classified information. Bill Moore has never forgiven Klass for this, and even Phil's skeptical protégé Robert Sheaffer agreed with me that *if* the documents were genuine, the public's right to know overrode any national security concerns.

Anyway, at NUFOC, Moore, Friedman, and Shandera officially released the MJ-12 papers to media and public—sort of. In his press conference presentation, Moore stated that when he received the papers, *nothing* was censored, yet the version he handed out to the press had the markings "Top Secret" and "Eyes Only" lined out, and copies distributed before the convention had different passages of text blacked out. I remember seeing four different versions, no two of which were exactly the same with respect to what could be read, although the underlying document was exactly the same. When I asked Bill about this, he said he'd done it to titillate the press. This crude stunt made a very bad impression on me and severely undermined what little inclination I had to believe the material might be authentic.

The key thing that turned me off, however, was the inclusion of Donald Menzel as an MJ-12 member and the emphasis this was given by singling him out in the briefing paper's text as being the one member who did not believe the crashed saucers and their unfortunate occupants came from Mars: "Since it is virtually certain that these craft do not originate in any country on earth, considerable speculation has centered around what their point of origin might be and how they get here. Mars was and remains a possibility, although some scientists, most notably Dr. Menzel, consider it more likely that we are dealing with beings from another solar system entirely."

Stan Friedman has made a big deal out of Menzel's alleged involvement, seeing it as strongly supporting the documents' authenticity. Stan claims that at first he was puzzled by *the* anti-saucerer being included, thinking it unlikely he would have been part of such a group. Then his research revealed Menzel had led what Friedman melodramatically called a "secret life," working as a code-breaker for the National Security Agency and doing other supersecret, behind-the-scenes deeds. None of this had anything even remotely to do with flying saucers, yet suddenly the light dawned for the Flying Saucer Physicist: Menzel's whole saucer-debunking career was just a diabolical cover operation, maybe even part of MJ-12's disinformation campaign to keep the Roswell secret under wraps.

I saw the matter somewhat differently, as I've said in print and told Friedman privately many times: Including Menzel and his alleged doubts about the saucers being from Mars was a hoaxer's very clever inside joke. Anyone who knew Menzel knew he had a fixation about *mythical* Martians. He wrote science-fiction stories about them. He doodled Martians and Martian scenes at scientific conventions. He sent out homemade Christmas cards, a couple of them to me, adorned with his sketches of cavorting Martians. He even did weird, silly paintings of Martians, four of which I bought, one autographed to me (see the photo section). None of this was a secret. Far from it.

If I knew nothing else about MJ-12, including Menzel eventually would have convinced me it was a hoax. What better way to "validate" the documents and the cover-up than to include ufology's most notorious (deceased) foe. After all, no smart hoaxer would do such a stupid thing, right? Including Menzel was a clever ploy and a subtle joke. And the joke's on Stan Friedman.

There is one other little angle I want to mention: the second saucer crash discussed in the briefing document. This supposedly took place in the "El Indio Guerrero area of the Texas-Mexico boder [*sic*]" on December 6, 1950. The location, date, and the few details about the crash and retrieval which were included were more than a little familiar to me. This was the big crash story Todd Zechel had been touting a few years before, and which he still claims to believe, while utterly rejecting Roswell. There was good reason to doubt this story during the 1970s and 1980s, and I did. Now there's every reason to completely dismiss it. Research done by "skeptical believer" ufologists Dennis Stacy and Tom Deuley has proven the origin of Zechel's (and MJ-12's) Texas-Mexico border saucer-crash story is very earthly. At the 1999 NUFOC in San Antonio, Texas, Deuley gave a talk in which he presented evidence that proved beyond any reasonable doubt that what had evolved into a 1950 saucer crash was actually the accidental fatal shoot-down of a Civil Air Patrol plane late in World War II.

So good old NUFOC had redeemed itself—and during a convention that actually turned a small profit, too, unlike the heavily promoted one in 1987. Oddly, despite all the advance publicity, the prospect of earth-shaking revelations, and a Los Angeles–area venue, the big MJ-12 NUFOC of '87 drew a disappointingly small crowd, and Bill Moore lost about two thousand dollars on it. Even so, and to his credit, Bill paid back every cent of the six hundred bucks I'd advanced him to cover early expenses, and I didn't even have to send the MIB after him to get it.

BIRDS of a FEATHER

Despite the financial setback of his NUFOC convention, Moore and his associates, buoyed by the interest and controversy they had stirred up, pressed on. It wasn't long before Bill was whispering to me of inside contacts he had in the U.S. intelligence community who were feeding him startling inside information on the UFO cover-up and human dealings with aliens. He gave these contacts code names, various sorts of birds, and collectively they became known as the Aviary. As this part of the saga began to unfold, I sought fame and cloak-and-dagger excitement by claiming to be a member of this elite group, labeling myself Oiseau (French for *bird*) and later Buzzard, alas, to no avail.

However, in September 1987 I became an Insider of sorts when I returned to Burbank at my own expense for the sole purpose of having a private showing by Moore and Shandera of videotapes they had made of a key Aviarian, the most mysterious Falcon. Selected, brief segments of some of these tapes were shown the following year on the dreadful television special *UFO Coverup?—Live*, which perhaps marked the high point of Bill Moore's saucering career.

I arrived in California firmly committed not to be hypercritical, but I just couldn't help being highly *un*impressed by all aspects of what I was shown. To begin with, there were the cheap theatrics of an alleged intelligence agent in shadow, with his back to the camera and his voice disguised electronically. If his disclosures were of matters of vital importance to the government, it wouldn't have been hard to figure out who Falcon was, though as far as I can recall, he never has been publicly identified despite a lot of informed and semi-informed guessing behind the scenes.

The content of the videos was, if anything, worse. Falcon raved at length about Jesus Christ being a spaceman; Earth being under alien surveillance for twenty-five thousand years; a shipwrecked saucer pilot kept alive by the U.S. government in a secret location, where he enjoyed strawberry ice cream and Tibetan music; and on and on and on. I remember going easy on Moore when I wrote this up in *Smear*, but Bill was sorely disappointed, as he'd hoped I would take a much more positive attitude toward what he had let me in on. He as much as told me that he hoped I would help convince The Field about the validity of his tapes (an interesting insight into Moore's judgment). He also tried to pump up my enthusiasm by telling me that there was more tape that was so secret he could not show it even to me, whom he trusted implicitly (see my above observation about his judgment).

Bill and I had several other meetings during the late 1980s, including a long, private lunch aboard the *Queen Mary* floating hotel in Long Beach, where I was staying. I've had enough "quality time" with Bill that I should be able to figure him out, yet he remains an enigma. I do remember that he once told me his religious beliefs are consistent with the idea that there are humanoid beings from other planets visiting here and the notion that Jesus was one of them. Did he invent MJ-12 and the Aviary and misconstrue Roswell to confirm his religious beliefs? Or were his motivations more down-to-earth, mere fame and fortune? Or was the whole thing a semiclever ploy to get the government to release The Truth by making up and promoting stuff that Moore considered shockingly close to the truth?

Whatever was behind what he did, it all ended in tragedy for Bill. At the very wild 1989 MUFON symposium in Las Vegas, I listened in great surprise as he delivered a long speech in which he confessed—or at least claimed—to having been in league with agents of U.S. intelligence in the early 1980s. He said he'd provided these agents with "harmless" information on various luminaries of saucerdom and even fed (harmless?) disinformation to The Field at their behest. This he did in the hope he would be given important inside saucer scoop. Instead, he said, he got only "crumbs." He also admitted that some of what Falcon and another Aviarian called Condor had said in the video clips shown during the *UFO Coverup?—Live* program the previous October wasn't true—but he didn't reveal what should or shouldn't be believed.

All in all, if this confessional was basically true, it simply proved the government was smarter than Moore thought himself to be. True or not, I think Bill expected to be hailed a Hero of Ufology and carried out of the hall on the shoulders of adoring saucer fiends. Instead, he barely got out of the place in one piece, ducking out the back way before anyone could ask a question or throw anything. Of course, it's also possible Bill's performance may have been a somewhat more dramatic version of Al Bender's way out of ufology so many years before. I suppose we'll never know for certain, but after this appearance, Moore's ufological star slammed to the ground faster and harder than a crashed saucer. Yet, amazingly, Roswell soared to even greater heights, becoming one of modern ufology's two Great Obsessions.

As for Bill Moore, in recent years he has stayed sporadically and enigmatically in touch with ufology through correspondence with Karl Pflock and me, some of which I've published in *Smear.* He now claims to have doubts about the authenticity of the MJ-12 documents he once so vigorously promoted, though he denies he had anything to do with hoaxing them. More interesting, perhaps, is this from a letter of his which I ran in the August 5, 1997, *Smear:* "I am no longer of the opinion that the extraterrestrial explanation is the *best* explanation for [the Roswell] event. . . . [I]t remains in the running as a *possible* explanation."

Bill Moore, an enigma wrapped in a questionable maybe-classified document, perched in an aviary from which all his birds have flown . . .

Life is just one damned thing after another.

—Frank Ward O'Malley

Ufologically speaking, I began the eighties with yet another lapse of semi-sanity. Despite my 1967 experience, I agreed to host the 1980 National UFO Conference, once again staging it in New York City.

The MIB MADE ME DO IT

In keeping with NUFOC tradition, I scheduled the con for the weekend closest to the anniversary of Kenneth Arnold's famed sighting, June 20–21, then began lining up speakers, hiring the hall, and so on. This joyful experience restored and confirmed forever my resolve always to give someone else the pleasure and prestige of hosting NUFOC, while I selflessly shoulder the drudgery of being a featured speaker and, usually, master of ceremonies.

The Doral Inn, located in midtown Manhattan, was the convention hotel, not nearly as grand as the Commodore of old, but a nice place nevertheless. The speakers slate kept changing almost up to the last minute, but in the final analysis, it proved to be a small but interesting group. Rick Hilberg, one of NUFOC's founding fathers, spoke on the history of UFOs from ancient times to the present. John Keel, in a rare public appearance, pontificated on his unique (that is, incomprehensible) philosophical insights into the saucer mystery. Charles Berlitz attempted to make a connection between the subjects of two of his best-sellers, the (shudder!) Bermuda Triangle and the (gasp!) Philadelphia (invisible ship) Experiment, but said not a word about Roswell, on which he was then writing his book with Bill Moore. Stan "The Flying Saucer Physicist" Friedman and Robert "The Cheery Negativist" Sheaffer perpetrated a first in the history of UFO conventions: a UFO Believer versus UFO Skeptic debate, in which both acquitted themselves well and with no rancor. (Boo! Hiss!) Stan later gave the con's closing lecture, in which he demonstrated with scientific precision and mathematical logic how close we were to a major ufological breakthrough. (We're still waiting, Stan.)

Also on the program was Betty Hill, who, since the untimely death of her husband and coabductee, Barney, in 1969, had been making wild claims of repeated UFO sightings and continuing contacts with the Space People. She told of a secret UFO landing field, where the saucers appeared to her almost nightly, and said she had taken dozens if not hundreds of photos of UFOs. She showed slides of these during her talk, and they were so obviously of aircraft navigation lights and other mundane things made streaky and strange by camera motion, lack of focus, and such, that the audience began to get restless. When she got to her outrageous tale of communicating with the Space People via a display of Christmas lights in her backyard, the crowd became downright rude. So I stepped in and insisted Betty be shown a little common courtesy. Those who remained for the balance of the presentation behaved themselves, thank goodness.

I felt very bad for Betty, who is a delightful if somewhat kooky lady. Personally, unlike my coauthor, I never thought the landmark abduction experience she and her husband reported having in 1961 was real. I'm sure they saw something in the night sky that terrified them, but I'm just as certain the answer to what they believed happened to them after that is more likely to be found in psychology than ufology. I remember watching Betty on a television talk show in 1975, part of the promotion NBC-TV was doing for the premiere of its movie based upon her UFO encounter story. To me, she was far too cheerful and enthusiastic about what most of us would consider a very frightening and degrading experience. This feeling has been reinforced during the few times I've met her since. I have no doubt Betty Hill is being entirely honest, that she believes everything she says, but I think her saucers and spacemen hail from her inner space rather than our outer space.

In a public sense, the grumbling of the masses during Betty's talk was the only significant problem I encountered during the con. In a private sense, I had a major problem with red ink. Despite a very good turnout of several hundred saucer fans, I managed to lose a couple thousand dollars, half of that on a private speakers' banquet for about twenty at Windows on the World, the restaurant that once topped the World Trade Center. Why I splurged like that is beyond me. I suspect MIB manipulation. Never again, you fiends!

The FICKLE FINGER of FATE

As far as I can recall, my first awareness of my coauthor's involvement in saucering came in late 1980, when I read an article by him in *Fate* magazine. This caught my interest because it claimed one of the last of my *Saucer News* lecture series speakers was a confessed hoaxer and, above all, because this person seemed to have totally taken in Fortean writer John Keel. Here's how I wrote up these shocking revelations in the October 25, 1980, *Saucer Smear* (as *Saucer Rear*):

> The November issue of "Fate" Magazine has an interesting article by one Karl T. Pflock entitled "Anatomy of a UFO Hoax." It tells how a young man named Tom Monteleone supposedly decided to have a little fun several years ago [in 1967], while a UFO contactee named Woody Derenberger was on a Washington, D.C. radio talk show. According to the article, Tom phoned the program, and told on the air how he had been to the same planet [Derenberger had traveled to] (Lanulos) but had seen things just a little differently there. Sure enough, Derenberger was glad to have the confirmation, and even adjusted his own story a bit to fit Monteleone's.
>
> According to Pflock, the whole thing would have ended there, except that Derenberger's manager Harold Salkin phoned Monteleone a little later, from the radio studio, and asked a lot more questions, as he was delighted to have someone back up his client's story. One thing led to another, and eventually the Monteleone contact was written up

> by Tim Beckley, John Keel, and others. Monteleone also lectured on his experience just once that we know of [in January 1970], for the SAUCER NEWS Lecture Committee (now defunct) in New York City.
>
> Your "Saucer Rear" editor was then running the New York lecture committee, and had the opportunity to talk to Tom quite a bit while he was in town. We came off with the impression (years before the present "expose") that Tom was one contactee who definitely did not believe his own story. Not only that, but he was totally different from the usual contactee profile. He was very bright & well educated [with a degree in psychology], not particularly religious, and oriented toward the reading and writing of science fiction. We made a mental note at the time that his UFO experience seemed totally out of character.
>
> As a result of the present "Fate" article, those who believed in Monteleone are justifiably upset. Salkin, who is a warm, likable, but somewhat gullible sort, still believes the story in spite of the "expose". He insists that he can prove Derenberger told him facts about Lanulos long before the radio broadcast which were then brought out on the show by Monteleone—thus proving the authenticity of both contacts.
>
> Most upset of all is John Keel, who is mentioned profusely in the "Fate" article, regarding his interviews of and writings about Monteleone. Keel has put out a Sheet which calls the "Fate" piece "an attempt to discredit my entire body of work and my professional reputation as a journalist for over thirty-five years." He intends to sue, he says. Keel's position seems to be that though *he* doesn't believe Tom Monteleone and never did, Monteleone still sticks to his story privately, and is denying it now just to get in good with the science fiction crowd. Could be!

It seems to me that no one is better qualified to further enlighten us on this interesting and amusing affair than my Esteemed Coauthor. So now I will turn over control of this book (briefly) to Karl Pflock.

Thanks, Jim. John Keel probably was correct about Tom Monteleone's motives for going public with a confession, but was entirely wrong about mine for writing my article. When I met Tom in 1974 we were budding science-fiction writers. The science-fiction community generally is not favorably disposed to UFOs and is downright death on contactee tales. I had the definite sense Tom wanted to distance himself from any intimation his contactee "career" was anything more than a youthful prank that got out of hand, and that he hoped anything I might write about it would help this along.

However, Keel—who, by the way, never followed through on his threat to sue me, *Fate*, and sundry others—was being less than candid in claiming never to have taken Tom's tale seriously. In his 1975 book *The Mothman Prophecies*, he discussed the case in detail and called it "one of the most puzzling contact stories in my files." He also made a particular point of Tom's profession of ignorance of flying saucers and famous saucer personalities. This was made during an interview in Tom's apartment, which was lined with bookcases jammed full of hundreds of science-fiction and related books—as well as Tom's psychology texts. In a number of magazine articles and at least one other book (*Operation Trojan Horse*, 1970), Keel mentioned the case and cited elements of Tom's story as evidence supporting his theories about UFOs and related spooky stuff like the Men in Black.

Speaking of the MIB, Tom told me the main thing that caused Keel to decide he was telling the truth was something he made up on the spur of the moment during their first meeting. Allegedly, Tom's "Lanulisians" had promised him a saucer flight to Lanulos. As Tom related this to Keel, he decided to add some peculiar details, just for the heck of it: The saucer had landed at a remote rural site, and the spacemen sent a car to take Tom there. This was a black 1955 or 1956 Buick Roadmaster that looked and even smelled brand-new and was driven by a silent, black-haired man in a dark overcoat.

Tom told me that when Keel heard this, he exclaimed (quoting from my *Fate* article), "That clinches it! You have just revealed to me important information that is not available to the public. There is no possible way you could have known about this unless it really happened to you. As a matter of fact, I investigated a case in which the same car was seen about three weeks ago in the Warrenton, Va., area, very close to here. This is conclusive evidence that they [the MIB] have been working in this area."

Quite by chance, Tom had "borrowed" key elements from MIB lore, which at the time were not generally well known outside fairly limited saucering and Fortean circles. Ironically, he hadn't added this new twist with the intention of convincing Keel of his truthfulness, but rather to make the story more outlandish. It was merely the product of a fertile, impish imagination and a remarkable stroke of—dare I say it?—fate.

My intention in writing the article (which I wanted to call "Keel-Hauled by a Flying Saucer," a notion vetoed by *Fate* editor Jerry Clark) was to show how credulous the "investigators" involved in the Monteleone case were. I hoped this would encourage both ufologists and UFO buffs to learn to think more critically about the stories they heard, wrote about, and read. Yet saucer skeptic James Oberg, one of Phil Klass's associates on the UFO Subcommittee of the Committee for the Scientific Investigation of Claims of the Paranormal, managed to conclude I was blaming Tom for all the confusion. In his book *UFOs and Outer Space Mysteries* (1981), Oberg took my passing observation that it is not a good idea to perpetrate hoaxes and construed it as an "ironic complaint" that "appeared to absolve the over-gullible investigators of any responsibility for careless and credulous acceptance of Monteleone's fabrications. [Pflock] . . . seemed to be saying that it wasn't their fault that they were hoaxed."

So I took heat from both sides of the UFO-belief divide, just as I have for my conclusions about the Roswell saucer non-crash. Looks like I was and still am doing *something* right!

I now return control of this book to you, Jim.

Thanks, Karl. Somehow, now seems just the right time for . . .

SEX and SAUCERS II

During the summer of 1981, at the urging of famed Bigfootologist Jon (now, for no apparent reason, Erik) Beckjord, I journeyed to a tiny rural-residential community in the Midwest to investigate a spate of Sasquatch (Bigfoot) reports that supposedly had a UFO connection. I had called ahead and arranged to stay several nights at the home of "Brenda," one of the two principal witnesses, both married women and very close friends. It seemed to me they were much closer than their conventional Midwestern neighbors might have imagined.

"Brenda," the woman in whose home I stayed, was middle-aged and clearly not happy in her marriage. She told me several times without any encouragement on my part that she and her husband hadn't had sex in many years (they later divorced). Her friend, "Laurine," who lived just a few doors away, was a very attractive young mother in her early twenties, married to a long-distance truck driver who sometimes was on the road for two or three weeks at a stretch. It was obvious to me that Brenda and Laurine were lonely and very much attached to each other.

The Great Bigfoot Flap had begun about a month before, with reports made by Laurine, who told Brenda and other neighbors a huge, hairy biped had been lurking around her home. Laurine's first awareness of this came as she was watching late-night television alone. She'd gotten up and closed the door to her children's playroom, and moments later heard "terrible noises" at the playroom window. Checking, she found part of the screen had been torn out and scratches had been made in the outside frame. (She showed me this damage, and it seemed unexceptional, something that easily could have been done by human hands and fingernails.)

Laurine immediately decided Bigfoot had a habit of watching her through the window, and he had become enraged when she blocked his view by closing the door. (Egads! Sasquatch is a Peeping Tom with a temper!) Terrified, she took her two small children and stayed at Brenda's house the rest of that night. Thereafter, concerned for her friend's safety, Brenda made a habit of spending considerable time at Laurine's, often sleeping over. Yet Laurine told me she had quickly decided there was nothing to fear from Bigfoot. In fact, she was contacting him psychically, inviting him to visit her, and was leaving her front door ajar so he could come inside.

Of course, I asked Brenda about Laurine's story. She confided that her friend's telepathic communication attempts had been amazingly successful. Bigfoot not only regularly and peacefully visited Laurine, he had become her lover!

Needless to say, I wasted no time arranging to ask Laurine about this in private. I was astounded when, without the slightest hesitation or embarrassment, she not only confirmed what Brenda had said, but volunteered that she preferred sex with Bigfoot over sex with her husband because Bigfoot's penis was smaller!

To my Humble Nonexpert mind, the Freudian and neighborly (not to mention Sasquatch research) implications of all this are, um, enormous. But I leave it to the Experts to sort everything out.

It was obvious that Laurine's tales—expurgated, of course—had infected her neighbors with Bigfoot fever, and many of them reported startling, frightening, but not X-rated encounters. The area where most of the sightings had been made included an extended lawn running seventy-five yards or more down from the row of houses in which Laurine's and Brenda's were located. The bottom of the lawn was bordered by a creek, beyond which were dense woods. Without binoculars, it was very hard to make out what one was or was not seeing in the woods, even in daylight. After talking with several Bigfoot sighters, I had little doubt that what they reported had been inspired and enhanced by fertile imaginations and a driving will to believe.

Several times I sat outside with Brenda, Laurine, or both of them until two or three in the morning listening to what they thought were Bigfoot calls (it sounded like birds to me) and hoping in vain for a sighting of the creature. On the night of a full moon, the neighborhood held a Bigfoot fish fry and lawn party, during which several ladies in the crowd endeavored to point out Bigfoot to me at various places in the woods. They could see him; I couldn't. When I insisted on going into the woods to take a closer look (and still saw nothing), the frightened ladies chose to stay behind—as did their husbands.

By odd, ahem, coincidence, I was away from my hosts' home one night when Brenda and her son saw a UFO land near the creek, to pick up Bigfoot, they thought. Brenda told me about this exciting event when I returned soon after, but a search of the area revealed nothing. (Curses!) However, early the next morning, the son shook me awake, shouting, "There's a flying saucer landing on the roof of this house *right now!*" I grabbed my camera and rushed outside, only to discover a rapidly descending hot-air balloon. There were three men in the balloon's basket, two of them dressed in dark business suits (MIB?). None bore any resemblance to Bigfoot. One of the well-dressed men leaned over to look at us gaping upward, smiled, and in a crisp British accent cheerfully said, "Good morning." Then the "saucer men" did whatever they had to do to take their balloon upward again and gradually disappeared in the sky. Brenda later claimed to have checked everywhere in the area, and there was no earthly place where the balloonists and their craft could have come from. Bigfoot's 4-D Hot-Air Balloon Rentals, perhaps?

I've long since gone as far as I can with this curious affair, but I understand Erik (formerly Jon) Beckjord currently is working on a book called *Sex and the Supernatural Sasquatch.* He definitely must include this case. Without it, his tome hardly could be considered definitive.

The (NOT SO) STRANGE CASE of MORRIS K. JESSUP

Morris K. Jessup was a real, if unconventional, scientist who in the 1950s wrote four books about UFOs and was a semiregular contributor to *Saucer News* (then called *Nexus*). He thereby established himself as an important second-tier figure in the early history of saucerdom. The first of Jessup's books was *The Case for the UFO* (1955), which really cemented Jessup's place in saucer lore when a weirdly annotated copy of it was sent to the U.S. Navy's Office of Naval Research.

Scientists at ONR contacted Jessup, who recognized the annotations, allegedly made by three people, as having been written by a single person calling himself Carlos Allende. This character, actually one named Carl Allen, had written Jessup four letters in which he offered a rambling commentary on the author's UFO ideas and claimed knowledge of a 1943 experiment in which the U.S. Navy had made a warship invisible, with all sorts of dire consequences. For some reason, a group at ONR took such interest in all this that they privately had the annotated book plus the four Allende letters done up together in a very small printing by the Varo Company, a Texas printer. This has since come to be known as "The Varo Edition," and its contents formed the basis for the Berlitz-Moore book *The Philadelphia Experiment* and all sorts of wild claims by a number of saucer fiends.

Apparently the Allende affair and Jessup's other saucering activities so tarnished his reputation in establishment science that he despaired of any future there. He tried various other ventures with not much success and seems to have made little money with his saucer books. Tragically, in 1959, at the age of fifty-nine and deeply depressed, he committed suicide.

Of course, many in saucerdom immediately leaped to the conclusion that Jessup's death was suspicious, and certain others, notably Gray Barker, delighted in taking advantage of this. In fact, Gray really seemed to enjoy perpetuating legends about Jessup, weaving the poor fellow's suicide in with other elements of UFO folklore. Besides publishing his own book *The Strange Case of Dr. M. K. Jessup* (1963) and many articles in his magazine and newsletter, in 1981 he released *The Jessup Dimension*, a peculiar volume by Anna Genzlinger. The psychically oriented, wealthy, and well-intentioned Mrs. Genzlinger had taken up an investigation of Jessup's death about twenty years after the fact, the results of which she reported in *The Jessup Dimension*. Of course, her research confirmed her conviction that Jessup's death wasn't suicide, but rather murder made to look like suicide. She even thought it might have been perpetrated via "mind control," by which They (whoever They are) made Jessup the innocent instrument of his own death.

Genzlinger *wanted* to believe Jessup's death was mysterious, just as so many today *want* to believe that the government or other mysterious forces are so concerned about saucerdom that The Field and leading saucerers are targets of disinformation campaigns, threats, surveillance, telephone taps, and so on. If Jessup knew something important enough for Them to drive him to suicide, then saucerers could vicariously feel a little more important. Their drab, dreary lives would be brightened up just a bit, knowing that Jessup knew something they didn't but which they might somehow, someday find out, knowing that they were a part of a Noble Quest for Truth.

In this case, the truth is that the objective evidence unmistakably pointed to more mundane conclusions about Jessup and his demise. No one who had met Carlos Allende, as I had, could ever take seriously anything he said, annotated, or wrote about. As even Genzlinger admitted, Jessup sent letters expressing a clear intent of suicide to Long John Nebel and others. The one to Long John, which I read at the time, included a description of an experiment Jessup wanted the radio talk-show host to try on the air. The idea was to see if Jessup could come back from the dead or at least be contacted on the Other Side under certain controlled conditions. I was to participate, but Jessup's widow threatened to sue the radio station if Long John followed through. Thus, the only "mysterious" matter associated with Jessup's death was never explored.

"I JUST DON'T HAVE TIME to MAKE IT MYSELF"

In late 1983 I relocated from dreary Fort Lee, New Jersey, to sunny, funky Key West, Florida, with a friend named Anna Montgomery (an arrangement that lasted for about three years until she decided to return to the frozen north). I bought a house in the Oldtown section of the city, and on the ground floor set up a pre-Columbian antiques business called Rose Lane Antiquities.

My inventory was mainly pre-Columbian pottery and other artifacts from Peru, which I had received in the early 1970s from another American grave robber living in Lima, who shall remain "Nameless" here. The laws governing importation of such things were beginning to change just then, but with effort I was able to clear everything through customs in New York. I then stored and sold it for Nameless and sent him the proceeds minus a fee. When I decided to move from one location in Fort Lee, to another, I asked Nameless to take back his remaining goods, which I estimated to have a retail value of about $70,000. Incredibly, he essentially refused to take anything back. So when I moved to Key West and launched my business, I had a very good start-up inventory at no cost.

So there I was, selling out of my own house, rent-free. My basic inventory was free, and the rest of what I sold—pre-Columbian items from countries other than Peru and some African primitive pieces—was on consignment from dealers I knew in New York. I had no investment in inventory and no overhead. Naturally, I made a fortune. Wrong.

During the five years I was in business, I barely broke even (my ever-shining business goal). In part this was because I plowed my profits back into advertising, but mainly it was because the primitive-art market is very small. There are just too few customers. Even though I was only a half-block off Duval Street, Key West's main drag, only five or six people would come in on a typical day.

I found that most gladly would buy the ordinary items priced at a couple hundred dollars or less, but they wouldn't take a chance on the better, more expensive stuff, even with my money-back guarantee. Faced with this, I didn't try to stock truly fine, expensive items, so that when the very few serious collectors who really knew what they were doing showed up, they didn't buy anything either. A case in point is the late actor Vincent Price, who came in with his wife. At the time he was one of the biggest collectors of pre-Columbian art in America. Both he and his wife were very cordial and quite polite about what I had to offer, but bought nothing.

Somewhere near the other end of the customer spectrum was a very well dressed, prosperous-looking black woman. She spent about five minutes looking at all the shelves without saying anything. Then she asked me in all seriousness, "Do you have this stuff brought in, or do you make it yourself?" Obviously, she thought I was selling Key West curios or other such souvenir junk. Wearily, I told her, "Lady, I'll have to confess to you that I have it brought in. I just don't have time to make it myself." She replied, "I thought so," and walked out without another word.

GRAY ROSCOE BARKER, 1925–1984

On December 6, 1984, I lost my best friend. After a long series of illnesses, Gray Barker died in a Charleston, West Virginia, hospital. He was fifty-nine, far too young. With his passing, the door fully closed on the "classic" era of saucering, though in truth, I suppose, that age really ended with the 1950s, leaving just a few of the old guard like Gray and me still kicking around. There's not much more to say, except perhaps as I tried to say it in this poem of sorts, which I penned not quite a year after Gray's death:

Back to You, Gray Barker

I tried to phone Gray Barker tonight
Like we used to do.
I dialed the 304 area code
(So close to 305, in Florida);
And the robot said,
"You can't dial him where he is now
The li-ons don't go out that far."
And I sassed the robot, saying,
"How far out do the li-ons go?"
And it replied, mockingly,
"Thank you for using AT&T."

I tried to write Gray Barker the other day
Like we used to do.
I put on a "D" stamp
(Was there *ever* a "C"?)
And the letter came back to me,
Together with a warning
Stamped on the envelope:
"For Domestic Use Only."
A man from the Post Office Department came by
And informed me
That R. E. Straith is dead.

I tried to reach Gray Barker the other night,
Telepathically, as if in a dream;
And I saw this circle of Beings
Clustered around a smoldering cauldron.
Here was Palmer and Arnold and Jessup and Wilkins;
And Layne and Edwards and Scully and Van Tassel;
All their differences forgotten;
And George Adamski, with his telescope;
And here too was Gray Barker
With a drink in his hand,
Stirring the cauldron so vigorously
That his hand shook;
So I asked him, "When may I join you?"
And George Adamski answered, for the group:
"Time Will Tell."

MYSTERIES of CORAL CASTLE—REVEALED

Early in February 1985 in an unsuccessful attempt to boost sales at Rose Lane Antiquities, I appeared on Miami radio station WGBS, discussing UFOs, ancient astronauts, and, of course, pre-Columbian South American art and artifacts with host Mike Spandell and call-in listeners. In the course of my ravings, I touched upon mysterious Coral Castle, a Florida tourist attraction a few miles south of Miami on U.S. 1. This fairyland-like structure consists of huge, beautifully carved rocks weighing many tons each. It was built single-handedly by a lovelorn Latvian immigrant named Ed Leedskalnin, who died in 1951 without revealing the secret of how he, weighing little more than one hundred pounds, had managed to transport, carve, and set the massive stones.

I explained how many people, including myself, had speculated that Leedskalnin—just as he'd claimed—had rediscovered the construction secrets of the Egyptian pyramids, or even that he had help from the Space People. Such notions have not been discouraged by those who owned Coral Castle over the years since its creator's death. Understandably, they're interested in making a buck or two.

I "discovered" Coral Castle in the late 1950s and wrote an article about it, which I ran in *Saucer News* (September 1963). This was a paraphrasing of a pamphlet that once was on sale at the castle souvenir stand, but which by the mid-1980s had been "suppressed," apparently as it could dampen any desire to take a paid tour of the place.

Gray Barker and I included this article in my 1967 anthology *Jim Moseley's Book of Saucer News*, which saucerer/science-fiction writer/artist Otto Binder then used as a reference for a discussion of Coral Castle in one of his books. Thereafter, the castle's owners framed the relevant page from Binder's book and hung it on the wall of the souvenir shop. Thus, the circle was completed, and once again I became an instant Expert, essentially just by having read and rewritten a pamphlet for sale in the very same shop. (*Sic transit* UFO research!)

When I appeared on the Spandell show, I still felt the castle was at least somewhat mysterious, but like other Fortean writer-researchers, I hadn't made any attempt to locate and interview people who might have known Leedskalnin when he was alive and shaping his labor of love. Such thoughts were discouraged by the castle tour guides' emphasis that Ed *always* worked alone, *always* stopping if anyone came to watch. So it seemed useless to pursue the matter.

As Spandell and I talked about Coral Castle, a listener named Earl Lee called in. He said he had been a friend of Leedskalnin and had watched him work during the late 1920s. This was a time when the construction was about three miles south of its present location. It seems that about 1935, Leedskalnin decided to move and took with him—by the mundane means of a truck—the huge rocks he had carved up till then, repositioning and adding to them at the current site.

A few days after the radio show, I located and interviewed Earl Lee. When Lee was a boy, he and several friends from the area had spent many hours talking with Leedskalnin and watching him work. (It was well known that Ed liked kids and enjoyed having them around, so this was credible.) Lee explained that the eccentric Latvian had built his mysterious castle with simple levers, counterweights, and very hard work, with not a bit of advice taken from ancient papyri or whispered to him by spacemen. Adding insult to injury, Lee also told me and I later confirmed that Coral Castle, which Leedskalnin called "Rock Gate," isn't made of coral at all, but rather of a stone called oolite.

Shockingly, the mundane facts are never mentioned at Coral Castle, where in the 1980s—and maybe still today—the mimeographed booklet *The Enigma of Coral Castle* by one Ray Stoner (!) was on sale. Therein, the author compared the castle favorably with the Great Pyramid of Egypt, Stonehenge, and Mexico's Pyramid of the Sun—all of which he found most mysterious. Stoner concluded that Leedskalnin's remarkable work was accomplished through esoteric knowledge, or, alternatively, that the man actually was a time traveler, an interdimensional being, or a spaceman! Stoner's only attempt to solve the mystery was through pseudomathematical mumbo-jumbo, the exposition of which took up most of his booklet.

Sic transit illusions about semi-ancient mysteries. And yet, let's not sell Ed Leedskalnin short. Probably no man in American history ever moved and positioned so many tons of stone all by himself, and then carved them into such interesting shapes to please the eye of the beholder. Hats off to you Ed, even though—no, *especially because* you weren't an extraterrestrial!

FIASCO NEAR FRISCO

In 1985 the glorious NUFOC sank to its all-time low, unmatched before or since. Our local sponsor and exactly one-half the speakers was a teenaged Kal K. Korff. Very intelligent and rather arrogant, as he remains today, Kal had already achieved a measure of ufological fame with his preliminary exposé of Swiss contactee Billy Meier, who among other things cranked out dozens and dozens of amazingly sharp photos of saucers from the Pleiades. In recent years, Korff has produced an incredibly detailed (yawn) book about Meier and another less weighty skeptical tome on the Roswell crashed-saucer affair, as well as being involved in some television exposés of sundry Fortean claims having to do with Bigfoot and the like. Although both of us have gone through the motions, we've never been able to develop any sort of rapport, and Korff now lives in Europe, which I suppose is America's loss.

I remember Kal best, if not fondly, for the '85 NUFOC, which (barely) took place close to, but unfortunately not in, San Francisco. Instead, it was held in the nearby metropolis of Fremont, Korff's hometown. I suspect this largely was because Kal was able to get free use of his high school alma mater's basketball auditorium. He also managed to save money by not doing any advertising, relying on mentions in *Smear* and, I suppose, word of mouth. In keeping with this "theme," Kal selected as the official NUFOC motel an establishment that for complicated reasons was so unsuitable not one convention participant stayed there. Topping things off, he failed to have the NUFOC Ufologist of the Year Award plaque ready in time. Fortunately, this was to be presented to Center for UFO Studies treasurer John Timmerman in absentia, so *its* absence wasn't a major problem. (John, have you ever gotten your plaque?)

For reasons known only to Korff, he would not allow any speakers but himself and his then-friend Bill Moore. The lone con session, on the evening of May 25, was attended by a pitiful "crowd" of thirty or so, including the speakers and the school janitor. I shared master of ceremonies duties with a malfunctioning microphone and a faltering sound system. Moore spoke well, on Roswell, of course. Korff's slide-illustrated lecture was a long-winded attempt to prove his contention that he was neither a skeptic nor a believer, but merely an objective saucer researcher, one of his recurring themes even today. He wound down about midnight, and the twenty-second NUFOC convention was history. At least Kal's minimal efforts averted a break in our world-record string of annual events. Fort be praised!

More interesting was a gathering two nights before the convention. Korff and I spoke at the monthly meeting of the Bay Area Skeptics, hosted by Robert Sheaffer. Speaking first, I told the group about four mysterious UFOish cases I'd personally investigated over the years, all of which turned out to have very mundane explanations. I emphasized that, unlike many who consider themselves skeptics, I did not conclude from this that there can't be other cases that truly are mysterious. My point, I said, was that after almost forty years, nothing really mysterious had yet been *proven* about *any* UFO case. In my Humble Opinion, this sort of critically thoughtful open-mindedness is genuine skepticism.

Following my presentation, Kal droned on about something I don't recall, likely why he's neither skeptic nor believer, and so on. There followed a lively discussion period, consisting largely of a long but interesting technical discussion between Sheaffer and Todd Zechel's old associate Brad Sparks. The two debated the evidence for and against the authenticity of what may be the two most famous of reasonably credible UFO photos, taken in May 1950 by McMinnville, Oregon, farmer Paul Trent. These show a classic flying saucer close to the ground and not far from the witness, and they stumped Condon Committee investigators. While I wasn't and still am not convinced the Trent photos have been proven genuine, it seemed to me Sparks won the debate hands down that night.

A weird touch was added to the proceedings by Bill Moore, who was in the audience. As I reported in *Smear* (July 1, 1985), he "shared with us the intriguing 'fact' that Phil Klass has threatened to kill him. When called on this, he retreated to the position that even if Klass did not mean the threat seriously, he is nevertheless 'sick'. All the Believers in the audience seemed to agree with this, with the exception of your editor," who was and is a Skeptical Believer.

Too bad I didn't think of asking Sheaffer to double bill his meeting as NUFOC 1985. Then *I* could have claimed credit for an interesting and entertaining event.

Let us give thanks for the fools. But for them the rest of us could not succeed.
—Mark Twain

Now we come to one of the wildest and most complicated cases in the annals of Recent Ufology, rivaled only by Roswell. It may (or may not) be that I am the only one who understands the essence of the whole caper—which I reveal here in semi-coherent form for the first time.

SPACE DOGS?

This bizarre saga supposedly began to unfold on the evening of November 11, 1987. About 5 P.M., Ed Walters, a very successful home builder-developer in the small Florida panhandle town of Gulf Breeze, was working in his home office when he saw a strange glow emanating from behind a pine tree in his front yard. When he went outside for a closer look, he spotted a flying saucer shaped like an old-fashioned child's humming or musical top. It had a row of portholes around its midsection and a brightly glowing ring on the bottom. The object was hovering fairly close to the ground, only about 150 feet from where Walters stood.

Ed ducked back into his office, picked up his old Polaroid camera, stepped back out, and snapped four pictures of the saucer as it slowly drifted from behind the tree. Out of film, Ed got more, took another photo, and then ran out into the street in front of his house, trying to get closer to the UFO, which by then was crossing the road. He planned to get more pictures, but suddenly the saucer was right above him, and he was hit by a bright blue beam that paralyzed and lifted him several feet off the ground (shades of Travis Walton). Ed smelled a foul odor, like ammonia mixed with cinnamon, and heard a weird, "computer-like" voice inside his head saying, "We will not harm you." He responded by screaming, whereupon a female voice began speaking to him and he saw images of dogs (!) flash before him. Then he was unceremoniously dumped on the road. Ed didn't see the saucer leave. It was just gone.

Inside the house, Ed's son, Danny, a high school senior, somehow had completely missed his father's frightening experience, and for some reason Ed didn't say a word to him about it. Instead, he waited until his wife, Frances, got home from a shopping trip and told her. She later claimed Ed was very frightened and said she could smell the strange, pungent odor on him. Later in the evening, Ed and Frances sat down with Danny and their daughter, thirteen-year-old Laura, and told them what had happened.

MR. X

About a week later, Ed went to see his friend Duane Cook, editor of the *Gulf Breeze Sentinel*, the local weekly newspaper. He showed Cook his saucer photos, claiming they had been given to him by one Mr. X, who was publicity shy. He also gave the editor a letter from X, describing what had happened on November 11. This actually was written by Walters and his wife. A couple of days later, Cook ran the photos and letter in his paper, along with a photo caption asking anyone who knew anything about the incident to come forward.

Before long, Ed, Frances, and, through them, their kids were claiming all sorts of close encounters with UFOs just like the one Ed had photographed and almost been space-napped by on November 11. Ed claimed he usually knew in advance when an encounter was going to happen, alerted by a mysterious hum only he could hear. He also received further telepathic communications during some of the encounters, with the alien stalkers calling him "Zehaas" (*Ed* in Reticulian?). A saucer landing "trace"—a twelve-foot perfect circle of dead grass—was "found" on the grounds of the high school near Ed's house. There were even "creature" sightings, my favorite being the big-eyed Peeping Tom clad in armor (?) and toting a glowing wand, who came out of the night in an attempt to spy on Ed and Frances in their bedroom.

Of course, Ed was getting many more amazing new photos of huge, glowing UFOs in the skies over Gulf Breeze—but, oddly, none at all of the beings who piloted them. This set off a local flap, in which many town and area residents reported sighting saucers identical to those shown in photos published in the paper—Ed's and others from two anonymous sources, "Jane" and "Believer Bill," who of course could have been, ahem, Mr. X.

IT'S a WRAP

The Walterses' experiences ended abruptly on May 1, 1988, with the twentieth UFO encounter in about six months, which was a real biggie. By this time, a special MUFON local investigative team had been at work for several weeks, with two major Serious Ufologists consulting. These were my old "friend" Budd Hopkins, who by then was the leading UFO abductions guru, and Dr. Bruce Maccabee, a U.S. government optical physicist and longtime independent UFO investigator specializing in photo cases. Hopkins had been called in by MUFON Florida State Director Donald Ware, who wanted him not only to look into possible abduction elements of the Gulf Breeze events, but also to give Ed Walters advice on what to do about a big-money book offer he had received. Hopkins met with Ed and his family in February 1988 and again on April 20, 1988, a week and a half before the experience Ed somehow knew would be his last, an experience during which he was (surprise) abducted.

Shortly after midnight on the morning of May 1, Ed was alone on a Gulf Breeze beach attempting to get scientifically measurable photos of one of the UFOs with equipment and instructions supplied by Maccabee. The UFO appeared, and the next thing Ed knew, it was more than an hour later. He was lying on the beach some yards from where he had been standing by his tripod-mounted camera. There were strange bruises and red marks on his face and he had some foul-smelling gunk under his fingernails (preserved for analysis, results never revealed, as far as I know).

Later, via regressive hypnosis, it was discovered Ed had been abducted and subjected to all sorts of "disgusting" indignities. Also unleashed by the hypnosis were memories of past abductions, including one of Ed's older brother. It seemed the aliens had been taking a long-term interest in "Mr. Ed" and his family, coincidentally, of course, a theme of Budd Hopkins's abduction findings.

INVASION of the MUFONITES

Right from the beginning, this case generated tremendous interest and controversy in saucerdom. With typical abandon, Walt Andrus decided Ed's story was true—even while the MUFON "investigation" was still underway. So naturally MUFON staunchly and publicly supported Ed. The leaders of CUFOS, somewhat less credulous than Walt in those days, expressed grave doubts and before long denounced the affair as an elaborate hoax.

One debunker himself resorted to a hoax in an attempt to discredit Walters. Learning that the Walters family had taken a vacation trip to New York City, Willy Smith, at the time a MUFON bigwig, had a professional photographer fake photos showing a "Mr. Ed saucer" hovering near the Chrysler Building, in the air near Ed's home, and so on, and then distributed them to various ufologists with a letter claiming they had been faked by Ed. (The photographer seems to have been innocent of what Smith was up to.) This stunt, exposed in *Saucer Smear*, led to Smith's expulsion from MUFON. As time went on and more was learned about Ed Walters and his activities, many MUFON leaders began to question the organization's blessing of Ed's claims and photos. But Walt would not be dissuaded, and others followed Willy Smith into exile.

When the story first broke in November 1988, I was eager to look into it myself. Not only was it a dramatic case, it was fairly close to my home in Key West. As interested as I was, I decided to wait for a few months after Ed's last reported experience before getting involved in person, meanwhile reporting latest developments and the antics of other involved saucerers in *Smear*. I didn't want to have to compete with all the MUFON investigators who were chasing after Ed and feeding his ego. Besides, by that time, I myself was (tah, dah!) MUFON state section director for Monroe County, Florida (Key West and vicinity), and snooping around in Gulf Breeze might have been seen by MUFON International Headquarters as poaching or some such and gotten me (horrors!) drummed out of the organization. (Which I all but was, eventually, the reasons for which along with the full exciting story of my MUFON career will be revealed in our next thrilling chapter.)

The ULTIMATE PRANKSTER?

While I waited and watched, the controversy continued to build. Nick Mock, a teenaged friend of Ed's son, Danny, went public with claims that Ed was known among local teenagers as a joker who had bragged before he started reporting UFO encounters that he was going to come up with the "ultimate prank." He said Ed entertained Danny and his school friends at his home, where he produced weird double-exposed photos for the kids' amusement. He also alleged Ed had taken him aside and warned him to stop calling him a prankster and joker.

The inevitable Phil Klass got into the act by digging into Ed's past and discovering that, while in college and still a teenager, he had been arrested for car theft and check forgery. Klass also found that Ed was simultaneously using the names Ed Walters and Ed Hanson, in an odd attempt to keep at least some of his friends and neighbors from knowing about his nefarious past. In a letter published in *Smear* (July 20, 1989), Ed admitted his youthful indiscretions and that he'd served two and a half years on the bad-check charge (the cars had been returned, so those charges were dropped). Still later, Ed got the governor of Florida to grant him a pardon, based on his twenty-five or more years of exemplary living, community service, and so forth, and in spite of his UFO-photos caper—though I suppose that, too, may have been considered community service, as it gave a nice boost to tourism in the Gulf Breeze area. Curiously, as far as I know, Klass has never publicly acknowledged Ed's pardon, which it seems to me is the fair thing to do.

POSSESSED!

I finally journeyed to Gulf Breeze on December 16, 1988, meeting with Ed and Frances in their luxurious home the next day. This was the first of several occasions I've spent time with the Walters. Both were genial and charming, and I rather liked them. On this visit, I spent several hours interviewing Ed, with Frances joining us now and then. Of course, Ed made every effort to refute the charges leveled against him by Nick Mock, Willy Smith, and others, and at the time much of what he said seemed reasonable.

One thing that raised very serious questions in my mind about Ed's claims was an infamous videotape, shot by his friend and *Gulf Breeze Sentinel* editor Duane Cook. This was done on January 24, 1988, when Ed supposedly found himself once again compelled to rendezvous with a UFO. Allegedly, he asked Cook to join him in the hope the newspaperman would see the saucer and become a supporting witness.

During my visit, Ed assumed I knew about the video and expected to see it. Actually, I'd never heard of it, but pretended I had. So, after sending thirteen-year-old daughter Laura to bed because he didn't want her to hear the language he used during the incident captured on the tape, we sat down for a viewing. Thus it was that I became one of a very few to see the entire forty-five minutes or so of this amazing "evidence," which Ed soon wisely decided to suppress.

The motif of this amazing production is less UFOs and more demon or evil-entity possession. Ed is driving his truck, while Cook is videotaping him from the passenger seat beside him. Ed keeps cursing a blue streak, wildly and excessively (in normal conversation, Ed rarely swears). He babbles on about how the entities/space beings are attacking him psychically, that he can *feel* it, that his face is contorted, with one eye being pushed out, and on and on. I almost laughed out loud when he asked Cook, "Isn't my face contorted?" and Cook replied, "No, Ed. You look about the same as you always do." Finally, Ed stops the truck, quickly gets out, Polaroid in hand, and snaps a picture of a UFO in the night sky. Cook is slower to leave the truck, and by the time Ed can point out the UFO, the thing's gone. Ed then shows Cook the photo he seemingly just took, and by what I call Saucer Logic, Cook declares that because he saw Ed take the picture, that proves a UFO was actually there, at least for a brief moment. (Here again I had to suppress an almost overwhelming urge to laugh my head off.)

I later learned from one of *Smear*'s army of Usually Reliable Sources that the same evening the video was taken, a Reliable Friend of my Source was present in Ed's home when Walters and Cook were viewing the tape. Both were laughing heartily about it. This is hard to square with the terror Ed allegedly was experiencing when he allegedly thought he was being taken over by evil space beings. However, it definitely is consistent with

Ed's really awful acting on the tape. It is beyond me how any pro-Ed person seeing the video could be anything but terribly disillusioned, yet one who has, Bruce Maccabee, remains a staunch Mr. Ed booster.

Of course, this *may* have something to do with the fact that Bruce reportedly got as much as $20,000 to write up the results of his photo analysis for Ed and Frances's (first) book about their experiences. This was *The Gulf Breeze Sightings* (1990), for which Maccabee wrote a long section "proving" the authenticity of Ed's photos, and to which Budd Hopkins contributed a substantial introduction (wonder how much he got?). Naturally, Ed and Frances did even better with the book than Bruce and Budd. According to the April 7, 1989, *Publishers Weekly*, William Morrow and Company paid them a $200,000 advance. The same article revealed they'd gotten another $100,000 (against a promised $450,000) from an unnamed television production company for a never-produced miniseries. The paperback edition came out in 1991, and it's a safe bet a pretty penny was paid for that, too. It appears Budd Hopkins's advice proved very helpful. Maybe he should give up abductology and become a literary agent.

DOUBLE EXPOSED

A couple of months after Ed and Frances's book was released, the *Pensacola News Journal*, published just across the bay from Gulf Breeze, reported that the new resident of the house the Walters had lived in at the time of their UFO sightings had found a saucer model in the attic. It looked exactly like the saucers in Ed's photos, and part of it was made from drafting paper, on the back of which were some notations in Ed's handwriting.

Of course, there was much convoluted disputation about who made the model and put it in the attic, when the model was made, and so on. Ed said the notes on the drafting paper were for a house he never built and were made in September 1989, long after his UFO experiences. Besides, he asked, if he were a hoaxer, would he be so foolish as to leave such damning evidence behind when he moved? Obviously, he and his defenders said, some evil debunker had fished the paper out of Ed's trash, built the model, and stashed it in the attic of his old house, a ticking time bomb waiting to be found and discredit him. Ed's detractors countered with various reasons why the paper and Ed's scribbles easily could have predated his saucering adventures. They also pointed out that Ed's "Would I be so dumb?" retort could be read as the response of a very clever man attempting to cover up a potentially devastating error by introducing reasonable doubt in the minds of those wanting to believe him.

As for me, since the model was found in a place where it was likely no one would come upon it for quite a long time, the skeptic-hoax idea makes no sense. Anyone trying to embarrass Ed would have picked a more accessible location. I think Walters deliberately put the model in the attic hoping it would be found years later, at a time when he could enjoy a hearty "gotcha" horselaugh. When fate thwarted this long-range scheme before Ed had milked everything he could from his UFO adventures, he was forced to resort to his "Would I be so dumb?" defense.

Whatever the truth may be, a week after the model swooped out of the attic, Tommy Smith came forward. He was the son of a prominent Gulf Breeze lawyer and a former friend of Danny Walters. Smith said the discovery of the UFO model inspired him to tell what he knew of Ed's activities. Smith claimed he, Danny, and another kid named Hank Boland had watched Ed make fake UFO pictures, using a model and double exposures. This, he said, was in early November 1987, and shortly afterward, Ed asked him to take five of the fake saucer photos to the *Gulf Breeze Sentinel* and claim he was the photographer, giving Ed a backup witness not cloaked in anonymity. Smith refused, saying he could understand a practical joke, but that Ed was taking things too far. Smith also claimed the entire Walters family was in on the gag, and that the "saucer landing" circle had been created by one or more of the Walters clan tromping on an upside-down trampoline.

Smith's revelations prompted a race to see who could get to Hank Boland first—Ed Walters versus Gulf Breeze mayor Ed Gray and town police chief Jerry Brown, both of whom had been outspokenly skeptical about Ed's tales from the beginning, apparently concerned Ed was giving their fair city a bad name. Boland had moved to Chicago, so the very determined Gray and Brown flew there to see him. They first met with Boland at his home, where he refused to confirm or deny what Smith had said. Later in the day, the two men confronted Boland at work. He then supported Ed Walters's side of the story. Ed may not have gotten to Boland first, but he seems to have been more persuasive when he did make the connection.

Days later, in the same Pensacola hotel where MUFON would stage its annual convention the following month, Walt Andrus held a press conference, Ed and Frances Walters at his side. Andrus declared his personal belief that the Walterses' experiences were real and proof of alien visitation. He pledged MUFON's continuing support, but then announced the organization was reopening its investigation (an odd way to show support, it seems to me). The reinvestigation was to be conducted by Rex and Carol Salisberry, MUFON state section directors for the Pensacola area and staunch MUFONites who, at the MUFON convention a couple of weeks later, received a special award from Walt for the quality and volume of their UFO-sighting case work.

Apparently, the Salisberrys didn't understand their marching orders from International Headquarters. They conducted a careful and apparently objective investigation of Ed's claims, and their "interim report" was very negative. Among other things, they interviewed one of the Walterses' neighbors, who told them that, from about 4:30 to 6:00 P.M. on November 11, 1987, he and two local salespeople were in his front yard negotiating some work to be done. The area where Ed's blue-beaming UFO was supposed to be lurking was in plain view the entire time. None of the three saw a UFO or even Ed with his trusty Polaroid in hand. In short order, the Salisburys were booted out of MUFON, and their report was tossed aside in favor of the results of another (surprise!) positive review of the case. None of this did MUFON any good, but Walt weathered the storm and ruled for ten more years.

The ESSENCE of the CAPER

There's more, like the six U.S. Army intelligence soldiers who went AWOL in Germany and headed for Gulf Breeze for mystical-ufological reasons unconnected with Ed Walters, but I think it's now time for me to give the world my take on this crazy affair. (Those interested in the full story of the "Gulf Breeze Six" will find at least most of it in the August 25, 1990, *Saucer Smear*, with follow-ups here and there in subsequent issues.)

As has already been revealed, Ed Walters had been something of a juvenile delinquent. As I got to know him, I came to feel he retained a rather hostile and sneering attitude toward society, but wisely decided to beat the system legally and properly, and so became a successful builder-developer. Still, his somewhat antisocial side was always lurking in the background, aided and abetted by a tremendous ego and a rather sick sense of humor. (Okay. Okay. Yes, it does take one to know one.)

When Ed's son, Danny, became a teenager, Ed decided to get involved in civic-minded, kids-oriented activities, including heading up a successful effort to build a community recreation center. He also began holding regular parties at his home for Danny's teenaged friends. That's when things started to get weird. During at least one of these parties, Ed made double-exposure photos, one of which showed the face of a "ghost demon" peering over a girl's shoulder. This was all fun and games, but it seems to me it reflected not only Ed's fun-loving side but also a dark side involving at least an interest in the occult.

After the success of the ghost-demon photos, Ed decided to go a step further and fake some UFO pictures, with the help of Danny, Tommy Smith, and Hank Boland. It was this that Smith exposed. Ed tried to poke holes in Smith's story, which was backed up by his socially very prominent parents, but he couldn't even dent the Smiths' character. He tried, calling Tom Smith Sr. a religious fanatic, which I found hilarious, as the Smiths were Episcopalians. I was raised an Episcopalian and know that members of that upper-crusty church are fanatical only about two things: money and social standing.

So the faking of UFO photos with teenagers was the second phase of Ed's activities. His submission of at least some of these photos to the *Gulf Breeze Sentinel*, allegedly on behalf of Mr. X, probably would have been the end of it all, but then MUFON got involved and made a big deal out of everything. In short order, Ed was being pursued by book publishers, writers wanting to coauthor books with him, television and movie producers waving contracts, and so on. Suddenly he realized there was real money to be made from UFO fakery. I'm absolutely convinced that if it hadn't been for MUFON, Ed never would have gone on to phase three, moneygrubbing. It was the gullibility of Walt Andrus and MUFON that raised an essentially harmless local hoax to the level of a nationally publicized piece of outrageous—and profitable—nonsense.

There are those who claim Ed couldn't have been a hoaxer, because he was a millionaire and didn't need the money. However, by strange coincidence, about the time Ed began his moneygrubbing phase, there was a period of a year or two when the local real estate market went into a major slump and Ed's building business dropped way off. The saucer bucks filled the gap very nicely for him.

Then came phase four. When the money stopped coming in and the whole thing got boring for Ed, he just completely withdrew from The Field. I remember that he had tried to start a national UFO newsletter, which was to be marketed through a professionally planned television advertising campaign. Ed tested the waters and found there was no money to be made there after all, so he dropped the idea like a badly faked UFO photo. I doubt his and Frances's second book, *UFO Abduc-*

tions in Gulf Breeze (1994), did very well either, another sign it was time to quit. Ed did try to stage a ufological comeback in 1997 (another business slump?), coauthoring the paperback *UFOs Are Real: Here's the Proof* with Bruce Maccabee. But that seems to have done even less well than his second collaboration with Frances, and Ed has been sticking to more earthly business since.

Something else that suggests to me Ed is not a "real" contactee/abductee is that his alleged experiences failed to change his life at all over the long term. Adamski, Fry, Berthurum, Angelucci, and all the others continued to have new adventures with the Space People throughout their lives, continued to spout spiritual nonsense they said they'd learned from their Space Brothers, and purported to have the course of their lives altered permanently, supposedly for the better. Walters just cut things off when it suited him, and went back to the life of an ordinary businessman.

Ed Walters and I had a friendly understanding. He didn't mind that I didn't believe his pictures and stories, but he quite naturally couldn't stand debunkers like Phil Klass, Willy Smith, and others who went after him. I told him I would not debunk him in *Smear.* (Professional courtesy? Maybe.) That was good enough for him, and we remained friends on that level.

I recall taking Ed and Frances to dinner near Gulf Breeze at the time when rumors were circulating that they were going to break up. The purpose of the dinner, from Ed and Frances's point of view, was to disprove the rumors, and they seemed and acted quite normal and friendly with each other. Having a somewhat different aim than theirs, after a couple of drinks, I pointedly said, "If you two should break up and either one of you should ever decide to change your story, please come to me and I'll be delighted to print it." They looked at each other quite deliberately for a long moment and said not a word.

Shortly after this interesting dinner, Ed and Frances did divorce, splitting $2.5 million down the middle. Neither one of them has come to me with a confession—yet.

PART 5

Back to the Future —Film title

This is fairy gold, boy, and 'twill prove so.

—William Shakespeare

Saucerdom has always had more than its share of paranoia, but in the 1980s such fears began to take over. By the early 1990s The Field was awash in it. Whoever thought up this popular bumper-sticker plea easily could have had late-twentieth- and early-twenty-first-century ufology in mind: "Help! The Paranoids Are After Me!"

Sex-crazed little alien Grays—not to mention rough Reptilians and icky Insectoids—were snatching and doing bad things to unsuspecting earthlings by the thousands—anally probing, stealing eggs and sperm, raping both women and men, creating alien-human hybrids, and playing weird mind games. Heavy-handed government thugs, and maybe a MIB or three, were intimidating those who Knew Too Much—especially about Roswell and other crashed-saucer affairs. There were even alien-earthling conspiracies, treaties under which, in exchange for at least some of their super-advanced technology, the space beings were given permission by the U.S. and other governments to abduct us at will, even process us as food in underground bases here on Earth. The government knew The Truth about all this, but refused to come clean.

Meanwhile, the dearth of plain old ordinary saucer sightings continued. Formations of silvery disks no longer whizzed through the skies. Garden-variety landings, close encounters, and little-men cases were passé—unless the witnesses, now more often known as "experiencers," said they were abducted. The few "conventional" sightings that came in no longer were of much interest to Serious Ufologists and certainly not to your average saucer fiend, unless an abduction connection or something similarly exotic could be divined. Not that a UFO sighting was required for an abduction claim to be linked to saucers by eager abductologists and their fans. If an experiencer thought he or, usually, she had been snatched, it had to be by aliens. Who else?

Somewhere along the way in the late 1980s, there had been a ufological watershed. The years that followed found The Field captured by abductions and wilder and wilder claims of government cover-up. And those beats go on today.

In retrospect, my investigation of Ed Walters's audacious antics seems to have been my own watershed. It was my last real, if semi-serious, foray into ufological investigation. Thereafter, I was quite happy to stick almost exclusively to just observing and commenting on the passing (almost non)saucer scene and, when the opportunity presented itself, making that scene more interesting by generating what controversy I could in the powerful pages of *Smear*—usually, as always, in the form of unstuffing a stuffed shirt or exposing some particular example of newly hatched or recycled looniness. For me, saucering was becoming progressively less interesting and fun, but there still were some important insights and good laughs to be had. In this and the following chapter I offer up a few that stick in my memory as capturing the True Character of ufology in the nineties and today.

WELL, IT'S NOT the BOOK-of-the-MONTH CLUB, BUT...

Those who choose to interpret the following sad tale as the reason for my final retirement from semi-real UFO investigations are free to do so. However, they will be wrong.

It may be recalled that, in 1974, Mutual UFO Network International Director Walt Andrus and the MUFON board unanimously rejected my application for membership, essentially because I was not considered sufficiently Serious. Several subsequent attempts to join were similarly rebuffed. Then, in 1980, I was granted the status of Contributing Subscriber. In other words, I was allowed to pay for a subscription to the *MUFON UFO Journal*, but not to become really and truly a *member* of the club.

My wonderful CS status and privilege of making annual contributions to Walt's treasury with nothing but the monthly magazine in return continued until May 1986, when Andrus personally blessed my elevation to real MUFONite. My friend Hal Starr, an old-time saucerer who was then Arizona MUFON state director, had prevailed upon Walt to relent. Much to my surprise, at the 1986 National UFO Conference in Phoenix, MUFON's Maximum Leader handed me a membership application, saying, "If you submit this, Jim, it will be given favorable consideration."

I did, and it was. Not only was I admitted to full membership, I was appointed MUFON Florida state section director for Monroe County, which includes all the Florida Keys and the southernmost fringes of the Everglades. Somewhere along the way, I also passed the MUFON field investigator exam with flying colors (it's an open-book test). I was now a real person in the eyes of MUFON. Whee! Not quite the same as being a Ground Saucer Watch Grand Dragon, but Whee! nonetheless.

This Honor came at a good time. A few months before, I had been cruelly abused by the Society for Scientific Exploration, an organization that encourages what it considers scientific approaches to the study of things Fortean and other sorts of scientifically fringy matters. In those days, the SSE was an august order confined to those who held Ph.D.s. Unaware that I, a mere Princeton dropout, wasn't qualified, I submitted an application for membership. I included a glowing recommendation from SSE member Dr. Thornton Page, a NASA astronomer who in January 1953 had served on the CIA-convened UFO review committee known as the Robertson Panel.

Before long, I received a letter from SSE Secretary Laurence Fredrick, informing me I had been accepted and asking me to return the enclosed personal information form with a check for six-months' dues. I immediately did so. Apparently I was honest about my academic (non)qualifications, as a few weeks later, I received another letter from Fredrick. This informed me he had erred in welcoming me to the bosom of the SSE and that the society would be returning my check. However, by then, said check had cleared my bank, so for the brief shining moment until a refund could be made, I was an SSE member. Which I guess means I'm now a member emeritus.

My bruised ego restored by Walt Andrus's magnanimity, I set about my duties as Key West's local MUFON power. Which is to say I did nothing to speak of. As I put it in *Smear* when I announced my new high status,

> I intend to do a sincere job of watching for anomalies in our little corner of the world. . . . However, it would indeed be embarrassing to us and all concerned if anything ufologically important happens around here any time soon. In view of our checkered past in UFO Research, someone might suspect (falsely, I assure you) that we were behind it, if a spectacular case developed in the near future in this particular area! The late, great Alexander King said, "Let this house be safe from tigers"—and *it was!* We say: Let Monroe County be safe from saucers. . . .

And it was. I do recall looking into a couple of highly nonspectacular UFO reports over the next few years, but fortunately, nothing Big happened. I must have been doing a good job. Then came the Mr. Ed case.

As we know, in June 1990 Ed Walters came under serious fire due to the revelations of Tommy Smith and the accidental and likely premature discovery of a saucer model in his former home. A few days later, Walt Andrus leaped into action, calling a press conference in Pensacola, where he defended Walters. The next day, I was in Gulf Breeze and mounted my own investigation, during which I made a courtesy telephone call to Charles Flannigan, the new Florida MUFON state director. He immediately attempted to *order* me not to interview Tommy Smith, Hank Boland, or Ed's son, Danny, *until after the MUFON hierarchy had done so.*

I was astounded (really). There was little doubt that the three boys were the keys to the case. Clearly, MUFON wanted to get to Boland and young Walters to plug any holes in their stories, and to Smith to punch holes in his. The MUFON Powers That Be were doing damage control and didn't want me interfering. Of course, I ignored Flannigan's orders and managed to interview Danny briefly by phone, while his father stood at his elbow. Of course, young Walters backed up his father.

I reported all this in *Saucer Smear* (July 10, 1990), and relations with my MUFON "superiors" were distinctly cooler thereafter. Now fast-forward to early 1992: On Flannigan's recommendation, Andrus demoted me to assistant section director for Monroe County—without appointing anyone to take my previous high office. Then, about a year later, I received a curt letter from the same dreaded Flannigan: "Toward the interest of increasing management effectiveness, I am recommending that Walt reassign you to Journal Subscriber (JS)."

Andrus acted on this recommendation, demoting me to JS, which had replaced CS as the lowest level of association with MUFON. At least the initials are less susceptible to misinterpretation, and I still proudly include them after my name on the *Smear* masthead.

It's too bad Gray Barker wasn't around for my final "humiliation." He always got a big kick out of the difficulty I had in gaining and maintaining membership in any organization. As he once put it, "Jim, you'd have trouble being accepted by the Book-of-the-Month Club."

INVASION of the NO-SEE-UM SAUCERS

While I was experiencing my meteoric rise and fall in MUFON, my old archenemy Budd Hopkins had established himself as *the* guru of abductology, and by the early 1990s it seemed almost anything he claimed was lapped up unquestioningly by eager abduction fiends. I well remember listening in amazed amusement to Hopkins's presentation in Richmond, Virginia, at the 1993 MUFON symposium (see the *Proceedings* of same). He said that, after a lecture in Brisbane, Australia, he was approached by a married couple, Sam and Jenny Washburn (pseudonyms), who handed him some oddly tinted photographs of seashore and beachside playground scenes. All but two showed no people.

Of the people-less snaps, Jenny told Hopkins, "The thing about these pictures is that we're supposed to be in them, and we're not. Sam took one of the boys and me, and I took two of him and the boys, and when we got the pictures back from the store, we weren't in them."

Hopkins said his "curiosity surged." Naturally, he persuaded the Washburns to let him hypnotically regress them. Lo and behold, except for Sam, the entire family had been abducted by a hovering UFO and, some time later, returned to the beach. Under hypnosis, Sam recalled that, while his wife and sons were in the hands of the aliens, he stood frozen on the playground, camera in hand. People passed by but did not seem to know he was there—not to mention not seeing the huge, low-hovering UFO.

Employing absolutely breathtaking Saucer Logic, Hopkins concluded from all this that Sam, his camera, and the UFO had been made invisible. The Washburns' photos—the negatives of which they had (surprise!) lost—proved it. According to Hopkins, the "photos, then, provide clear, though indirect, physical evidence of the phenomenon of invisibility [during some UFO abductions]. They buttress the near impossibility of a *visible* Sam not attracting attention while remaining absolutely frozen, camera to face, for perhaps an hour in a busy playground."

He then went on to say, "Surely at some point all four Washburn family members were literally invisible to everyone nearby. . . . And . . . a temporarily invisible camera recorded the invisibility of the Washburns against a visible landscape—the images caught in tones of red on temporarily invisible Kodak film!"

Because the Washburns were not shown in the photos—or, perhaps, because their nonimages somehow were?—the pictures prove the family was invisible. The Red Queen and the Mad Hatter, not to mention George Adamski, would be proud of this reasoning. As soon as Hopkins wrapped up his talk, I headed for the bar to consult a more reliable source of wisdom, a glass of good scotch.

COULD I INTEREST YOU in a BRIDGE, MR. PEREZ de CUELLAR?

I suppose Hopkins's no-see-um tales shouldn't have surprised me or anyone else who had attended the MUFON symposium the year before in Albuquerque. I was in the audience there when Hopkins unveiled what would prove to be his most controversial abduction case. In this instance, the aliens seem to have had their invisibility device turned off. According to Hopkins's later statements and writings, this was deliberate and for the purpose of making a display of their great powers to a major world political figure.

In Albuquerque, the Great Abductologist informed one thousand or so assembled gaga saucer fiends that, at about 3:15 on the morning of November 30, 1989, a woman whom he called Linda Cortile was abducted from her twelfth-floor apartment in lower Manhattan by three typical big-eyed Grays. The aliens transported Linda right through the glass of her living-room window, and the party of four, Linda in a flowing white nightgown, was beamed up to a huge, glowing saucer hovering above the building. This somewhat unusual event was witnessed by two unnamed members of an unnamed government security agency and the unnamed "major political figure" whom they were guarding in a car about two blocks away. Supposedly, Linda's snatching also was observed by an unnamed woman who was driving across the nearby (named) Brooklyn Bridge.

I remember thinking at the time, Well, at least now we know the subject of Budd's next book. In 1996 my powers of precognition were proven when his *Witnessed: The True Story of the Brooklyn Bridge UFO Abductions* was published.

When Hopkins finished speaking, he presented Linda to the audience. An attractive woman in her forties, she opened her brief remarks with unconscious humor by asking, "Are there any questions?" There certainly were, but there were very few responsive answers from either her or Hopkins. However, I learned many interesting things during private conversations at the convention and later with George Hansen, Joseph Stefula, and Richard Butler, former associates of Hopkins who had been looking into the case independently. What they told me made it pretty clear there were more holes in the story than in a Swiss cheese. Moreover, as I listened to what they had to say, it seemed to me the case was more suited to an investigation by the late, great Sigmund Freud than by an abstract artist turned abductologist.

It turned out Linda's real last name was Napolitano. (I revealed this to the world in the September 5, 1992, *Smear*, much to the chagrin of Hopkins and his very vehement supporters, notably CUFOS Leading Light Jerry Clark.) It also transpired that the story hadn't begun with Linda's amazing abduction. She had been a member of Hopkins's abductee "support group" for more than six months before that event, drawn there by having read his second abductions book, *Intruders* (1987), which she claimed to have picked up by accident, thinking it was a mystery novel. It seemed that, on reading the book, Linda suddenly realized she'd been abducted several times in her childhood and youth.

I also learned that the two security agents supposedly were named Dan and Richard. Hopkins had received a number of letters and audiotaped messages from these two mysterious characters. And who were Dan and Richard guarding in the wee hours of November 30, 1989? It was none other than then–United Nations Secretary General Javier Perez de Cuellar. Apparently, he was the great personage the Linda-nappers were trying to impress.

It gets even better. While Dan and Richard were in touch with Hopkins and Linda in various ways after the abduction, to this day Hopkins has never met them, and if they ever existed at all, they didn't meet Linda in person until early in 1991, when they supposedly showed up at her apartment, where she lived with her husband and two sons. On another occasion, they kidnapped her on the street, forced her into a black Mercedes sedan, and drove around New York City for several hours while questioning her and (egads!) examining her feet. The latter was because they suspected she was an alien "half-breed," and something about her feet supposedly would reveal this.

And it gets better still. On October 15, 1991, Dan, acting alone, grabbed Linda off the street and drove her to a house far out on the north shore of Long Island. There he demanded she put on a white nightgown and made sexual advances. At one point, he went crazy and tried to drown her in the ocean, but a "mysterious force" drove him away from her, and she ran off down the beach. Then Richard showed up, slipped Dan a "mickey," and drove Linda back to Manhattan. Before she and her spy in shining armor left the beach house, Linda spotted some CIA stationery in a desk drawer (no wonder that outfit had so much trouble trying to assassinate Castro!).

And still better. On December 14, 1991, Dan sent Linda a Christmas card with a long, rambling message. It seemed the security man was by then in a mental hospital and that he believed Linda definitely was an alien-human hybrid. Here is part of his "holiday greeting," as published in the September 5, 1992, *Smear:*

> Dear Pretty Linda—MERRY XMAS!
>
> By the time this Xmas greeting reaches you, I will have managed to get out of this place successfully. If you don't see me, then you'll know that I'm still in here thinking my way out. Did you believe that I would let you go so easy?
>
> The staff here usually keeps me pretty much sedated. You see, they like me and give me special favors. This is how I was able to get this letter started. . . . I'm trying to get a holiday pass so I can come and see you. This pass may last me a life time (with you).
>
> It seems like yesterday when I wanted you to go back from where you came. I hated you because I needed to live a normal and stress free life again, but the thought of you wouldn't let me. Sometimes the hate still creeps out of me, until I think about looking into those big, deep brown eyes of yours. Then the hate goes away. In fact, I can't wait to watch you move, as you walk by. I'm going to kiss that pretty nose and inscribe our names with my lips, on that full, heart shaped mouth that looks unhappy only when it's with me. . . .
>
> Linda, you don't belong here. But I'll find a place for you. When I do, you'll teach me your ways and your special language.
>
> Everyone thinks I'm crazy you know. It's because they have never

seen or heard what I have, coming out of you. Richard and the other man [Perez de Cuellar] just let me sit in this place, knowing full well that I'm not crazy. They saw the very same things I saw in you.

I want you to know that we have done our homework over all these months. To prove it, I have some information that no one else would have but you and your doctor. I told you that I would prove the difference in you. Linda, it isn't just in your eyes [what about her feet?]. It's in your cell structure. You didn't think I knew, did you? You can't pretend it isn't true, because it's there. We know you were put here on purpose, but we don't know exactly when.

You do make good things happen to others, and it's no coincidence. I'll bet something nice has happened to everyone you've been close to or touched. But it hasn't happened to me yet.

If you show this letter to anyone, you know that they won't believe me because I'm supposed to be crazy. That's clever, Linda. But, what if they give me the benefit of the doubt? Then they'll find out that you're a halfbreed.

We'll be covering a lot of miles, Linda. Prepare yourself for a happy and comfortable life abroad. Pack your toothbrush, in order to travel lightly at any time. You'll make a beautiful bride, dressed all in white, just like the morning of November 1989.

If you see Richard, tell him I said "Go to Hell."

If I don't get out of here, I'll be thinking of you. If I do, I'll be looking at you.

Happy Holiday, pretty. /s/ Danny

Despite this and other at least equally absurd stuff, and the admonitions of Hansen, Stefula, and Butler and a number of prominent ufologists, all of whom tried to convince him the whole weird tale was a complex hoax, Hopkins gave Linda, Dan, and Richard the "benefit of the doubt" and then some. He pressed on with his "research" and the writing of his book. And, shades of his threats against me over the O'Barski anniversary happening, he vowed to denounce Hansen and his two friends as government agents if they tried to stand in his way.

Ignoring Hopkins's fulminations, the intrepid trio pressed on, too, eventually publishing a long paper called "A Critique of Budd Hopkins' Case of the UFO Abduction of Linda Napolitano" (1993). Therein, they revealed that in April 1989, the same month Linda began meeting with Hopkins, a science-fiction/spy novel called *Nighteyes* had been published. Intriguingly, they discovered over a dozen specific points of similarity between the novel and Linda's adventures with the Grays, Dan, and Richard.

They also charged that Hopkins failed to make a thorough search for backup witnesses among the tenants in Linda's large apartment complex. Similarly, they wrote, he seemed to have made no effort to interview the complex's security guards to see if any of them had seen or had reported to them sightings of a very brightly lit saucer hovering outside Linda's window. And on and on and on.

Needless to say, this paper brought on a firestorm of attacks from Hopkins and his boosters. This culminated in the March–April 1993 issue of the CUFOS magazine *IUR*, with a cover-story diatribe by Hopkins and a companion editorial by Jerry Clark entitled "Saucer Smearers" (Yay!). Nineteen of the magazine's twenty-four pages were devoted to the Napolitano case, eleven of them to Clark's and Hopkins's pieces, in which both focused on attacking the character and personalities of Hansen, Stefula, and Butler—oh, yes, and Yours Truly.

Hopkins wrote that I was "a dubious personage," publisher of a "scandal sheet" who, as a "cynical and parasitic journalist immediately accepts the Linda-as-diabolical-hoaxer theory, perhaps because he himself once perpetrated a successful UFO hoax." As for Hansen and company, he compared them to the Muslim extremists who bombed the World Trade Center in February 1993, stating, "Killing American office workers can no more accomplish [their] goal than Hansen's character trashing can accomplish whatever it is he thinks is his goal. The more broadly he indulges his arm-flailing and reputation-bashing, the more the cruelty of his own brand of fanaticism reveals itself."

Ah, there's nothing like dispassionate scientific restraint. Still more revealing of Hopkins's qualifications as an objective, scientific investigator, however, was the cover of the magazine. It carried a photograph taken by Hopkins and captioned: "Stereo view of the Brooklyn Bridge from the approximate position of 'Dan's' car at the time of the abduction. The New Jersey side is across the river on the left, and Manhattan is out of sight to the right." Well, not quite. Manhattan was out of sight, all right, but behind the camera, and unfortunately for Hopkins, a longtime resident of lower Manhattan, the Brooklyn Bridge runs from (yes) lower Manhattan, where Our Hero stood to take his photo, to (yes!) Brooklyn. Of course, New Jersey also was out of sight, several miles *behind* Hopkins and his camera. Perhaps, unbeknownst to him, Budd was getting a little help from the aliens who made the "Washburns" invisible. Whatever the reason for his confusion, I gleefully reported it in *Smear* under the headline "How Can Budd Hopkins Sell Us the Brooklyn Bridge When He Doesn't Even Know Where It Is???"

I really don't know exactly what to make of the Linda case, except that I'm certain *someone* pulled a hoax. Just who and why, I'm not sure. I have some ideas, which the libel and slander laws prevent me from airing here. Suffice to say that I've met and spoken with Linda a few times and found her a very pleasant, rather charming person, a seemingly quite normal middle-class New York housewife who very definitely was enjoying her fifteen minutes of fame. I wouldn't be a bit surprised if the whole crazy case grew out of what we might call Bored House Frau Syndrome, with Linda looking to add a little excitement to her life and finding a bit more than she'd bargained for. A couple of years ago, she hinted she knew that what happened or at least what was behind it was very different from Hopkins's "interpretations," but she also made clear she had no intention of saying anything more specific. If she ever does, it should be very interesting, and I will be cynically and parasitically waiting to reveal all in the scandalous pages of *Smear.*

BIG MACK

In the early nineties, an apparently professionally qualified new researcher strode onto the abductology stage, stealing a bit of Budd Hopkins's limelight. This was Dr. John Mack, a Harvard Medical School psychiatrist who had written a Pulitzer Prize–winning autobiography of Lawrence of Arabia some years before. Serious Ufologists, always looking for a respectability enhancement for ufology, eagerly embraced the good doctor, and he became very popular on the speakers' platforms of saucerdom. But while Mack was professionally qualified, it soon became apparent he had an agenda of his own.

The April 25, 1994, issue of *Time* magazine featured an article entitled "The Man from Outer Space," followed by this teaser line: "Harvard psychiatrist John Mack claims that the tales of UFO abductions are real. But experts and former patients say his research is shoddy." For good measure, *Time* threw in a deliberately goofy-looking photograph of Mack.

The most devastating part of the article was the testimony of Donna Bassett, a professional writer who had infiltrated Mack's inner circle with a fake abduction story and with the deliberate intent of exposing him to ridicule. Bassett's most amusing account was of the session she had with Mack, lying on a bed in a darkened room in his home and supposedly under hypnosis. She "recalled" being on board a saucer with John F. Kennedy and Nikita Krushchev during the 1962 Cuban missile crisis, and told Mack she had comforted Krushchev by sitting on his lap. When the abductologist heard this, he "became so excited that he leaned on the bed too heavily, and it collapsed." Apparently, the famed shrink actually believed the yarn.

Soon after reading this article, I discovered that Bassett's husband, Ed, also a professional writer, had once worked for *Aviation Week and Space Technology*. Since arch-anti-UFOlogist Phil Klass had been an editor on that magazine for many years, I suspected he had put the Bassetts up to their plot against Mack. It turned out I was wrong, although I found out that Klass had gotten in touch with them after the *Time* exposé appeared and tried to steer their intended book to Prometheus Books (whatever happened to that project?).

Anyway, after some considerable sleuthing, I reached the Bassetts in North Carolina by telephone. They told me that, after breaking with Mack, they received threats from the "Mackies," as the psychiatrist's hard-core abductees were called, forcing them to move from one location to another. They explained that they had serious legal and moral objections to Mack's methods as well as his conclusions.

They weren't the only ones. One of my nonsubscribers familiar with the Mack story wrote (*Smear*, June 15, 1994):

> Certainly, even for those who believe in alien abductions, Mack is someone to watch out for. He's not professional, he doesn't do follow-up research, he treats his clients with indifference, and all of his clients seem to walk into his office confused and needy, and walk out infused with millennial New Age self-confidence and political and cultural views identical with Mack's. This is what I keep trying to tell my abductee friends who worship Mack just because he has a Harvard professorship. Avoid any UFO investigator who has a political agenda and who is more interested in New Age religion than in science. That means Mack. . . . It's the Space Brothers all over again. . . . And why is it that only Mack's abductees have these spontaneous past-life regressions all the time? And why is it that these past lives are all of the clichéd kind, like Egyptian hieroglyphic [*sic*] painters and American Indian warriors? I mean, *come on!* . . .

HATS OFF...UH...ON

Hopkins and Mack, of course, are not the only abduction gurus. There are others on the scene, such as history professor David Jacobs, who's convinced we're under genetic siege by malevolent space beings, and best-selling horror novelist Whitley Strieber, who claims to be personally under siege/instruction/something by what he calls The Visitors, who come from he's not sure where. But Hopkins paved the way, and Mack lent abductology respectability of sorts.

So it is that today thousands of people think, or at least suspect, they've been abducted by alien beings, nasty or benevolent depending on their choice of guru. And for many in and outside ufology, UFOs and abductions go hand in hand, and the latter usually far overshadow the former. As for me, I'm really not sure what's going on. However, I do agree with the late Carl Sagan that the mere fact that so many people think they've been snatched and manipulated by beings from outer space (or wherever) is highly significant and worthy of serious scientific study.

On the other hand, maybe Nevada inventor Michael Menkin has the answer. He recently announced that he has developed a hat he says prevents alien abductions. According to an article in the March 23, 2000, *Las Vegas Star Ledger*, the hat is a leather motorcycle cap with added layers of an antistatic material normally used to protect printed-circuit boards. Menkin says the chapeau works as a "thought screen" and claims his research proves it is "100 percent effective in preventing alien abductions." His proof? No one wearing the thing has been abducted.

Of course, this is Saucer Logic at its finest, a near-textbook example of the logical fallacy of the excluded middle. While I concede Menkin's claim *may* be true, however wildly unlikely, it does not in any way follow from the reported fact that no one wearing his headgear has been snatched by alien beings. Still, given a choice between Menkin and Hopkins, Mack, and their ilk, I say hats off (or on) to Menkin.

It ain't over 'til it's over.

—Yogi Berra

According to the Hickory, North Carolina, *Catawba Valley Neighbors* (October 29, 1999), North Carolina MUFON state director George Lund, a U.S. Army Reserve retiree, claimed he once was discussing UFOs with some fellow reservists when an officer with a top-secret security clearance joined them. Lund recalled, "He said they [UFOs] simply don't exist and turned around and walked out. That tells me he knew something and didn't want to talk about it."

Well, maybe I'm naive or duped by the propaganda of the UFO-cover-up machine, but it seems to me that, if the guy knew something he didn't want to talk about, he wouldn't have said anything at all. Lund's thinking is Saucer Logic in spades.

William J. Birnes takes the opposite view. When Those Who Know say nothing at all, They speak volumes. Birnes, now publisher of the California-based *UFO* magazine, coauthored *The Day After Roswell* with the late Lt. Col. Philip J. Corso. That's the book in which the good colonel recounted how he launched the modern technological age by clandestinely seeding American industry with alien technology taken from the wrecked Roswell saucer. During an online question-and-answer session (Compuserve, August 10, 1997), Birnes was asked if Corso was fulfilling a long-range Pentagon plan to gradually "desensitize" the public to the existence of visiting space beings and, therefore, had not violated any secrecy oaths.

Birnes answered, "Somehow, I think this argument holds a lot of water. When you realize that no one in the Pentagon or in government has stepped forward to challenge Corso's story, . . . you begin to see that the Pentagon may actually be supporting Corso even if only by default. . . . So I tend to think that the Colonel is part of the disclosure on a grand, gradual scale."

Corso was not charged with revealing classified information. No official attempt was made to refute his story. Therefore, his tale must be true and part of a larger government plan to reveal The Truth about alien visitation according to some Master Plan of the cover-up cabal. The absence of an official response proves it. Of course it does.

This is akin to a ufological mantra coined by Roswell-crash advocate Stan Friedman: Absence of evidence is not evidence of absence. While this is literally true, the real message, conveyed with body language and a knowing nod, is subliminal: Therefore, evidence really does exist—Roswell crashed-saucer parts, alien cadavers, "smoking-gun" documents, you name it. This bit of Saucer Logic is more subtle than most, making the spoken words seem to mean *much* more than they actually do. In truth, the absence of evidence after a thorough investigation is a strong clue that what was not found does not exist or did not happen, and common sense says go with that until contrary clues show up.

The most recent gem of Saucer Logic to tickle my fancy is the failed lie detector test that actually confirmed the veracity of the person who failed it. Over the past several years, a California man named Timothy Cooper has been the subject of much interest in ufological circles. The self-described private investigator has produced reams of alleged highly classified government documents—more than three thousand pages worth!—which he claims to have received at his post office box and through personal contacts. Among other things, these documents purportedly prove a saucer crashed at Roswell and the existence of MJ-12, the mysterious group said to be responsible for covering up the U.S. government's recovery of and research on that crashed saucer and others—

and, of course, the bodies of their crews. Cooper fed these papers to the father-and-son UFO research team of Robert and Ryan Wood, who champion them as authentic government documents. According to the Woods, some reveal The Truth, while others are disinformation to help keep it concealed. With their backgrounds in the defense and computer industries, they should know better, but the true saucer fiend's will to believe is a powerful thing.

In 1999, publicly prodded into it by veteran ufologist Robert Durant, Cooper submitted to a polygraph examination, paid for by Durant. Quoting a press release issued by the Woods on August 15, 1999, Cooper "did not do well." Asked three times if he lied when he said he received the documents in his post office box, he answered, "No." The Woods reported that Cooper's answers "clearly indicated deception," but concluded, "This deception is to be expected, based on his determination to conceal the identity of the other [non-mailbox] sources."

How's that again? The repeated question had nothing to do with the identity of Cooper's sources, but only with where he claimed to have found the documents. Yet the Woods decided the man's "clearly indicated deception" was consistent with his intent "to protect the identity of his two other sources besides the mailbox . . . source."

Note that all of these Saucer Logic gems have in common the theme that the government has proof of the reality of UFOs, where they come from, and who's flying them. All but one share Roswell as the focus of the Big Cover-Up, or, as Stan Friedman calls it, the Cosmic Watergate, and it's a safe bet Roswell was in the back of North Carolina MUFON official George Lund's mind when he was being interviewed, and not very far back either.

LEGEND CONQUERS REALITY

Roswell. Sigh . . . This infamous case has become the eight-hundred-pound Yeti of saucerdom. Along with abductions, it defines Ufology As We Know It. It's a household word. Ask anyone what Roswell is, and even if they know or care nothing about flying saucers, odds are they will say something like, "That's where that UFO crashed back in the forties with all those dead aliens and stuff, isn't it?" Amazingly, a Zogby International poll taken in early 2001 found that one-third of all American adults believe a saucer crashed near Roswell and that the government has the thing secretly stashed away somewhere.

Yet, as my Esteemed Coauthor exhaustively demonstrates in his book *Roswell: Inconvenient Facts and the Will to Believe* (2001), the *credible* evidence very convincingly shows that there was no saucer crash, no alien bodies, no government threats against the witnesses, and so on. What it does show almost as convincingly is that what fell out of the southeastern New Mexico sky during the summer of 1947—during the first flying saucer flap—probably was a huge array of balloons, radar targets, and scientific instruments. This thing had been launched from near the town of Alamogordo, about one hundred miles west of Roswell, as part of a top secret army air forces research program called Project Mogul.

The evidence also shows that Roswell fans are right about at least one thing: there was a cover-up. However, it was to protect Project Mogul, not the secret of a crashed saucer. Thus, ironically, government secrecy was the seed from which the whole gigantic Roswell myth has grown.

This all sounds right to me. Still, I sometimes wonder if something else—like the accidental dropping of an atomic bomb with a release of dangerous radiation—might not also have been involved. Esteemed Coauthor says not. Still . . .

Anyway, never fear. I'm not going to rehash the Roswell debate for the umpteenth time here. I'll leave such exercises in futility to the Experts. After all, isn't that what Experts are for? As a Humble Nonexpert on Roswell, the things I find most interesting are how the case survived Bill Moore's self-immolation at the 1989 MUFON symposium and all the wonderfully wacky stuff that has grown up around it since.

Even as Moore was speaking in Las Vegas, aiming at his foot and shooting himself in the head, a new team of Roswell investigators was hard at work. Not long before, the Center for UFO Studies decided to sponsor a close look at the case by the two-man team of Donald Schmitt, then CUFOS director of special investigations and board member, and Kevin Randle, a longtime semi-skeptical ufologist. At first, these two worked closely with Stan Friedman, who had decided to change horses after various difficulties with Moore. Later, Friedman and Moore, independently and unsuccessfully, would attempt to stop or stall publication of Randle and Schmitt's first Roswell book.

In the fall of 1989, only a couple of months after Moore's MUFON speech, the television show *Unsolved Mysteries* aired a segment about Roswell, complete with appearances by Friedman and Randle and dramatic reenactments—if that's the right word for dramatizations of nonevents. *Unsolved Mysteries* succeeded in doing what *The Roswell Incident* had failed to do nine years before: capture the imagination of the general public. It also brought phone calls from several people who claimed to have knowledge of what happened and even to have been directly involved. One man, Gerald Anderson, told how, when he was a boy, he and members of his family stumbled upon a crashed saucer and not only dead aliens but one live one. Still another, Robert Smith, said he'd been one of the military men who'd helped load the saucer debris on airplanes at the Roswell army air base. Another, who didn't call in but was found by Friedman when he was in Roswell working on the show, was Glenn Dennis, the now infamous good ol' boy mortician who claimed he was told about alien bodies by a nurse friend, who (surprise!) disappeared mysteriously after Saying Too Much.

The Roswell saucer legend was off the ground, and it really got flying in 1991, with the publication of Randle and Schmitt's *UFO Crash at Roswell*, the first of their two books on the case (their second, published in 1994, has the amusingly curious title *The Truth about the UFO Crash at Roswell*). CUFOS held a big book-launch press conference and even published its own companion volume. While spokespeople for the group carefully asserted that CUFOS had not made up its official mind about the story, it was obvious that it had: a saucer had crashed, and the government secretly was holding it and the bodies of its crew. In 1991 CUFOS had been on the financial edge for some time, and I suspect its leaders saw the exciting and mysterious Roswell tale as the perfect ticket to solvency. (It didn't work.) Whatever the original motivation, CUFOS has long since dropped any pretense of objectivity about the case and is the one UFO group that unwaveringly stands behind it without qualification.

ROSWELL (THE TOWN) CATCHES ON

Down in Roswell itself, Glenn Dennis, Walter Haut (the man who put out the announcement that the army had "captured" a flying saucer), and town business power Max Littell launched the International UFO Museum and Research Center. Supposedly, this was to be a serious research institution while also helping to draw tourists to the town. Guess which competing interest won out.

At first, the city fathers found the idea of boosting Roswell as the UFO capital of the world too embarrassing, but before long, the lure of the long green overcame this. In 1995 Roswell staged its first saucer-crash festival. It and the one the following year were warm-ups for the big fiftieth anniversary event in 1997.

Of course, I was there in 1997, one of about forty-five thousand who showed up, doubling the town's population for a few sweltering July days. Luckily for the Roswell Police Department, the rock concert for "less than 150,000 people" never materialized. William Shatner of *Star Trek* fame canceled. The crowds were somewhat smaller than anticipated, despite millions of dollars in free nationwide publicity (who'd ever have imagined an alien would be on the cover of *Time*?). My own informal survey showed that there were hotel and motel vacancies throughout the event, which I thought was not a good sign for the future. Still, the hordes that did show up were treated to a town where nearly every business joined in the lighthearted alien motif (today, even the town's streetlights sport alien eyes). At the center of everything was the International UFO Museum, with backup from another, now defunct and more fun and funky establishment called the UFO Enigma Museum, which was located just outside the old Roswell army/air force base main gate.

For me, a major highlight of the festival was the debate between Kevin Randle and Karl Pflock, sponsored by the Enigma Museum. Of course, Kevin argued that there was a saucer crash. Of course, Karl made his case for a Mogul gadget. I was on Karl's side, but Randle won the debate by dramatically whipping some balloon and foil fragments out of his pocket, ripping them up, and throwing the pieces in the air like confetti. Also, it didn't hurt that all but a few in the audience already had their minds made up. Ain't science grand!

Another high point of equal scientific significance was a presentation by movie and television producer Paul Davids, notorious ufologist and self-described alien hunter Derrel Sims, and others, who held a press conference to exhibit an "authentic" Roswell-saucer fragment (one of many that have come and gone). After their pitch, all of the principals except Davids left hurriedly before the press could ask questions, taking their precious alien junk with them. They literally ran out the back door and jumped into a car waiting for them with its engine running. Science on the run!

Speaking of Roswell saucer fragments, in its July 2000 newsletter, the International UFO Museum, which continues to draw over one hundred thousand visitors a year, announced it would pay as much as $1 million for the "first scientifically verified piece of debris from the legendary 1947 crash of an alien spacecraft near Roswell." Apart from the publicity value of such an offer, it's my guess that the museum elders are attempting to recover from the disaster of a few years ago when they made a very big and very public deal out of a slice of Roswell saucer that proved to be a piece of jeweler's scrap. If someone does come in with something, before handing over the money, the museum folks better be certain there's not a car waiting out back with the engine running.

Returning to Roswell 1997, my personal high point of the festival was being interviewed by famed *Washington Post* science and feature writer Joel Achenbach, who quoted me in his article about the Big Event. Asked my opinion of the affair, I said, "It's the greatest celebration of a non-event that I've ever experienced." In ufology, that's saying something.

GUTS! or—CHILI, ANYONE?

Probably the most audacious exploitation of the public's fascination with the Roswell noncrash is the Amazing, Incredible Alien Autopsy Film. In January 1995, via a British television interview with rock star Reg Presley of the appropriately named group the Trogs, the ever-primed world of ufology learned that British music promoter Ray Santilli had acquired film of the autopsy of one of the Roswell aliens. Soon after, Santilli himself made it known that he'd bought the film from the man who'd shot it in 1947, a conveniently dead American named Jack Barnett.

Over the next few months, Santilli very cleverly dribbled out bits and pieces of tantalizing information, and eventually, in May 1995, he previewed the film at the London Museum. Over one hundred ufologists, journalists, and, most important, television and film producers turned out. After the showing, wily Ray opened the bidding for the right to be first to exhibit the film publicly. Before long, Santilli struck a deal with independent television producer Robert Kiviat, who licensed exclusive first broadcast rights in return for a fee of $125,000. Kiviat then did a deal with the Fox Broadcasting Company for a one-hour prime-time special.

While Kiviat's project was in production, Santilli put together a videotape called *Roswell: The Footage* and began promotion of it, capitalizing on public excitement over the upcoming Fox special. The video sold thousands of copies, including two to me (don't ask!), a "bargain" at $59 a copy.

Santilli's marketing campaign for the video was brilliant. Exciting hints were dropped on the Internet and in interviews: President Truman could be seen in some of the footage. There were scenes at the crash site, showing doctors examining one, maybe even two alien bodies. Others showed weird wreckage. Cleverly, Santilli and his cronies never quite promised that Truman and all the rest would be shown on the Fox program or in the video. And (surprise!) he wasn't and it wasn't, but the television show was a huge ratings success and Santilli cleaned up with the video.

When I first saw the latter, I couldn't believe anyone could take it seriously. For example, the "doctors" performing the autopsy were wearing unsealed protective suits. The alien itself obviously was a dummy, looking like a prop rejected by the director of a very bad 1950s science-fiction flick. It almost seemed whoever had put the film together didn't mean for it to be taken as anything but a gag.

Worst of all was the ridiculous way the actors, uh, doctors handled the alien entrails, not to mention the entrails themselves. After cutting the dummy's, uh, alien's abdomen open, the quacks scooped out masses of dark, gloopy stuff with their hands and dumped them into containers without performing the slightest examination. When I watched this absurd production again in the video room at the 1995 Gulf Breeze UFO Conference (held in Mobile, Alabama, due to a hurricane), I deliberately sat in the front row, eating a bowl of chili, which bore an uncanny resemblance to the dark mush being so unceremoniously extracted from the alleged alien on the TV screen. For some reason, no one wanted to sit near me! Too bad more people didn't take a similar attitude toward the whole goofy business before Santilli, Kiviat, and Fox raked in the dough.

But the perfect finishing touch didn't come until December 1999, when Kiviat and Fox wowed the world with another special, *The World's Greatest Hoaxes: Secrets Finally Revealed.* This time, without a word about their own role in helping to promote the alien autopsy film as real, they exposed it as a hoax.

At least we did get to see one of the whispered about but previously unreleased scenes. This showed two men in surgical gowns—neither of them Harry Truman—working in a tent at the Roswell crash site. They were attempting desperately to save the life of a barely surviving alien. But then Kiviat spoiled the fun by using some sort of image analysis that led to the identification of one of the valiant doctors as an Elliot Willis, a British film technician. Willis was then interviewed on camera, and he spilled the chili. It seemed that AK Music, a company he had worked for, had created the tent sequence for Santilli. Best of all, Willis's companion in the scene was a local butcher!

ROSWELL EXPLOITERS MAY COME and GO, BUT...

Roswell will go on forever. There has never been a UFO case like it, and I doubt there will ever be another. At least a dozen books and countless magazine articles have been written about it. There have been as many or more television specials entirely or at least partially devoted to it, and in 1994 the aforementioned Paul Davids cranked out a made-for-television movie, cleverly entitled *Roswell*, based upon Randle and Schmitt's first book. The International UFO Museum keeps pulling people in, and although the emphasis wisely seems to be shifting away from UFOs to something more like a huge street fair and carnival, the town continues with its annual "crash and burn" fest. And, of course, there are the Friedmans, Corsos, Coopers, and Woods, and a host of lesser players.

The objective facts about what actually happened and the truth about so many Roswell "witnesses," no matter how painstakingly presented by researchers like my Esteemed Coauthor, make no difference to those who Want to Believe. Neither do scandals like those that blew up around CUFOS Roswell investigator Donald Schmitt a few years ago.

In 1995 it was disclosed that Schmitt had grossly misrepresented how he makes a living—he is a rural mail carrier, not a commercial artist and undercover drug agent—and his academic credentials—he has a junior college degree and isn't a Ph.D. candidate. He also dissembled concerning important elements of his Roswell "research." All of this was much to the chagrin of his former partner Kevin Randle, whom I consider an honest if somewhat deluded man. Finally, CUFOS was forced to accept Schmitt's resignation as both director of special investigations and a member of the center's board. Yet today he's back spinning new Roswell tales and publishing articles in the CUFOS magazine *IUR*.

Whee! Roswell the Legend Lives!

This little ditty—meant to be sung to the tune of Danny and the Juniors' classic song "Rock 'n' Roll Is Here to Stay"—really says it all:

The Roswell crash is here to stay
It will never Die.
It was meant to be that way
Though I don't know why.
I don't care what the people say
The Roswell crash
is here to stay.

Whee!

WALT ANDRUS'S LAST UFO(O)LOGICAL ADVENTURE

The cover of the March 1999 *MUFON UFO Journal* carried a full-page photograph of MUFON Maximum Leader Walt Andrus, dressed in shorts and droopy socks, smiling like a kid who'd just found a new toy. In fact, he had. In the photo, he holds a very large, oval piece of plaster of paris in which is embedded a mystery skeleton (pictured in the photo section). This, Walt claimed in his accompanying article, just might be the bones of an alien killed in the crash of its saucer over a hundred years before.

The story was rather convoluted, but fit rather nicely with the famed Aurora, Texas, saucer crash of 1897. Of course, the Aurora case has long been generally accepted in The Field as a hoax, as detailed by UFO historians Ronald Story and Jerry Clark and such others as Dr. J. Allen Hynek and investigators of Andrus's own MUFON. But, then, all of saucerdom once considered *Roswell* a hoax or at least a case of misidentification.

Anyway, as Walt explained, according to a letter written in 1925 and rediscovered some time after that, two cigar-shaped spaceships landed near Ladonia, Texas, on the night of April 16, 1897. Little men were seen moving about in the vicinity of the landed ships, one of which supposedly had crashed the next day in Aurora, slightly less than one hundred miles from Ladonia. (It really does start to sound like Roswell again, doesn't it—except that the event took place over one hundred years ago, and none of the alleged eyewitnesses are still living.)

Our saga now moves on to sometime after 1929 (Walt didn't make the exact date clear). A strange skeleton was dug up near Ladonia and shown to Dr. Bob Slaughter, a well-known paleontologist who lived in the area. The thing was about forty inches tall, had mostly hollow bones and humanlike teeth, and, most interestingly, was clad in some sort of armor and an ornate belt from which hung a ceremonial sword. There was some resemblance to the dreaded Grays of modern saucer mythology, but Walt, always the careful researcher, cautiously stated, "MUFON is making no claims that the skeleton is of an extraterrestrial alien . . . [but] the similarities are sufficient to make it very exciting for future study." In fact, to my semi-expert, semi-serious eye, the similarities seemed much closer to Bugs Bunny's outer-space nemesis, Marvin the Martian.

Andrus noted in his article that Dr. Slaughter, an accomplished sculptor as well as a paleontologist, had written a book dealing with strange bones and fossils from around the world, which was published in 1996. Unfortunately, Slaughter died in early 1998, just months before Walt tried to contact him. All the other key figures in the case also were dead or missing. Clearly, researching the origins of the weird skeleton would not be easy, but in a telephone interview with me, the intrepid Andrus vowed to go on trying, which he did until I and others dug up the all-too-obvious truth.

While Walt went his merry way, I contacted Slaughter's widow, Judith. She very kindly sent me a copy of her late husband's book, which I found highly illuminating. The title? *Fossil Remains of* Mythical *Creatures* (emphasis mine). The first chapter is called "Alien" and deals with the Ladonia skeleton. There follow chapters about fossil mermaids, leprechauns, and so on.

Perhaps most interesting of all is the introduction, supposedly penned by a friend of Slaughter's named George Toomer, a professor of comparative religion at (surprise! nonexistent) Ladonia University. Here are a few excerpts:

> If one mythological example is accepted, then it becomes hypocritical to disregard another. Can we laugh at Santa Claus, the Easter Bunny and the Tooth Fairy while placing a call for an exorcist to chase away a demonic possession? . . . A true believer in one mythical standard can't in good conscience pooh-pooh the standard of another. . . .
>
> The question of authenticity is no more important than that of religious relics. . . . There is really no right or wrong answer when dealing with the mystical—one accepts or rejects according to one's current popular faith in such things. . . .
>
> A hoax is when someone is fooled. It's different from a lie in my opinion. Generally, only a fool can be a victim of a hoax, while the victim of a lie is usually one who had the faith to believe and was misled. . . .

Thus ufo(o)logy as it soars into the New Millennium.

It is the dull man who is always sure, and the sure man who is always dull.
—H. L. Mencken

So here we are at the beginning of the New Millennium and (whew!) very near the end of this book. No doubt there is something Significant about this coincidence (coincidence?), but I don't have the vaguest idea what that might be. It's rather like where I am and what I know and think after all these years of saucering and tweaking other saucerers.

Back in the Old Millennium, Phil Klass, ufology's own Great Satan (and proud of it!), sent me this very interesting letter, which I published in the October 10, 1983, *Saucer Smear:*

> THE LAST WILL AND TESTAMENT OF PHILIP J. KLASS:
>
> To ufologists who publicly criticize me,...or who even think unkind thoughts about me in private, I do hereby leave and bequeath:
>
> THE UFO CURSE:

> No matter how long you live, you will never know any more about UFOs than you know today. You will never know any more about what UFOs really are, or where they come from. You will never know any more about what the U.S. Government really knows about UFOs than you know today. As you lie on your own death-bed, you will be as mystified about UFOs as you are today. And you will remember this curse.

What Klass was trying to say, and what he continues to say every chance he gets, is that there is no real mystery—just misinterpretations of mundane things, deluded people who see and believe in things that aren't really there and don't exist, and, of course, hoaxes. I believe there is a real mystery, but Klass's Kurse, taken literally, might nevertheless be valid. Maybe we will never find the solution to the Secret of the Saucers, at least not in *my* lifetime. (But see the epilogue that follows this chapter.)

Still, my (egad!) half century in ufology has been a lot of fun. All along, cleverly couched in mirth and mischievous verbal mayhem, I have had a serious purpose all too often missed or ignored by others: Encourage others to *think* in new ways and to question their unproved assumptions. I have attacked both True Believers and True Unbelievers with, I believe, equal justification and evenhandedness. Am I unbiased? Hardly! But by regularly filling the pages of *Saucer Smear* and its ancestors with letters and commentary by writers who oppose my views—and each other's—I have created a forum that is found nowhere else in The Field. I have entertained and, I hope, on occasion have even enlightened.

Over the years, particularly the past twenty or so, the ufological middle ground has shifted ever further into left field. Stories that would have been considered too far-out for belief by ufologically conservative minds are now accepted routinely by most of The Field's leaders, Serious and Not-So-Serious Ufologists alike. It seems that anything goes, no matter how absurd and unlikely—and this includes many of the "explanations" cooked up by debunkers.

Very recently, there has been another troubling trend—the exploitation of UFO beliefs to push political agendas. Most prominent of late is the Disclosure Project headed up by Dr. Stephen Greer, a former emergency-room physician. Greer began his ufological career several years ago by going out into the countryside with flashlights, with which he signaled the Space People. Of course, they came to him in their saucers, and he began to develop communications with them. This inspired him to establish the Center for the Study of Extraterrestrial Intelligence (CSETI), which has developed quite a loyal following of flashlight-toting fans and which should *not* be confused with SETI—the Search for Extraterrestrial Intelligence pursued by scientists who, unlike Greer, are still looking for ET.

Over time, Greer learned that the Space People are opposed to the development of ballistic missile defenses and weapons in space. (So am I, but not because of anything the Space People told me.) They also are concerned about the state of the earthly environment. (As for me, I refuse to breathe any air I can't see.) And—when we are sufficiently Enlightened, of course—they will give us the benefit of all their wondrous technology, which will solve our problems forever and ever, amen. Of course, our government has already unlocked at least some of these scientific and technological secrets, via "back engineering" the stuff from the Roswell crash and so on, but of course, it is keeping this knowledge from us for base economic reasons. Now Greer is touring the country with twenty or so alleged former military and civilian cover-up insiders, pressing for the government to reveal The Truth about UFOs and to adopt the political policies the Space People know are Good for Us.

Of course, the contactees of old did this sort of thing, too. George Adamski preached the Space Brothers' warnings of nuclear doom. Gabriel Green ran for president ("Abe in 1860. Gabe in 1960!") on a platform vaguely based upon Wisdom from space. But there was a certain innocence about it then. Not today. Greer's basic message really isn't much different from that of the contactees, but there is a Dark, troubling tinge to it.

Unlike Greer and so many others who have come and gone on *all* sides of the ufological belief divide (yes, I know what I just wrote), after almost fifty years of saucering, I have learned not one Great Truth. Not a single one. As I explained in my prologue, I think UFOs are just one of a vast spectrum of so-called Fortean phenomena that *may* be unsolvable, but which at least should convince us that the universe is much more complex than most people—even those in ufology—have ever imagined. I suspect the UFO Mystery is very much intertwined with the most fundamental mysteries of human life: Where did we come from? Why are we here? Where, if anywhere, do we go next? These questions can be "answered" through religious faith and "anti-answered" through smug skepticism. Questions about UFOs tend to be dealt with in the same way.

But *I* have no real answers, other than my semi-serious 4-D Theory. I think it's *possible* UFOs come from other planets, but it's much more likely that, whatever they may be, they are a permanent part of Earth's environment—whatever that may mean. The Christmas 1983 issue of

Time magazine carried a wonderful article called "What Does Science Tell Us About God?" Therein, a leading contemporary biologist whose name I don't recall was quoted as saying, semi-facetiously,

> There's one theory of the universe that I rather like. Suppose our planet is a "zoo for extraterrestrial beings." They planted the seeds of evolution on earth, hoping to create interesting, intelligent creatures. And they watched their experiment, interfering hardly at all, so that almost everything we do comes out according to the laws of nature. But every now and then they see something that doesn't quite look right. For example, they see that the zoo is going to kill itself off if they let mankind do this or that. So they insert a finger and change some little thing. And maybe these are the miracles which religious people like to emphasize.

Substitute the *Cosmic Tease* for *extraterrestrial beings, UFOs* for *miracles,* and *ufologists and ufoologists* for *religious people,* and this is very close to my view of the UFO phenomenon—whenever I'm forced to think about it seriously, as my Esteemed Coauthor is making me do now.

The difficulty for ufology today is that whatever it is that UFOs are and wherever it is they originate, they very well may be beyond proof. Therein lies the problem. Most people eventually tire of a mystery that can't be solved. Plain vanilla unidentified *flying* objects are bad enough, but what can be done about abductions, where the "proof" seems to be purely subjective? If abductions continue to be just about the only UFO-related events happening, ufology as a separate Fortean "discipline" may soon die out, its New Agey remnants merging back into the sort of occult subcultures from which they came back in the mid-1940s. What The Field desperately needs right now is some good pilot sightings, landings by *live* little men, treetop-level saucers close enough to shoot at, and Unkowns that zip all over radar scopes, as in days of yore. Alas, this doesn't seem to be part of the Cosmic Tease's game plan.

Enough profundity. A couple of years ago, former *MUFON UFO Journal* editor Dennis Stacy labeled me the "Reigning Court Jester of Ufology." At first, I wasn't sure how to take that. Should I consider it an honor or a slam? Then I received a letter from the mysterious Harry Lime of Vienna, Austria. It seems Lime is a friend of Carlos Mentira, a very longtime *Saucer Smear* nonsubscriber, and Mentira has been passing along copies of *Smear* to him. In one of these, Lime read of my reluctance to accept the jester mantle.

In reaction, he wrote, "The ancient tradition of the wise fool, he who could with impunity tell a crowned head The Truth—including especially pointing out his majesty's own stupidities—is an honorable and most valuable one. The jester combines wisdom with humor to convey unpalatable realities. Isn't that what you do, O Wise Ufool?"

These words put things into focus for me. While I hesitate to characterize my thoughts and writings as anything close to wisdom, I think Lime is in essence quite right. As I've long since given up taking the trouble to research UFO events in great depth, and as I *do* have some original thoughts on various ufological topics, the only reasonable role for me in The Field is that of court jester, chiding and poking fun at Serious and Semi-Serious Ufologists and other Leading Lights in such a way that they're not moved to cut me off completely—but may be moved to rethink their various notions and nostrums. So even though I didn't really plan it this way when I got into The Field back in 1953, I have found my legitimate role in ufology, and it was astute of Stacy and Lime to see this.

So let us carry on seriously, but not *too* seriously, groping for The Truth. I plan to continue tweaking the noses of my "betters" for some years to come. We shall see just how long that may be and what good it might do. As George Adamski was so fond of saying, time will tell.

. . . your belief will help create the fact.

—William James

The April 1, 1982, *Saucer Smear*, then as today an eight-page publication, carried the following item:

FLYING SAUCER MYSTERY SOLVED AT LAST????

Just as we were "wrapping up" this issue for the printer, we received startling information from a new research group called the Fortean Investigation Bureau, headquartered in Nutley, N.J. According to their release, a computer study of over 20,000 UFO cases has revealed a relatively simple pattern, which, if properly understood and correlated with other data, gives a simple and *unquestionably true* solution to the entire flying saucer mystery! Needless to say, your humble editor was astounded—and even saddened—to realize that in all his years of research he had overlooked the rather obvious facts which have now

> been revealed to the public by the Nutley group. In a nutshell, the secret becomes clear and even obvious when (continued to Page 9)

Once again, the Secret of the Saucers—The Fact, as Ray Palmer called it—had eluded an attempt to expose it publicly. Similarly, if Palmer really knew The Fact as he claimed he did, he took this Dangerous Knowledge with him to the grave, probably having no choice in the matter. The Fact is a shadowy, slippery thing, determined to remain forever just out of the grasp of mere mortals.

Yet true saucer fiends never give up their quest to reveal The Fact and add the Secret of the Saucers to the tree of human knowledge, a mystery no more. So it is that I have woven The Fact into my narrative. Somewhere in this tome, it lurks, unknown (I think) even to my Esteemed Coauthor, waiting for the discerning eye and clever mind to recognize it.

The reader who discovers The Fact herein and is the first to accurately identify it and provide a clear and entertaining explanation of why it is indeed The Fact (write: The Fact, PO Box 1709, Key West, FL 33041-1709) will receive a lifetime nonsubscription to *Saucer Smear*, for him- or herself or any other person he or she may name. Two other readers who in the judgment of my coauthor and myself made the most creative attempts to finger and explain The Fact will receive one-year *Smear* nonsubscriptions for themselves or whomever else they designate.

If The Fact is identified, I will attempt to publish it and the discoverer's name and explanation in *Smear*, but there is no guarantee The Fact will permit this. I should be able to get away with publishing the efforts of the runners-up—unless, of course, they are Too Close to The Truth.

Time will tell.

Finally, a couple of helpful hints: The Fact is *not* in this epilogue. A vital Clue is.

This appendix makes conveniently available for the first time in decades two Classics of 1950s saucering. The first of these is a copy of the original, signed Straith letter, which Gray Barker and I cooked up and sent to George Adamski. My Esteemed Coauthor discovered it in 1997 while sleuthing through the Gray Barker Collection in the Clarksburg-Harrison County Library in West Virginia. The other is the complete special issue of *Saucer News* in which I collected all of the articles I had published in *Nexus/Saucer News*, from January 1955 on, exposing Adamski's now rather nostalgically appealing Space Brothers scam. This Historic Issue appears in facsimile just as it was published at the height of the Golden Age of Flying Saucers. Those readers who lust to add a quality full-size, separate copy to their saucer-lore collections should write Tom Benson, PO Box 1174, Trenton, NJ 08606-1174 for price and availability information.

DEPARTMENT OF STATE
WASHINGTON

Prof. George Adamski
Star Route,
Valley Center
California

My Dear Professor:

For the time being, let us consider this a personal letter and not to be construed as an official communication of the Department. I speak on behalf of only a part of our people here in regard to the controversial matter of the UFO, but I might add that my group has been outspoken in its criticism of official policy.

We have also criticized the self-assumed role of our Air Force in usurping the role of chief investigating agency on the UFO. Your own experiences will lead you to know already that the Department has done its own research and has been able to arrive at a number of sound conclusions. It will no doubt please you to know that the Department has on file a great deal of confirmatory evidence bearing out your own claims, which, as both of us must realize, are controversial, and have been disputed generally.

While certainly the Department cannot publicly confirm your experiences, it can, I believe, with propriety, encourage your work and your communication of what you sincerely believe should be told to our American public.

In the event you are in Washington, I do hope that you will stop by for an informal talk. I expect to be away from Washington during the most of February, but should return by the last week in that month.

Sincerely,

R E Straith

R. E. Straith
Cultural Exchange Committee

RES/me

SPECIAL ISSUE #1
(Whole Number 27)

SPECIAL
ADAMSKI EXPOSE ISSUE

Printed Oct. 1957
Price: $1.00

SAUCER NEWS

OFFICIAL PUBLICATION OF THE SAUCER AND UNEXPLAINED CELESTIAL EVENTS RESEARCH SOCIETY

MAILING ADDRESS:
P. O. BOX 163, FORT LEE, N. J.

EDITOR:
JAMES W. MOSELEY

WHICH TWIN IS THE PHONY? Of the two photos above, one is an alleged flying saucer seen and photographed on December 13th, 1952, by George Adamski, co-author of "Flying Saucers Have Landed" and author of "Inside the Space Ships". The other is a photograph of a small model, and was published in the May, 1954 issue of "Yankee" Magazine. The Editor of "Yankee" has written us that their model was made from a Chrysler hub cap, a coffee can, and three ping pong balls. It is our contention that there is a striking similarity between these two pictures! (See Page 6 for the answer to the mystery of which photo is of the "genuine" Adamski saucer.)

CONTENTS OF THIS ISSUE

FEATURE ARTICLES:

Some New Facts About "Flying Saucers Have Landed" - by James W. Moseley......Page 2

Further Revelations about Adamski - by Irma Baker..............Page 12

"Inside the Space Ships" - a book review by Lonzo Dove.........Page 16

SAUCER NEWS is published approximately bi-monthly in Fort Lee, New Jersey, by the Saucer and Unexplained Celestial Events Research Society. Editor: James W. Moseley; Managing Editor: John Marana; Overseas Editor: Bryan Essenhigh; Photographic Consultant: August C. Roberts; Special Projects Consultant: William Albert; Associate Editors: Richard Cohen, Dominic Lucchesi, and Fred Broman. Subscription price: $2.00 per year, $3.50 for two years. Address all correspondence to P.O. Box 163, Fort Lee, New Jersey.

2.

EDITOR'S NOTE: The following article originally appeared in the January 1955 issue of "Nexus" (former name of SAUCER NEWS). Due to the great amount of public interest stirred up by the article, it was reprinted in February, 1955. This third printing is being made in October, 1957.

SOME NEW FACTS ABOUT "FLYING SAUCERS HAVE LANDED"
- by James W. Moseley -

During the past few years, numerous accounts have been given concerning alleged landings on this Planet by space ships, i. e., flying saucers, from other worlds. It is my intention in the following article to consider in detail the most widely publicized of these stories, namely, the one told by Mr. George Adamski. This story is given in detail in "Flying Saucers Have Landed" (British Book Center, published 1953). It is probable that most "Nexus" readers have read this book, which is co-authored by Mr. Adamski and Desmond Leslie; but for the benefit of those who are not familiar with the book, a brief resume of Adamski's portion of it is given below:

George Adamski's Story

Mr. Adamski begins his section of the book by stating that he is a "philosopher, teacher, student, and saucer researcher." Also, for several years he has been an amateur astronomer, and has in his possession two small telescopes: one a 15-incher, housed under a dome, and the other a 6-incher. Though he lives on the slopes of Mt. Palomar, California, where the giant 200-inch telescope is located, Adamski concedes that he has no connection with Palomar Observatory.

Adamski has long been interested in the possibility of life on other planets, but his first attempts at photographing flying saucers came only when, in late 1949, he was visited by two men - J.P. Maxfield and G.L. Bloom - of the Point Loma Navy Electronics Laboratory near San Diego. These men assured Adamski that flying saucers are probably interplanetary, because an Earth government is also making them. They also asked his co-operation in trying to get photographs of these strange craft, on the assumption that Adamski's 6-inch telescope could maneuver more easily than the large telescope at the Observatory. They told Adamski that they planned to make a similar request for photographs from the Observatory itself. Later, on a subsequent visit to Adamski's home at Palomar Gardens, Mr. Bloom confirmed a radio report of a flying saucer said to have landed in Mexico City.

Thus, having been asked by "the military" to co-operate with them in taking saucer photographs, Adamski proceeded to buy more photographic equipment. To quote the book, "Since then, winter and summer, day and night, through heat and cold, winds, rains, and fog, I have spent every moment possible outdoors watching the skies for space craft....Night after night I stayed outdoors watching the heavens....The cold winds wrapped me round and seemed to penetrate the very marrow of my bones. And steaming hot coffee was incapable of warming me. Once I caught such a cold that it took me many weeks to recover, but still I persisted."

Even though Adamski's liason with the Point Loma technicians soon fell through, he continued his efforts at saucer photography, and gradually his efforts were rewarded by an increasing number of good photos, though most of his pictures did not turn out well enough to prove anything. All through this

3.

period, Adamski hoped that some day the time would come when he could make a personal contact with a man from another world. Many times he wandered out onto the desert in hopes of such a contact, but it was not until November 20th, 1952 that he succeeded in making this wish a reality.

In August of 1952 Adamski became acquainted with Mr. and Mrs. Al Bailey of Winslow, Arizona, and Dr. and Mrs. George Williamson of Prescott, Arizona. (See Footnote #1 below.) The Baileys and Williamsons were as interested in making a contact as was Adamski, and they asked to be invited along the next time he made a trip into the desert. Accordingly, Adamski phoned Williamson on November 18th and arranged to meet the two couples near Desert Center, California, on November 20th. Accompanying Adamski to the rendezvous were Alice Wells, owner of the Palomar Gardens Cafe, and Lucy McGinnis, Adamski's private secretary.

These seven people met on schedule, and proceeded to a point on the highway about 11 miles from Desert Center. The Baileys brought a movie camera, the Williamsons had a still camera, and Adamski brought his 6-inch telescope, binoculars, and a case containing his still camera and gadgets for attaching the camera onto the telescope; also, he had seven film holders and a cheap Brownie camera. Thus, the party was quite well prepared in case they should see a saucer or a space man.

The first unusual occurrence was the sight of a large "mother ship" type of saucer,which appeared at high altitude and was seen by the whole party. As the group was camped right next to the highway when they made this sighting, the "mother ship" could have been seen by any passing motorist, says Adamski.

But Adamski had the feeling that this would not be the spot where he would make contact with a space man. Accordingly, he had Lucy drive him to a place a half mile or so from the highway. He requested that Lucy return and wait with the others for a period of one hour, after which time he would rejoin the group. Thus, for one hour Adamski remained alone on the desert,while the other members of the party watched his activities as best they could from a distance of between a half mile and a mile.

Adamski set up his telescope and other equipment, and within five minutes was rewarded by the sight of a small "scout ship" type saucer some distance away from him. He took seven photos of this "scout ship", though as he notes further along in the story, none of these pictures turned out well for some reason. Not long thereafter, Adamski saw a man approaching him. As Adamski walked up to the man and took a good look at him, he realized that he was looking at a human being from another world. The Visitor looked basically similar to an Earth man, though different in many details of his clothing and personal appearance. But the thing that made it obvious to Adamski that this stranger was indeed from Space, was the beautiful feeling that the sight of the man

Footnote #1: Bailey and Williamson later co-authored a book of their own called "The Saucers Speak", based on alleged radio and ouija board contacts with space men. Bailey later dropped out of saucer research, but Williamson has remained active. He organized the Telonic Research Center in Arizona, which published a bulletin for about a year. This organization and bulletin are now defunct, and Williamson's activities have shifted to Peru, where he currently heads the Brotherhood of the Seven Rays, a mystic philosophical organization. He has also recently published a second book called "Other Tongues, Other Flesh".

4.

caused him. To quote the book: "The beauty of his form surpassed anything I had ever seen.....I felt like a little child in the presence of one with great wisdom and much love, and I became very humble within myself, for from him was radiating a feeling of infinite understanding and kindness, with supreme humility."

The meeting lasted exactly long enough to use up the remainder of the hour Adamski had allotted himself;During this time Adamski learned,by using mental telepathy and gestures (as the stranger spoke no English), that the man was from Venus, and that his visit here on Earth was due in part to concern over our use of atomic weapons. To express the idea of atomic explosions, the Visitor said "Boom! Boom!". Unfortunately, the man would not allow Adamski to take a photograph of him.

Toward the end of the interview, the Venusian made a point of calling attention to his own footprints. It developed that the soles of the Visitor's shoes were inscribed with significent markings. After the Venusian returned to his "scout ship" and departed, Adamski rejoined his friends. Dr.Williamson happened to have with him a small package of plaster of paris, as "on this trip we tried to be prepared for any eventuality". Plaster casts were therefore made of the footprints, and over the subsequent months attempts have been made to interpret the strange symbols thereon.

In the course of his talk with Adamski, the Venusian had asked permission to take one of Adamski's film packs, with the promise that it would be returned to him before long. Sure enough, on December 13th (i.e., about three weeks later), the same scout ship flew over the vicinity of Palomar Gardens, and Adamski's space friend dropped the film pack out the window. When the film was developed, more strange symbols were found, and they too are now being interpreted by Adamski and his co-workers. On December 13th Adamski succeeded in getting several good photos of the "scout ship". These are reproduced in the book, and one of them is also shown on the cover of this issue. Adamski's account also states, "It (the 'scout ship') was seen and photographed by others." Though these "others" are not named in the text, one of them must be Jerrold Baker, for a blurred close-up shot of a "scout ship" is given in the photographic section of the book, with the following caption: "Flying Saucer Passing Low Over Trees: This photo, taken a few minutes later (i.e.,a few minutes after Adamski's series of Dec. 13th) was made by Sargeant Jerrold E. Baker with a Brownie Kodak camera as the saucer flew away and passed rapidly over the low hill on which he was standing. The blurred effect is due to the rapid speed at which the craft was moving."

As if this were not confirmation enough, Adamski's account is further strengthened by the inclusion in the book of sworn statements by each of the six people (other than himself) who were present at the November 20th contact. These affidavits read as follows: "I/we the undersigned, do solemnly state that I/we have read the account herein of the personal contact between George Adamski and a man from another world, brought here in his Flying Saucer "Scout Ship"; and that I/we was/were a party to and witness to the event as herein recounted."

Adamski's portion of "Flying Saucers Have Landed" concludes with an appendix, which describes a meeting held on June 1st, 1953, at which flying saucers were discussed by several qualified men. The most noteworthy features of this appendix are some remarks attributed to Al Chop, former Public Inform-

5.

ation Officer at the Pentagon, and the following statement attributed to Pev Marley, a cameraman for Warner Brothers Studios in Hollywood. Mr. Marley is quoted as having said that Adamski's pictures, if faked, were the cleverest he had ever seen, rivaling a Houdini. Marley pointed out that the shadows on the saucers, and also on the ground, correspond to such a remarkable degree that they could not be faked, and to fake such pictures would require costly equipment which Adamski obviously does not possess and which, even then, would not assure such a result.

Some of the Flaws

I have done my best to relate the above account without sarcasm or prejudice of any kind, though in view of the detailed study I have made of this story, I must admit that I find it difficult to present it without editorializing a little here and there. However, if I have made my account too brief to suit those of you who have not yet read "Flying Saucers Have Landed", it is merely because of limitations of space; and if I have seemed to emphasize some phases of the narrative more than others, it is because I now intend to raise an objection to nearly every portion of the story as I have presented it above.

There are others besides myself who have studied the Adamski story, and their conclusions vary according to their own particular "bent" and also according to how thoroughly and open-mindedly they have studied the evidence. To two of these fellow researchers- namely Mr. Jerrold Baker and Mr. John Pitt, of Surrey, England - I am deeply indebted for some of the material I am about to present. I am also indebted to other informants whom I am not at liberty to name. But in all due modesty, I must say that to the best of my knowledge, very few researchers have made as complete a survey of the Adamski tale as I have. I have traveled personally through Arizona and California, interviewing all the principals mentioned in the story, with the exception of Mrs. Bailey. Through interviews and lengthy correspondence I have made it my business to obtain all possible details concerning the "inside story" of Adamski's portion of "Flying Saucers Have Landed". Therefore, I now proceed to give you - not opinions - but to the best of my knowledge and ability, facts, fully mindful of the libel laws which compel me not to deviate from the truth.

Point One: Taking these points more or less in the order of their occurrence in the narrative, the first objection I raise is that Mr. Bloom, of the Point Loma Navy Laboratory, stated to me on the phone when I was in San Diego that he has been grossly misquoted in "Flying Saucers Have Landed". In particular, he claimed to have no knowledge whatsoever of a saucer landing in Mexico City.

Point Two: In the book (but omitted in my summary)is the following statement by Adamski: "If these (saucers) were secret experimental military devices, I would not be allowed to copyright my photographs and send them so publicly through the mails. And I sent a set of them to Wright-Patterson Air Force Base. In the interests of national security they would have stopped me, if I was photographing our own secret craft. They never have." This statement is, in all probability, true; but the same arguments would apply if Adamski was photographing extraterrestrial craft, if we are to assume that there are extraterrestrial aircraft in our atmosphere, and that the Air Force does not want details or proof in regard to these objects to be given out to the public. The obvious conclusion is that Adamski is not photographing any sort of craft at all, that the Air Force knows this, and therefore does not bother him. (Note:

6.

Adamski has run into really serious difficulty with "officialdom" only once, as far as I know, and that was for circulating among a group of "intimates" a ridiculous letter purporting to show that certain military officials back up the authenticity of his story and photos.)

Point Three: When I first read "Flying Saucers Have Landed", I was impressed by the fact that Adamski's story was backed up by four people (the Baileys and the Williamsons) whom Adamski knew only slightly. Although the text does not explicitly say so, I came to the conclusion (as many other readers did, no doubt), that these four were impartial, reasonably conservative, well educated people, not prone to indulge in hoaxes or be easily swayed by a hoax perpetrated upon themselves. I learned, however, from my own investigations, that all four were already ardent "Believers" before they made the November 20th contact, and that none had any particular educational advantages that would qualify them as expert or impartial observers. In particular, Williamson, though a pleasant enough young man, admits that he has no degree entitling himself to be called a "doctor", even though he allows himself to be called "Dr. Williamson" throughout the book - just as Adamski, among his friends and admirers (though not in the book), is known affectionately as "professor", without benefit of any degree. Put together, I think these facts add up to an entirely new picture of Adamski and his six witnesses. When we remember that two of Adamski's witnesses were close personal friends (one the owner of the property where he lives and the other his secretary), and when we find that none of the other four can be called either impartial or objective, then, I believe, a new light is thrown on the whole situation.

Point Four: The photographs: This subject has already been partly covered in the paragraph on the cover of this volume. Incidentally, it is the photo on the right that is the "phony", and the one on the left is the "genuine" "scout ship" photographed by Mr. Adamski. Additional remarks will be made further along concerning the photograph bearing Jerrold Baker's name; and indeed, a veritable volume could be written concerning the other photographs, some of which appear as "scout ships", others as "mother ships", and still others as mere spots of light without any definite form. But perhaps it will suffice here to quote a few of the remarks made by Arthur C. Clarke in the Journal of the British Interplanetary Society, March, 1954:

"Mr. Adamski's hobby is photographing flying saucers, and he undoubtedly is the most successful at this interesting art.....There are (in the book) several close-ups of space ships, leaving no doubt that they are artifacts. The uncanny resemblance (of the 'scout ships') to electric light fittings with table tennis balls fixed underneath them has already been pointed out.....To us, the perspective is all wrong, and though this is a qualitative impression perhaps not susceptible to rigorous proof, the pictures seem to be of small objects photographed from very close up and not of a large object seen through a telescope. Many people, including, we suspect, Mr. Adamski, do not realize that a large object seen through a telescope bringing it to within 20 feet looks quite different from an object itself 20 feet away....

"We have a much more serious comment, however, to make on photograph #3, which purports to show a fleet of saucers taking off from the Moon. Alas, something has gone wrong here. We would like Mr. Adamski to account for the fact that one of his saucers appears to be <u>inside the telescope</u>. This would not be apparent to anyone who was unacquainted with lunar geography, but an inspection of the background shows that the line of saucers is not clear of

7.

the Moon's edge, as appears at first sight, but extends off the field of view of the lens altogether. It is odd to say the least that Mr. Adamski's discriminating telescope is able to see a saucer and to ignore the Moon shining around it."

Point Five: Disagreement among witnesses: At least one of Adamski's six sworn witnesses no longer upholds the account as presented in the book. Mr. Al Bailey, who is a railroad worker in Winslow, Arizona, told me in a personal interview that he did not see the space man with whom Adamski allegedly talked, nor did he see the "scout ship" that allegedly landed on the desert. He did see the "mother ship", and some flashes of light in the direction where Adamski was supposed to be during the contact. To the best of his knowledge, no one else present saw any more than he did. Furthermore, a drawing in the book, supposedly made by Alice Wells while watching Adamski and the Visitor through binoculars, could not in Bailey's opinion have been made from that distance (i. e., about a mile away), nor was it made that day as far as he knows. Although Bailey admits that Adamski's account is not true in all details, he feels that Adamski's contact may actually have taken place, though he himself cannot vouch for it. I therefore feel that, if a hoax was involved, Mr. Bailey was duped rather than being in on it, for he further states that he believes that the advance text of the book sent him by Adamski, and on the basis of which he made his sworn statement, was not the same text actually used in "Flying Saucers Have Landed". (See Footnote #2 below.)

These points are further borne out by a letter from Bailey to Mr. Baker, dated June 1st, 1954, from which I now quote: "I am well aware of the placement and disposition of all members of the party that day (November 20th, 1952.) I also feel sure that no one saw any more than I did. (Italics mine.) There is a possible exception, and it is this: At the time of returning to the spot where Adamski was, he took Williamson off alone to the spot where the alleged footprints were. Just what transpired then, I have no way of knowing, nor did I make any inquiries at the time....There is a remote chance that during this interval he too saw the space man....I will no longer place myself on record to back up or refute anyone in such a controversial escapade again with no better proof than was mine at that time."

Point Six: Mr. Al Chop, who, it has been noted, is quoted at length in the appendix of the book, told me in a personal interview that he is misquoted, and that he has considered suing Mr. Adamski because of this fact. Similarly, in a phone conversation with me, Pev Marley denied having made the statements attributed to him, and also denied the rumor, circulated by Adamski and a few of his admirers, that Marley had blown up one of the Adamski "scout ship" photos and found, in the blow-up, the head of a man looking out of one of the "portholes".

Point Seven: Burning questions left unanswered by the book: How did the Venusian's footprints turn out so well on desert sand, in an area in

---

Footnote #2: Bailey apparently made his sworn statement based on Adamski's original manuscript, which was later edited, expanded, and "improved" by a mysterious "C.L.J.", whose editing is acknowledged by Adamski in some editions of "Flying Saucers Have Landed", and omitted in others. As we revealed in our February-March 1957 issue of SAUCER NEWS, "C.L.J." is Clara L. John, a Washington D. C. friend and admirer of Adamski, and currently the editor of "The Little Listening Post".

8.

which, according to a West Coast informant, there had been no rain for several months?

In the book (but omitted from my summary) Adamski says that American aircraft were seen overhead several times during the November 20th contact. These planes were apparently trying to catch the "mother ship" and the "scout ship". Why, therefore, were the saucers not reported by the pilots of these aircraft? If any such confirmatory evidence were available, Mr. Adamski would have it by now. The fact that he does not have it seems to indicate that there were no airplanes overhead that day.

If the space man was indeed from Venus, how was he able to defy every scientific principle by existing so easily and comfortably in the Earth's atmosphere, since it is a well known fact that the atmosphere, etc., on Venus is entirely different from ours? And how was the Venusian able to defy every law of probability by looking so similar to earth men?

Why did no one succeed in taking any movies or decent still pictures of the saucers seen during the November 20th contact?

And last but not least, what was the necessity of Adamski having his companions remain at such a great distance during his contact? Could this have been to make it easier to perpetrate a hoax on some of his friends (those who were not co-conspirators)?

The Evidence Presented by Mr. Jerrold Baker

Jerrold Baker is a young saucer researcher who, after his discharge from the Army a few years ago, became personally acquainted with Frank Scully (author of "Behind the Flying Saucers") and George Adamski. From November 12th 1952 until January 12th, 1953, Baker lived and worked with Mr. Adamski at Palomar Gardens, earning his board and keep by working as a secretary, chauffeur, and general handyman. Thus, Baker was present during the critical period covered in "Flying Saucers Have Landed" The reader will recall that November 20th and December 13th are the two important dates in Adamski's narrative.

I met Jerrold Baker at Scully's home some time ago, but did not know then of Baker's intimate knowledge of the details of the Adamski story. Now, in a letter dated September 11th, 1954, Baker writes me the following startling facts: "1. I did not take the Brownie snapshot accredited to me; 2. This was not the only Brownie picture taken; 3. George Adamski was the photographer, and the other Brownie pictures were destroyed at his request by Lucy McGinnis; 4. The photograph was not taken on the date indicated (i.e., not on December 13th); 5. The desert contact was pre-planned and Adamski related the details to me of what was to take place there previous to the venture.... 6. Lucy (McGinnis) purchased the plaster of paris in Escondito (Calif.) with me, and it was Adamski who carried it (on November 20th), not Williamson."

At this point I wish to state that whereas I do not know Mr. Baker well, and therefore cannot be absolutely certain of his motives for coming forward at this time, I nevertheless do know this: (1) That I have offered Baker no money or other inducement; (2) That by admitting that he was duped by the Adamski hoax he is gaining nothing, as far as I can see, except the knowledge that through his efforts and mine, the truth on the Adamski matter is at last coming to light; (3) That much of his evidence corresponds with information I have received from other reliable sources, and which I therefore readily accept as true; (4) That no one, other than Adamski and his six witnesses, has as great a first-hand knowledge of the incidents described in "Flying Saucers Have Landed" as does Mr. Baker.

Baker's information is contained in a number of letters and other documents that he has kindly lent me. Therefore, rather than run the risk of coloring Baker's information by putting it into my own words, I will tell his story mainly by quoting from these various documents.

First, here, in part, is a sworn statement made by Mr. Baker on June 29th, 1954: "To whom it may concern: In a recent book, "Flying Saucers Have Landed," an alleged photograph of a flying saucer was credited to Sargeant Jerrold E. Baker. I, the undersigned, am the said party....I make this statement in hopes of separating facts from fiction, truth from lies, and the real from the unreal. I did not take the alleged photograph accredited to me. The alleged photograph was taken with the Brownie camera, along with three or four similar photos, by Mr. George Adamski, on the morning of December 12th, 1952, and not on December 13th, 1952, as indicated (in the book)".

In a letter to me dated November 18th, 1954, Baker states: "Shortly after beginning work at Palomar Gardens, I had a long discussion with George Adamski, in which I tried to point out his slipshod manner of publishing what saucer photographs he had taken during the five years previous. In the discussion, I suggested that he not be the only photographer present during a flight of saucers over Mount Palomar.....It was my suggestion that he be located at one spot with his telescope and camera while I or any other individual be located at another spot on the property with a different type of camera.....Much to my amazement, within a week after this suggestion, George Adamski early one morning disclosed the fact that he had taken pictures with the Brownie camera, adjacent to his cabin. The date of the photography was December 12th. I chauffeured Alice Wells to Escondito to purchase the week's supply of restaurant articles. On our return, there was a fire on the slopes of Mount Palomar, and we stopped at the ranger station to ascertain its location....I insert this to perhaps give you some means of substantiating my whereabouts. Alice Wells liked me very much and if anyone would reveal the truth, she would be the one, but her admiration for George Adamski proves the greater, and I feel she would be likely to protect him.

"However, there are two other people who can provide you with the necessary proof of my claims regarding the photographs. They are: (1) Mr. Detwiler, the professional photographer who processes Adamski's work. (See Footnote #3 below.) He must fully recall the dates on which the photographs were presented to him. Secondly, he also developed the additional negatives to substantiate the erroneous fact of merely one Brownie photo. (2) Mr. Hal Nelson, who was and is presently an investigator for the United States Civil Service. ...Hal was present the morning Mr. Detwiler and his wife delivered said photographs to Palomar Gardens, and can verify seeing more than one Brownie snapshot."

Here I must interrupt Baker's account for a moment, to state that although I met Mr. Detwiler while I was in California, I did not yet know of the controversy over the Brownie photo, and therefore did not ask him about

---

Footnote #3: Detwiler has died since this account was written in 1954.

10.

it. However, I did ask Detwiler what he thought, in general, of Adamski's photographs, and his answer was as follows: He himself does no "fakery" in the processing of the pictures, and he receives genuine negatives from Adamski. Therefore, if Adamski's pictures are not genuine, then the "fakery" on Adamski's part does not consist of retouched negatives, but rather, it consists of the use of models. Detwiler says that he has no way of knowing whether or not Adamski uses models, or whether the photographs are of genuine saucers.

Now back to Baker's account. This time, I quote from a letter from Baker to Frank Scully, dated January 31st, 1954: "Case 'A': He (Adamski) has taken hundreds of photographs. Here are the most astounding photographs obtained thus far on the elusive saucers. This man claims he has spent untold hours watching and waiting, both day and night, to obtain the pictures. (See Page 2, next to last paragraph.) This is not true. I know that he knows exactly when a (space) ship is coming, and is there at the precise instant to snap the picture. It is a planned, purposeful action, not the mere chance which he implies. Why the necessity of the deception? Is it as he claims? Perhaps yes; but more likely, NO.

"Case 'B': Contact with space man on the desert: Here again, misleading, untrue stories are concocted to have the public accept what is supposed to be a fact....It is too purposeful, planned, and with peculiar motives. I was with Lucy when the plaster of paris was bought prior to the trip. I purchased the photographic plates myself. And, I accidentally heard a tape recorded account of what was to transpire on the desert, who was to go, etc., several days before the party left Palomar Gardens. Though this recording was a 'communication through psychic means', the account as presented (in the book) is entirely untrue. Regardless of the reasons presented to you or me, the witnesses, or the reading public, its manner of presentation to the public has been misleading and false."

In another letter, Baker expands on this point: "The tape recording I heard was a metaphysical discourse received through Professor Adamski approximately one week before the desert contact. I had heard about ten minutes of the tape-recorded talk when Lucy came to the office and advised me not to play the tape recorder. From this brief behind-the-scenes listening, I was able to determine that the desert contact was not a mere stab in the dark or a picnic on the desert, but a planned operation."

"Case 'C' (again quoting from Baker's letter to Scully): The Brownie Snapshot: You are presently familiar with this episode so I will not have to go into it again. However, in talking with this man (Adamski) when we met in town last week, he urged me to continue using my name on the picture because, 'You have to enter the back door sometimes to get the truth across.' What kind of a fool does he think we are, Frank? And actually, what kind of imbiciles are we to pledge our support to such stories? Is not all this a corruption of the truth? I say it is! I know it is! I will not condone it or support it any longer."

The above letter was written on January 31st, 1954. On November 2nd, 1953, Adamski, in an obvious effort to induce Baker to "stay in line", had written Baker as follows: "Now you know that the picture connected with your name is in the book, too - the one taken by the well with the Brownie. And with people knowing that you are interested in flying saucers as you have been, and buying the book as they are.....you could do yourself a lot of good.

For you have plenty of knowledge about these things (i. e., saucers), whereby you could give lectures in the evenings. There is a demand for this! You could support yourself by the picture in the book with your name. Remember that you are as much publicized in the book as I am, as far as the picture is concerned. And having the knowledge you have of these things, you have your break right here."

Notice that Adamski does not say "the picture in the book which you took", but rather, "the picture in the book with your name". Has not Baker proved his contention right here? Furthermore, if the blurred effect in the "Baker photo" is due to the saucer being out of focus rather than, as Adamski claims, in motion - then the "saucer" must be less than ten feet from the camera, as anything beyond ten feet is in focus with a Brownie!

Yes, Adamski attempted to bring Baker "back in line", as noted above, but the present state of the controversy can be summarized by the following letter from Baker to Desmond Leslie dated August 4th, 1954. After reiterating that he did not take the Brownie photograph, Baker states: "I am fully cognizant that words and accusations that prove unfounded are vain. So - with such an awareness and knowledge - I am proceeding to take whatever action I deem congruent with the nature of the Adamski fabrications, being confident that sufficient evidence to substantiate my claims is in my possession at this time. I readily admit that I fell victim to a hoax. I sustained the blow, and condoned the erroneous stories. But I have not supported them in any way, shape or form. And presently, under existing conditions, I will no longer continue to condone the erroneous stories or fabrications of any party connected with flying saucers...."

Finally, here is one more extract from a personal letter written by Baker to a friend of his: "Shortly before his disappearance, Karl Hunrath called a number of people. (See Footnote #4 below.) Among these were Frank Scully, Manon Darlaine, and Mrs. Wilkinson.....He denied Adamski's pictures as being real. He even told Mrs. Darlaine he saw the model. This I cannot confirm or deny. However, I can truthfully state that both Karl and I did see something one morning on our way down to the Palomar Gardens Cafe from our cabin, that closely resembled a skeleton for a saucer mock-up. It was a piece of wooden frame in a circular shape with strips of copper, about one inch in width, strung in circles on this wooden frame....We both questioned George Adamski about this paraphernalia behind his cabin, at which he grew somewhat uneasy, (italics mine), and assured us that what we saw was his own television antenna. I cannot say one way or the other, that it was or that it wasn't. But it is interesting and important considering the mathematical analysis made by several astronomers, who claim the photos couldn't be of anything but a small model."

This same information has been conveyed to me by other reliable informants.

Conclusion

The parade of evidence in regard to "Flying Saucers Have Landed" could go on almost indefinitely. Naturally, I have used my most sensational

Footnote #4: The mysterious disappearance of Karl Hunrath and Jack Wilkinson is another very interesting story, but outside the scope of the present article.

12.

material in this article, but were it not for limitations of space, I could give dozens of other examples, from Baker's files as well as my own, which would show other small and large matters of fact on which Mr. Adamski has "slipped up". If there is sufficient reader demand, I will give some of this additional information in a future issue of "Nexus".

In the meanwhile, let us remember that I am not saying - nor is Mr. Baker, that George Adamski's account is necessarily entirely untrue. In the final analysis, the true story may be known in its entirety only by Adamski himself. All any outsider can do, in regard to what another man claims to have seen and done, is to point out flaws in that man's narrative. However, I do believe most definitely that Adamski's narrative contains enough flaws to place in very serious doubt both his veracity and his sincerity. Furthermore, I am hoping that in the light of all the previously unpublished facts contained in this article, the reader will be moved to make for himself a careful re-evaluation of the worth of the Adamski book.

One final note: On my own part, at least, I am moved by no personal antagonism of any kind toward either George Adamski, Desmond Leslie, or any of the other principals in this narrative. Ever since my meeting with Adamski about a year ago, I have been convinced that he is a kindly man who would do harm to no one. If he has written a fraudulent book, perhaps he did so not so much for personal profit, but to put across, in dramatic form, philosophical principles in which he sincerely believes. In any case, his book has entertained thousands, and injured no one. But I sincerely believe that if the truth concerning the flying saucers is ever to be arrived at, someone must now and then perform the rather thankless task of sifting away the "saucer fiction" from the "saucer facts". It is with this goal in mind, and no other, that I have written the above account.

....

EDITOR'S NOTE: The following article originally appeared in the June-July 1955 issue of SAUCER NEWS. It is written by the woman who was later to become Jerrold Baker's wife. She gives an excellent picture, in our opinion, of the strange behind-the-scenes happenings at Palomar Gardens around the time that the events in "Flying Saucers Have Landed" took place. The article was written in answer to counter-charges made by Desmond Leslie as a result of the article you have just read.

FURTHER REVELATIONS ABOUT ADAMSKI
- by Irma Baker -

I met George Williamson and Al Bailey first a day or two after the Desert Contact. I saw Williamson only one other time until he moved bag and baggage to Palomar Gardens. At this time, Lucy McGinnis and George Adamski told me that Williamson was having trouble and had been ever since his arrival, with "low spirits" taking over his body, and that George was trying to help him, as Williamson was now controlled by this "low element".

On January 3rd, 1953, I drove to Palomar Gardens again with friends. We were approached by Lucy very confidentially for funds, as no one there had money (nor ever did, for that matter), and by then work was being done to prepare another half-finished cabin and furnish it for three men- George Williamson, Karl Hunrath, and Jerrold Baker. These three were to form the "Adamski Foundation". We were told that Karl Hunrath was an inventor par excellence, and was having his equipment shipped from the east for use on George's property. Some of this equipment consisted of magnetic frequency machinery designed with an eye to contacting a saucer and bringing it down on Palomar.

On January 10th I revisited Palomar and viewed the photographic plate - the one with hieroglyphics, supposedly dropped on George's premises by a saucer. I viewed this on a screen through a projection machine rigged by Karl Hunrath. I will only say at this time that I feel a space man capable of space travel, superior intelligence, and such a superior way of life as described by George, should have figured out an easier way of communicating with our present level of evolution!

Another thing that troubled us all was the manner in which Hunrath, Williamson, and Baker all disappeared from the Cafe after viewing the plate, whereas prior to this they had been most friendly toward us, and Williamson had danced original Indian dances, etc., for our benefit. I was puzzled and of course suspicious.

Two days later, on January 12th, 1953, I received a tearful and pathetically distraught telephone call from Lucy McGinnis, from a tavern just below Adamski's property. (George did not have a phone.)

"Irma", said Lucy, "Please do something fast. Professor Adamski said to call you and that you would know just who to phone. This is an emergency. The 'boys' are threatening to shoot down our own jets with that awful machine!" She continued by saying that the machine she had told me about had arrived, and that Hunrath said he would just as soon bring down our own jets with it as a saucer. She said that the Professor had become righteously indignant and ordered them off the premises, and that they- the Professor, Lucy, and Alice Wells (owner of Palomar Gardens) - were frightened to death that "the boys" would return and do them harm.

By this time, I was a bit punchy! I told Lucy to remain by the phone. I took her number and said I would call her back.

First, I called a close friend, a Lieutenant in Navy Meteorology, stationed in San Diego. He advised me not to get involved but suggested that I call the O.S.I. or Army Intelligence.

I called the office of the O.S.I. I reported exactly what Lucy had told me, and gave them her name and telephone number. They assured me they would call her immediately,and that they would also call the F.B.I. The O.S.I. did this as I waited.

I was intrigued. I couldn't resist the urge to learn more about all this, because by then I was well aware that every story told by George and his disciples could be interpreted to have a different meaning. So I gathered three other people in my car, and drove to Palomar Gardens. We arrived shortly after dinner. The F.B.I. and O.S.I. men were already there. Here are some of the highlights of what George said to these men in the presence of myself and three other witnesses:

Adamski's Statements to the F.B.I. and O.S.I. Agents

1. Karl Hunrath (whom George had formerly called an esteemed col-

14.

league and close friend) was now a beast, an uncontrolled monster, and a sadist. He had an ego complex and was anti-female to the point of insulting the women. He had stated that it was irrelevent if he brought down American jets by use of the magnetic machine in his quest of grounding a saucer. He was practicing occultism, but had only progressed to the point of "being taken over by a beast". He had threatened George all of a sudden - "a weak, feeble old man, afraid for his very life." (George is really quite strong, and much bigger than Hunrath.)

2. Dr. George Williamson wasn't really a doctor at all. He only posed as one, and used an honorary degree to gain recognition. (This is really true, and is common knowledge in select circles, but this is a case of the pot calling the kettle black.) Williamson was on Palomar to have Professor Adamski help him. He was constantly being taken over by a "low element" of spirit which would put him out cold for sometimes as long as an hour at a time. Of course, no good "element" would think of doing such a thing. Williamson was <u>posing</u> as a medium, but was a <u>fake,</u> because Adamski had proved many times (to his own satisfaction) that when Williamson went into a trance, he was only putting on; - and his study of Indian lore, etc., enabled him to pretend as though an Ancient Being was speaking through him as a guide. (By this time the F.B.I. men must have inwardly burst into convulsions of laughter!) Williamson was weak and spineless, and had left his poor pregnant wife. (It is true that he did for a time, but not with intentions of separation.) He had left her to treck up to Palomar and stay there eating the food from Adamski's poor table. George asserted to the F.B.I. that he knew this as <u>he</u> was a <u>real</u> medium. He related experiences to them of tests put to him by his Teachers. Lucy's head bobbed up and down all the time in silent agreement with every word Adamski said. The F.B.I. and O.S.I. men sat silent and wide-eyed. "I am the only real medium", George repeated to them many times. (The poor F.B.I! What they go through to earn the taxpayers' money! I'll bet this was a new experience for them!)

3. Jerrold Baker was a nice quiet boy - always writing letters to his mother. He seemed like such a good fellow. He must have been really taken in by the other two. Of course he (George) wasn't always too sure about Baker. He did seem to have a weak character. He always agreed with everybody, and wasn't ever disagreeable. George sometimes wondered if maybe he was a secret investigator, "but then you fellows can find out better than I can about that, ha-ha!" - Anyhow, Baker did receive regular checks from the American Air Force while he was here at Palomar, but never paid any rent. "I would like to collect that, of course", said George. (No mention was made of the work Jerrold did there and which I witnessed, from typing by the hour, chopping logs, and washing dishes, to waiting on tables in the Cafe, etc. The statement about the checks was another falsehood, but I didn't learn that till later.)

All three men were accused of having attempted to hi-jack the Professor's mail. Lucy was supposed to have called the police to stop them. All this took place in Escondito. (The true story is that Hunrath, on being confronted by Lucy in Escondito, called a policeman to make this fanatical woman let them alone, as she threatened all sorts of things if they <u>left</u> Palomar. Jerry had been delegated to pick up Adamski's mail as a representative of Palomar Gardens. This Adamski had to admit to the F.B.I. when questioned. The fact that they were bringing George's mail back with their own to the Cafe did not come out till later, when it was learned that the fracas in Escondito occured <u>before</u> they had packed the car with their personal belongings. At the time of the fracas their belongings were still in the cabin on Adamski's property, to which they had every intention of returning.)

It seemed apparent that any and all means to discredit these three must be made that night. But why? Because they wished to leave the Adamski stronghold. Why should that disturb him so? I couldn't help but see just how disturbed he was - shaken and scared. The F.B.I. agents assured him repeatedly that they didn't believe the men intended to return to Palomar to attempt to harm him. It seemed to me that there was only one answer: "Hell hath no fury like a woman scorned." Adamski, although a man, had obviously been scorned. The three new disciples had walked out, and for a reason. What that reason was I was determined to find out, and did. It was also obvious that three disciples don't up and leave the "Master" unless they have discovered that his feet of clay are showing!

Adamski made no mention that night of any money stolen by anyone, although he did later. They had all the mail there. The F.B.I. determined that, and George reluctantly admitted that "they hadn't made off with a thing, of course, but they might have but for Lucy." George added as a further thought, "Hell, there might have been a check in the mail for all I know. People are always sending me donations."

"Was there?" asked the F.B.I.

"I don't think so, but I haven't opened all the mail yet," George answered. But if any chance or opportunity to pin a theft on anyone had arisen, he would have done so then and there! The present answer is pretty damned obvious!

....

My friend the meteorologist went to the F.B.I. some time later, and checked this whole affair for me. He disbelieved in Adamski, and relished the opportunity to get his own story on him, which of course he did. The F.B.I. was then watching George for more "slips" in his oratory efforts in the Cafe, in which he often elaborated on his confidential knowledge of troop, atomic, and secret military movements, supposedly passed on to him by his military contacts and informants. The F.B.I. had him listed as a complete crackpot, and completely discredited his report on Hunrath, Williamson, and Baker, as the ravings of a jealous madman. (George would often elaborate on stories he heard in the Cafe from servicemen, and because of his exaggerations, a private or corporal in passing his story would be identified as "the military" or a "top notcher". Much of Adamski's pattern today is precisely the same. He continually uses witnesses' testimony, which he perverts to use in furthering his beliefs.)

Some Further Points Regarding Adamski's Claims

1. Mayme Maum was not present the day Detwiler returned the Brownie snapshots to Adamski, in spite of Desmond Leslie's claim that she was. I confronted her at the recent saucer convention at Giant Rock, California, and she admitted that she and I went up to Palomar together and arrived at a later time. When invited to walk the length of two automobiles to meet the Nelson Brothers who were present when the Brownie photos arrived, she reneged and backed down completely.

16.

2. Mr. and Mrs. Frank Scully, as well as Hal and Wally Nelson, witnessed my efforts the same day as the Giant Rock Convention (March, 1955) to engage George Adamski in an out and out discussion of the Brownie snapshot. I challenged him and he evaded me for three solid hours.

3. Adamski has changed his space man story distinctly from the way it was the first several times I heard it. I took notes at the time,and therefore am sure that the story has changed.

4. The original communication between Adamski and the space man consisted purely of telepathy. His later meetings with these space men (after publication of "Flying Saucers Have Landed") always were in a bar in Los Angeles, where they met him and then supposedly drove him (as he can't see well enough to drive himself) to isolated spots for conferences. If space men are meeting people like George in bars, I feel that I prefer not to meet one myself!

5. I questioned George Williamson in April of 1954, to find out whether or not he ever saw the space man during the November 20th 1952 contact, and he answered me a straight NO! Furthermore, I told him I thought Adamski was lying about the material facts of the meeting, and that I believed if it happened at all it was spiritual in nature - and he agreed!

This was the point Adamski and I fell out on first. I contended that the law of averages prohibited life on other planets from being exactly as we are, because atomic nuclei respond differently to different atmospheric conditions. He replied that in order to get across to the people his teachings and philosophies, he couldn't be too"mystical", as he put it, and that he must present all the happenings on a very material basis because that is how people want them. I contended that this was as good as lying! He answered, "Sometimes to gain admittance, one has to go around by the back door." To gain admittance to what? The cloud of literary achievement? Or public acclaim? The latter I do not agree with!

....

EDITOR'S NOTE: The following article is a review of "Inside the Space Ships", the book that Adamski wrote as a sequel to "Flying Saucers Have Landed". The article originally appeared in the October-November 1955 issue of SAUCER NEWS. Lonzo Dove, the author, is an amateur astronomer of considerable standing.

INSIDE THE SPACE SHIPS
- Reviewed by Lonzo Dove -

I feel that "Inside the Space Ships" deserves some blunt remarks to show it up for what it is. If the Space Men really spoke as quoted therein, their wisdom reflected in their space-craftmanship is utterly contradicted by their spoken ignorance of even the basic principles of the sciences of astronomy, optics, and biology.

On Page 76 of the book, Adamski, inside a saucer, views the Earth from a distance of 50,000 miles, and declares the apparent size of the Earth to be the same as that of the Sun. He also states that the planet Earth appears less bright than the Moon. Now, out there in open space, he did not have to guess. By turning his head he would have seen both the Sun and Moon, as

17.

well as Earth, and from out there the Sun would appear the same size as from sunny California. The facts: From Earth, the Sun and Moon appear the same size, and subtend the same angle of 1/2 degree of arc. The Moon is 240,000 miles from Earth, and the diameter of the Moon is about one fourth that of Earth. The 50,000 mile viewpoint is about 1/5th the distance from Earth to Moon. If the Moon were only that far away, it would then appear 5 times larger in diameter, i. e., it would then subtend $2\frac{1}{2}$ degrees of arc. Since the Earth is 4 times larger than the Moon, from the same distance the Earth must appear 4 times 5, or 20 times larger than the Moon or Sun appear from the Earth's surface. In order to see the Earth as small as the Moon and Sun appear from Earth, the space ship would have to be somewhat over a million miles away, not a mere 50,000 miles. Even without the Sun out there to compare with, it would be hard to mistake a difference of 20 to 1 in size!

As for the brightness of the Earth as seen from space, it would be about the same as the similar planet Venus, which reflects 8 times more light than the Moon does. Earth and Venus are covered by highly reflective clouds and water surfaces, while the Moon is unobscured dark rocky material that reflects only 7 percent of the sunlight falling on it. Therefore, 50,000 miles away, the planet Earth, being larger and more shiny, would outshine the Moon by more than 3,000 times!

Adamski also says that the surface features on Earth were invisible from "up there". But just look at the published photographs taken from actual outer space rockets. The ground surface of Venus, far away as it is, shows enough through the denser clouds to enable me, by the help of a clue from the real flying saucers, to determine the axis rotation of that planet as 125.64 hours. Adamski, with all his claimed first-hand knowledge about Venus, could not tell us how long the Venusian day and night is!

On Page 158-159, Adamski betrays complete ignorance of the axis of rotation of our closest neighboring world, the Moon. Actually the Moon rotates relative to the Sun and stars in a period of about 27 1/3 days, with its axis poles at the North and South limbs of the globe as seen from Earth. The sunlight goes around the Moon in a West to East direction as it does around Earth from East to West. Therefore the temperature on the hidden side of the Moon is the same as on the side always turned toward Earth. And Adamski's statement about a temperate zone around the visible edges of the Moon is a physical absurdity. On the Moon, the zones of lesser sunlight are to the North and South, as on Earth and on Venus and Mars. The twilight zone moves around the Moon with its rotation, and we see the line cut the disk into the progressive phases from Full to Quarter to New, in shadow of night there.

On Page 86: Contrary to what is dogmatically stated here by Adamski, astronomers have never found a single group of 12 suns or stars revolving around a larger body, nor is such a system meant when astronomers speak of "island universes". This term means clusters or galaxies of numberless stars, each cluster isolated by the vastness of space. Furthermore, there are not 12 planets revolving around our Sun or star. Even if there were 3 more planets beyond the orbit of Pluto, where already the Sun is so far away that it looks like a bright star and gives out as much heat and light, such outer planets would be so dark and cold that organic molecules could never organize for the evolution of life. Mars is near the outer limit of the zone of life in the Solar System, and the next planet, Jupiter, is eternally frozen in mid-day sunshine.

18.

It is ridiculous for Adamski to speak of "horses" and "cows" and "human beings" on Saturn or its satellites, or for that matter, on the Moon or Venus or Mars - unless they were transported there from the place of their origin, the Earth. Biological forms evolving on different planets would not take the same structure. Even on Earth, where all life arose from one source, but later became separated by wide barriers, animals adopted to similar environments. Though they develop similar habits, and may have similar size and general external form, they are not the same species. In Australia there are dog-like and bear-like animals, but they are marsupials, not mammals. If the isolation were more complete and for a longer time, perhaps man-like marsupials would have arisen; but they would not be human beings, and there could be no mating between the two groups, though both would be on the same planet and from the same earlier biological origin. How much more different man-like creatures of different planets must be by the chance orders and kinds of environments and ultimate origins on the molecular level. For example, I have determined that living cells on Mars are composed of deuterium, i. e., heavy hydrogen, instead of universally-abundant ordinary hydrogen as on Earth. In that case, they could not even eat food grown on Earth, nor could we do well on Martian vegetation, as proved by experiments in the laboratory with heavy hydrogen. Multiply such differences, and you can dismiss all "Venus Men".

On Page 78: Meteors darker than the darkness of outer space? Nothing can be darker than the background of empty space or the absence of reflected light. From a viewpoint far out in space, away from the shadow cone of the Earth or other heavenly body, any meteor close enough to be seen would be reflecting sunlight, and so would appear bright like stars, though meteors do not become self-luminous till they reach the friction of an atmosphere around a planet.

Adamski stalls us regarding that 6-foot telescope lens which he claims to have seen in the floor of the space ship, and through which he merely, without eyepiece, looked down upon Earth from "many miles high" and saw details on the ground - at midnight and with only a thin crescent Moon in the sky one February 18th! He says this machine was not like our man-made telescopes, and in this I agree. Aside from the impossibility of viewing a scene directly through an objective lens at one's feet, it is impossible to see more than a tiny point at a time, or to see in darkness. Even Adamski's alleged mysterious rays cannot do away with the blurring effect of a turbulent atmosphere which makes impossible any magnification beyond a certain limit. The larger the lens, the more collection of this blurring effect. A large lens alone does not mean high magnification, which depends on the distance the image is formed behind the lens, and the power of the little eyepiece by which the image is viewed. To say nothing of the mystery of Adamski's seeing the "black shadows" and "curving sides"of the cigar-shaped space ship down against the dark background of the Earth on a moonless midnight. (See Pages 51-54 and 157.)

The only way to observe fine details at great distance is to plant on the scene a transmitting instrument, under remote control from the flying saucer. This Adamski thinks of on pages 122 and 147-148, an idea original with me in my 1950 statements on the subject of flying saucers. But if the saucer has inside it the marvelous telescope described in the story, and if this telescope is able to look directly on a scene below it, then why the superfluous nonsense of sending out any observing devices? That marvelous upside-backward telescope was good enough to see the barnyard animals on Venus, which scenery Adamski then saw for the first time - though this contradicts his own statements about having seen the wonders of Venus <u>before</u> the amazing episode related in "Inside the Space Ships".

I will pass over Adamski's unscientific "science" about the Sun not being hot, and about radiation not being heat until it passes through a planetary atmosphere, which automatically increases the heat and light to human needs according to the distance from the Sun. Adamski apparently does not realize that radiation mass-energy decreases with the square of the distance from a given area, and that the atmosphere of Saturn cannot increase this radiation to human tolerence level, nor can the atmosphere of Mercury, such as it is, decrease the close heat very much. If anyone wants to test this, merely place a thermometer inside a vacuum jar, and it will be discovered that the same temperature is registered in the vacuum as in atmosphere. The contrary statements are on Pages 51, 87, 89, and 158 of Adamski's book.

In the same unscientific class is the statement that ordinary sounds on Earth can be picked up miles away without a transmitter on the spot. Sound waves diminish with distance through air, and at a certain distance, according to the strength of the sound, it is completely masked by surrounding noises, and no amount of filtering or magnifying can bring the original sound to its original form. This corresponds to the blurring of fine visual details. See Pages 46 and 80 for the reversal of this fundamental law of nature!

Having passed over these errors and much more of the same sort, I now come to my favorite topic, those ever-present-with-Adamski photographs of space ships over the Moon or somewhere. In this his latest book, the alleged picture of the Moon can hardly be recognized as such. If his telescope is that bad, how could he get the earlier photos he claims to have taken? I have seen better, sharper photos of the Moon taken through a small toy telescope. Let us assume, however, that it is really the Moon in these photos, and not some unreasonable facsimile thereof. If the saucers over it are "near the Moon", then their size must be 25 to 150 miles in diameter, since the Moon from edge to edge is about 2,000 miles across. It is simply a matter of proportion and perspective.

Now to those relatively close-up photos of the cigar-shaped ship with port holes on the side, showing the faces of Adamski in one hole and of his Venus Man in the adjoining one - or so the book tells us. The book also says that these photos were taken with a camera that leaves no negatives for inspection, and that it was by artificial lighting from a scout ship whose pilot was taught the art of using this Earth gadget. Why the highly-advanced space travelers lacked a better picture-taking device is left dangling as one of the abtruse mysteries. Did the light shine on the whole side of the cigar-shaped ship, or just in a strip along the port holes? Is that elongated fuzzy blur the outline of the cigar-shaped space ship? If so, from the proportion of these windows to the whole image, those faces must be yards wide! This was, so Adamski says, a ship large enough to carry many regular saucers of the 30-foot variety. But let us assume that the holes are only as large as the faces show. The holes are described as being 6 feet through. Imagine a window as wide as a man's face and 6 feet through, like a long tube! It's no good for looking over the outside scenery of space, for the angle is too narrow. This would make the holes about 6 feet apart. A camera at several hundred feet away could barely see through both holes at once to show the two faces behind them, and at a hundred foot distance the inner ends of both tubes couldn't be seen as shown

20.

in the picture. At the several hundred feet distance, human faces would not be identifiable. It is a matter of optical parallax and photographic resolution. But to cap the climax, out there in open space, 2½ hours by saucer from Earth, according to our Authority, why resort to artificial lights to take this blur of a photo, since the full sunshine blazed at all hours upon the polished silvery sides of the space ship?

It would be unfair to reveal what those nebulous patches of light with port holes and faces pasted on actually were originally, for that would spoil the fun of debunking the story the photos were meant to prove. Adamski himself, on page 248, admits how bad these photos were, and puts the blame on mysterious rays from the saucers. It happens that radiation spoilage of photographic materials can be identified. It does NOT blur the image placed there by the proper exposure, but it only superimposes upon the photograph a fog or spotty appearance evenly, most visible in the dark parts of the picture. So, this picture appears just as intended to appear - a blurred elongated nebulous light with a background of darkness. Why Adamski didn't include the Earth or Venus, by that marvelous television machine on the saucer, as added evidence, only he can answer. He has photos of saucers over the Moon, so when he had the chance of a lifetime, how could he miss the opportunity to take a photo of the cigar-shaped ship with the Earth as a distant background decoration?

In conclusion, let me affirm that I am not "scoffing at the new wonders" of Adamski, as he predicts in this book that the critics will do; but I am merely pointing out the demonstrable flaws in a few of the crucial details of his story, with the honest hope that rational people will decide positively whether they still believe Adamski took his rides in a flying saucer <u>or ever took a photo of a saucer, with or without his telescope.</u>

ARE YOU ON OUR SPECIAL NEWSLETTER MAILING LIST? Since December, 1955, irregularly-issued Newsletters have been made available to SAUCER NEWS subscribers who want to be on the <u>inside</u> of the strange and baffling behind-the-scenes events in saucer research. These Newsletters often contain material that we consider "too hot to handle" in the regularly-scheduled issues of our magazine. Any SAUCER NEWS subscriber can be placed on the special Newsletter mailing list for an indefinite period of time for the price of $1.00. Recent Newsletters have dealt in detail with the current Peruvian adventures of George Williamson, key witness to Adamski's 1952 desert contact. As of this writing, Williamson appears to have given up his Peruvian metaphysical colony at least temporarily, and is rumored to be heading back to the United States for a lecture tour. Future issues of the Newsletter will tell you about these and other equally interesting events, just as soon as sufficient information is received here at our Headquarters. Don't miss out! Send us your name and address today, while you're thinking about it, and let us put you down for the Newsletter. We can't guarantee when or where something sensational will break, but when it does, our organization will have the inside facts, through our world-wide network of correspondents, clipping services, and other informational sources.

NEW AIR FORCE STATEMENT AVAILABLE: A new "fact sheet" was issued by the Air Force in October, 1957, and can be obtained without cost by writing to the following address: Major L.J. Tacker, Information Services USAF, Pentagon (Room 4C-916), Washington 25, D. C. - Meanwhile, you can still obtain the 80-page-long Project Bluebook Special Report #14 by sending $1.50 to Dr. Leon Davidson, Box S, 64 Prospect St., White Plains, New York.

Adamski, George. "Adamski Answers Washington Denial Regarding R. E. Straith." *Flying Saucer Review* (January/February 1959): 8–9.

———. *Flying Saucers Farewell.* New York: Abelard-Schuman, 1961.

———. *Inside the Space Ships.* New York: Abelard-Schuman, 1955.

Allingham, Cedric. *Flying Saucer from Mars.* New York: British Book Centre, 1955.

Angelucci, Orfeo. *The Secret of the Saucers.* Amherst, Wis.: Amherst Press, 1955.

———. *Son of the Sun.* Los Angeles: Devorss and Company, 1959.

Arnold, Kenneth, and Ray Palmer. *The Coming of the Saucers: A Documentary Report on Sky Objects That Have Mystified the World.* Boise, Idaho, and Amherst, Wis.: Authors, 1952.

Barker, Gray. *Gray Barker at Giant Rock.* Clarksburg, W.Va.: Saucerian Publications, 1976.

———. *Gray Barker's Book of Saucers.* Clarksburg, W.Va.: Saucerian Books, 1965.

———. *MIB: The Secret Terror Among Us.* Jane Lew, W.Va.: New Age Press, 1983.

———. *The Silver Bridge.* Clarksburg, W.Va.: Saucerian Books, 1970.

———. *They Knew Too Much About Flying Saucers.* New York: University Books, 1956 (reissued with a foreword by John Keel; Lilburn, Ga.: IllumiNet Press, 1997).

———, ed. *Bender Mystery Confirmed.* Clarksburg, W.Va.: Saucerian Books, 1962.

———. *Saucer News Non-Scheduled Newsletter* (March 10, 1968–August 17, 1970). For availability and prices of facsimile copies write: Tom Benson, PO Box 1174, Trenton, NJ 08606-1174.

———. *Saucer News* (spring 1968–spring 1970). For availability and prices of facsimile copies write: Tom Benson, PO Box 1174, Trenton, NJ 08606-1174.

———. *The Strange Case of Dr. M. K. Jessup.* Clarksburg, W.Va.: Saucerian Books, 1963.

———. *A UFO Guide to "Fate" Magazine.* Clarksburg, W.Va.: Saucerian Press, 1981.

Barry, Bill. *Ultimate Encounter.* New York: Bantam Books, 1978.

Baxter, Marla [Constance Menger]. *My Saturnian Lover.* New York: Vantage Press, 1958.

Bender, Albert K. *Flying Saucers and the Three Men.* Clarksburg, W.Va.: Saucerian Books, 1962.

———, ed. *Space Review: Complete File of the Publication Issued by the International Flying Saucer Bureau, Bridgeport, Conn., from October, 1952, through October, 1953, Inclusive.* Clarksburg, W.Va.: Saucerian Publications, 1962.

Berlitz, Charles, and William L. Moore. *The Roswell Incident.* 1980; reprint, New York: Berkley, 1988.

Bethurum, Truman. *Aboard a Flying Saucer.* Los Angeles: DeVorss and Company, 1954.

Binder, Otto O. *Flying Saucers Are Watching Us.* New York: Belmont Books, 1968.

Black, Victor. "The Flying Saucer Hoax." *American Mercury* (October 1952): 61–66.

Bloecher, Ted. *Report on the UFO Wave of 1947.* Washington, D.C.: Author, 1967.

———. "The Stonehenge Incidents of January 1975." In *Proceedings of the 1976 CUFOS Conference,* edited by Nancy Dornbos, pp. 25–38. Evanston, Ill.: Center for UFO Studies, 1976.

Blum, Ralph, with Judy Blum. *Beyond Earth: Man's Contact with UFOs.* New York: Bantam Books, 1974.

Cahn, J. P. "Flying Saucers Swindlers." *True* (August 1956): 36–37, 69–71.

———. "The Flying Saucers and the Mysterious Little Men." *True* (September 1952): 17–19, 102–12.

Clark, Jerome. *The UFO Encyclopedia: The Phenomenon from the Beginning.* 2d ed. Detroit: Omnigraphics, 1998.

Corso, Philip J., with William J. Birnes. *The Day After Roswell.* New York: Pocket Books, 1997.

Darrach, H. B., Jr., and Robert Ginna. "Have We Visitors from Space?" *Life,* April 7, 1952, 80–84, 89–92, 94, 96.

Davidson, Leon. "The CIA and the Saucer: The Significance of the Socorro Symbol." *SBI Report* 3, no. 6 (1982): 18–20.

———. "Why I Believe Adamski." *Flying Saucer Review* (January–February 1960): 3–8.

———, ed. *Flying Saucers: An Analysis of the Air Force Project Blue Book Special Report No. 14.* White Plains, N.Y.: Editor, 1956.

Dickinson, Terence. *The Zeta Reticuli Incident, with Related Commentary by Jeffrey L. Kretsch, Carl Sagan, Steven Soter, Robert Sheaffer, Marjorie Fish, David Saunders, and Michael Peck.* Milwaukee, Wis.: AstroMedia, 1976,

———. *Zeta Reticuli Update.* Fredericton, N.B.: UFORI, 1980.

Eberhart, George M., ed. *The Roswell Report: A Historical Perspective.* Chicago: Center for UFO Studies, 1991.

Editors of United Press International and Cowles Communications. *Flying Saucers, A* Look *Special.* 1967.

Edwards, Frank. *Flying Saucers—Serious Business.* New York: Lyle Stuart, 1966.

Fort, Charles. *The Books of Charles Fort.* New York: Holt, 1941.

Friedman, Stanton T. *Top Secret/MAJIC.* New York: Marlowe and Company, 1996.

Friedman, Stanton T., and Don Berliner. *Crash at Corona: The U.S. Military Retrieval and Cover-up of a UFO.* New York: Paragon House, 1992.

Fry, Daniel W. *Alan's Message: To Men of Earth.* Los Angeles: New Age Publishing Company, 1954.

———. *The White Sands Incident.* Los Angeles: New Age Publishing Company, 1954.

Fuller, John. *Incident at Exeter.* New York: G. P. Putnam, 1966.

———. *The Interrupted Journey: Two Lost Hours "Aboard a Flying Saucer."* New York: Dial Press, 1966.

Genzlinger, Anna Lykins. *The Jessup Dimension.* Clarksburg, W.Va.: Saucerian Press, 1981.

Gilmour, Daniel S., ed. *Final Report of the Scientific Study of Unidentified Flying Objects* ("The Condon Report"). New York: Bantam Books, 1969.

Goerman, Robert A. "Alias Carlos Allende." *Fate* (October 1980): 69–75.

Good, Timothy. *Above Top Secret: The Worldwide UFO Cover-up*. New York: William Morrow, 1988.

Gross, Loren E. *Charles Fort, The Fortean Society, & Unidentified Flying Objects*. Fremont, Calif.: Author, 1976.

———. *UFOs: A History, 1896, 1946–1959*. Fremont, Calif.: Author, 1974–2000.

Hall, Richard H. *The UFO Evidence, Volume II*. Lanham, Md.: Scarecrow Press, 2001.

———, ed. *The UFO Evidence*. Washington, D.C.: National Investigations Committee on Aerial Phenomena, 1964.

Heard, Gerald. *The Riddle of the Flying Saucers: Is Another World Watching?* London: Carroll and Nicholson, 1950. Published in the U.S. as *Is Another World Watching? The Riddle of the Flying Saucers* (New York: Harper, 1951; rev. and expanded ed., New York: Bantam, 1953).

Hickson, Charles, and William Mendez. *UFO Contact at Pascagoula*. Tucson, Ariz.: Wendelle C. Stevens, 1983.

Hill, Betty. *A Common Sense Approach to UFOs*. Greenland, N.H.: Author, 1995.

Hopkins, Budd. *Intruders: The Incredible Visitations at Copley Woods*. New York: Random House, 1987.

———. "Sane Citizen Sees UFO in New Jersey." *Village Voice*, March 1, 1976.

———. *Witnessed: The True Story of the Brooklyn Bridge Abductions*. New York: Pocket Books, 1996.

Hynek, J. Allen. *The Hynek UFO Report*. New York: Dell, 1977.

———. *The UFO Experience: A Scientific Enquiry*. Chicago: Regnery, 1972.

Hynek, J. Allen, and Jacques Vallée. *The Edge of Reality: A Progress Report on Unidentified Flying Objects*. Chicago: Regnery, 1975.

Jacobs, David M. *Secret Life: Firsthand Accounts of UFO Abductions*. New York: Simon and Schuster, 1992.

———. *The UFO Controversy in America*. New York: Signet/New American Library, 1976.

Jessup, M. K. *The Case for the UFO*. New York: Citadel Press, 1955.

Keel, John A. *The Mothman Prophecies*. New York: Saturday Review Press, 1975.

———. *Our Haunted Planet*. Greenwich, Conn.: Fawcett Publications, 1971.

———. *Strange Creatures from Time and Space*. Greenwich, Conn.: Fawcett Gold Medal, 1970.

———. *UFOs: Operation Trojan Horse*. New York: G. P. Putnam, 1970.

Keyhoe, Donald E. *Flying Saucers from Outer Space.* New York: Holt, 1953.

———. *The Flying Saucers Are Real.* New York: Fawcett Gold Medal, 1950.

———. "The Flying Saucers Are Real." *True* (January 1950): 11–13, 83–87.

Klass, Philip J. *The Real Roswell Crashed-Saucer Coverup.* Amherst, N.Y.: Prometheus Books, 1997.

———. *UFO Abductions: A Dangerous Game.* Updated ed. Amherst, N.Y.: Prometheus Books, 1989.

———. *UFOs—Explained.* New York: Random House, 1974.

———. *UFOs—Identified.* New York: Random House, 1968.

———. *UFOs: The Public Deceived.* Amherst, N.Y.: Prometheus Books, 1983.

Layne, N. Meade. *The Ether Ship and Its Solution.* Vista, Calif.: Borderland Sciences Research Associates, 1950.

Leslie, Desmond, and George Adamski. *Flying Saucers Have Landed.* New York: British Book Centre, 1953.

Lorenzen, Coral E. *Flying Saucers: The Startling Evidence of the Invasion from Outer Space* (original title: *The Great Flying Saucer Hoax*). New York: Signet/New American Library, 1966.

Lorenzen, Coral, and Jim Lorenzen. *Abducted: Confrontations with Beings from Outer Space.* New York: Berkley, 1977.

———. *Encounters with UFO Occupants.* New York: Berkley, 1976.

———. *Flying Saucer Occupants.* New York: Signet/New American Library, 1967.

———. *UFOs Over the Americas.* New York: Signet/New American Library, 1968.

McAndrew, James. *The Roswell Report: Case Closed.* Washington, D.C.: U.S. Government Printing Office, 1997.

Mack, John. *Abduction: Human Encounters with Aliens.* Rev. ed. New York: Ballantine, 1994.

Matheson, Terry. *Alien Abductions: Creating a Modern Phenomenon.* Amherst, N.Y.: Prometheus Books, 1998.

Menger, Howard. *From Outer Space to You.* Clarksburg, W.Va.: Saucerian Books, 1959.

Mentira, Carlos, and Fred Broman. *An Inferential Guide to Parallel Universes (With Notes Toward Future Investigations).* Philadelphia and Hamilton, Bermuda: Invisible Triangle Press, 1961.

Menzel, Donald H. *Flying Saucers.* Cambridge: Harvard University Press, 1953.

Menzel, Donald H., and Ernest H. Taves. *The UFO Enigma: The Definitive Explanation of the UFO Phenomenon.* Garden City, N.Y.: Doubleday, 1977.

Menzel, Donald H., and Lyle G. Boyd. *The World of Flying Saucers: A Scientific Examination of a Major Myth of the Space Age.* Garden City, N.Y.: Doubleday, 1963.

Moore, William L. *UFOs and the U.S. Government: Spies, Lies & Extraterrestrials, An Exposé in Four Parts* (includes the complete text of Moore's 1989 MUFON International UFO Symposium speech). Burbank, Calif.: Fair-Witness Project,1990.

Moore, William L., with Charles Berlitz. *The Philadelphia Experiment: Project Invisibility—An Account of a Search for a Secret Navy Wartime Project That May Have Succeeded—Too Well.* New York: G. P. Putnam [Grosset and Dunlap], 1979.

Moseley, James W. "Curse of the Quishuarni Treasure." *Fate* (May 1957): 62–68.

———. "Inca Treasure—by the Ton!" *Argosy* (June 1964): 44–49, 90–94.

———. "Peruvian Desert Map for Saucers?" *Fate* (October 1955): 28–33.

———. "UFOs Out West." In *UFOs 1947–1997: From Arnold to the Abductees, Fifty Years of Flying Saucers,* edited by Hilary Evans and Dennis Stacy, pp. 53–59. London: John Brown Publishing, 1997.

———. "UFOs, the Universe, and Mr. John M. Cage." *Fate* (September 1962): 78–84.

———. "What I Really Believe." *Caveat Emptor* (spring 1972): 9–12; (winter 1972–1973): 5–6, 21–22.

———. *The Wright Field Story.* Clarksburg, W.Va.: Saucerian Books, 1971. Revised and reissued as *UFO Crash Secrets at Wright-Patterson Air Force Base* (New York: Abelard Productions, 1991).

———, ed. *Jim Moseley's Book of Saucer News.* Clarksburg, W.Va.: Saucerian Books, 1967.

———. *Saucer News* [as *Nexus,* July 1954–May 1955] (July 1954–winter 1967–1968). For availability and prices of facsimile copies write: Tom Benson, PO Box 1174, Trenton, NJ 08606-1174.

———. *Saucer News Non-Scheduled/Confidential Newsletter* (December 5, 1955–November 10, 1967). For availability and prices of facsimile copies write: Tom Benson, PO Box 1174, Trenton, NJ 08606-1174.

———. *Saucer Smear* [under various other titles, February 1976–May 20, 1981] (February 1976–present). For a nonsubscription ("love offering" gratefully accepted) and back issues (2001–present, $1.00 each) write: *Saucer Smear,* PO Box 1709, Key West, FL 33041-1709; for availability and prices of back issues, 1976–2000, write: Tom Benson, PO Box 1174, Trenton, NJ 08606-1174.

Moseley, James W., and Karl T. Pflock. "Saucer Logic." *Fate* (November 2000): 19–21.

Nebel, Long John. *The Way Out World.* Englewood Cliffs, N.J.: Prentice-Hall, 1961.

Oberg, James E. *UFOs and Outer Space Mysteries: A Sympathetic Skeptic's Report.* Norfolk, Va.: Donning Company/Publishers, 1981.

Peebles, Curtis. *Watch the Skies! A Chronicle of the Flying Saucer Myth.* Washington, D.C.: Smithsonian Institution Press, 1994.

Pflock, Karl T. "Anatomy of a UFO Hoax." *Fate* (November 1980): 40–48.

———. "I Was a Ufologist for the CIA—Not!" *UFO* (November/December 1993): 25–30.

———. "Mojave Time Warp." *Fate* (August 2001): 26–29.

———. "NUFOC Report." *Fate* (January 2000): 20–23.

———. *Roswell: Inconvenient Facts and the Will to Believe.* Amherst, N.Y.: Prometheus Books, 2001.

———. "What's Really Behind the Flying Saucers? A New Twist on Aztec." *Anomalist* (spring 2000): 137–61.

Pflock, Karl T., and James W. Moseley. "UFOs: 3-D or 4-D+?" *Fate* (September 2000): 22–24.

Randle, Kevin D., and Donald R. Schmitt. *The Truth About the UFO Crash at Roswell.* New York: Evans, 1994.

———. *UFO Crash at Roswell.* New York: Avon, 1991.

Randle, Kevin D., Russ Estes, and William P. Cone. *The Abduction Enigma: The Truth Behind the Mass Alien Abductions of the Late Twentieth Century.* New York: Forge, 1999.

Rupplet, Edward J. *The Report on Unidentified Flying Objects.* Garden City, N.Y.: Doubleday, 1956; expanded ed., with three additional skeptical chapters, 1960.

Sagan, Carl, and Thornton Page, eds. *UFOs—A Scientific Debate.* Ithaca, N.Y.: Cornell University Press, 1972.

Scully, Frank. *Behind the Flying Saucers.* New York: Holt, 1950.

Sheaffer, Robert. *The UFO Verdict: Examining the Evidence.* Amherst, N.Y.: Prometheus Books, 1981.

Stanford, Ray. *Socorro "Saucer" in a Pentagon Pantry.* Austin, Tex.: Blueapple Books, 1976.

Steinman, William S., and Wendelle C. Stevens. *UFO Crash at Aztec: A Well-Kept Secret.* Tucson, Ariz.: UFO Photo Archives, 1986.

Story, Ronald D., ed., and J. Richard Greenwell, consulting ed. *The Encyclopedia of UFOs.* New York: New American Library, 1980.

Stringfield, Leonard H. *Inside Saucer Post . . . 3-0 Blue.* Cincinnati, Ohio: Author, 1957.

———. *UFO Crash/Retrievals, Status Reports I–VII.* Cincinnati, Ohio: Author, 1978, 1980, 1982, 1985, 1989, 1991, 1994.

Tomlinson, Bracey, and Egon Spunraas. *We Have Seen the Saucers and Those Who Pilot Them.* Edinburgh, Scotland: Ormuss-Puller Editions, 1954.

United States Air Force. *The Roswell Report: Fact versus Fiction in the New Mexico Desert.* Washington, D.C.: U.S. Government Printing Office, 1994.

Vallée, Jacques. "Anatomy of a Hoax: The Philadelphia Experiment Fifty Years Later." *Journal of Scientific Exploration* (spring 1994): 47–71.

———. *Messengers of Deception.* Berkeley, Calif.: And/Or Press, 1979.

Vallée, Jacques, and Janine Vallée. *Challenge to Science: The UFO Enigma.* Chicago: Regnery, 1966.

Van Tassel, George W. *The Council of the Seven Lights.* Los Angeles: DeVorss and Company, 1958.

———. *I Rode a Flying Saucer! The Mystery of the Flying Saucers Revealed.* Los Angeles: New Age Publishing Company, 1952.

Von Däniken, Erich. *Chariots of the Gods?* New York: G. P. Putnam, 1970.

Walters, Ed, and Bruce Maccabee. *UFOs Are Real: Here's the Proof.* New York: Avon, 1997.

Walters, Ed, and Frances Walters. *The Gulf Breeze Sightings.* New York: William Morrow, 1990.

———. *UFO Abductions in Gulf Breeze.* New York: Avon, 1994.

Walton, Travis. *Fire in the Sky.* New York: Marlowe and Company, 1996.

———. *The Walton Experience.* New York: Berkley Books, 1978.

Welch, Len. "Flying Saucer 'Passenger' Declares A-Bomb Blasts Reason for Visits." *Phoenix Gazette,* November 24, 1952.

Williamson, George Hunt. *Other Tongues—Other Flesh.* Amherst, Wis.: Amherst Press, 1953.

———. *Road in the Sky.* London: Neville Spearman, 1959.

———. *Secret Places of the Lion.* London: Neville Spearman, 1958.

Williamson, George Hunt, and Alfred C. Bailey. *The Saucers Speak! A Documentary Report of Interstellar Communication by Radiography.* Los Angeles: New Age Publishing Company, 1954.

Williamson, George Hunt, and John McCoy. *UFOs Confidential! The Meaning Behind the Most Closely Guarded Secret of All Time.* Corpus Christi, Tex.: Essene Press, 1958.

Zinsstag, Lou, and Timothy Good. *George Adamski—The Untold Story.* Beckenham, England: Ceti Publications, 1983.

Achenbach, Joel, 318
Ackerman, Forrest ("Mr. Science Fiction"), 72
Ackerman, Wendayne ("Mrs. Science Fiction") 72
Adams, Tom, 256
Adamski, "Professor" George, 27, 31, 37, 44, 59–62, 63–70, 73–74, 79, 80, 82, 85, 94, 109, 110, 124, 125–27, 129, 134, 136–37, 139, 161, 184–85, 186, 208, 280, 295, 304, 325, 327, 331. *See also appendix*
Adickes, Robert, 43
Alexander (a MIB?), 172–74
Ali, Muhammad, 222
Allen, Carl M. *See* "Allende, Carlos Miguel"
Allen, Steve, 135
"Allende, Carlos Miguel" (Carl M. Allen), 244, 277, 278
Anderson, Gerald, 316
Andreasson, Betty (Betty Luca), 252
Andrus, Walter H., 225–26, 251, 256, 288, 292–94 passim, 301, 302, 303, 321–22
Angelucci, Orfeo M., 73–76 passim, 161, 167, 295
Arnold, Kenneth, 13, 113, 199, 204, 205, 231, 240, 241, 261, 269, 280
Auriche, Edmundo, 145, 146–47

Bachmeier, James, 95–96
Bailey, Alfred C. "Al," 60–62, 63, 65, 74. *See also appendix*
Bailey, Betty (wife of Al Bailey), 61, 62. *See also appendix*

Baker, Irma (wife of Jerrold Baker). *See appendix*
Baker, Jerrold E., 61, 64, 68–69, 74, 77, 108. *See also appendix*
Baldwin, Robert, 172
Barbieri, Joseph, 40
Bardi, Pedro, 141–42
Barker, Gray Roscoe, 38, 42, 98–99, 103–11 passim, 118–27, 135, 139, 156, 161, 163, 168, 169, 171–72, 173–74, 175, 180–82, 182–83, 190, 200–201, 204, 205, 210, 214, 218, 222, 224–25, 235, 277, 279–80, 281, 303, 331
Barnes, Harry, 47
Barnett, Jack, 318
Bassett, Donna, 309–11
Bassett, Ed (husband of Donna Bassett), 310
"Baxter, Marla." *See* Menger, Constance
Bean, Norman, 101
Beckjord, Erik (formerly Jon), 274, 276
Beckley, Timothy Green ("Mr. UFO"; "Mr. Creepo"), 111, 182, 214, 218, 238–39, 272
"Believer Bill" (Ed Walters?), 287
Bender, Albert K., 14, 15, 32, 38–39, 41–42, 46, 72, 98, 108, 116, 118, 120–21, 122, 123, 126, 171, 173–74, 175, 210, 268
Bender, Mrs. Albert K., 14, 174
Benevidas, General (president of Peru), 146
Bennett, Terry, 213
Benson, Tom, 331
Berlitz, Charles, 113, 262–63, 270
Berry, Robert, 232
Bethurum, Truman, 73, 75, 161, 166, 295
Big Bo (Venusian dog), 156
Binder, Otto, 281
Birnes, William J., 312–13
Black, Victor, 84–85
Bloecher, Ted, 108, 125, 236, 237–38, 262
Bloom, G. L. *See appendix*
Blum, Judy (wife of Ralph Blum), 232
Blum, Ralph, 232
Boland, Hank, 292, 294, 302
Booth, Lloyd C., 51–52
Boyd, Mrs. Lyle G., 185
"Brenda" (friend of "Laurine," Bigfoot's friend), 274–76
Brewster (Republic Aviation executive), 43
Broman, Francis, 94–95
Broman, Fred, 108
"Brother Philip." *See* Williamson, "Dr." George Hunt
Brown, Fred, 101
Brown, Harold, 196
Brown, Jerry, 292
Brown, T. Townsend, 129
Bunch, David, 49–50, 82
Burke, Alan, 210
Burrell, John, 88
Burrell, Mrs. John, 88
Burroughs, Edgar Rice, 99
Bush, Vannevar, 263
Butler, Richard, 305, 307–308
"Buzzard" (failed secret agent), 266

Cahn, J. P., 78–79, 82, 93

Campbell, Rose Hackett, 129
Carr, Robert Spencer, 232
Carson, Johnny, 160, 201
Carter, Horace, 51–52
Carter, James E. "Jimmy," 232
Carter, John (of Mars), 99
"Case, Justin" (George Mackas), 85, 108, 117
Chambers, Elmer, 48–49
"Chicken Queen, The" (daughter of Harlan Sanders), 222
Childers, Lee ("Prince/King Neosom" of planet Tythan), 156, 157–59
Chiles, Clarence S., 53, 76
Chop, Albert M. "Al," 80–84. *See also appendix*
Clark, Jerome, 121, 138, 178–79, 215, 231, 233, 239, 243, 245, 273, 305, 308, 321
Clarke, Arthur C. *See appendix*
Clinton, William J. "Bill," 140
Cohen, Richard, 105, 129
Colderin (a Grapalin; channeled space entity), 240
Comella, Tom ("Peter Kor"), 108
Condon, Edward U., 196, 209, 212, 215–17, 218
"Condor" (alleged secret agent), 268
Conger, George, 31
Conrad, Mikel, 76–77, 82
Cook, Duane, 286, 290
Cooper, Timothy, 313–14, 320
Copeland, James, 47
Corso, Lt. Col. Philip J., 313, 320
"Cortile, Linda." *See* Napolitano, Linda
Criswell, Jeron King ("Criswell Predicts"), 73
"d'Obrenovic, Michel D. M." *See* Williamson, "Dr." George Hunt
"Damsky, I. Givva" (??), 108
"Dan" (alleged security agent), 305–307, 308
Darlaine, Manon, 70–71, 71–72, 73–75, 80, 87, 124–25. *See also appendix*
Darnell, Linda, 69
Davids, Paul, 317, 320
Davidson, Leon ("Dr. D"), 108, 114–17
Davis, Isabel, 108, 125
Dennis, Glenn, 316
Derenberger, Woodrow W. "Woody," 272–73
Desvergers, D. S. (Dunham Sanborn) "Sonny," 83, 101
Detwiler, D. J., 63–64, 65. *See also appendix*
Deuley, Thomas P. "Tom," 266
Dickinson, Terence, 249–50
DiMeola, Lorrayne, 39–40
DiMeola, Margurete, 39–40
Dimmick, Ray, 94
Docker, Beth ("Princess/Queen Negonna" of planet Tythan), 157, 158
Douglass, Earl, 180
Dove, Lonzo, 108, 110, 126. *See also appendix*
"Dr. D." *See* Davidson, Leon
"Dr. Gee." *See* GeBauer, "Dr." Leo
Ducker, W. L., 55–56
Dunmier, Margo, 172
Durant, Robert, 314

Earley, George, 204

Eaton, John, 88–89
Edwards, Frank, 72, 199, 202, 204–205, 280
Eichler, Werner, 84–85, 86
Einstein, Albert, 36, 66
Eisenhower, Dwight D., 46, 73, 263
Elizabeth II, 26
Emerson, Col. Robert B., 40–41, 55

"Falcon" (alleged secret agent), 267, 268
Farish, Lucius "Lu," 226
Fawcett, George W., 38
Feifer, Marilyn, 108
Fish, Marjorie, 249–50
Flader, Herman, 78, 93
Flammonde, Paris, 204
Flannigan, Charles, 302–303
Foley, J. B., 31, 37
Ford, Gerald R., 193, 195
Forrestal, James V., 263–64
Fort, Charles Hoy, 33
Fortner, Yonah ("Y. N. ibn A'haron"), 122, 183–84, 191
Foutz, Robert, 89
Fowler, Raymond E. "Ray," 252
Fredrick, Laurence, 301
Freiberg, Libby (wife of Warren Freiberg), 238–40
Freiberg, Warren, 238–40
Freud, Sigmund, 305
Friedman, Stanton T. ("The Flying Saucer Physicist"), 14, 95, 201–202, 249, 253, 262–65, 270, 313–16 passim, 320
Friend, Lt. Col. Robert J., 175–76
Fry, Daniel W. "Dan," 161, 166–67, 204, 295
Fuller, Curtis, 143
Fuller, John G., 175, 190–91, 215, 229
Fulton, Harold, 42

Gallo, Mujica, 150
Gamow, George, 100
Gardner, Louis, 36
Gardner, Robert Coe, 82
Garland, Brig. Gen. William, 82
Gatti, Attilio, 26
GeBauer, "Dr." Leo ("Dr. Gee"), 76, 77–79, 87, 92–95, 113
Geller, Uri, 189, 247
Genzlinger, Anna, 277–78
Gernsbach, Hugo, 99
Gersten, Peter, 243
"Ghoul, Joseph C." (Jim Moseley), 106
Gleason, Jackie, 169
Golka, Bob, 222
Good, Timothy, 70
Gort (Klaatu's robot sidekick, *The Day the Earth Stood Still),* 20
Graits, Agatha, 108
Gray, Ed, 292
Green, Gabriel, 162–63, 195, 325
Greenfield, Allen H. "Al," 203
Greer, Stephen, 324–25
Guzman, François, 140, 141, 148

Hall, Richard H. "Dick," 108, 131, 169, 191–92, 204, 246
Hams, William, 56
Hancock, Douglas, 156, 157, 158
Hansen, George, 305, 307–308
"Hanson, Ed." *See* Walters, Edward
Harder, James, 227, 249, 250, 251
Hart, Carl, Jr., 55–56
Haut, Walter, 316
Heard, Gerald, 27

Hershey, Joe. *See* Sheehy, Joe
Hewes, Hayden, 182
Hickson, Charles, 226–27, 228, 249
Hill, Barney, 22, 175, 191, 204, 249, 270
Hill, Betty, 22, 175, 191, 204, 249, 270–71
Hillberg, Rick R., 203
Hillenkoetter, R. Adm. Roscoe H., 264
Hopkins, Budd, 236–38, 239–40, 252, 287, 288, 291, 303–305, 307–309, 310–11
Horton, Ralph, 54, 262
Howard, Dana, 21, 164
Howe, Linda Moulton, 255–56
Hudson, Barbara, 208, 211, 212, 218, 222
Hughes, Howard R., 245
Hunrath, Karl, 73–74. *See also appendix*
Hunt, Ruth C. (mother of Ted Hunt), 36
Hunt, Theodore "Ted," 36
Hutchinson, Mrs. W. J., 50–51
Hutchinson, W. J., 50–51
Hynek, J. Allen, 121, 188–89, 192, 193, 195, 199, 202, 224–25, 227, 228–29, 229, 231, 241–42, 249–52 passim, 321

"ibn A'haron, Y. N." *See* Fortner, Yonah
Isquith, Ben, 122–23

Jacobs, David M., 215, 310
"Jane" (Ed/Frances Walters?), 287
Jessup, Morris K., 108, 129, 130, 276–78, 280
Jesus Christ (as spaceman), 267
John, Clara L., 108, 129. *See also appendix*
Jones, Candy (wife of Long John Nebel), 247, 263
Jones, James Earl, 250
Joquel, Arthur, 73

Keane, Jack, 123
Keel, John A., 42, 175, 204, 206, 210–11, 231, 234, 270, 271–74
Kelly, Brig. Gen. Joe W., 73
Kennedy, Bob ("The Other Bob Kennedy"), 185, 186, 196
Kennedy, John F., 215, 309
Kennedy, Robert (the Peruvian one), 142–43, 144, 145, 146, 147, 148, 149, 152
Kerkendall, Brig. Gen. J. P., 54
Keyhoe, Donald E., 20, 27, 35, 44–46, 47, 48–50 passim, 54, 80–81, 83, 86, 90, 93, 102, 108, 110, 113, 129, 130, 155, 169, 191–92, 196, 204, 218, 222, 223
"King Neosom." *See* Childers, Lee
King, Alexander, 302
Kiviat, Robert, 318–19
Klaatu (benevolent spaceman, *The Day the Earth Stood Still)*, 20, 22
Klass Philip J., 132, 188, 227, 229–30, 243, 245, 252, 264, 274, 284, 289, 295, 310, 323–24
Koehler, George, 92, 93
"Kor, Peter." *See* Comella, Tom
Korff, Kal K., 282–84
Kover, Jonas, 158
Krippine, Ken, 26, 27, 29–30, 66, 89, 98, 100, 102, 140
Krushchev, Nikita, 309–10

Lady ("Snippy," unfortunate Earth horse), 255
Lansing, Stela, 240
Larsen, Sherman, 228
Laughead, Charles, 137
Laughead, Lillian (wife of Charles Laughead), 137
"Laurine" (close friend of Bigfoot), 274–75
Layne, N. Meade, 108, 137, 230, 280
Lee, Earl, 282
Leedskalnin, Ed, 281–82
Leigh, Vivian, 241
Leslie, Desmond, 27, 31, 35, 37, 59–60, 108, 110. *See also appendix*
LeVan, Leon, 169
Leyden, James, 31
Lime, Harry, 326–27
Littell, Max, 316
Little Bucky (Venusian redneck), 156
Loftin, Robert, 211
Lorenzen, Coral E., 40, 121, 124, 131, 222–24, 225, 228, 241–42, 251, 256
Lorenzen, Leslie James "Jim," 131, 222–24, 228, 232, 241, 251, 252, 256
Low, Robert T., 209
Lowery, Fannie, 157
Luca, Betty. *See* Andreasson, Betty
Lucchesi, Dominick (occasionally, Dominic) C. "Dom," 32–33, 37, 40, 41, 70, 98, 104–106, 118, 207–208
Lund, George, 312, 314
McDonald, James E., 195, 229, 230
McGinnis, Lucy, 61. *See also appendix*
McLean, C. F., 49–50, 51, 82
McLean, Clyde, 49–50, 54, 102
McLean, Mrs. C. F., 49
McNeil, Alex, 209
Maccabee, Bruce S., 287, 291, 295
Mack, John, 309–11
Maddox, Lester, 198–99
Manak, Allan J. "Al," 203
Mann, Michael G., 138, 158
Manning, Robert, 43
Mannor, Frank, 192
Mannor, Ronald, 192
Mantell, Capt. Thomas F., Jr., 13, 27, 199
Marana, John, 108, 112
Marcel, Maj. Jesse A., 253, 262
Marley, Pevernell, 69. *See also appendix*
Marlo, George, 169, 173
"Martinez, Isabel," 144, 146–48 passim
"Matthews, A. G.," 124
Maum, Mayme. *See appendix*
Maxfield, J. P. *See appendix*
Mayher, PFC Ralph, 101, 185, 188
Mebane, Alexander "Lex," 108, 109, 125
Meier Eduard A. "Billy," 283
Menger, Constance "Connie" ("Marla Baxter"; Connie Weber; second wife, space soulmate of Howard Menger), 133, 135, 136, 170, 171, 206
Menger, Howard ("the East Coast Adamski"), 133–36, 169–71, 204, 206

Menger, Rose (first wife of Howard Menger), 134
Menkin, Michael, 311
Mentira, Carlos, 326
Menzel, Donald H., 36, 47, 57, 58, 93, 95, 99, 100, 101, 109, 185–86, 188, 229, 264, 265
Meyer, F. W., 92
Michel, Aime, 108
Mika (space animal), 165
Miller, Dick, 137
Miller, Max, 72, 75–76, 85, 98, 103, 108, 159, 167, 206
Mingus, Charlie, 206
Mock, Nick, 289, 290
Monteleone, Thomas F. "Tom," 271–74
Montgomery, Anna, 278
Moore, William L. "Bill," 113, 253, 262–65, 266–68, 270, 283, 284, 315
Moseley, Elizabeth Barber "Betty" (daughter of Jim Moseley), 186, 187, 222
Moseley, Florence Barber (mother of Jim Moseley), 25, 26
Moseley, Maj. Gen. George Van Horn (father of Jim Moseley), 25, 125
Moseley, Lt. (later, Capt.) James W. (*not* the coauthor of this book), 119, 139
Moseley, Sandy. *See* "Swendsin," Sandy
Mothman (winged, red-eyed ??), 210
"Mr. Creepo." *See* Beckley, Timothy Green
"Mr. R." *See* Streeter, Lyman
"Mr. UFO." *See* Beckley, Timothy Green
"Mr. X" (Ed *and* Frances Walters), 286–87, 294
Mundo, Laura, 124, 171

"Nameless" (grave robber in Peru), 278
Napolitano, Linda ("Linda Cortile"), 304–309
Nash, William B. "Bill," 100–101, 108
Nebel, John "Long John," 122–24, 133, 135, 157, 169, 175, 184–85, 189, 193, 204, 205, 247, 278
Neff, Earl, 203
Neiman, Daryle, 164–65
Nelson, Buck, 156, 157
Nelson, Hal. *See appendix*
Nelson, Wally. *See appendix*
Newton, Silas Mason, 73, 76, 77–79, 87, 92–95, 113, 233, 261
Nixon, Richard M., 72, 221, 245
Norman, Lewis, 47–48

O'Barski, George, 236–38, 240, 252, 307
Oberg, James E., 274
Ogden, Richard, 110, 139, 186, 187
"Oiseau" (failed secret agent), 266
Olsson, 1st Lt. Robert, 83
Orthon (Venusian Space Brother), 60, 61, 63–64, 65, 67, 68, 94. *See also appendix*
Oscar (Peruvian tour guide), 141, 148, 149
Otto, John, 97–98, 108

Page, Thornton, 195, 301
Palmer, Raymond A. "Ray," 123, 143, 204, 205, 280, 329
Parker, Calvin, 226–27, 228, 249
Parsons, Estelle, 250
Pauling, Linus, 163
Pelley, William Dudley, 74, 136–37
Perez de Cuellar, Javier, 304 (as "major political figure"), 305
Pett, Saul, 35–36
Pflock, Ernst H. (father of Karl Pflock), 19, 20
Pilar (Peruvian actress, wife of Dick Weldy until she met John Wayne), 27
Pitt, John. *See appendix*
Prado, Manuel, 150
Presley, Reg, 318
"Prince Neosom." *See* Childers, Lee
"Princess Negonna." *See* Docker, Beth
Probert, Irene (wife of Mark Probert), 165
Probert, Mark, 165
Professor Ne-Lah, 168–69

Quazgaa (space alien), 252
"Queen Negonna." *See* Docker, Beth
Quintanilla, Maj. Hector, 188

Randi, James "The Amazing/ Amusing," 175, 189–90, 193, 204, 221
Randle, Kevin D., 256, 315–17 passim, 320
Reiche, Maria, 148, 149
Reid, Frank, 108
Rhanes, Aura (sexy Clarionite saucer commander), 75, 166
Rhein, Robert, 89
Rice, Hugh, 36
"Richard" (alleged security agent), 305–307
Riedel, Walther, 69, 72, 84
Ritchey, James, 47
Roberts, Alvira (second wife of Truman Bethurum), 166
Roberts, August C. "Augie," 31–34, 37–41, 70, 98, 104–106, 110, 206
Rockmore, Eliot, 133
Rohrer, Joseph, 90–92, 94
Rosiechi, Zenon, 164
Rost, Andy, 140–41, 142, 143, 148
Ruppelt, Capt. Edward J., 20, 80–84, 89–90
Russell, Jane, 241

Sagan, Carl, 195, 250, 311
Salisberry, Carol (wife of Rex Salisberry), 293
Salisberry, Rex, 293
Salkin, Harold, 238–39, 271, 272
Samwick, Charles, 132
Sanders, Col. Harlan, 222
Sanders, Mrs. Harlan, 222
Sanderson, Ivan T., 119, 175, 204, 206
Santilli, Ray, 318–19
Schirmer, Herbert, 247
Schmitt, Donald R., 315, 316, 320
Scully, Frank, 27, 66, 73–76 passim, 77–80, 82, 87, 92–95 passim, 108, 109, 113, 161, 233, 244, 280. *See also appendix*
Severson, Thor, 95
Shandera, Jamie, 263–64, 267
Shatner, William, 317

Sheaffer, Robert, 264, 270, 283–84
Sheehy, Joe, 112, 113–14
Sheets, John, 200
Shreibstein, Norman, 171–72
Simon, Benjamin, 191
Sims, Derrel, 317
Sinatra, Andy ("The Mystic Barber"), 159–60
Sinatra, Giovannina (wife of Andy Sinatra), 160
Slaughter, Bob, 321–22
Slaughter, Judith (widow of Bob Slaughter), 322
Slipher, E. C., 56, 57–58, 97
Smith, Robert, 316
Smith, Tom, Sr. (father of Tommy Smith), 294
Smith, Tommy, 292, 294, 302
Smith, Willy, 288, 290, 295
"Snippy." *See* Lady
Soloma (spacewoman), 164–65
Spandell, Mike, 281
Sparks, Brad, 243, 244, 284
Spaulding, William H. "Bill," 242, 245, 250
Sperry, Willis, 76
Spielberg, Steven, 121
Sprinkle, R. Leo, 250, 251
Squires, William, 96
Stacy, Dennis, 266, 326
Stanford, John, 137
Stanford, Ray, 137, 246–47
Starr, Hal, 301
Stefula, Joseph, 305, 307–308
Steiger, Brad, 231
Steinberg, Eugene "Gene" ("Richard E. Wallace"), 179, 182, 191
Steinman, William, 95
"Stevens," Sandra. *See* "Swendsin," Sandy
Stevens, Wendelle, 95
Stoner, Ray, 282
Story, Ronald, 168, 321
"Straith, R. E. (Reynold)," 124–27, 280. *See also appendix*
Stranges, Frank E., 167–68, 204
Streeter, Lyman, 60–62, 63 (as "Mr. R"), 65, 74
Strieber, Whitley, 311
Stringfield, Leonard H., 108, 113, 114, 117, 233, 234, 243, 247, 253–55, 261, 263
Sullivan, Ed J., 72, 84–86
Svendsen, Sandra. *See* "Swendsin," Sandy
"Swendsin," Sandy (Sandra "Stevens"; Sandra Svendsen; ex-wife of Jim Moseley), 180, 186, 187
Swords, Michael D., 138

Talman, William ("Hamilton Burger"), 71
Tarzan (of the Jungle), 99
Teddy (Earth dog), 156, 157
Tellefsen, J. A., Jr., 180
Teller, Sanford "Sandy," 184, 185
Thinnes, Roy, 195, 204, 208–209
Thomas, Lowell, 72
Thor, Valiant (yet another Venusian), 168
Thorne, Clarence, 113–14
Timmerman, John, 283
Tiny ("Tiptoe Through the Tulips") Tim, 187
Todd, Robert G., 21
Tombaugh, Clyde W., 56–57, 72
Tombaugh, Mrs. Clyde W., 57

Toomer, George, 322
Totten, Bertram, 48–49
Trent, Paul, 284
Troncosco, Domingo, 141–42
Truman, Harry S, 96–97, 180–82, 241, 263–64, 319

Urey, Harold, 97

Vallée, Jacques, 231
Van Tassel, George, 73, 75, 158–61 passim, 162, 163, 165, 166, 195, 280
Vandenberg, Gen. Hoyt S., 53, 82
Vertlieb, Erwin, 171–72
Villas-Boas, Antonio, 223
Vinther, Laurence, 95–96
Vivian, Weston E., 193
von Däniken, Erich, 148, 149, 183

Wales, Jim, 171
Walker, Bob, 197
"Wallace, Richard E." *See* Steinberg, Eugene
Walters, Danny (son of Ed Walters), 286, 289, 292, 293–94, 302
Walters, Edward "Ed" ("Ed Hanson"), 285–95, 300. *See also* "Mr. X"
Walters, Frances (ex-wife of Ed Walters), 286–87, 289–90, 291, 292,
294–95. *See also* "Mr. X"
Walters, Laura (daughter of Ed Walters), 286, 290
Walton, Travis, 250–52, 286
Walton, Vivian, 111 (as "a woman"), 112, 113–14
Ware, Donald, 287
"Washburn, Jenny," 303–304, 308
"Washburn, Sam" (husband of "Jenny Washburn"), 303–304, 308
Watters, Edward, 53
Wayne, John, 27
Webb, Marlo, 89
Webb, Walter N., 175, 249
Weber, Connie. *See* Menger, Constance
Weldy, Dick, 26, 29, 98, 100, 102
Wells, Alice K., 61, 64. *See also appendix*
Welo, Jerome, 73
Wentworth, Ted, 164
"Werner, Fritz," 233
Whitted, John B., 53, 76
Wilhelm, Charles, 255
Wilkins, Harold T., 108, 280
Wilkinson, Mrs. Wilbur J. *See appendix*
Wilkinson, Wilbur J. "Jack," 73–74. *See also appendix*
Williamson, Betty (wife of George Hunt Williamson), 61, 74, 137. *See also appendix*
Williamson, "Dr." George Hunt ("Brother Philip"; "Michel D. M. d'Obrenovic"), 61, 62–63, 65, 73, 74, 75, 79, 136–38, 151, 167, 246. *See also appendix*
Willis, Elliot, 319
Winchell, Walter, 72
Winters, Cliff, 168
Wolfer, George, 111–12
Wood, Robert, 314, 320
Wood, Ryan, 314, 320
Woods, William, 157, 158

Yada di Shi'ite (channeled ancient entity), 165

"Zachary, Ted." *See* Zechel, W. Todd
Zamora, Lonnie, 116, 187–88, 189, 193, 247
Zechel, W. Todd ("Ted Zachary"; "Ted Zilch"; "Todd Zilcovich"), 233 (Dec. 1975 letter to Jim Moseley), 242–46, 266, 284
Zehaas (*Ed* in Reticulian?), 287
"Zilch, Ted." *See* Zechel, W. Todd
"Zilcovich, Todd." *See* Zechel, W. Todd